Literature and Architecture in
Early Modern England

Literature and Architecture in Early Modern England

ANNE M. MYERS

The Johns Hopkins University Press
Baltimore

© 2013 The Johns Hopkins University Press
All rights reserved. Published 2013
Printed in the United States of America on acid-free paper
2 4 6 8 9 7 5 3 1

The Johns Hopkins University Press
2715 North Charles Street
Baltimore, Maryland 21218-4363
www.press.jhu.edu

Library of Congress Cataloging-in-Publication Data

Myers, Anne M.
Literature and architecture in early modern England /
Anne M. Myers.
p. cm.
Includes bibliographical references and index.
ISBN 978-1-4214-0722-7 (hdbk. : acid-free paper) —
ISBN 978-1-4214-0800-2 (electronic) — ISBN 1-4214-0722-1
(hdbk. : acid-free paper) — ISBN 1-4214-0800-7 (electronic)
1. English literature—Early modern, 1500–1700—History and
criticism. 2. Architecture and literature—History—16th
century. 3. Architecture and literature—History—17th
century. I. Title.
PR408.A66M94 2013
820.9'357—dc23   2012012207

A catalog record for this book is available from the British Library.

The illustrations in Chapter 6 are reproduced by permission of the
Huntington Library, San Marino, California, from *Parallel of the
Antient Architecture with the Modern*, by Roland Fréart, translated by
John Evelyn (London, 1664, pp. 17, 34, 43, 93, 45, and 47, resp.).
All photographs are by the author.

*Special discounts are available for bulk purchases of this book. For more
information, please contact Special Sales at 410-516-6936 or
specialsales@press.jhu.edu.*

The Johns Hopkins University Press uses environmentally friendly book
materials, including recycled text paper that is composed of at least
30 percent post-consumer waste, whenever possible.

Contents

List of Illustrations vii
Acknowledgments ix

Introduction: Building Stories: Writing about Architecture in Post-Reformation England   1

1 Loss and Foundations: Camden's *Britannia* and the Histories of English Architecture   23

2 Aristocrats and Architects: Henry Wotton and the Country House Poem   50

3 Strange Anthologies: *The Alchemist* in the London of John Stow   77

4 Restoring "The Church-porch": George Herbert's Architectural History   105

5 Construction Sites: The Architecture of Anne Clifford's Diaries   132

6 Recollections: John Evelyn and the Histories of Restoration Architecture   160

Coda: St. Helen's Bishopsgate: Antiquarianism and Aesthetics in Modern London   191

Notes 205
Bibliography 229
Index 245

Illustrations

Two-story porch at St. Nicholas, King's Lynn, Norfolk	112
Three-story porch at St. John the Baptist, Cirencester, Gloucestershire	113
North porch at St. Mary Redcliffe, Bristol, Gloucestershire	114
Porch at St. Peter and St. Paul, Eye, Suffolk	129
Dole table in porch of St. Peter and St. Paul, Eye, Suffolk	129
Inscription on porch of Mallerstang Chapel, Cumbria	139
Motto on gatehouse of Skipton Castle, Yorkshire	140
Inscription on Anne Clifford's tomb, St. Lawrence Church, Appleby, Cumbria	145
Plaque above gatehouse of Brougham Castle, Cumbria	148
Illustration of Doric order from Roland Fréart's *Parallel of the Antient Architecture with the Modern*, tr. John Evelyn (London, 1664)	166
Illustration of Doric order on Sepulcher near Terracina, from Fréart's *Parallel of the Antient Architecture with the Modern*, tr. Evelyn (London, 1664)	167
Illustration of Ionic order, Baths of Diocletian, from Fréart's *Parallel of the Antient Architecture with the Modern*, tr. Evelyn (London, 1664)	181
Illustration of Trajan's Column, from Fréart's *Parallel of the Antient Architecture with the Modern*, tr. Evelyn (London, 1664)	182
Palladio and Scamozzi on the Ionic order, from Fréart's *Parallel of the Antient Architecture with the Modern*, tr. Evelyn (London, 1664)	184
Serlio and Vignola on the Ionic order, from Fréart's *Parallel of the Antient Architecture with the Modern*, tr. Evelyn (London, 1664)	185
Redesigned interior of St. Helen's Bishopsgate, London, looking east	193
Redesigned interior of St. Helen's Bishopsgate, looking west	194
Redesigned interior of St. Helen's Bishopsgate, northeast corner of nave	195
Redesigned interior of St. Helen's Bishopsgate, from the south transept	196

Acknowledgments

I could not have completed this book alone, and I am glad to have this opportunity to acknowledge a few of the many institutions and individuals that have supported the project. First, the book has benefited from several sources of financial assistance. I am grateful to the University of California, Los Angeles, for the dissertation and travel fellowships that enabled its early stages, and to the University of Missouri for the teaching leave and summer research grants that allowed for its completion. I am equally indebted to the Huntington Library for a short-term Francis Bacon fellowship and to the Newberry Library and British Academy for an exchange fellowship.

One of the most exhilarating aspects of my interdisciplinary research has been the variety of invaluable collections to which it has led me. I would like to thank the staff of the British Library, the Huntington Library, the Newberry Library, the Guildhall Manuscripts Library, the Folger Shakespeare Library, the Getty Research Institute, and the Cumbria Archive Centre in Kendal for their assistance in locating materials and for access to these incomparable resources. Special thanks, as well, are due to Anne Willoughby, who graciously made special arrangements for me to see and photograph the church porch and dole table at St. Peter and St. Paul, Eye. Quotations from Anne Clifford's Great Books, appearing in Chapter 5, are reproduced with the kind permission of the Cumbria Archive Centre, while quotations related to the Consistory Court hearings concerning St. Helen's Bishopsgate appearing in the Coda are included by the joint permission of the London Metropolitan Archives and the Registry of the Church of England Diocese of London. Reproductions from Roland Fréart's *Parallel of the Antient Architecture with the Modern* appearing in Chapter 6 were supplied by the Huntington Library and are reprinted here by their permission.

An earlier and considerably shorter version of Chapter 5 appeared in *ELH* 73 (2006): 581–600, and a version of Chapter 4 appeared in *ELR* 40 (2010): 427–457.

I am grateful to the Johns Hopkins University Press and *ELR*, respectively, for allowing me to include some of this previously published material here.

It is with pleasure and deep gratitude that I reflect on the many colleagues, friends, and mentors who have offered their encouragement, expertise, and guidance and who have all, in their separate ways, made it possible for me to see the book through to its conclusion. I am particularly grateful to A. R. Braunmuller and Devoney Looser for graciously sharing their expertise and insight at every stage of the writing and publishing process. My scholarship and research will always remain indebted to the training and generous attention of my long-time friends and advisors from UCLA, A. R. Braunmuller, Jonathan Post, Robert N. Watson, and Debora Shuger, who taught me both to love research and to do it well. For fruitful, stimulating conversation as well as incisive criticism and feedback, I am especially grateful to Sean Silver. I will always remember our long talks in the paradisiacal surroundings of the Getty Research Institute and, later, during summers at the British Library. For her constructive suggestions and unfailing encouragement, I thank Melissa Sodeman. Thanks are due to other readers as well, including Patricia Fumerton, Holly Crawford Pickett, Devoney Looser, and the anonymous reviewer for the Johns Hopkins University Press. The final stages of this project benefited greatly from the rigorous standards of Frances Dickey and Alexandra Socarides, who managed to balance candid criticism and motivational encouragement in an intensely helpful way. Special mention is due to my department chair at the University of Missouri, Patricia Okker, for taking up my cause with a vigorous and successful campaign to fund our campus's access to Early English Books Online. I would also like to acknowledge my research assistant, Ruth Knezevich, who helped me with the tedious tasks of fact and quote checking with efficiency, meticulousness and good humor. I am grateful to my editor at the Johns Hopkins University Press, Matt McAdam, for his interest in my work, for seeing the project through the approval process, and for his patient answers to my numerous queries. This book has also benefited from the careful attention and helpful suggestions of copy editor Anne Whitmore.

Finally, I must thank my parents, Linda and David Myers, who have never questioned the value of my work and who, in an act of true dedication, helped me to proofread the entire manuscript. I will always be thankful for the many opportunities that have enabled the completion of this book, and my collaboration and conversation with fellow scholars and mentors have proven among the project's greatest pleasures.

Literature and Architecture in
Early Modern England

INTRODUCTION

Building Stories

Writing about Architecture in Post-Reformation England

In approximately 1536, John Leland began the first of several journeys around various parts of England with the goal of rescuing English history. Leland was driven by a special sense of urgency; for him, the dissolution of the monasteries threatened the loss of England's historical record. Monasteries and their associated churches had long been both the sources and the repositories of the nation's most important "antiquitees" and "monumentes," words that, in Leland's usage, referred most often to written historical documents and records.[1] According to Leland's admirer and fellow antiquarian John Bale, these valuable items were being recklessly sold off and put to undeserved and undignified uses: grocery wrapping, for instance, and toilet paper.[2] Leland went mad and died before publishing a single word of his notes, but Bale would plead with Edward VI in 1549 that Leland's recuperative project be continued and that ancient written histories be "by the art of pryntynge... brought into a nombre of coppyes."[3]

This dispersal of the contents of monastic libraries was in part occasioned by the destruction of the library buildings themselves. As Leland's notes reveal, monastic and ecclesiastical structures were sold off, converted, pulled down, or allowed to fall into the evocative ruins that were by then frequent features of the landscape. Even to strongly Protestant writers such as Leland and Bale, the Reformation produced a sense of loss, as England's religious houses—which numbered six hundred forty-five, their antiquarian successor William Camden would report—were abandoned and disavowed as part of a Catholic past.[4] To Leland's antiquarian eye, architectural and written forms of history were necessarily intertwined: buildings, like documents, communicated history. We might say that for Leland and others, architecture itself was in danger of becoming illegible, no longer clearly tracing the human histories which had produced it and which it, in turn, preserved and contained. The contents of Leland's written itineraries are not merely descriptions or catalogues of monastic libraries or even of the monasteries themselves, although these are included. They are also extensive topographical accounts that take note of many building types in every stage of construction, use, or decay, including castles, country houses, churches, and Roman ruins. In Leland's project of recovery, both buildings and written documents helped to construct the histories that he meticulously wrote down. Buildings, like written "monumentes," told stories, of the people who built them, destroyed them, owned them, lived in them, died in them, and inherited them, and of those who recorded their histories. It is with this interdependence—between architectural and written records of human history—that this book is primarily concerned. Modern readers of sixteenth- and seventeenth-century literature have much to gain by recognizing this relationship; sensitivity to the historical and narrative functions that architecture can fulfill expands our understanding of how a range of early modern writers viewed and made use of the material built environment that surrounded them.

Leland was not the only English writer to understand architecture and narrative as related forms of storytelling; this perception permeates many sixteenth- and seventeenth-century works, though scholars today rarely focus on these interrelations. Influenced by the aesthetic theories of classical architecture and the Italian Renaissance, modern art and architectural historians often assume that architecture is experienced only visually and spatially and, as a result, that it is most naturally interpreted and talked about in those terms. Suna Güven, for instance, observes, "Standing out as innate to architecture are the components of visuality and space. Visual history and spatial history each constitute a self-referential equation peculiar to the architectural brand of history."[5] We can see this equation at work in the way we organize our academic disciplines. Architectural history is quite often placed by modern universities in art history departments, which, as Dana Arnold writes, "has serious consequences for the way in which the history of architecture is studied," since the work is made the "institutional preserve" of a discipline "whose primary concern is properly with aesthetics."[6] As a result, perception of the relationship between architecture and narrative, or storytelling, has become institutionally marginalized.

It may seem surprising, but this marginalization has been dominant even in literary scholarship. Arnold's statement might be perceived as a conservative characterization of the broad fields of art and architectural history in general, but it accurately describes the ways in which these fields have been received by literary studies. So far, studies comprising both the architecture and the literature of the sixteenth and seventeenth centuries have relied mainly on periodization and aesthetic preference to construct analogies that forge synchronic relationships among works in different media. David Evett, for instance, has written eloquently of how constructing analogies among poetry, painting, sculpture, and architecture can help the scholar "learn" or know more thoroughly the members of each group. In the service of this argument, he compares "traditional and renascence styles" and refers to categories such as "earlier Tudor art, whether visual or verbal."[7] Murray Roston has defended the practice of "inferential contextualization," in which works in one group might be used to deduce the historical and aesthetic pressures and conditions to which works in another responded. Thus, as Roston argues, we might use sixteenth-century country houses such as Hardwick Hall to better understand the "complex yet integrated structure of Shakespeare's plays" as "not only a mark of the dramatist's personal talents, but part of a larger Renaissance sensibility."[8] Lucy Gent similarly argues for analogous aesthetic preferences in the painting and poetry of the Elizabethan era, despite the fact that "the obvious clues in literature do not lead to actual pictures" and "the poets' descriptions cannot be related to their pictorial counterparts."[9] In each case, these scholars offer us useful ways of imagining or explaining the development of certain formal and aesthetic features in both visual and written media, but those ways do not allow us to look in a nuanced way at how early modern writers consciously created an engagement between the two.

    I argue that in sixteenth- and seventeenth-century England, much writing about architecture belonged more properly to the fields of literature and historiography than to the fields of visual and material culture. We must recognize that, in the early modern era, talking about buildings was a way to tell human stories, to reflect on history, to discover it or make it up. Using new analyses of texts by a diverse set of authors whose works represent a range of genres (histories, dramas, poems, diaries, and architectural treatises), I examine the narrative dimensions of England's built environment from the late sixteenth century through the late seventeenth. The texts I consider in each chapter are united by two distinctive qualities. First, all point to features of a real built environment that existed outside their pages. Second, all use those features as a means of telling stories.

    It is not only, however, that architecture contributes to the study of early modern literature and historiography; these texts also supplement or revise what has appeared to some scholars to be a paucity of information concerning the way architecture was regarded and interpreted during this period. An English Short Title Catalogue search for "architecture," for instance, will turn up only two pre-Restoration works originally written in English: John Shute's *First and Chief Groundes of Architecture* (1563) and Henry Wotton's *Elements of Architecture* (1624). Allowing for translated works, we can include Hans Blum's *Booke of Five Collumnes* (1601) and Sebastiano Serlio's *Five Books of Architecture* (1611) on the list. Architectural historians, among them Eileen Harris, have usefully pointed out and described a variety of other texts that we might see as supplementing our knowledge of English building practices of the time, including works on carpentry and measurement, such as Leonard Digges's popular *A Boke Named Tectonicon* (1556) and Richard More's *The Carpenters Rule* (1602).[10] Judged against the great Continental and classical treatises of their predecessors, however, the English treatises by Wotton and Shute are disappointing. Both Wotton and Shute were readers of Vitruvius, but Wotton's short treatise deals only with country houses, whereas Vitruvius treats the design and construction of cities and temples, in addition to private buildings. Shute's (like Blum's translated work) discusses only the five orders—or types of columns—and Shute, who was trained as a painter-stainer, was quite possibly more interested in the engraving techniques of this richly illustrated work than he was in the construction of buildings.[11] And while Serlio's *Five Books* does constitute a comprehensive treatise on building, design, and ornament, Anthony Wells-Cole has demonstrated that in England the work seems at first to have functioned mainly as a pattern book for woodwork, masonry, and plasterwork: "The appearance of Serlio's *Architettura* did not change the course of architecture in England overnight ... but it had an irreversible impact on architectural decoration."[12]

Literary and historical texts might expand our knowledge of early modern architecture in another way, contributing not so much to our knowledge of its design or construction as to our sense of how it was valued and understood. Pre-Restoration printed treatises on architecture provide evidence of an interest in both building and buildings, but even taken together they do not allow us to construct the comprehensive or systematic aesthetic theory that was exemplified by their classical and Continental predecessors. Put differently, they do not provide a complete methodology or vocabulary for understanding, designing, or evaluating architecture as a visual art. Among others, Gent has lamented that early modern Britain's "traditions in architecture and painting are relatively voiceless." The "architectural remains," she argues, "are surrounded by a singular degree of silence," because "prior to the assimilation of continental treatises, building in England lacks a body of theory."[13] But this deficiency appears only if we search for accounts of aesthetic tastes or detailed descriptions of what buildings looked like. By understanding architectural writing as a form of narrative or storytelling, we might make the opposite claim: in sixteenth- and seventeenth-century England, the built environment was far from voiceless. Rather, it inspired an unusual amount of literary and historiographic production. Recently, Maurice Howard has noted the possible influence of literature on the way early modern viewers were "prepared" for the "visual exploration" of various building types; I contend that the built environment likewise affected the way writers were prepared to approach, in writing, the representation of historical places and literary settings.[14]

Leland's writings answer the methodological question at the center of this book: What do the architecture and literature of early modern England have to do with each other? He suggests answers to this question that have not been recognized by modern scholarship. First, Leland demonstrates how an author might perceive architectural evidence and narrative as related and often interdependent forms of storytelling. A specific example is Leland's description of Malmesbury, a name that designated both a Wiltshire town and an abbey that had been dissolved in 1539. As we might expect, Leland notes the remaining contents of the monastery's library, which included works by Apuleius, Tertullian, Albinus, John Scott, and the twelfth-century monk William of Malmesbury. In addition, though, he describes the "very feble" walls of the town, a now-vanished castle "sum tyme... of greate Fame, wher yn the Toun hath syns bene buildid," and "a right fair and costely Peace of Worke in the Market Place made al of Stone, and curiusly voultid for poore Market folkes to stande dry when Rayne cummith." The church formerly attached to the abbey, once "a right magnificent thing," was by then partly a ruin, including "2... Steples, one that had a mightie high *pyramis*, and felle daungerusly *in hominum memoria*, and sins was not reedified," and part of which had been converted to a parish church, and "The fair square Tour in the West End... kept for a dwelling House." In a second church on the abbey grounds, "Wevers hath now lomes... but it stondith and is a very old Pece of work."[15] Here we see Leland's combined interest in written and built monuments and the range of buildings to which he attends. A similarly wide range of significant architectural settings will be examined in this study.

More important, though, the history of Malmesbury's architecture was also a history of its human inhabitants, both past and present. The salient qualities of architecture—even monastic architecture—described by Leland are not those that his post-Reformation historical moment might lead us to anticipate. Rather than mostly evoking reactions to the Catholicism of England's past, the architecture divulged to him a much more varied range of content. Leland's architectural description does reflect England's changing political and religious identities, but it also speaks of the particular biographies attached to those buildings and remains: "The Saxons first caullid it *Ingelburne*. And after of one *Maidulphus* a *Scotte*, that taught good Letters there and after procurid an Abbay ther to be made, it was *Maidulphesbyri*: *Maidulphi curia*. The King of the *West Saxons* and a Bishop of *Winchestre* were founders of this Abbay. *Aldelmus* was then after *Maiduph* Abatte there, and after Bishop of *Shirburn*. This *S. Aldelme* is Patrone of this place."[16] A bit later, Leland notes, "Ther was a litle Chirch joining to the South side of the *Transeptum* of th abbay Chirch, wher sum say *Joannes Scottus* the Great Clerk, was slayne about the Tyme of *Alfrede*, King of the *West-Saxons*, of his own Disciples thrusting and strikking hym with their Table Pointelles." And then we return to architectural history: "Ther was an Image set up yn thabbay Chirch yn Honour of this *John Scotte*. This is *John Scotte* that translatid *Dionysus* out of *Greke* into *Latine*."[17] Then Leland records the legal fate of the property and writes of the next generation connected to Malmesbury: "The hole logginges of thabbay be now longging to one *Stumpe*, an exceeding riche Clothiar that boute them of the King. This *Stumpe*s Sunne hath maried Sir *Edward Baynton's* Daughter. This *Stumpe* was the chef Causer and Contributer to have thabbay Chirch made a Paroch Chirch."[18]

In such passages, we see that Leland's antiquarian brand of architectural history is anchored in the physical materials of Malmesbury's buildings but does not rigidly adhere to only a description of them. Instead, the notation of physical features—"an Image set up yn thabbay," for instance—branches off into the story of the people responsible for or associated with them, in this case, John Scott. And here, the description of Scott's architectural monument nicely enfolds the history of precisely the sort of written literary or historical "monument" in which Leland was equally interested. Conversely, the retelling of human history feeds back into the description of the building, as one narrative thread leads us from the "hole logginges of thabbay" to the acquisitions of the "exceeding riche Clothiar" Stumpe, to the marriage of Stumpe's son, before returning to the building itself, when Stumpe is represented as an instrument of architectural change, the story of how "thabbay Chirch" was "made a Paroch Chirch." Throughout the *Itinerary*, as here, Leland's architectural descriptions differ from those of a modern architectural history, being richly studded with the names of owners, occupants, and important historical figures, rather than with names of architects and with architectural terms. Such emphases change the way we see architecture itself, making it part of the historical record, rather than an expression of a particular aesthetic style or of a single architect's skill.

In his attention to real architectural materials that existed outside the pages of his notes, Leland offers a way of formulating the relationship between architecture and literature that differs from the synchronic, aesthetic, and analogy-based approaches that characterize much modern inter-art scholarship. He also perceives a relationship between the two that is not strictly conceptual or immaterial. Scholars such as Roy Eriksen and A. W. Johnson have located the intersection of architecture and literature in metaphor, noting numerous examples in which the processes of building and composition or the qualities of architectural and textual structures are seen as representing each other.[19] Here, for instance, we might place John Donne's determination to "build in sonnets pretty rooms" or Ben Jonson's famous assertion that "in the constitution of a poem, the action is aymed at by the poet, which answers place in a building; and that action hath his largeness, compass, and proportion."[20] Here we might also locate the tradition of memory houses, in which imagined architectural structures are used as mnemonic devices and which have been thoroughly discussed by Frances Yates and Mary Carruthers.[21]

Endorsing the value of Leland's method does not invalidate these other approaches or disprove the importance of architecture as metaphor in Renaissance thought. It does, however, suggest that literature and historiography might engage architecture in a way that is both more literal and more self-conscious. Critics can construct analogies between one work and another without claiming that the two were deliberately positioning themselves in relation to each other or that writers and artists were mindful of the cultural conditions to which they responded. For Leland, as for the other writers I consider here, the interrelation between written text and built environment was quite consciously perceived: it is one thing to write a poem that shares some general aesthetic characteristics with contemporary country houses; it is another to write a poem about a specific country house. It is certainly possible to argue that the fragmented and often disordered quality of Leland's historiography reflects the disorder of the built environment he confronted.[22] But the relationship between the buildings Leland observed and the stories he wrote down was not one of analogy or shared style. It was one of contingency: the stories emerged from the process of architectural description itself, and they depended on buildings outside their pages to be remembered and told. Without the looms and dwelling houses in Malmesbury Abbey, for instance, there would have been no occasion to tell the story of the wealthy clothier Stumpe. Conversely, architectural description required narrative; Leland's *Itinerary* could not have been fully expressed in maps or diagrams, even if Leland had had the technical skill to produce such items. Instead, his notes require characters and verb tenses as they imagine biographies and move, diachronically, between present and past. Howard Marchitello and others have explored the temporal dimensions of cartographic development during this period, especially in chorographic texts such as Leland's: "In both instances," Marchitello writes, "the representations produced (maps and chorographies) are images of the world engendered by a narrativizing of topography and history: both are made to tell historical tales, and these tales, moreover, are deployed in the service of specific political and cultural ideologies."[23] By spanning the gap between verbal history and a built environment, Leland introduces us to a kind of architectural history that is not entirely invested in either architecture or history; it is not a study of architectural structures in their own right, but its stories continually gesture toward buildings which, from Leland's perspective, were real and at least partly present. A building, to Leland, was an object of explication and interpretation, but it was not a figure of speech.

Leland's perception of a close relationship between material or built architecture and verbal narrative as two forms of historical record illustrates a complex understanding of a very basic literary term: setting. Here, architectural setting acts as source material, contributing content that, like any other literary or historical source material, was adapted by authors to various strategic ends. For Leland these ends were both antiquarian and nationalistic; architectural description was a way of preserving what Bale would call the most "worthy monumentes" and "noble Antiquitees" of England's past and of mapping the expanses of his nation.[24] (When the project was done, Leland would claim, Henry VIII, to whom he intended to give the work, would have his "worlde and impery of Englande ... sett fourthe in a quadrate table of sylver."[25]) The generic variety of the texts I consider here demonstrates the very broad range of stories architecture can be used to tell. In order to perceive this dynamic sense of architectural setting in sixteenth- and seventeenth-century texts, however, modern readers must dismantle the categories that have isolated the academic disciplines of literature and architectural history from each other. Once we develop a broader sense of what architectural writing as a category might comprise, we come to see the sophisticated and conscious ways that texts traditionally classified as literature or history engage the real built environment.

Leland's attention to the dissolution of the monasteries also grounds the particular modes of architectural interpretation with which this book is concerned in a specific time and place. An analogic or inferential approach might be used to connect the literary and architectural developments of any period or location, but Leland's view of this connection is quite clearly a post-Reformation idea.

This is not to claim that the texts I discuss in this book are all in some way about the Reformation; it is to suggest that certain effects of the Reformation provide a useful way of accounting for or tracing the history of characteristics that these texts share with Leland's writing and with one another. James Simpson has recently praised studies that historicize both the "break" between the pre- and post-Reformation periods "and, more profoundly, the forms of understanding that flow from it."[26] I focus here on how Leland models the development of a "form of understanding" that has particularly to do with architecture. As Jennifer Summit shows, "Leland's project was to rewrite the violence of the Reformation and to reincorporate the ruins it left into a topography of the newly Protestant nation."[27] The broad strokes of this project—using the stories of buildings to remake the past and adapt it to the interests of the present—apply as well to the aims of several of the later writers I discuss here.

It is important, however, not to overemphasize Reformation rupture or controversy as the lens through which the architecture of this period might have been viewed. As Leland shows, although many of the histories that architecture preserved or implied were necessarily by or about Catholics, they were not, in themselves, histories of Catholicism. Camden, for instance, would praise William of Malmesbury, "unto whom for his learned industry, the Histories of England both civill and Ecclesiasticall are deeply indebted," and Philip Schwyzer has noted that few literary works of the period deal with the subject of monasteries.[28] When it comes to architecture, we might see the Reformation inheritance of these texts differently, not as a preoccupation with the architectural relics of the Catholic past, but as a distinct approach to the built environment more generally, one that focuses on the excavation and retelling of history rather than on the judgment of religious categories or identity. Taking Leland's account of Malmesbury once again as an example, we can see how a former monastery is made to tell stories on several topics, from a dinner-time death to a present-day marriage. Freed of the notion that the post-Reformation built environment produced only traumatic reminders of an inconvenient historical truth, we are better able to see how that environment offered an attractive subject to sixteenth- and seventeenth-century writers working in a range of historiographic and literary genres.

Recent scholars in many fields have attempted to transcend the boundaries of aesthetic judgments and genealogies by replacing the term "visual arts" with "visual culture," what Norman Bryson, Michael Ann Holly, and Keith Moxley have designated a "history of images" rather than a "history of art."[29] This shift in terminology, they argue, "offers the prospect of an interdisciplinary dialogue" between art history and cultural studies in other fields.[30] With regard to the early modern period specifically, studies of funeral monuments by Nigel Llewellyn and Peter Sherlock have amply illustrated the alternative cultural and historical fields in which funerary sculpture might participate.[31] Countering the art historical periodicity of such works as Margaret Whinney's *Sculpture in Britain* (1964), Llewellyn (2000) asserts that "quite anachronistically, post-Reformation monuments have invariably been judged according to Italian criteria and the narrative history of English art has been presented as a series of steps towards or away from such criteria." In fact, Llewellyn argues that "we should instead establish an account grounded in a unique set of circumstances: for every funeral monument, there was a funeral; for every funeral a death; for every death a life."[32] Once these historical meanings are taken into account, it comes as no surprise that funeral monuments were a favorite subject of sixteenth- and seventeenth-century antiquarians, who deplored their destruction and decay.[33]

Early modern descriptions of architecture such as Leland's prompt a reconsideration of the word "visual" as well. Although Llewellyn, Paul Hunneyball, and others have fruitfully questioned the usefulness of judging English patrons and craftsmen by Italian standards that they were not, in many cases, trying to imitate, the Italian Renaissance has continued to influence our conception of painting, sculpture, and architecture as related and primarily visual forms of expression.[34] The concatenation makes sense when applied to Italian luminaries such as Michelangelo, whose genius was manifested in all three media, but early modern England does not afford us such examples, and it is difficult to imagine that sixteenth- and seventeenth-century English writers or viewers shared this sense of the field. Thus, while the change in terminology—from "visual arts" to "visual culture"—has admitted a much greater range of materials and interpretive methods, it has not really redefined our sense of where the word "visual" might be applied. While it is certainly true that architecture itself is perceived visually and that sixteenth-century English people evidently enjoyed looking at it, Leland's record reminds us that it is possible to write about it in a way that renders its appearance the least interesting or dependable of its features.

To some degree, the concept of spatial practice and experience has supplanted or supplemented the study of aesthetics in architectural history over the past several decades; and, at a distance, literary and historical criticism of early modern architecture and culture have followed this shift. In the 1957 treatise *Architecture as Space*, Bruno Zevi famously argued that space is "the protagonist of architecture," and many studies over the past two decades have turned on the idea of social space.[35] Following Michel de Certeau's assertion that "everyday stories ... are treatments of space," these approaches draw on patterns of use and daily habit to translate the discussion of architecture from the realm of the aesthetic to that of the "everyday."[36] The synthesis of these studies often consists of classification, as locations are designated public or private, male or female, urban or domestic. The work of Lena Cowen Orlin has been particularly influential in this regard.[37] Such work has provided a liberating opportunity to talk about buildings that may have been designed with use, much more than aesthetics, in mind. It has been of particular interest with respect to London architecture, which, as archaeologists such as John Schofield have pointed out, often appears hardly to have been designed at all, except insofar as its space might have been useful to someone who was willing to pay for it.[38] In viewing architecture from the perspective of users, instead of architects or elite connoisseurs, these studies have taken into account the perceptions and habits of a much broader range of social classes.[39]

At the same time, however, these approaches are less attentive to other dimensions of architectural description that appear in texts such as Leland's. Few spatial depictions of early modern architecture exist, and such artifacts as the floor plans of Ralph Treswell, the—never realized—sketches of John Thorpe, and the city views of Wenceslaus Hollar have received much attention partly because they are such rare examples.[40] The classification of these cultural spaces is historical only from our modern point of view; for early modern viewers and users, these perceptions and spatial practices would have been contemporary. Yet architecture often had a historical dimension, even from the perspective of sixteenth- or seventeenth-century writers, readers, and viewers. For Leland, as for the other authors discussed in this book, the practices that defined the built environment were narrative as much as spatial; architecture was necessarily positioned in time as well as space. Malmesbury Abbey, for instance, appeared to Leland both as what it had been and what it was; change and history were constitutive features of its identity.[41] Moreover, early modern descriptions of architecture tend to be far more interested in the extraction of particulars and idiosyncrasies than in the identification of cultural or aesthetic categories. The most prominent qualities of Malmesbury Abbey lay not, from Leland's perspective, in its representation of religious, political, or social ideology but in a dinnertime stabbing, a sheaf of manuscripts, and the benefactions of a wealthy clothier named Stumpe. Different as they are from one another, the authors I discuss shared an interest in particular architectural histories that preserved individual identity. Part of a building's utility consisted in the stories it might inspire and its capacity to say things that might be written down and retold for various purposes, to be something more than material and produce something more than space.

Despite these differences between the texts I consider here and modern practices of architectural history, recent work on the development of architectural historiography helps us to imagine and perceive these alternative forms of architectural writing. Critical examinations of genre in architectural historiography allow us to "unthink" some of the categories that have excluded the sorts of texts this study comprises. Among many others, Gent, Catherine Belsey, and Arnold have questioned approaches that cast the architectural history of this period as a halting but inevitable progress toward the classical ideals of the eighteenth century, judging even indigenous traditions by a standard that was not yet available.[42] At the very least, as Belsey acknowledges, "this was not a smooth and easy transition."[43] Following the Second World War, as Arnold has pointed out, scholars began attempting to establish relationships between England's architectural history and that of the Continent.[44] Classicism, according to Arnold, has generally been accepted as the conceptual framework that enables such comparisons. In these comparative methodologies, early modern England invariably comes up lacking, and scholars are forced to admit that during this period, at least, England never achieved the equivalent of the Italian Renaissance in the visual arts. The Palladian-style works of Inigo Jones have certainly received a disproportionate amount of attention, in part because when classicism is the standard, they contribute so readily to a sense of architectural progress. Jones's genius was indeed singular and his career worthy of attention,[45] but it is precisely this singularity that makes them a slippery ground on which to construct a general account of how the English perceived architecture during this period.[46] John Wilton-Ely, for instance, has noted that "significant as Jones is as the first true architect in the modern sense, his career is unrepresentative of the general current of English architecture until the latter half of the eighteenth century, when the idea of a single figure, responsible for both design and supervision, began to be widely accepted."[47]

Because Leland grounded his intensive study of architecture in the English Reformation, his *Itinerary* overturn an ingrained explanation of the differences between English and Continental architecture. The general explanation for the belated development of classical architecture in England is that the English were Protestants and that their suspicion of religious imagery and church ornament extended to every field we have subsequently designated a visual art. John Peacock, for instance, considers these iconoclastic impulses to be one of the challenges Jones himself faced in introducing the principles of classical aesthetics to his countrymen: "Like other Protestant states, England had developed a culture wary of the visual arts."[48] Without entirely disproving this possibility, Leland, along with the writers treated in subsequent chapters, suggests that the Reformation did not inhibit England's interest in architecture—at least, it was not that simple. Instead, the peculiar characteristics of the post-Reformation built environment produced an alternative tradition manifested in a form of description that was carried out in narrative rather than visual terms. Nor does writing influenced by this tradition generally show any awareness of, or interest in, classical style. Nonetheless, each chapter of this book demonstrates that the art of architectural interpretation in early modern England was sophisticated, well developed, and ingeniously employed. The authors I consider allow us to speak of architecture—and of writing about architecture—during this period in terms of its content and contribution, instead of its deficiency and absence. They provide us with possible solutions to what Belsey has identified as the "difficulty for us now of recovering the meanings and values that preceded a world influenced by the Renaissance appropriation of classical models."[49]

This book's approach, then, might be called predisciplinary as much as interdisciplinary. It is less an attempt to impose the methodologies of one academic discipline on the materials of another than it is an exploration of a historical moment in which architecture and literature were not yet separated but, in fact, overlapped each other in their interests and emphases. In her recent book, *Reading Architectural History*, Arnold has pointed out two other generic limitations, besides a penchant for classicism, that have characterized the architectural history of the twentieth and twenty-first centuries: an overemphasis on the career of the architect and on the art historical aesthetic period (gothic, classical, perpendicular, Palladian, etc.). These organizing principles, Arnold proves, are historically acquired, with the former being linked to the rise of the architectural profession—which arguably remained incipient in England until after the Restoration—and the latter arising after the Second World War as an attempt to create a nationalistic idea of style that then subjugated the idiosyncrasies of the individual to a broader sense of cultural progress.[50] Both, Arnold notes, have been well established since the appearance of seminal and authoritative works of architectural history such as John Summerson's *Georgian London* (1945), *Architecture in Britain, 1530–1830* (1953), and Howard Colvin's *Biographical Dictionary of English Architects* (1954).[51]

It is worth calling attention to these conventions here precisely because they are so familiar to most modern readers and were so entirely unfamiliar to sixteenth- and seventeenth-century writers, readers and viewers of architecture. Even in the very few instances when the names of architects are known, the buildings seem often to have been the collaborative effort of a builder or surveyor with practical skills and an amateur patron; Robert Smythson's work for Bess of Hardwick at Wollaton Hall and Hardwick Hall is perhaps the most famous example of this model. William and Robert Cecil, as well, are well known to have played important roles in both interior and exterior designs at Theobalds and Hatfield House.[52] Only two of the works I study in detail mention the names of particular architects: Henry Wotton's *Elements of Architecture* (1624) and John Evelyn's translation of Roland Fréart's *Parallel of the Antient Architecture with the Modern* (1664). Both works were attempts to import the principles of foreign treatises to English soil, but, as architectural historians have noted, neither work had much direct impact on English building. Moreover, despite Wotton's exact contemporaneity with Inigo Jones, the architects he mentions are all classical, French, or Italian. Evelyn is the only author in this study to show either a sophisticated awareness of architectural styles or the capacity to associate them with different historical periods, and his treatise was not published until after the Restoration. In the sixteenth century and early in the seventeenth, buildings were instead dated in human terms, that is, not through their associations with particular architects, but through their associations with owners, occupiers, and local histories. In texts they are also sometimes located within the scheme of human generations, either through their inclusion in aristocratic pedigrees or through their retention in human memory. Leland's phrase "*in memoria hominum*" is a popular antiquarian tag, along with such variations as "in our grandfathers remembrance," "in our fathers remembrance," or "to our fathers daies."[53]

Early modern texts, then, often do not reflect the interests of much of modern architectural history. By attaching their texts to a built environment that existed beyond their pages, however, they have seemed conveniently to share a focus with some recent studies in material culture. In the influential collection *Subject and Object in Renaissance Culture*, Margreta de Grazia and Maureen Quilligan call for a study of Renaissance culture that will "insist that the object be taken into account." "With such a shift," they write, "it is hoped that new relations between subject (as position, as person) and object (as position, as thing) may emerge and familiar relations change."[54] Leland seems already to be carrying out such a project; one way to characterize the *Itinerary* is as a sustained study of objects, with the human subjects of the narrative being mainly introduced and defined through their relations to historical things. The same might be said of other texts: in country house poems, for instance, it might be argued that the house creates its owner as much as the owner creates the house. Speculating on a fourteenth-century inscription—"This made Roger"—at her beloved Brougham Castle, Anne Clifford framed the question in grammatical terms: "Which words are severally interpreted for some think Hee meant it Because Hee built that, and a great part of the said Castle ... And some think hee meant it, Because hee was made in his fortune by marriage with Isabella de Veteripont, By whome hee became possessor of this Castle."[55] It is unclear to Clifford, in other words, whether the inscription means that Roger made the building or the building made him, because both are, in some sense, true. In its solidity and duration, architecture may seem to be an obvious topic for object-centered reconstructions of the past, and Gent has argued that, in the absence of a clearly articulated body of aesthetic theory, the architecture of this period will become accessible only through "an intervention on behalf of materiality."[56]

Subsequent critics have questioned what they see as the underlying fantasy of studies in material culture, that is, the notion that the unselfconscious material byproducts of everyday life allow us to perform an end run around the obfuscations of authorial self-fashioning and hence to achieve a moment of unmediated contact with a moment in the past. The result, Alan Sinfeld says, has been "attention to clothes, pots and pans, needles and pins, *as objects*, they are, after all, *stuff*, they are *made of* material, let's *touch* them, you can't get more material than that."[57] Jonathan Gil Harris has also challenged the premise that studies of the material open wormholes to synchronically perceived points in history. Objects, he points out, cannot be interpreted independently of their "diachronic trajectories ... through time and space" or outside the contexts in which they arrive as much as those in which they originated.[58] It is true that the idea of material culture has penetrated the study of literature so thoroughly that many scholars have sometimes come to take things more seriously than words. Writing about seventeenth-century developments in antiquarian historiography, for example, Graham Parry writes, "What the study of antiquity needed was more attention to Things: inscriptions, coins, physical remains from the earth—other forms of evidence than the verbal."[59] Fikret Yegül voices a common assumption about the study of architectural evidence when he writes that architecture "has little use for traditional, written text, and can be considered to be relatively free of textual distortions. Dealing directly with the raw material of building, it evades . . . linguistic instabilities of meaning."[60] If architecture is less eloquent than poems or treatises or plays, it seems, it is at least less capable of active self-fashioning or misrepresentation.[61]

Rational as Yegül's statement may be from an archaeological perspective, it does not accurately represent the view of architecture we encounter in early modern texts.[62] Jonathan Gil Harris and Natasha Korda have noted a reductive tendency "to equate the 'material' with the 'physical'," and in early modern texts architecture is both physical and not.[63] Far from viewing architecture as a site of unmediated contact with the conditions of either past or present, these authors used it precisely as an opportunity to mediate that experience; it was the intervention of authors and texts between readers and environment that made writing about architecture such an attractive prospect. Regarding antiquarian writing in particular, Angus Vine has argued that "English scholars and writers . . . sought not only to collect the scattered traces of the past, textual, material, and so on, but also to restore that past through the process of writing."[64] In my study, we see a similar approach to material "traces" of both past and present but across a broader range of sixteenth- and seventeenth-century authors and genres. Moreover, these authors' relationships to their physical subject matter were, in most cases, more skeptical than those of many modern studies of material culture; underlying the possibility of direct contact was always the unavoidable—and fortunate—necessity of mediation. The translation between media, from building to text, created a space that allowed for reinvention, for interpretation, as well as sometimes for fiction.

Clearly, my study is indebted to recent scholarship in material culture insofar as it examines not only texts but their relationships to objects and places. Each chapter of this book is partly grounded in features of the material post-Reformation built environment. At the same time, though, this book might be seen as a rejoinder to such approaches, in questioning the degree to which such distinctions—between the verbal and the material—are necessary or, indeed, actually relevant to some early modern texts. Jonathan Gil Harris, drawing on Nietzsche for his terminology, characterizes the material aspects—real or imagined—of several Renaissance texts as "untimely," that is to say, that "like a palimpsest," a material aspect "exhibits a temporality that is not one."[65] Harris's choice of the word "untimely" evokes Freud's concept of the "uncanny" (and indeed Harris goes on to use the word "*unheimlich*" in a subsequent chapter); and this, along with his overarching figure of the palimpsest, aggressively scraped and imperfectly erased, suggests that the perception of multiple time frames is somehow antagonistic, traumatic, or unsettling.[66] In fact, as I argue in Chapter

1, to view matter through multiple temporal lenses is not necessarily as strange or disorienting—to early modern writers or to us—as Harris's "untimely" would suggest. It is the work that narrative does all the time, through either the construction of linear histories or the collation of sometimes incongruous sources. In Chapter 3, I replace Harris's figure of the palimpsest with that of the anthology, in discussing Stow's and Jonson's descriptions of London architecture, suggesting a less fractious interplay between past and present yet still accounting for the multiple histories that the architecture of the city can encode. As a whole, my approach softens distinctions between extratextual material and more traditionally "literary" matter. Each chapter recentralizes textual interpretations of the architectural environment, rather than seeking to decode them in search of something that is more solid and authentic because less consciously intended. For these authors, architecture became significant in part because it was made so through storytelling. They did insist on the reality, and to some degree the authority, of objects, but they also insisted on writing about them. Their texts do not represent their architectural settings transparently, but as literary scholars we ought to be interested in their textual reinventions and authorial strategies not as the obfuscations of material truths but as original and valuable productions in themselves.

Leland's writing thus illustrates the relationship between architecture and literature—as interdependent forms of storytelling—with which each chapter of this book is concerned. Each author I treat here contributes to a new and more inclusive sense of what architectural writing might comprise. From this revised and broadened category emerges a more complex and interdisciplinary view of their literary and historiographic productions; we come to understand not only that literature and history might participate in the field of architectural history but that architecture and its histories might participate in the creation and significance of literary and historical works. Architectural setting, even when attached to the physical environment, becomes a dynamic category that contributes its own adaptable source material; it is not a static spatial or scenic detail that anchors a text in a solid layer of reality.

Chapter 1 lays the groundwork for my study by turning to William Camden's *Britannia* (Latin 1586, English 1610), the first printed work to realize Leland's plans for a comprehensive historical topography of Britain. Like Leland, Camden extracted history from buildings, including former monasteries, Roman remains, castles, churches, cathedrals, and dwelling houses. The *Britannia*'s wide readership during the seventeenth century suggests that interest in Camden's approach extended far beyond an antiquarian audience, and Chapter 1 uses this work to illustrate and project three important characteristics of the period's architectural writing that will be taken up in subsequent chapters. First is Camden's mixture of archaeological, documentary, and what we might call literary or folkloric forms of evidence, all of which converge in his narratives about buildings and architectural remains. Second is Camden's attention to the connections among architecture, landscape, and aristocratic history. Third is the secular nature of most of the *Britannia*'s architectural histories, which disproves the persistent critical assumption that architecture was necessarily associated with Catholicism and idolatry. Even as Camden follows an antiquarian tradition that emerged from the Reformation, his focus is not post-Reformation polemic. Rather, the description of buildings—even of religious buildings—turns to miscellaneous storytelling, about people who lived in them, died in them, paid for them, inherited them, destroyed them, and wrote their histories. In providing an alternative to both classicism and Protestantism as lenses through which to interpret architecture, the *Britannia* illustrates the other kinds of stories that architecture might be used to tell.

Chapter 2 turns to what is generally considered the first Vitruvian-style architectural treatise in English, Sir Henry Wotton's *Elements of Architecture* (1624). I examine the tensions that emerge as Wotton attempts to impose the visual aesthetic models of Vitruvius, Alberti, and Palladio on the native, historical modes of architectural interpretation that characterize such works as the *Britannia*. As Camden's work reveals, country houses in particular invited historical interpretations, because they provided opportunities to celebrate the ancestral authority of the house's current owner. Pairing *The Elements of Architecture* with seventeenth-century country house poems by Ben Jonson ("To Penshurst" c. 1612), Thomas Carew ("To My Friend G.N. from Wrest," 1639), and Andrew Marvell ("Upon Appleton House," c. 1654), I argue that each work acknowledges conflicts between visual and historical approaches to architectural writing. Wotton clearly designates his treatise a manual for the gentleman amateur, that he "may ... be made fit to judge of examples."[67] Each of these poems offers its own lesson in the judgment of architecture, and each pointedly rejects visual perception as a way of comprehending a building's significance. Faced with these traditions, Wotton strategically adapted his Continental sources; and, despite its classical and Italian trappings, *The Elements of Architecture* grows equally out of English soil. Wotton understood that aesthetics must reinforce, rather than efface, the story of the patron, and that the measured proportions of the Italian villa must not erase the historical dimensions of the English country house. In elaborating the differences between visual and historical ways of "seeing" a building, the chapter casts the period's architectural history in a new set of terms; less than a competition between native and foreign architectural aesthetic styles, we witness a tension between conflicting modes of architectural literacy.

Stemming from the discussion of Wotton's *Elements* and the country house poems is an examination of the architectural profession in early modern England. Taken together, I argue, these texts identify problems that the figure of the professional architect presented to the antiquarian views exemplified in the *Britannia*. English writers of this period conceived of architecture in a way that is more indebted to the profession of the antiquarian chorographer or estate surveyor than to the practically and aesthetically skilled architect described in classical and Continental treatises. In an interpretive tradition that understood architecture through its relation to both landscape and the history of its owner or patron, there was simply no room for the professional architect, and his influence was deliberately marginalized in literature about the English country house. The work of Wotton and the country house poets suggests a reason for the scarcity of professional architects in pre-Restoration England: the skill of the architect was irrelevant or even inimical to the ancestral stories a building was meant to tell.

In Chapter 3 we move from the country house to the architecture of early modern London, juxtaposing two very different texts about the city. John Stow's *Survey of London* (1598) and Ben Jonson's comedy *The Alchemist* (1610) transpose historical modes of architectural interpretation from the ostensibly stable world of the country house to a London environment where architecture visibly implied the political and social disruptions of post-Reformation English history. Stow's *Survey* presents to readers a cityscape haphazardly made over by rapid population growth and the conversion of monastic properties. Former churches had become stables and storehouses, while monasteries and nunneries were used as dwelling houses, armories, or, in the case of Jonson's Blackfriars, theaters. I argue that Jonson also responds to—and exploits—the problems of crafting coherent narratives about an architectural setting that points constantly to change. As "To Penshurst" is unmistakably a country house poem, we might equally view *The Alchemist* as a kind of city house play. In *The Alchemist* the absence of a genteel landowner breaks down the ancestral narratives that order accounts of the English country house, and the alchemical process itself emerges as an alternative form of history that might serve to legitimize claims to ownership and social status. If realized, the culmination of the alchemical process would solidify the possibility of a new social hierarchy. Like the country house poems, Jonson's play shows how literature might adapt antiquarian ideas by using architecture as a way to think about history. In both the *Survey* and *The Alchemist*, however, the kinds of stories that organize the country house poem are evoked only to be dismantled, revealing the instability of London's future through an exploration of its past.

Chapter 4 explores forms of local history that were originally associated with the parish church porch. Centering on George Herbert's neglected poem "The Church-porch" (1633), the chapter argues that the poem's proverbial style and didactic content—features that modern readers have found distasteful—are deliberate reflections of its architectural setting. Although "The Church-porch" has been marginal in recent scholarship, the church porch itself would not have been at all marginal in seventeenth-century parish life: the first part of the baptismal and marriage ceremonies, for instance, were solemnized in the church porch, where also children were taught, contracts witnessed, alms disbursed, and debts paid. In the church porch, religious principle met secular practice, and the life of the individual intertwined with the traditions, histories, and values of a community. Herbert's didactic and moral precepts thus represent a common verbal and moral currency whose circulation and constant reuse mirror the kind of public exchange that took place in the church porch. Sources in local history and ecclesiology reveal earlier associations of this poem's architectural setting, and we see that even church architecture can be viewed from a historical, rather than a doctrinal, perspective. In fact, as the traditional centers of local history, religious buildings are particularly susceptible to this sort of interpretation.

In Chapter 5, my reading of the late diaries and architectural works (1650–1676) of Anne Clifford entwines several threads from previous chapters: the capacity of architecture to record ancestral and individual histories, the narrative interrelation of built environment and written text, and the antiquarian's use of architecture as a way of discovering the past. In 1605, when Clifford was fifteen years old, her father died, leaving his lands to his brother and his brother's heirs, rather than to his only child, a daughter. She and her mother spent years attempting without success to prove that his bequest was illegal. Not until her cousin died without issue in 1643 did Clifford inherit the properties. In 1649 she traveled north to her holdings in Cumberland, Westmorland, and the West Riding of Yorkshire. There, she dedicated herself to two interdependent pursuits: the compilation of autobiography and family history and an aggressive program of architectural repairs to her castles and their surrounding churches. I argue that Clifford's written and built works shaped each other. First, Clifford's diaries—journals that were as much legal as personal documents—were meant to point outside of themselves, asserting ownership over buildings and places known to the writer and, presumably, the reader. Explicating the significance of real castles and monuments, they are patterned, in part, after architectural inscriptions. At the same time, the buildings themselves were shaped by the concerns of legal documents; Clifford inscribed each building with a triumphant proclamation of her ownership, creating a record that was not confined to the pages of her books. I argue that, as the diaries and architectural works shaped each other, both were in turn influenced by seventeenth-century antiquarian writing—such as the *Britannia*—with which Clifford was familiar. Surprisingly, such works informed not only her books but her buildings; the plaques, initials, arms, and funeral monuments with which she adorned them were exactly the sort of features that itinerant antiquarians like Leland, Camden, and Stow used to tell the histories of great families. In her architecture, then, Clifford practiced a kind of forward-looking antiquarianism; her castles and churches both record the past and anticipate their inclusion in some yet unwritten antiquarian text. Clifford's conversation with these writers counters the modern scholarly treatment of antiquarianism as an isolated (and entirely male) tradition and demonstrates that in the seventeenth century, antiquarian approaches to architecture were current enough to influence the logic of both built and written works.

Chapter 6 extends my analysis past the Restoration, which is generally viewed as a turning point in English architectural history.[68] At last, architectural historians observe, the influence of Continental models produced such skilled and aesthetically inspired professionals as Christopher Wren. In this period of newness, however, John Evelyn displayed an acute sensitivity to the connection between architecture and historical narrative. Even as he dedicated his 1664 translation of Roland Fréart's *Parallèle de l'architecture antique avec la moderne* (Paris, 1650) to the newly restored Charles II, Evelyn attempted to integrate visual aesthetics with the historical interpretation of architecture. He sought to introduce classical and Continental models into England but also to make them tell the story of a new English king. I argue that for both Evelyn and Fréart, the figure of the virtuoso—a collector of *virtù*, or antiquities and curiosities—becomes the model for a new kind of architectural patron. The disarticulation and disintegration of history are precisely what allow architectural fragments of the classical world and the Italian Renaissance to be realigned and rearranged under the guidance of a new collector, to be enlisted in the construction of histories that are geographically and temporally distant from their own original sites. Through the reordering of ancient and foreign architectural artifacts, the patron becomes an architect of history, with the capacity not only to recollect the past but to repair its discontinuities. While post-Restoration architecture and architectural writing fit much more easily into art historical categories of period and aesthetic style than do earlier English examples, this chapter demonstrates that the historical modes of architectural interpretation and writing traced in previous chapters did not become obsolete. Instead, they remained legible and relevant to post-Restoration authors as a way of imagining and describing both present and past.

The Coda traces the afterlife of this balance among history, fragmentation, and aesthetics in the architecture of one modern London building. In 1993, the medieval church St. Helen's Bishopsgate, which had survived both the Great Fire and the air raids of World War II, was partly destroyed by a series of IRA bombs. Architect Quinlan Terry was hired to redesign the church. Terry has been styled a "new classicist" and professes to believe that the proportions of the classical orders (or types of columns) were divinely communicated to Moses for use on the Temple of Solomon. The controversy produced by Terry's redesign centered partly on the conflict between architecture's capacity to preserve layers of history—what we might call its accretive or antiquarian function—and its capacity to reflect the aesthetic integrity of an architect's unified design. Visually, Terry's restored church recalls Evelyn's use of the architectural artifact. Medieval, Jacobean, and Victorian furnishings, along with a fine collection of funeral monuments, have been neatly rearranged, balancing historical with aesthetic integrity and creating a symmetry and order that is carefully reconstructed from the material fragmentation of the past.

The Coda finds Leland's antiquarian footsteps in the twentieth century. The assertion that even contemporary architecture can speak on narrative and historical registers, even as it attends to visual aesthetics, brings *Literature and Architecture* back into conversation with the modern critical questions raised in this introduction. As mentioned, architectural historians have recently explored alternatives to visual aesthetics and periodic classification as the organizing concepts of architectural history and design. Taken as a whole, this book adds a historical dimension to these discussions: questions about how architecture is perceived and written about are not new, and approaches that appear to be the products of modern theoretical inquiry might be equally understood as the most recent chapters in a long and largely unexamined story.

CHAPTER ONE

Loss and Foundations

Camden's Britannia *and the Histories of English Architecture*

Quite rationally, most histories of English architectural writing begin with books that are actually about architecture. As the introduction to this study points out, this is a sparse and attenuated category in pre-Restoration England. Nonetheless, a handful of original and translated treatises by John Shute, Hans Blum, Sebastian Serlio, and Henry Wotton lay out elements of building design, or of classical and Renaissance aesthetics, in ways that recognizably relate to our modern sense of the architectural profession.[1] William Camden's *Britannia* (Latin 1586, English 1610), by contrast, is not concerned with any of these topics. But if the *Britannia* tells us little about the history of architectural theory in England, it undoubtedly tells us more about the history of actual English buildings than all of these early treatises combined. Shute, Blum, Serlio, and Wotton together mention a total of one real English building, while the *Britannia*'s survey stretches easily into the hundreds, locating in the English landscape more than 100 former monasteries, more than 150 country houses or palaces, more than 130 castles or other fortifications, and at least 60 churches or cathedrals.[2] The first printed work to realize John Leland's ambitious vision of a complete historical and topographical survey of Britain's counties, the *Britannia* comprehends nearly every type of building and positions these structures in a history that stretches from Roman Britain to Camden's day. Thus, while early treatises tell us more about how the English came to understand and assimilate the aesthetic traditions of the classical world and the Italian Renaissance, the *Britannia* gives a much fuller idea of how its author and contemporary readers thought about the built environment that already existed around them and how they interpreted architectural landmarks and remains that had been coming into and fading from existence for more than a thousand years.

In this chapter, the *Britannia* is used to lay historical groundwork for the many types of architectural writing we will see in subsequent chapters. Camden's popular chorographic work illustrates three important patterns and features that will recur in texts throughout this study and will be detailed below. It also provides a way of tying the emergence of these patterns and features to antiquarian thought and to Camden's own post-Reformation moment. While modern scholarship has most often praised the *Britannia* for its proto-archaeological method and its capacity to separate solid empirical evidence from fiction and fantasy, the work does not consistently authorize things over words, and even when Camden attempts to sort historical truth from wishful mythology, he tends to include both.[3] Documentary and written evidence, oral tradition, and visible architectural remains combine in the *Britannia*'s depiction of the physical landscape, with the result that architecture is very often positioned through its relation to narrative records and traditions, viewed through the lens of the stories that had been written and told about it.[4] As Angus Vine has written, "One moment an antiquary might be describing the tessellated fragments of an unearthed Roman pavement, whilst the next he might report an oral tradition or rumour associated with the same place. He might then switch his attention to the ancestors of the local gentry. The point is to note how easily and readily the antiquaries moved from one context to another."[5] Sometimes, in fact, architecture survived for Camden only in writing. In the flexibility and variety of its narratives, the *Britannia* prepares us for the wide range of authors and texts that would make use of architecture over the course of the seventeenth century. Architecture in the *Britannia* is valued for the stories it might tell, and its particular locative qualities lend themselves to a strand of antiquarian writing that diverges from the histories of collecting with which antiquarianism is now most often identified.[6] Inalienable from its original site and resistant to physical preservation, architecture encourages a form of antiquarian production that expresses itself most fully in narrative genres and culminates in the reproduction and circulation of texts, not the acquisition and display of rare or antique objects. For both practical and methodological reasons, in this approach, architecture and storytelling are interdependent practices. Architecture is experienced as a process of reading, rather than solely of seeing.

The *Britannia*'s narrative and historical descriptions of architecture coalesce into recognizable models and genres that were consciously appropriated by contemporary and subsequent writers. Again for practical and methodological reasons, particular kinds of stories became associated with certain kinds of buildings, and these stories were told in formally similar ways. In perhaps the most pervasive and widely adapted of these patterns, descriptions and celebrations of the country house placed these buildings at the center of a narrative genre invested in the compilation, and manufacture, of ancestral history and social legitimacy. In these written works, the current genteel and aristocratic owners are made to rest—literally—on ancient foundations, becoming the capstones of histories that channel the description of the architecture toward celebration of the family's stability and their connections to the landscape that Camden's *Britannia* surveys.

The *Britannia* will also be used to break down a series of common critical assumptions about the causal relationship between the Reformation and English perceptions of architecture during this period. It has generally been assumed that architecture as a discipline carried some kind of doctrinal marker or that it produced a range of associations that might account for England's differences from the Continent. Converted monasteries, monastic ruins, and certain features of churches, for instance, could be associated with a Catholic past, while classical style in general might be suspect for its Roman heritage. Alternatively, scholars have suggested that classicism was consciously appropriated as part of a Protestant iconography.[7] More broadly, it has been suggested, architecture's visual vocabularies might have alienated a Protestant audience with an inherent distrust of images.[8] While Camden cannot be used to represent every case, he does present an alternative model, in which architecture—even religious architecture—is not understood through these sorts of doctrinal connotations. Buildings are instead mined for the array of idiosyncratic and secular stories that could be told about them—in short, we might say, for the human stories they could tell.

For obvious reasons, the thousand or so folio pages of the 1610 *Britannia* are rarely read cover to cover today, and the work is primarily studied in the context of other antiquarian and chorographic enterprises by such authors as John Stow, John Selden, James Ussher, William Dugdale, and Roger Dodsworth. But the *Britannia* was, in its day, a very popular book, and this small band of antiquarian scholars does not accurately represent the apparent breadth and variety of its sixteenth- and seventeenth-century readership. Unlike most pre-Restoration architectural treatises, the *Britannia* enjoyed a publication history any modern academic press would envy, running through six successively enlarged Latin editions (1586, 1587, 1590, 1594, 1600, 1607) before being translated into English by Philemon Holland in 1610.[9] While the *Britannia* is readily available (often in multiple copies and editions) in rare book libraries across the United States and

Great Britain, John Shute's *First and Chief Groundes of Architecture* (1563), survives in only five copies. Henry Wotton's *Elements of Architecture* (1624) was not republished until after the Restoration.[10] An additional edition appeared after Camden's death in 1637, and in 1695 Edmund Gibson orchestrated a completely new translation augmented with additions and corrections by multiple contributors. Although the *Britannia* seems originally to have been written for a community of foreign scholars, its publication history, and especially its eventual translation, indicates that it appealed to an English audience with a broader range of social and educational backgrounds. Holland's translation, writes Graham Parry, "became a common item in gentlemen's libraries, and did more to create a readership for antiquarian writings than did any other volume of the age."[11]

It seems likely, then, that the *Britannia*'s approach to the interpretation of architecture was at least as influential and interesting to English readers as the precepts expounded in architectural treatises, and that its perception of architecture as both the object and the source of historical narrative could have become characteristic of English texts in many genres over the course of the seventeenth century. The *Britannia* was known to several of the authors considered in the coming chapters: Ben Jonson was Camden's pupil at Westminster school, and in Epigram 14, he praises Camden's "sight in searching the most ántique springs!"[12] John Stow was a fellow member of the Society of Antiquaries. Later in the century, Anne Clifford would cite the *Britannia* in her Great Books and include it among the volumes depicted in the Great Picture (1646) of her family. At the end of the century, John Evelyn contributed notes on the county of Surrey for the new translation of 1695.[13] It is not that the *Britannia* provides source material for all of these works, but it elaborates a historical view of architecture that is common to them all, revealing their—often as yet unnoticed—indebtedness to antiquarian habits of thought.

Scholars have found it difficult to say exactly what the *Britannia* is about, but architecture has never been a candidate.[14] The work has generally been classified according to three of its main, and admittedly overlapping, interests: the rediscovery of Roman Britain, post-Reformation antiquarian study of a vanishing Catholic past, and chorography, which, broadly defined, is the historical description of landscape and cartographic space. Viewed through these multiple lenses, the *Britannia* appears to be several different books. Stuart Piggot, for instance, writes, "I do not think we can escape from the conclusion that the *Britannia* was originally planned to elucidate the topography of Roman Britain . . . which would enable Britain to take her rightful place at once within the world of antiquity and that of international Renaissance scholarship."[15] As Parry points out, though, even the first edition of 1586 "made evident, from the abundance of material remains, that there was much more history to be investigated than that relating to the Roman occupations."[16] And this broader focus is not surprising when we consider Camden's debt to Leland's *Itinerary*. (The outraged herald Ralph Brooke would accuse Camden of unacknowledged plagiarism in 1596.[17]) It is in this tradition of "British Antiquarian Research... conducted with reference to field work" that T. D. Kendrick places the *Britannia*.[18] Bernhard Klein offers another perspective, contending that the *Britannia* is mainly "preoccupied with names and boundaries," so that "even when the description follows a county's rivers, these are shown to be flowing exclusively around stately mansions, ancient castles, and private parks."[19] Despite the diversity of these assessments, it is difficult to disagree with any of them because, depending on the pages or passages we select from this vast work, all are at once correct.

It is the layering and simultaneous presence of these interests that draw the *Britannia*'s focus so often to buildings and that produce the work's distinct approach to architectural description. All these emphases interpret architecture through its relationship to both landscape and history, as a plot point in the map of an ancient Roman town, for instance, an object observed during itinerant antiquarian "field work," or as a visible reminder of a family's long-standing connection to a measured expanse of land. In each tradition, architecture accrues its significance from its association with particular human ancestors, not to abstract aesthetic ones. Whatever their state of completion, destruction, or decay, buildings were the marks of a history that comprised conquest and failure, devotion and decadence, prosperity and decline. The simultaneity and diversity of these foci contribute to the flexibility of architecture's possible significance, broadening the range of historical events and periods in which it might be implicated.

CAMDEN'S INTERDISCIPLINARY APPROACH

William Camden's reliance on firsthand observation and his skepticism of "fables" and "extravagant digressions" are often hailed as advancing a methodology that would push the study of history toward the solid ground of the social sciences and away from the muddy waters of literature and mythology.[20] The empirical and the literary are frequently cast by modern scholars as competing historiographic modes that pull in entirely different directions. While the study of literature and philology—at least as the vehicles of history—is often portrayed as the unfortunate residue of the Middle Ages, empirical observation of material evidence is viewed as looking forward to later developments in historical method, archaeology, and natural philosophy. Both Parry and Marjorie Swann have placed the *Britannia* at the beginning of a shift, over the course of the seventeenth century, from the study of words to the study of things, imagining Camden as an early adopter of the empirical method or of the late-seventeenth-century Baconianism that would be taken up in earnest by post-Restoration collectors and members of the Royal Society. Parry sees a parallel between the *Britannia*'s archaeological strands of inquiry and Bacon's *Advancement of Learning*, in which, he says, "Bacon... rightly drew a distinction between 'Words' and 'Things' as unprofitable and profitable means of inquiry." While Camden did not have "the benefits of an archaeological outlook," his "attention to Things," Parry argues, was "what the study of antiquity needed."[21] From Parry's perspective, therefore, the *Britannia* might be seen as participating in the development of objectivity, in both of the senses defined by Julie Robin Solomon: "the holding in abeyance, or erasure, of the individual mind's desires, interests, assumptions while that mind is in the process of knowing the material world" and "the idea that the material world is itself capable of authorizing knowledge."[22]

In its solidity and materiality, architecture might seem to contribute to this objective emphasis. Camden's interest in observation of the built environment could then appear to indicate a divergence of the two fields—literature and architecture—that this study is meant to unite. And on the one hand, this view of the *Britannia* is partly accurate. Camden purports to have undertaken the work in "a firme setled study of the truth," and he dismisses Geoffrey of Monmouth and the medieval Brutus myth because he can find no corroborating evidence ("Author to the Reader," [7]). In addition, successive editions of the *Britannia* acquired more and more maps, illustrations, and descriptions based on the firsthand observation of places and artifacts. But, it is difficult chronologically to cast Camden as the intellectual offspring of Bacon when influential works such as the *Advancement of Learning* (1605) and the *Novum Organum* (1620) were not published until the *Britannia* had gone through several editions.[23] And, as F. J. Levy has pointed out, Bacon himself was not particularly Baconian in his study of history. He did not write history according to his own standards for the investigation of natural philosophy, nor, really, to his own standards for writing history.[24] More important to my argument here is that the *Britannia* does contain literary sources, folkloric traditions, and verbal modes of inquiry, in abundance.[25] Long blocks of Latin poetry, some of it by Camden himself, stand out on the page; and even after acknowledging that philology is a speculative and imperfect art, he frequently resorts to it. Classical texts carry at least as much weight as Roman artifacts, and it is telling that when Camden does reflect on the corroborative "unity" of words and things, he refers not to Bacon but to Plato's *Cratillus*, authorizing archaeological study through recourse to a classical text ("Author to the Reader," [5]). Jennifer Summit has persuasively softened Parry's distinction between the ways "words" and "things" operate in the *Britannia*; Camden's method, she says, is a "literary archaeology," which does not so much distinguish between things and written sources as it transforms written sources into artifacts. Furthermore, these written artifacts require the interpretation and reframing of the Protestant historiographer: "Manuscripts," writes Summit, "will not speak the truth themselves; instead, they must be made to do so through active intervention."[26] It is not, then, that Camden's sources, whether verbal or material, speak for themselves with an authentic immediacy; rather, it is the work of the *Britannia* to locate them temporally and to extract their significance through mediation and explication.

Despite this pervasive formal and methodological interdisciplinarity, Camden is often praised today for his ability to keep disciplines apart, to separate history and poetry, and, as Wyman Herendeen says, to give them "styles and importance proper to themselves."[27] To characterize Camden as the great divider of literature and history, of philology and archaeology, is to miss the degree to which the *Britannia* does not separate words from things, stories from material objects, or known fables from ostensible facts.[28] On the contrary, the chorographic organization of the *Britannia* as a journey from one place to the next means that such sources are often aligned with one another, if not through a shared vision of history then through their attachment to a single place. In his address to the reader, Camden defends the thoroughness of his research in a way that repeatedly places material or archaeological forms of evidence in parallel with written and orally related stories:

> I have in no wise neglected such things as are most materiall to search, and sift out the Truth. I have attained to some skill of the most ancient, British, and English-Saxon tongues: I have travailed over all England for the most part, I have conferred with most skillfull observers in each country, I have studiously read over our owne countrie writers, old and new, all Greeke and Latine authors which have once made mention of Britaine. I have had conference with learned men in other parts of Christendome: I have beene diligent in the Records of this Realme. I have looked into most Libraries, Registers, and memorials of Churches, Cities, and Corporations, I have poored upon many an olde Rowle and Evidence. ("Author to the Reader," 4)

Interestingly, the passage begins with what we might think of as an archaeological metaphor ("sift out the Truth"), but much of what Camden considers most "materiall" is not material in a literal sense at all. This protestation is immediately followed by an assertion of his skill in philology, and conversation ("I have conferred") is juxtaposed in grammatical parallel to direct observation ("I have travailed"). Further, despite the *Britannia*'s chorographic and topographical emphasis, Camden claims that his research has been largely a process of reading and talking. The "Records of this Realme" are presumably written documents here, as are "Libraries, Registers, and memorials of Churches, Cities, and Corporations," "Rowle[s]," and "Evidence." Significantly, when Camden mentions the "memorials" of the churches and cities, context suggests that he is referring to these documents, not to the built architectural memorials that he also sought out on his travels. Very often, historiography is not a matter of sorting or separating types of sources but of collecting them in a way that evinces their interrelations. As Vine convincingly argues, "Archaeology . . . was only one aspect of early modern antiquarianism, no more or less important than many other fields, from etymology and epigraphy to numismatics and numerology."[29] Words were valuable to Camden as the philological wormholes to the map of Roman Britain, but they were also a means through which things themselves were understood and interpreted. Verbal narrative was not simply corroborated or effaced by archaeological evidence; it equally had the capacity to confer meaning on the artifacts of the past.

The chorographic organization of the *Britannia* produces the effect of an anthology, rather than a hierarchy, of Camden's various kinds of sources. Literary, folkloric, and documentary evidence are bound to architecture or architectural remains through their attachment to a place. As an example, I take Camden's description of the dwindling town of Richborough, Kent, formerly the flourishing Roman settlement of Rhutupiae:

> [W]riters record, that it was the Roiall palace of *Ethelbert* King of Kent and *Bede* gave it the name of a City. But ever since, it beganne to decay: neither is the name of it read in any place afterward, as farre as I knowe. . . . Now hath time razed out all the footings and tractes thereof, and to teach us that Cities as well as men have their fatall periods, it is a verie field at this daie. . . . [W]hen the corne is come uppe a man may see the draughts of the streetes crossing one another: (For, wheresoever the streetes went, there the corne is thinne) which the common people terme Saint *Augustins Crosse*. And there remaine onelie certaine walles of a Castle of rough flinte, long Britain brickes in the form of a quadrant, and the same cemented with lime, and a most stiffe binding sand, mightily

strengthened by tract of time, so that the cement is as hard as stone. Over the entrie whereof is fixed a head of a personage engraven in stone, some say it was Queene *Berthas* head, but I take it to be a Romane worke. (341-342)

In this description, multiple kinds of research converge, and the built environment is understood and interpreted both through an examination of its physical fabric and through compilation of the stories and documents surrounding it. On the one hand, Camden deploys what we might call an archaeological method, and in judging the castle to be Roman work, he does choose one story over another. As he knew from his observations throughout the country, "Britain brickes" were characteristic of Roman architecture, and he was familiar, as well, with Roman building techniques such as the compounding of lime and mortar (349). It is not surprising, then, that subsequent scholarship has judged Camden to be correct in the matter; stretches of the Roman walls remain today, and this history is part of the way Richborough markets its interest to present-day tourists.[30]

On the other hand, archaeology produces only half of Camden's account, and the remains of Richborough are enfolded in texts and stories. In the first sentence "writers record," and the historian Bede calls it a city. Significantly, as well, Camden is as inclusive as he is discriminating, retaining a story he does not actually believe to be true, and thus compiling his sources, rather than sifting for truth. Bertha and Augustine belong to the same history: Bertha was the wife of King Ethelbert at the time of England's conversion to Christianity, and Camden says that she founded a church for Christian worship in Canterbury before Augustine's arrival (338). Surviving in the lore of "the common people," and uncorroborated by material evidence, this might seem exactly the kind of misleading fable that Camden claims to have avoided. In contrast to Camden's pronouncement that architectural materials indicate "a Romane worke," the names of Augustine and Bertha introduce an entirely different conception of the relationship between words and things, one that we might call imaginative or evocative rather than empirical or evidentiary. St. Augustine's Cross, marked out by the absence of seasonal grain, is clearly not, in any literal or direct way, the imprint of Augustine's presence; and Queen Bertha's face is imagined over material effacement, read backwards onto the worn features of an unidentifiable head. In a moment that reverses the process of empirical deduction involved in Camden's observation of the "Britain brickes," the remains of the built environment are understood through the terms and names of a popular story.

Even as Camden evaluates his sources objectively, then, the *Britannia* produces the impression that buildings accrue stories, both fanciful and true. In this respect, it illustrates a principle common to several of the texts discussed in the chapters that follow. The story of Rhutupiae is not the only case in which imaginative or literary and empirical observations are brought together by Camden, even when one fails to corroborate the other. In Oxfordshire, he views the tomb of Henry II's celebrated mistress Rosamund and comments on the surviving palace and park nearby: "so much were our ancestours ravished with an extraordinarie delight in hunting." In the following lines, archaeological and narrative forms of evidence diverge: "Our Historians report, that King Henrie the second being enamoured upon *Rosamund Clifford* . . . to hide her out of the sight of his Jealous *Juno* the Queene, he built a Labyrinth in this house, with many inexplicable windings, backward and forward: Which notwithstanding is no where to be seene at this day" (375). The complete lack of architectural evidence seems to relegate this story to the realm of literature or fable, an effect that Camden reinforces by describing Henry's queen through an allusion to Roman mythology.

As the story of St. Augustine's Cross has already demonstrated, these imaginative interpretations of architectural evidence often comprise folkloric and popular traditions in addition to literary or historical ones. At Redcastle, coins and Britain bricks once again speak to the presence of a Roman settlement, yet, Camden adds, "the neighbour inhabitants . . . report that it was a most famous place in King Arthurs daies, as the common sort ascribe whatsoever is ancient and strange to King Arthurs glory" (594). And at Dover in Kent, Camden describes "A most stately castle like unto a pretty Citie. . . . The common sort of people dreameth, that it was built by *Julius Caesar,* and verilie I suppose by the British Bricks in the Chappell there, that it was built by the Romans, who used such in their great buildings" (344). Camden's verb "dreameth" seems to acknowledge that the association with Caesar is untrue or unlikely. Nevertheless, he weaves the threads of this narrative through the fabric of the building itself, allowing imaginative storytelling to color the disciplined observation of familiar Britain bricks. Single sites thus collect multiple forms of history—architectural remains, written evidence, and reported or dreamed local mythologies—and conjoin these sources in different ways. At times, various forms of evidence and interpretation seem to contradict one another; at others, they become collaborative components of the same narrative.

The co-identification or conflation of architectural and textual forms of evidence is most complete in the many instances in which buildings survive only as text. Even though Camden personally visited the supposed sites of many former buildings, he often used texts in lieu of absent architectural evidence; so text rather than building material fills out the architectural setting of some histories. We read of Deorhurst, in Gloucestershire, a small town mentioned by Bede, which "had in it sometimes a little Monasterie, which being by the *Danes* overthrowen flourished againe at length under *Edward the Confessor*; who, as we read in his *Testament*, assigned *The religious place at Deorhirst and the government thereof to Saint Denis neere unto Paris*. Yet, a little while after, as *William of Malmesbury* saith, It *was but a vaine and void representation of antiquitie*" (360). To read this narrative is something like looking at the building—a flourishing "little Monasterie"—through its own photographic negative—"a vaine and void representation"—which is itself produced through the layering of interposed texts. The monastery is available to Camden only through the practice of reading records that, even in the day of William of Malmesbury, indicated the absence of the original object. When multiple, nonidentical narratives compile, the materiality of the lost architecture recedes from the reader and singular objects dissolve under the varying layers of textual evidence. In a description of the ruined church of St. Augustine's, Canterbury, the reader is led into a building which is itself no longer extant—"now ... at this day ... buried under his owne ruins, and the rest ... converted to the Kings house"—to examine an epitaph that is no longer physically there. There are two surviving stories about St. Augustine's epitaph. One records it as a brief Latin couplet "witness[ed]" by Thomas Spot, and the second reproduces a much longer prose inscription, also in Latin, "as *Bede* reporteth, who is rather to be credited," and Camden asserts that "this is the more ancient Inscription of the tomb" (337–338). Viewed through conflicting stories, architecture is fuzzily reconstructed and the object of observation either becomes a blurry image or recedes to an inaccessible vanishing point. Rather than consistently discriminating "between 'Words' and 'Things' as unprofitable and profitable methods of inquiry," as Parry suggests Bacon did, the *Britannia* elaborates and allows for many possible relationships between them.

On the whole, it is not surprising that so many of the buildings the *Britannia* describes had fallen to ruin or disappeared altogether. Architecture that had outlived its original uses was resistant to preservation. There would have been little point, in Camden's day, in reconstructing a Roman fortress or a decrepit monastery, even if the extraordinary means to do so had been available; and, as the previous examples show, it was precisely the impracticality of preserving architecture itself which made architectural description particularly dependent on textual records. As the object of historical or antiquarian study, architecture had other qualities that made it particularly susceptible to inclusion in narrative and literary traditions. The study of architectural remnants culminates in the reproduction and circulation of texts, ideally ones that are not rare or singular but abundantly reproduced, or, as John Bale put it, "by the art of pryntynge ... brought into a nombre of coppyes."[31]

It is often taken for granted now that whatever their differences, antiquarians of Camden's time shared "the antiquarian mania of collecting and conserving," as Jonathan Gil Harris has called it. Speaking of the London chorographer John Stow, whose *Survey of London* (1598) will be treated in Chapter 3, Harris writes, "Saving the past's material traces from extinction is Stow's cause."[32] For practical reasons, this desire is difficult to apply to architecture, so saving architecture's material traces must often be done through writing and textual production. In contrast to coins, whose integrity, Camden points out, was often protected by law, the stones and timber of defunct buildings were dispersed and scavenged for use in new and more serviceable structures.[33] Architecture demanded a different kind of antiquarian activity, one that relied more on the acquisition, transmission, and survival of stories and interpretations than of original objects themselves. Introducing his completely new translation of the *Britannia* in 1695, Gibson observed that it was not buildings but books about them that would be renovated and preserved; it was not the built environment but the *Britannia* that would penetrate the present moment. Whereas the deeds of dead men do not change, he says, "the Nature of the Work makes a large difference.... [T]he condition of places is in a sort of continual motion, always (like the Sea) ebbing and flowing. And one who should attempt such a complete Description of a single Town, as might serve for all Ages to come, would see his Mistake by the experience of every year, every month, nay almost of every day."[34] The histories of collected objects often entail their provenances, what Harris has called "the diachronic trajectories of things through time and space."[35] In fact, we might call many of Camden's architectural histories reverse provenances; they are stories of how things came to disappear.

As Gibson suggests, in the *Britannia*, one of architecture's most reliable qualities is its tendency to dematerialize; when defunct or superannuated, it must either be renovated under a new identity or linger to speak of absence and recession as much as of discovery, illumination, or the immediacy of the past. As time moves forward, the object does not; eventually, material history disappears and the verbal narrative is all that remains. At "old Winchester," for example, a "large rampier" pointed to the city it no longer protected: "by report, there stood in old time, a cittie, but now neither top nor toe, as they say remaineth of it: so as a man would quickly judge it to have beene a summer standing campe, and nothing els" (269). At Selsey, in Sussex, "remaineth onely the dead carkasse, as it were, of that antient little citie ... and the same quite hidden with water at everie full sea, but at low water, evident, and plaine to be seene" (308). At Dorchester, "of late by turning London high way from thence, it hath decreased so, as that of a citie it is scarse able now to maintaine the name of a towne, and all that it is able to doe, is to shew in the fields adjoyning ruines onely and rubbish, as expresse tokens of what bignesse it hath beene" (384). Abandoned by their original occupants and surroundings, it is these buildings' very stability that renders them unstable over time; they don't move, but other things do. The ramparts of old Winchester watch vacantly over a camp that has passed like a summer; Selsey disappears as its land is tugged gently out from under it, "quite hidden with water" at every high tide. Dorchester shrinks away from its very name "of a citie" as the road turns away to leave it desolate.

Several of England's most famous early collectors and collections do appear in the *Britannia*, and their presence shows how Camden's treatment of architecture differs from the usual antiquarian treatment of objects. *Britannia* mentions, among others, the famous manuscript library of John Stow, Bishop Frances Godwin's collection of "antique inscriptions," and, several times, Sir Robert Cotton's house at Connington, where Cotton, "having gathered with great charges from all places the monuments of venerable antiquity... [began] a famous Cabinet" (820, 637, 500).[36] Camden recognized the rise of an economy of collecting, in which scarcity, rather than inherent quality, would beget value. Near Kilman Lhyd, Caermardenshire, there had been discovered a certain kind of coin "which among Antiquaries" was considered "of the greatest price and estimation, as being most rare of all others" (650). In comparison to a coin, however, architecture is far less susceptible to being collected, moved, and rearranged; and to tour the buildings of the *Britannia* one turns away from Cotton's cabinet and walks down another path altogether, gaining access to a strand of antiquarianism that we might broadly call local history. Architectural inscriptions were sometimes collected and moved to new locations, but their presence pointed evocatively to what could not be relocated, even if it had survived. Cotton himself "translated" from Richmondshire to Huntingdonshire a plaque that Camden took to commemorate renovation of a Roman bath house, although others had postulated that it recorded the name of a town. "Heere," he writes, "must I cause them to forgoe their error, who by this inscription falsely copied forth, whiles they red untruly BALINGIVM for BALINEVM.... But if a man look neerer to the words, hee shall find it most evidently engraven in the stone BALINEVM, that is, a BATH, or Hotehouse" (732). In such examples we become aware that architecture defies reappropriation. The study of material artifacts bleeds into philological speculation, and the absence of either town or bath house, as much as the inscription's odd new situation in Cotton's collection, reminds the reader of what could not have been collected, even if it were still available to be observed.

For the antiquarian tourist of Camden's day, then, the built environment contained its own verb tenses: what had been a present-tense artifact for one writer or observer could be viewed by another only in the past tense. The *Britannia* contains many examples in which the passage of time slides between words (such as names or inscriptions) and things (such as architectural remains). The two no longer match each other, but neither is false. Put differently, Camden could only describe defunct buildings—monasteries, for example—in terms of what they *had been*; a monastery could not be, to him, what it was to Bede, or to William of Malmesbury, or to any of its vanished monks. And Camden's present followed the course of his narrative: his account of the Benedictines at Glastonbury illustrates how his temporal perspective differed from that of his historical sources. This powerful order "reigned as it were in all affluence 600. yeres (for all their neighbors round about were at their beck) they were by King Henry the Eighth dispossessed & thrust out of all, & this their Monastery, which was growen now to be a prety Citie, environed with a large wall a mile about, & replenished with stately buildings, was raced and made even with the ground: and now onely sheweth evidently by the ruines thereof, how great and how magnificent a thing it was" (227). One "now" comes up against another "now" ("growen now" and "now only sheweth"), compiling two definitions of the present, since the two do not refer to the same time period. Similarly, architectural evidence can point in two temporal directions at once. In Camden's narration, "a prety Citie" is both remembered and "raced" by the observation of its own "ruines." What is "evidently shew[n]" is not only what was once there but that it no longer is. In the final phrase, the former "great and ... magnificent ... thing," which the passage as a whole has helped us to imagine, is suddenly reduced and removed from the present by the final verb, "was."

In such cases, description implies the passage of time; it is the mediation of narrative, with its temporal inflections, which makes it possible to reassemble history at all. Harris has compared the built environment of this period to a palimpsest, a surface on which the marks of one historical period were aggressively but imperfectly erased to make way for the constructions of another.[37] The result is a perception of topography that he calls "polychronic," collating a series of historical moments in the same material object or geographical space. This effect of temporal depth and collation is what narrative expresses all the time, of course. One way to negotiate a polychronic or multitemporal view of something is to tell a story about it, which may easily comprise past, present, and future. As much as it might produce a sense of what Harris calls the "untimely," this experience of the polychronic is not necessarily disjointed or unsettling, to early modern antiquarians or to us. An antiquarian view of the built environment produced historical narrative, spinning out the threads of various stories as the perception of multiple time frames was negotiated and expressed through language.

Narrative becomes part of the process of architectural description. Historical buildings are understood in part through written historical sources. Because of their immobility, buildings tend to inspire records whose complexities are mediated by verb tenses and other temporally inflected words. The relationship between words and things in the *Britannia* becomes complementary, rather than necessarily corroborative, and fluid, rather than hierarchical. Sometimes, material remains are used as the starting point for observations or conjectures about the past. Equally often, this process is reversed and architectural evidence accrues meaning through the stories that survive about it. An example is Corf Castle, Dorsetshire, which comes into view only in the light of the historical narrative Camden relates, not through his observation of the building itself. The castle "after a long combat with time somewhat yeelded ... until of late it hath beene repaired and is a notable testimonie an dmemoriall [*sic*] of a Stepmothers hatred." This sensational detail is apparently not inscribed anywhere on the building, so it is not a memorial to anything until we are told by Camden's text to remember it that way. Camden activates the architecture's commemorative capacity by telling the story of Aelfrith, who, wishing "to make way for her owne sonne *Etheldred* to the Crowne," murdered her son-in-law Edward while he was on a hunting expedition at the castle. Camden's description of the deed is unusually graphic: Aelfrith "set some villaines and hacksters to murder him, and like a most wicked Stepdame fed her eies with his bloud" (211). Later, gratifyingly wracked with guilt, the unhappy Aelfrith founded a monastery. Camden's goal here is not to preserve architectural evidence or even to describe it. Instead, he attaches a story to a visible feature of the built environment, providing his reader with access to the landscape through the process of retelling and moralizing the past. The object sponsors the relation of history but is itself partly displaced by the story, for it is largely through this interpretive act of retelling that the building is really "seen."

ARCHITECTURE, ANTIQUARIANISM, AND ARISTOCRACY

As buildings become inseparable from narratives about them in the *Britannia*, certain types of buildings become associated with certain types of narratives, creating a series of subgenres that we might roughly classify as castle stories, country house stories, monastery stories, and so forth. In the second of these categories, to be examined in greater detail in the next chapter, architectural history is structured around the familial histories of England's genteel and aristocratic families. These stories are "streamline[d]," (to use Klein's term) and directed in a way that contributes to the celebration of those families, and the narratives culminate in the names and praises of landowners at the time of writing.[38] In fact, Camden's country house narratives differ in tone from many of the other architectural stories of the *Britannia*; they are less wandering and more focused, less speculative and more certain as the strands of history are resolutely directed toward a common end. Ancestral and architectural histories shape each other; while the buildings are mined for their heraldic possibilities, the locative nature of architectural description provides a way of collating these stories, producing impressions of coherence and continuity, even when historical fact did not readily lend itself to that end.

I have chosen this type of narrative because it seems to have been among the most attractive to writers in several genres over the course of the seventeenth century, serving their social priorities in a variety of ways. John Stow would attempt to apply its conventions to the architecture of early modern London (producing a very different result from the *Britannia*). Ben Jonson's "To Penshurst" and *The Alchemist* both seem to adapt the antiquarian country house narrative, to very different effect. Henry Wotton would defer to these traditions in *The Elements of Architecture*; Anne Clifford would exploit them in both her diaries and her buildings; and in his post-Restoration translation of Roland Fréart's *Parallèle de l'architecture antique avec la moderne*, John Evelyn would display a sensitivity to the well-established relationships among architecture, history, and aristocratic patronage. Modern scholarship has focused mainly on the social and political contexts in which these narratives functioned.[39] While attending to these contexts, Chapter 2 also establishes an ancestry for the genre itself, tying both its form and content to particular currents of antiquarian thought and methodology. Country house narratives were strategically constructed, but as the product of an antiquarian tradition that understood architecture through its relation to written history, these narratives were also shaped by the documents that survived about them and that they themselves often physically preserved.

Country houses are not the only buildings that generated recognizable narrative patterns, but it seems likely that writers found their stories especially serviceable, for social, legal, and political purposes. Because they dealt with buildings occupied by socially prominent families, country house narratives provided points of entry to significant contemporary conversations about legitimacy, social ascendance, and patronage in ways that other building stories did not. As a point of contrast, it is worth pausing to look at the types of narratives associated with a different kind of building: the castle. Because castles were originally fortifications, which became unnecessary and impractical as rulers or enemies faded away, narratives about them tend not only to account for their material degeneration but to extend those observations into reflections about decay and the wear wrought by the passage of time. In Shropshire, wrote Camden, "these castles with others which I am scarce able to number and reckon up, for the most part ... are now ruinate not by the furie of warre, but now at length conquered even with secure peace, and processe of time" (593). At Marlborough, Wiltshire:

> wee read, that John surnamed *Sine terra*, that is, *Without Land* (who afterwards was King of England), had a Castle here, which when hee revolted from his brother King Richard the First, Hubert Archbishop of Canterburie, tooke by force: and which afterwards was most famous by reason of a Parliament there holden ... But now being daunted by time, there remaineth an heape of rammell and rubbish witnessing the ruines thereof, and some few reliques of the walles remaine within the compasse of a dry ditch, and an Inne there is adjoyning thereto, which in stead of the Castle, hath the signe of a Castle hanging out at it. (255–256)

Like a country house, the castle's significance is defined in terms of socially and politically important figures associated with it, and the building is made to gesture toward its human—rather than aesthetic—ancestors. But the motion of the story is toward dissolution not monumentality, focusing on time's capacity to erase identity and influence rather than to bolster and create them, in the way that the preservation of ancestral history would do. The disappearance of the physical architecture renders history elegiac and reductive. While the *Britannia* records the history of former rulers and statesmen involved with castles, Camden concludes by telling us that the architectural evidence has forgotten them; kings and parliaments and archbishops are counterbalanced in Camden's story by "an heape of rammell and rubbish ... some few reliques of the walles" and—"in stead of the Castle"—a faint echo of its memory preserved on the sign of an inn.

There would have been little point in celebrating one's family or a prospective patron with the observation that glory fades, and country house narratives produce the opposite impression: status continues and, in fact, accumulates as time passes. On the one hand, as critics have observed, descriptions of the country house during this period were often nostalgic, evoking comparisons to a golden age or an idealized past.[40] On the other hand, Camden reminds us, country houses were emphatically imagined in the present tense, and history was enlisted insofar as it served a celebration of a present moment. As an example of the country house narrative's most common characteristics, we might take Camden's description of The Vine, in Hampshire:

> a verie faire place, and Mansion house of the Baron Sands, so named of the Vines there, which wee have had in Britaine, since Probus the Emperour's time.... The first of these Barons was Sir William Sands, whom King Henrie the Eight advanced to that dignitie, being Lord Chamberlaine unto him, & having much amended his estate by marrying Margerie Braie, daughter and heir of John Bray, and cousin to Sir Reinold Bray, a most worthy Knight of the Order of the Garter, and a right noble Baneret: whose Sonne Thomas Lord Sands, was Grandfather to William L. Sands that now liveth. (269)

The passage combines architectural history (the "Mansion house") with natural history ("so named of the Vines there"), familial history (the Sands and Bray lineages), and political history ("whom King Henrie the Eight advanced") in order to promote the name and titles of the present landowner ("William L. Sands that now liveth"). Details cluster around the story of the family, which is introduced through its connection to a specific architectural setting. Extending historical associations to the Emperor Probus, the name of the house—The Vine—lends the family even deeper roots, so that the architecture constructs lineage and history as much as these lenses enable the *Britannia*'s description of architecture itself. Similarly, in Derbyshire, a description of Hardwick Hall both shapes and is shaped by the history of its owners:

> upon a rough and a craggie soile standeth *Hardwic*, which gave name to a family in which possessed the same: out of which descended Lady Elizabeth Countesse of *Shrewsbury*, who beganne to build there two goodly houses joining in maner one to the other.... This now giveth the title of Baron to Sir *William Cavendish* her second sonne, whom King James of late hath honored with the honor of Baron *Cavendish of Hardwic*. (555–556)

It is through their ownership of "two goodly houses" that the Cavendish family is tied to the "rough and ... craggie soile" of Derbyshire. The end of the story collapses the identities of owner and architecture, as "Hardwic" comes to designate both William Cavendish (as part of his title) and the place to which he is attached. Architecture becomes both the expression and the creator of human identity as it moves from objective ("beganne to build... two goodly houses") to active grammatical roles ("This now giveth the title of Baron to Sir *William Cavendish*").

In these examples, then, as elsewhere in the *Britannia*, architecture mediates between the *Britannia*'s relation of human history and its description of the landscape, with the building itself hinging these two elements of the story. In the case of the country house narrative, the effect is both to naturalize aristocratic power by rooting these narratives in topography and to make the landscape more artificial, an emblem as much as a thing in itself. The vines of Hampshire are transposed from their literal referent to the house itself, while the house becomes a heraldic object in which family history might be recorded and discerned. As Richard Helgerson has pointed out, many early modern maps of England imposed the arms of prominent families over portions of the landscape where they lived.[41] In the *Britannia*, architecture often serves the same function, as buildings are explicated in the same terms with which one might decode the language of a heraldic escutcheon. In Cornwall, for instance, Camden describes Lhanheron, "the seat of the Arondels, a familie of Knights degree, who for their faire lands and large possessions were not long since called, the *Great Arondels*. In some places they are written in Latin *De Hirundine*, and not amisse, if my judgement be ought: For *Hirundo*, that is, a Swallow, is named *Arondell* in French: and in a shield sables, they beare for their armes six Swallowes argent. Certes, a very ancient and renowned house this is, spreading far and neere the branches of their kinred and affinity" (193). Through its context in the *Britannia*, the "seat" of the Arundels is located firmly in Cornwall, but rapidly, features that might be understood on a literal level in a naturalistic description of the landscape (here, the swallow) become philological and symbolic abstractions, transfigured from features of the Cornish countryside to the stylized ornaments of a "shield sables." By the end of this passage, the physical house presumably indicated in the "seat of the Arondels" has also become the symbolic "house" of a dynasty, which is in turn re-anchored to the landscape through the locative phrase "far and neere." Architecture thus becomes a strategic point of contact between physical and political understandings of the landscape, which early modern maps strove so often to combine.

As we see in each of these examples, by joining human and natural histories and by allowing many stories to accumulate on a single geographical site, architectural description could thread together disparate histories and manufacture a sense of continuity and longevity from stories that might otherwise appear disjointed and abrupt. Architectural and geographical continuity might thus conveniently stand in for the continuity of an ancient lineage. Appearing at the culmination of a country house narrative, the socially ascendant William Cecil acquires a longer and more illustrious history than he possessed through ancestry alone. At Welland, Northamptonshire, wrote Camden, "Ladie Margaret Countesse of Richmond, king Henrie the Seaventh his mother built a goodly faire and stately house." Camden then manufactured a sense of continuity by ignoring the fact that there was no direct family connection between the Countess of Richmond and the house's subsequent owners, the Cecils. What might be perceived as historical rupture is glossed over by the seamlessness of the narrative: "Now by this time is *Welland* come to *Burghley* whereof the most prudent and right honorable Councellour *Sir William Cecil,* Lord high Treasurer of England, yea a singular treasure and supporter of the same, received the title of *Baron Burghley,* for his great good deserts, at the hands of Queene ELIZABETH. Which title hee adorned with the lustre of his vertues, and beautified this place with magnificent sumptuous buildings, adjoining thereto a large Parke encompassed about with a stone wall of a great circuite" (514). In this passage, Cecil acquires with his house a history that is not his own, in part erasing the newness of his social prominence. His moral and political credentials are reinforced by his position in this country house narrative, for Camden makes his tenure the stable capstone of a longer architectural history. The identification between architectural and human narratives is cemented in the final line of the description, where personal virtues and architectural beautifications are placed parallel as joint expressions of Cecil's worth. The conventions of the country house narrative seem to carry authority here, legitimizing Cecil.[42]

Similarly, Penshurst, in Kent, was "the seat anciently (as it seemeth by the name) of Sir *Stephen de Penherst* who also was called *de Penchester* a famous Warden of the Cinque ports." In Camden's day, though, the house belonged to Robert Sidney (brother of the poet Philip Sidney), whom "*James* our soveraigne King, made right honorable, first by the title of *Baron Sidney of Pensherst,* and afterwards, of *Vicount Lisle*" (329). Camden's story is really the history of a title and a place, rather than of a person or family, because the designation "of Penshurst" floats from one owner to the next. The title is conveyed with the house, so it is architecture that provides the coherence in this case, rather than human lineage. Through architectural description, then, Camden is able to insert Robert Sidney into a history that is not his, granting him pride of place in both narrative and geographical terms.[43]

Camden, like some other writers who would adapt the country house narrative, clearly uses these aristocratic foci as indices of social and political concern, in acts of deference to prominent individuals who had served or might serve as patrons. But attention to such concerns was also born of more practical historical contingencies and from antiquarian methodologies that affected the emphases of Camden's stories and affect how buildings become legible to readers of his text. As mentioned, Camden's view of the landscape was heavily mediated by his access to texts and documentary evidence, and country houses tended both to generate and to preserve particular kinds of documents, which supplied and shaped the content of country house narratives. Being the objects of expenditure, ownership, and inheritance, these buildings were also frequently the subjects of deeds, wills, inquests, and accounts. They also preserved such records over time. As Lena Cowen Orlin has pointed out, documents, as well as buildings, have "spatial histories," and one reason records about wealthy households of the time tend to have survived is that wealthy households had good reasons and good places to keep them.[44]

Tracing expenditures, deaths, rewards, marriages, and inheritances—points at which properties changed or changed hands—these documentary sources are often easily discernible in Camden's architectural histories; buildings are described in a way that clearly reflects the content of their own libraries and muniment rooms. Many stories, rather than being based on visual artifacts, are compilations of legal agreements and official papers. It was with such sources that Camden could document that the dwelling named Nonesuch had originally been Henry VIII's palace. "Yet Queene *Marie* made it over to Henrie *Fitz-Alan* Earle of Arundell for other Lands: and he, when he had enlarged it wirh [sic] a Librarie passing well furnished, and other new buildings, passed over all his right when he died to the *L. Lumley*, who for his part spared no cost . . . and from him now is it returned againe by compositions and conveiances to the Crowne" (299). And we read of Einsham Abbey, in Oxfordshire, "which, *Aethelred* King of England in the yeere of salvation 1005. confirmed to the *Benedictine Monkes*, and in his confirmation *signed the priviledge of the liberty thereof* (I speake out of the very originall grant as it was written) *with the signe of the sacred Crosse*: but now is turned into a private dwelling house and acknowledgeth the Earle of Derby Lord thereof" (374). In each case, Camden pieced together architectural description from a series of legally significant documents about the house. The distinctive features of the country house narrative, which would appear in many incarnations over the course of the seventeenth century, can thus be traced to exactly the sort of interdisciplinary antiquarian method described in the first section of this chapter. Country house stories were not only opportunistic social constructions; they were the products of an approach to historiography that saw architectural and written forms of evidence as complementary and mutually productive ways of remembering and retelling the past.

THE REFORMATION AND ENGLISH PERCEPTIONS OF ARCHITECTURE

It is perhaps to be expected that Camden's stories about country houses are frequently secular in nature. More surprising, however, is that this statement also applies to his treatments of religious buildings, such as churches and monasteries. I suggest two ways in which the *Britannia* undermines the relationships scholars have traditionally formulated between architecture and religion in post-Reformation England. First, *The Britannia* fails to support the notion that classical and Renaissance architectural styles were associated with Catholicism and with Rome, and second, it demonstrates that religious architecture was not always viewed through the lens of post-Reformation polemic and classified as either Catholic or Protestant, Laudian or Calvinist.[45] Instead, Camden values churches and monasteries for their important role in curating England's historical record. As the long-established centers of parish and local history, they preserved history of many kinds and were particularly susceptible to historical and antiquarian interests and interpretation.

In modern scholars' attempts to explain the obvious differences between the architecture of the Italian Renaissance and the architecture of early modern England, the most common explanation has been that to a Protestant audience, classical and Renaissance styles were suspect, either because they were a potentially idolatrous form of visual display or because they were derived from Roman architecture. If anyone could have made this sort of conceptual association, it was Camden, a virulent Protestant and an internationally connected humanist scholar. But Camden does not resort to this idea. The *Britannia* does refer to Vitruvius more than once, but always as a historical source for ancient Roman history, never as an aesthetic or practical treatise that might be used by modern builders or applied in the judgment of modern buildings. For instance, Camden tells the story of a gardener in Flintshire who, "digging somewhat deepe into the ground, happened upon a very ancient peece of worke, concerning which there grew many divers opinions of sundry men." Vitruvius is evoked not as a building manual, exactly, but as the source Camden uses to identify this artifact: "hee that will with any diligence read *M. Vitruvius Pollio*, shall verie well perceive, it was nothing else but a Stouph or hote house begunne by the Romans, who as their riotous excesse grewe together with their wealth, used bathes exceeding much"

(681). Whatever Camden's interest in the aesthetics of Roman architecture, it is not apparent in the *Britannia*. Vitruvius functions as a document about Roman history and culture, but not as a manual of style.

Camden, in fact, rarely comments on architectural aesthetics at all—beyond calling certain buildings "fair"—and only once does he associate architectural display with Italy. Near the ancient castle of the Corbet family in Shropshire, Camden tells us: "[W]ithin our remembrance, *Robert Corbet*, carried away with the affectionate delight of Architecture, began to build in a barraine place a most gorgeous and stately house, after the Italians modell: But death prevented him, so that he left the new worke unfinished and the old castle defaced" (594). If Camden had wanted to taint Renaissance architectural styles with suggestions of Catholicism, this example would have provided him the opportunity, since the charge could easily have strengthened this mild critique of Corbet's overreaching. Instead, Camden demonstrates his capacity to associate a certain architectural style with Italy—knowledge which, Llewellyn and Hunneyball have argued, many English people would not have shared—but the building still does not carry any religious or doctrinal marker for him.[46] Although his failure to comment on architectural aesthetics might be read as a pointed Protestant rejection of such concerns, it seems more likely that Camden either did not associate classicism with Catholicism or found the idea irrelevant to the historical interests and, mainly narrative, form of the *Britannia*.

A second hypothesis about the relationship between the Reformation and English perceptions of architecture seems to fit more readily on the *Britannia*. Rather than parsing England's new building projects in search of classical inflections, several scholars have focused on the provocative features of religious architecture, including churches and ruined or converted monasteries. It has generally been assumed that the English viewed such buildings through the lens of Reformation polemic, and that the structures were of interest for their Catholic or Calvinist characteristics. The *Britannia* does not support this premise. While churches and monasteries appear in abundance throughout its pages, they are not defined in terms of an implied or explicit polemical context. Instead, they are presented as places that preserve history and about which history has been preserved. As libraries were dispersed and funeral monuments defaced, it was not only England's religious past that became suddenly more interesting. The *Britannia* and other antiquarian texts reflect an awareness of many types of history associated with such architectural features. Expressions of Camden's judgment of the monasteries and of England's Catholic past are remarkably sparse and inconsistent, and they seem to depend on the documents he had to hand rather than on any predetermined polemical stance from which he himself viewed the past. And many of the historical documents on which he depended could not have had anything to do with the Reformation, because they were written long before it happened.

Monasteries and churches were, of course, objects of special interest to Camden and other antiquarians. It was the imminent loss of monastic libraries that had spurred Camden's predecessor, John Leland, into the commencement of his journeys. Leland was vehement in his condemnation of Catholic institutions, but his admiration for their libraries was equally strong. "I dolorouslye lamente so greate an oversyghte in the moste lawfull overthrow of the sodometrouse Abbeyes & Fryereys," he wrote, "when the most worthy monumentes of this realme, so myserably peryshed in the spoyle. Oh, that men of learnyng & of perfyght love to their nacyon, were not then appoynted to the serche of theyr lybraryes, for the conservacion of those most noble Antiquitees."[47] In the *Britannia*, as well, monasteries and churches are frequently useful by virtue of the histories they might have preserved. About Monks Weremouth, in the Bishopric of Durham, Camden quotes William of Malmesbury, whom he has already lauded for "learned industry" in "the Histories of England both civill and Ecclesiasticall": "Benedict *Bishop* beautified with Churches and built Abbaies there, one in the name of Saint Peter and the other of Saint Paule. The painfull industry of this man hee will wonder at, who shall read his life; for that he brought hither great store of Bookes" (242, 742–743). In addition, the funeral monuments these buildings contained were often adorned with arms and inscriptions that recorded names, births, deaths, marriages, and progeny. In 1600, Camden published a transcription of the funereal inscriptions in Westminster Abbey, and he attends to inscriptions in the *Britannia* as well. At Arundel, in Sussex, for instance, he wrote, "in the Church are some monuments of the Earles there enterred, but one about the rest right beautifull, of *Alabaster*, in which lieth in the mids of the Quire Earle *Thomas*, and *Beatrice* his wife, the daughter of John King of *Portugall*" (310). At Bildas Abbey in Shropshire, "there flourished a faire Abbay, the Sepulture in times past of the noble familie of the *Burnels*, Patrons thereof" (593).

As these examples show, churches were objects of aristocratic expenditure; as such, they generated and preserved both written and architectural evidence of aristocratic investment and wealth. In some cases, then, the histories of churches fulfilled the same functions as those of the aristocratic or genteel country house. In addition to surviving in the pages of grants, deeds, and accounts, the names of donors and founders were sometimes inscribed in the fabric of parish churches themselves, so that the history and presence of a wealthy family were—literally—integrated into the space of the local community. At Chippenham, in Wiltshire, the *Britannia* recounts, "Nothing is there now worth the sight but the Church, built by the Barons Hungerford, as appeareth every where by their coats of Armes set up thereon" (243). And at York Cathedral, following a fire: "*John Roman* Treasurer of the Church laid the foundation of a new worke, which his son John, *William Melton*, and *John Thoresby*, all of them Archbishops, brought by little and little to that perfection and beauty which now it sheweth, yet not without the helping hand of the nobility and gentry thereabout, especially of the *Percies* and the *Vavasours*, which the Armes of their houses standing in the very Church, and their images at the West gate of the Church doe shew, *Percies* pourtraied with a peece of timber, and *Vavasours* with a stone in their hands" (706). As we see in these images of helpful aristocrats, church building and identity building become inseparable activities. To Camden, in this case, one of England's most impressive cathedrals functions as a slate on which local and ancestral histories are inscribed.

The stories of defunct monasteries in some cases resemble those of the country house, in that history from diverse sources tended toward the consolidation of aristocratic power. At the end of the seventeenth century, Thomas Tanner would defend his abridged translation of William Dugdale and Roger Dodsworth's massive monastic history, the *Monasticon Anglicanum* (1655), on the grounds that the work was relevant to contemporary aristocratic land rights. "[T]he Monks," he wrote, were "so accurate in Registering the Donations, and preserving all Charters, Leases, and other Deeds, relating to their possessions not only after, but also before it came into their hands."[48] As Tanner suggests, lands and rents were frequently recorded in the transactions between monasteries and aristocratic founders or benefactors, again intertwining architecture, aristocracy, and landscape, but monastic architectural histories also allowed the antiquarian to combine the adumbration of ranks and titles with reflections on the spiritual and moral nobility that ideally accompanied social status. Camden, like Tanner, was willing to exploit monastic history for its lofty social connections, as opposed to its Catholic ones. At Hertland, in Devonshire, "famous in old time for the reliques of that holy man Saint Nectan," Camden wrote, "there was erected... a little Monasterie, by *Githa* Earle Goodwines wife, who had this Nectan in especiall reverence, for that she was perswaded, that for his merits her husband had escaped the danger of shipwracke in a violent and raging tempest" (206). This story of devotion is quickly capped by another, more legally serviceable, account of the monastery's foundation: "Howbeit afterwards, the *Dinants*, who are also named *Dinhams*, that came out of *Bretagne* in France, whose demeans, as in see it was, were counted the founders thereof: and from them descended *Baron Dinham*, Lord high Treasurer of England, under K. Henrie the Seventh, by whose sisters and heires, the inheritance was divided between Lord Zouch, Bourchier Fitz-warin, Carew, and Arundell" (207). Rather than traumatic occurrences that ruptured the present with reminders of the Catholic past, monasteries represented to Camden and other antiquarians a source of legal, political, and ancestral documentation.

Camden does occasionally comment on the monasteries as abandoned Catholic institutions, but his conclusions are ideologically inconsistent, ranging from predictable Protestant denigration to what might look suspiciously like wistful Catholic nostalgia. As Camden switches allegiances, though, his methodology remains constant: his depictions are contingent on the documents he summarizes and compiles. At Bolton Abbey, Staffordshire, for example, a snatch from a "Leger-Booke" records the founder's extravagant payments of protection money—*"that his donation might stand good and sure"*—to *"every bishop . . . beside to* Alfrick *Archbishop of Canterbury."* Here, Camden's reflection ironically reverses any nostalgic idealization of the medieval church by replacing the "golden world" of a longed-for past with the gold which greased the palms of greedy church officials: "[W]e may understand, that there was a golden world then, and that gold swaid much yea in Church matters, and among church men" (586). In an introductory section on "the Division of Britaine," however, financial and legal accounts of the dissolution produce the opposite result: "England groned" at the overthrow of "the greatest part of the Clergie, together with their most goodly and beautifull houses . . . under a faire pretence & shew of rooting out superstition" (163). In light of the cash sums obtained through the sale of monastic properties, England's conversion changes from a transition between Catholicism and Protestantism to one between religious and secular forms of acquisition and investment. Emptied of their specifically Catholic value, but retaining their religious associations, the monasteries became "[m]onuments of our forefathers pietie and devotion, to the honor of God, the propagation of Christian faith and good learning, and also for the reliefe and maintenance of the poore and impotent" (163).

A pair of examples illustrates the flexibility and variety of Camden's monastic histories. Viewed with the aid of documents and legends from both the pre- and post-Reformation periods, not solely from the perspective of post-Reformation polemic, monastic architecture becomes susceptible to a much greater, and far more unpredictable, range of meanings. These meanings tend to be local and idiosyncratic, reflecting the whims, desires, and commitments of individuals rather than abstract doctrinal principles. At Whorwell, in Hampshire, we again encounter Queen Aelfrith, the murderous stepmother connected to Corf Castle. Aelfrith, it turns out, was a great beauty and a busy murderess; at Worwhell she endowed a monastery in order to "expiate" her soul and "wash out" her evil deeds, which included not only the untimely dispatching of her stepson but the murder of "her former husband *Aethelwold* a most noble Earle, whom King Edgar trained forth hither a hunting and then strake him thorow with a dart, because hee had deluded him in his love secrets, and by deceitfull and naughty meanes prevented him and gotten for himself this same *Aelfrith* the most beautifull Ladie that was in those daies" (262). At another site, the monastery at Peterborough, which had been sacked by the Danes, was "re-edified" in atonement for a less malicious manslaughter, with "the helping hand especiall of K. *Eadgar*, and *Adulph* the kings Chancellor, who upon a prick of conscience and deepe repentence, for that hee and his wife together lying in bed asleepe had overlaid and smothred the little infant their onely son" (512). There is no set of broad polemical or doctrinal categories that would allow us to equate monasteries with "love secrets" or squashed babies, yet when they are viewed as both historically and geographically local, these are the sorts of stories that monasteries tell.

Taken together, the features of Camden's *Britannia* outlined here prepare us for the many kinds of building stories the coming chapters will examine. By connecting those stories to patterns of post-Reformation antiquarian thought indebted to the chorographic project of John Leland, these shared features also ground the development of these stories in the specific historical and cultural conditions of sixteenth- and seventeenth-century England. What becomes clear in the *Britannia* is that the architectural writing of this period is as deeply implicated in the production of narratives and texts, in the fields of literature and historiography, as it is in those of visual or material culture. As much as it anticipates the perspectives of Baconian empiricists, it also looks back to Leland with a post-Reformation sense of loss, to a model that is far less invested in the preservation of things than in the circulation of texts, and less interested in touching the physical artifacts of the past than in telling its stories.

CHAPTER TWO

Aristocrats and Architects

Henry Wotton and the Country House Poem

What happens to the figure of the architect in the narrative and historical modes of architectural description of early modern England exemplified in William Camden's *Britannia*? Most histories of English architecture have tracked the development of the professional architect primarily through the assimilation of classical and Continental models and design principles, as they appear in both written works about architecture and built architecture itself.[1] The early to mid-seventeenth century offers sparse material for this approach, since Renaissance aesthetic styles seem to have leaked slowly into England, and even then, only in disarticulated bits and pieces.[2] Inigo Jones (1573–1652) frequently stands out as the only figure of his time whose career united what Vitruvius called "both practice and reasoning," with practice being "the constant, repeated exercise of the hands" and "reasoning" consisting of the ability to "explain the proportions of completed works skillfully and systematically."[3] In this union of the theoretical and the practical, it has been argued, Jones himself was England's best approximation of the professional architect both described and embodied by the architect-authors of Continental and classical treatises.[4]

By positing a close association between the practices of the architect and of the antiquarian chorographer during this period, this study takes a different tack. The *Britannia* offers an alternative history by describing architecture in a way that is dependent on neither architect nor aesthetics. Camden rarely identified architecture with Italianate or any particular style. For him, architecture offered an occasion for telling human stories, and these stories often celebrated patrons and landowners. This alternative tradition allows us to see differences between England and the Continent not as a result of England's conscious resistance to the foreign but as the result of competing modes of architectural literacy.[5] While historical and narrative perceptions constituted a response to the local political, religious, and architectural changes of the post-Reformation period, they also presented a challenge to Continental models that centralized the skill of the architect and the "systematic" visual assessment of a building's aesthetic qualities. English writers of the period conceived of the architect in a way that stemmed more directly from the related practices of the antiquarian chorographer and estate surveyor than from those of the professional designer imagined in Continental treatises.[6] As a result, English and Continental models relied on very different constructions of the architect and the architectural profession. While previous studies have noted the lineal relationship of surveyor to professional architect, less attention has been paid to the ways in which these divergent models implied and produced different methods for seeing, judging, and interpreting buildings.[7] For English writers, a building's significance depended little on the visual evaluation of façades, proportions, or symmetries and more on its relation to both landscape and human history. At times, these differences manifested themselves in physical perspective—English estate description often looks outward from the house rather than at it—but they also changed the way architecture was written about and what its most important qualities were perceived to be.

Here, I use these competing models of the architectural profession as lenses through which to examine four seventeenth-century texts about the architecture of the English estate: Sir Henry Wotton's *Elements of Architecture* (1624), Ben Jonson's "To Penshurst" (c. 1612), Thomas Carew's "To My Friend G.N., from Wrest" (1639), and Andrew Marvell's "Upon Appleton House" (c. 1654). All are partly structured around a tension between English and Continental perceptions of the architect and between resultant ways of seeing and writing about architecture. The *Elements*—frequently hailed as the first Vitruvian-style architectural treatise written in English—attempts to integrate these Continental and English traditions in order to package Wotton's knowledge of Italian art and architecture for prospective English patrons. The three well-known country house poems also offer lessons in architectural connoisseurship.[8] As they instruct the reader in the proper understanding of the country estate, each text implicitly or explicitly marginalizes the skill of the architect in order to promote the authority of the patron, and each argues against visual perception itself as a way of comprehending architecture's significance. Precisely because they were sponsored by an awareness of the tension between antiquarian and aesthetic approaches to architecture, these texts also confront questions about the differences between England and the Continent that continue in current critical discussions of England's architectural history. While English architecture and architectural writing of this period often do not reflect the terms employed by classical and Continental treatises, discussions of history, ancestry, and landscape play prominent roles. Taken together, these writers allow us to see England's architecture as the product of an alternative and highly developed tradition.

To understand how sixteenth- and seventeenth-century English writers imagined the architectural profession, one must know a bit about the history and profession of estate surveying during the period. In England, as architectural historians have noted, the estate surveyor provides the most direct ancestor of the modern professional architect. In his history of surveying manuals, Andrew McRae has shown that surveyors of the sixteenth and seventeenth centuries were already engaged in negotiating a new, more technical and codified position for the profession. They, much like the literary and architectural texts to be discussed, strategically handled tensions between innovative professional developments and older, more paternalistic and strictly historical ways of imagining the estate.[9]

Rather than combining abstract theoretical aesthetic principles with manual skills, as the Vitruvian architect did, the surveyor joined practical building skill to the historiographic practices of the antiquarian chorographer. In a surveying manual of 1533, John Fitzherbert defines the title of surveyor: "the name of a Surveyour is a frenche name, and is as moche to saye in Englysshe, as an overseer."[10] But the surveyor was an overseer in several different senses, performing at once the duties of engineer, assessor, cartographer, and historian. He needed some knowledge of building materials, but surveying was also a descriptive practice. The surveyor mapped or measured the boundaries of an estate, and, in a role that has no direct parallel in classical and Continental conceptions of the architect, he dredged up those aspects of the estate's history that documented the landowner's rights to the rents, contributions, and loyalties of his or her tenants.[11] "[T]o that end," John Norden wrote in *The Surveyors Dialogue* (1607), "it is ... expedient, that Lords of tenants have due regard of their owne estates, namely of the particulars of all their tenants landes, and that by a due, true, and exact view and survey of the same, to the end the Lord be not abused, nor the tenants wronged & grieved by false informations, which commonly grow by privat Inteligencers, & never by just Surveyors."[12] Fitzherbert's early instruction manual also reveals an overlap in the research methodologies of antiquarian and surveyor. Fitzherbert demands that the surveyor search for "rentes/fees, customes,

& services, the lorde oughte to have of his tenauntes" through the consultation of "evydence" such as "courte rolles, rentayles, and suche other presidentes, and specially by the originall dedes of their tenaunts."[13] The description anticipates Camden's antiquarian inquiries, as he documents them in the *Britannia*'s prefatory material: "I have poored upon many an old Rowle, and Evidence: and produced their testimonie (as beyond all exception) when the cause required, in their very owne words."[14]

As we have seen in the *Britannia*, buildings were more often associated with aristocratic owners and patrons than with the names of architects. Viewed within the purview of the surveyor, the processes of building and estate description are also tied less to aesthetics or artistry than they are to the construction of aristocratic prerogative. The builder of houses was also a builder of maps and histories—not his own, but those of the owners of the estates. As Norden's word "dialogue" suggests, building becomes one part of an imagined exchange between surveyor and landowner in which the professional architect—as distinct from the surveyor—has no part. McRae has described land surveying and antiquarian chorography as parallel developments of the late sixteenth century, but in the works of writers such as John Leland and John Norden, the two converge.[15] Leland, at least according to his posthumous commentator John Bale, had proposed to Henry VIII the simultaneous rescue of historical manuscripts and the mapping of the nation, promising the king, "thys your worlde and impery of Englande so sett fourthe in a quadrate table of sylver . . . that your grace shall have ready knowledge at the fyrst sighte of many right delectable, fruteful, and necessary pleasures, by contemplacion thereof, as often as occasyon shall move yow to the syghte of it."[16] Norden, one of the cartographers responsible for the county maps of the *Britannia*, also published county descriptions that were heavily indebted to the *Britannia* itself, inquiring after the etymologies of place names, the abundance of natural resources, and the legal and political histories that attached to various sites.[17] In *The Surveyors Dialogue*, Norden offers the description of land in visual form: "a plot rightly drawne by true information," which "describeth so the lively image of a Mannor, and every branch and member of the same, as the Lord sitting in his chayre, may see what he hath, where and how it lyeth."[18] As McRae has shown, some early modern estate maps supplemented visual information with narrative forms of description. In speaking of Cyprian Lucar's 1590 *Treatise Named Lucarsolace*, McRae points out Lucar's suggestion that the margins of maps "should be used to record a vast range of additional information, from the quality of the soil to 'the disposition, industrie, studies, manners, trades, occupations, honestie, humanitie, hospitalitie, apparell, and other morall vertues of the inhabitants.'"[19] The work of builder, antiquarian chorographer, and cartographer thus converged in the figure of the surveyor, and all of these activities were dedicated to recording and securing historical relationships among landlord, land, and tenant.

The second part of Norden's *Surveyors Dialogue* is presented as a conversation between a surveyor and a lord who might possibly employ him. This understanding of building and estate management as part of a dialogue between surveyor and landlord—rather than as the aesthetic conception of an architect—helps to explain some strange features of what is often called the first architectural treatise written in English: Sir Henry Wotton's *Elements of Architecture* (1624). Wotton openly acknowledges his classical and Continental sources, so it is not surprising that his implicit deference to English traditions has been less often noticed. On its surface, the treatise is an eclectic compilation of material from sources that include Vitruvius's *Libri decem de architectura* (c. 30–20 B.C.), Leon Battista Alberti's *De re aedificatoria* (1485), Philibert de l'Orme's *Nouvelles inventions pour bien bastir* (1561) and *Le premier tome de l'architecture* (1567), and Andrea Palladio's *I quattro libri dell'architecttura* (1570). Wotton also displays his knowledge of textual commentary on Vitruvius, and alongside the familiar names of these Continental masters appears another set of names perhaps less well known to the modern reader: Philander, Gualterus Rivius, and Barnardino Baldi, Abbot of Gustalla.[20] "I am but a gatherer and disposer of other mens stufffe," he admits in the Preface, "at my own best value."[21] Despite the apparently broad scope of Wotton's reading, the scope of the treatise itself is comparatively narrow. Wotton covers only topics that might be applied to the English country estate, in contrast to his sources, who take up towns, temples, public buildings, and military architecture as well.

The compilation that results is a strange generic hybrid. Part building manual for an architect designing a house and part guidebook for the gentleman connoisseur, the *Elements* is a book about building that could not really have been used to build, and a guide to connoisseurship that rested largely on principles of construction. The treatise vacillates between practical, mechanical advice and disavowals that such knowledge is necessary. In a complicated piece of logical diplomacy, the reader is both freed from and indebted to the sort of practical information that the *Elements* compiles. At the end of the Preface, Wotton suggests that his purpose is to make the reader "fit to judge of *examples*," but the *Elements* then goes on to discuss such topics as the depth of foundations, the firing of brick, and the compounding of lime and mortar, none of which would necessarily have belonged to the knowledge of the gentleman connoisseur (A 2 v).

Still, the treatise ends with an assertion about the value of "censuring," that is, judgment, disjoined from the science of construction: "I should thinke it almost harder to be a good *Censurer*, then a good *Architect*: Because the *working* part may be helped with *Deliberation*, but the *Judging* must flow from *extemporall habite*." Wotton stuffs most of what he says about construction into the category of connoisseurship, being "desirous to shut up these building *Elements*, with some *Methodical* direction how to *censure* Fabriques alreadie raised" (115), yet this "*Methodical* direction" seems to depend on a thorough understanding of what he calls "the *working* part" of architecture: "[L]et him [the censurer] suddenly runne backewardes, (for the *Methode* of *censuring* is contrary to the *Methode* of *composing*), from the *Ornaments* . . . to the more essentiall *Members*, till at last hee be able to forme this *Conclusion*, that the *Worke* is *Commodious, Firme*, and *Delightfull*; which (as I said in the beginning) are the three capitall *Conditions* required in good *Buildings*, by all *Authors* both Ancient and Moderne" (116). "[E]*xtemporall habite*," in this case, emerges only from a systematic knowledge of the careful deliberations required to produce a building in the first place.

These strange vacillations—between the concerns of building and censuring—are explained by the absence or redefinition of the central figure, who, in Wotton's models, is meant to unite the theoretical and practical skills of the professional architect. In Wotton's sources, this figure joins the manual and the intellectual, the technical requirements of structural soundness and the abstract aesthetic requirements for visual beauty. Rather than basing his conception of the architect or builder primarily on the professional of foreign treatises, however, Wotton drew on a combination of two figures who were, for him, closer at hand: the landowning gentleman amateur and the surveyor. This modification is in part due to Wotton's own goals for the treatise; his own background as reader, traveler, and purveyor of foreign goods; and his own pressing needs within the patronage system. For practical reasons, Wotton was not only interested in promoting new models—for both architects and architecture—but in reinforcing and commending native social and architectural structures that were already in place.

According to Vitruvius, an architect ought to know everything. His ideal list of accomplishments includes knowledge of letters, draftsmanship, geometry, optics, arithmetic, "a great deal of history," philosophy, physiology, music, law, medicine, and astronomy. Of course, Vitruvius concedes, "[n]o one . . . can possibly master the fine points of each individual subject," but it is through perception of "the relationship of all the branches of knowledge" that the architect "climb[s] step by step . . . to reach the loftiest sanctuary of Architecture."[22] This elite education is translated into concrete terms as Book II takes up the topic of building materials, including consideration of timber and brick, as well as at least six other types of masonry. Alberti held that an architect "should strive constantly to exercise and improve his ability through a keen and animated interest in the noble arts," cultivating the capacity "by sure and wonderful reason and method... both how to devise through his own mind and energy, and to realize by construction, whatever can be most beautifully fitted out for the noble deeds of man, by the movement of weights and the joining and massing of bodies."[23] De l'Orme's list is similar to Alberti's and particularly promotes the importance of geometry and arithmetic.[24]

There are traces of this extensive program of education in the *Elements*, but Wotton does not consistently extol the marriage of theoretical and practical knowledge—what Alberti calls the ability to "realize by construction"—in the same way that his sources do. In fact, he often seems at pains to separate them. To begin with, he apologizes for the concatenation of intellectual and material concerns, or at least prods it gingerly from a safe distance. "Surely," he writes, "it cannot disgrace an *Architect*, which doth so well become a Philosopher, to looke into the properties of *Stone* and *Wood*... Nay, to descend lower even to examine *Sand* and *Lyme*, and *Clay* (of all which things *Vitruvius* hath discoursed, without any daintines, & the most of new Writers)" (10–11). Vitruvius, says Wotton, "much commendeth in an *Architect*, a *Philosophical* Spirit, that is, he would have him (as I conceave it) to be no superficiall, and floating *Artificer*; but a *Diver* into *Causes*, and into the *Mysteries* of *Proportion*" (54–55). For Vitruvius, this diving and philosophizing would not, indeed must not, interfere with the acquisition of mechanical knowledge; but for Wotton they seem at times to be mutually exclusive, or at least he seems to think that his readers will believe they are. The architect's knowledge distinguishes him from the craftsman rather than joining craft and intellectual conception.

In such passages, Wotton's emphasis is shaped by both the limitations of his own credentials and by the education he would have expected his prospective patrons to possess. Wotton himself could not claim the same kind of knowledge or practical experience as the architect-authors from whom he gathered his material. As Wotton says in the Preface, "It will be said that I handle an *Art*, no way suteable either to my *employments*, or to my *fortune*" (A 1 r). The conventional modesty of the claim does not preclude its truth: it is unlikely, given his background, that Wotton could have executed his own advice, about laying foundations, for instance, or firing brick, or engineering vaults and arches. His name is not associated with the creation or design of a single building in England: the "elements" assembled in his treatise were never assembled in timber or stone. His sources differed substantially from one another in their training and experience, ranging from Alberti, the great humanist scholar, to Palladio, who rose under the auspices of Daniele Barbaro from his trade as a mason, but Wotton displays significantly less practical experience or knowledge than any of them.[25] Much of his advice about materials and construction remains at a level so obvious it is nearly funny. Of roofs, for instance, he writes, "There are two extremities to be avoyded ... That it be not too *heavy*, nor too *light*," and of types of stone, "that some, are better within, and other to beare *Weather*" (79, 11). In a discussion of floor plans, he specifically characterizes himself as a "speculative" writer, who is "not bound, to comprise all particular Cases, within the Latitude of the *Subject*" but only to give "Generall Lights, and *Directions*, and pointings at some faults." The work of the architect once again becomes secondary to the promotional concerns of the treatise, as the builder is here left to wrestle with practicalities, being put to "ingenious"—and here undescribed—"shifts" in order to deal with the "scarsitie of *Ground*" (74).

The *Elements* was produced by an extensively traveled diplomat, dilettante, and spy seemingly as part of a desperate bid for patronage. It was churned out and, Wotton himself would write, "printed sheet by sheet, as fast as it was born, and it was born as soon as it was conceived."[26] In 1624, after seventeen years as James I's ambassador to Venice, Wotton heard that his post had been given away to Sir Isaac Wake. Taking this news as a bad sign, he returned home to England in search of a new employer and a new job. "I am left utterly destitute of all possibility to subsist at home," he wrote to George Villiers, Duke of Buckingham, "much like those seal-fishes, which sometimes, as they say, oversleeping themselves in an ebbing water, feel nothing about them but a dry shore when they awake."[27] Seeking appointment to the lucrative provostship of Eton College, Wotton whipped up this short treatise of 125 pages and sent presentation copies to a number of influential prospective patrons, including King James, Prince Charles, Lionel Cranfield the Lord Treasurer and Earl of Middlesex, and George Abbot the Archbishop of Canterbury.[28] His efforts, along with some other trading and politicking, were ultimately successful, and Wotton would hold his post as provost of Eton until his death in 1639.[29]

The *Elements*, then, is informed by Wotton's own abilities and experience, but it equally defers to the capacities and interests of the aristocratic patrons Wotton hoped would help him secure the appointment. Although architecture was becoming a fashionable interest for gentlemen in early-seventeenth-century England, students of the art were actively encouraged not to become acquainted with its grittier aspects. In his 1607 pedagogical handbook, *The Institution of a Young Noble-Man*, James Cleland outlines what he considers a gentleman's education in architecture. First, he recommends that young men read John Dee's preface to Henry Billingsley's 1570 edition of Euclid, in which Dee cites both Vitruvius and Alberti, not as building instructors, but as sophisticated mathematicians. In addition, the gentleman should learn the "principles of *Architecture* ... not to worke as a Maister Mason, but that he may, be able, in looking upon any building, both naturallie in respect of it selfe, and in respect of the eie, to tel what is *Frontispice, Tympane, Cornishes, pedestals, Frizes,* what is the *Tuscane, Dorik, Ionik, Corinthian,* and *composed order,* like a *Surveyor.*"[30] The gentleman, in this case, was emphatically a "censurer" rather than a builder, and the term "surveyor" here seems designed to distinguish the overseer of a work from the craftsmen who actually construct it.

Wotton rarely defines the role of architect precisely, and he never does so in Vitruvius's explicit terms. When he does discern the architect's distinct hand in a building's production, he reimagines the production of a building as a collaboration between architect and surveyor, rather than adhering to a three-part Vitruvian collaboration among lord, architect, and artisan. It may, on the face of it, seem odd that Wotton would omit the very collaborator to whom the treatise was supposed to appeal. I argue, however, that Wotton's formulation conflates the roles of patron and architect, in order that Wotton may attribute the greatest influence and prestige to his aristocratic audience, not to the professional architect, a socially indeterminate employee. Near the beginning of the *Elements,* Wotton writes:

> To redeeme this Profession, and my present paynes, from indignitie; I must heere remember that to choose and sort the *materials,* for every part of the *Fabrique,* is a Dutie more proper to a second *Superintendent,* over all the Under Artisans called (as I take it) by our Author, *Officinator lib 6. cap.11.* and in that Place expressly distinguished, from the *Architect,* whose glory doth more consist, in the Designement and *Idea* of the whole *Worke,* and his truest ambition should be to make the *Forme,* which is the nobler Part (as it were) triumph over the *Matter.* (11-12)

On its own, this passage seems another attempt to slice the practice of architecture away from the practice of the manual arts more cleanly than Vitruvius and his followers had done. The topic, however, appears more sensitive when juxtaposed with the passage from Vitruvius that Wotton cites but does not exactly translate:

> Now the exact type of material that should be used is not under the architect's control, because all types of building material do not occur in all places. ...

Besides, it is the owner's prerogative [*in domine est potestate*], to build in brick or concrete or squared stone as he wills. Therefore, the test of all architectural works should be made on the basis of three things. . . . When a magnificently completed work is looked upon, the lavishness is praised, this is the owner's domain [*a domini potestate inpensae laudabuntur*], when it is completed with superior craftsmanship, the standards of the artisan [*officinatoris . . . exactio*] are what is approved. But when the work has a masterful beauty because of its symmetries and their harmony, then the glory goes to the architect.[31]

In Vitruvius's account the roles themselves differ and different duties are assigned to each. Here, the selection of building materials is not left to the architect at all; it is the "prerogative" of the lord, the most highly positioned in social rank, if not in the hierarchy of talent and skill. Wotton's rearrangements are original; the commentaries of Barbaro, Baldi, and Philander, all of whom Wotton claims to have consulted in the preparation of the *Elements*, do not interpret the passage this way.

Wotton's strategy is logical, if complicated. Eileen Harris suggests that, although "Wotton's hierarchical distinction between architect and artificer is contrary to . . . the Vitruviuan idea of a *uomo universale*, uniting theory and practice," it is "part and parcel of the larger division of form and matter, thought and action, which he derived from Plato and the neo-Platonists, Ficino and Alberti."[32] It seems likely, though, that Wotton's motives were more social than philosophical. In the context of the passage from Vitruvius, the architect—not the patron—is the one who transcends the realm of purely practical knowledge and influence, who is responsible for the most comprehensive role in the planning of the work, and who is therefore the object of the most admiration. In a similar vein, Alberti states that the architect ought to insist on the recognition of his preeminence by eschewing patrons who were unappreciative of his genius: "What can I gain if I explain my valuable and useful proposals to some completely untutored person . . . ? If you have gained some benefit from my experience, and this has saved you substantial expense or made a real contribution to your comfort and pleasure, do I not, for heaven's sake, deserve a substantial reward?"[33] De l'Orme, likewise, instructs that once an architect has been selected, his freedom ought to be "exempt from all constraint and subjection of spirit."[34] This sort of presumptuous and demanding professional was useless and even inimical to Wotton's purposes in the *Elements*. In search of aristocratic sympathy, it was beneficial for Wotton to attribute the greatest share of the prestige to his elite audience, not to someone who was, like himself, a dependent, rather than a benefactor, in the patronage system.

In combining the roles of patron and architect, then, Wotton accommodated his own interests, but he also promoted those of the aristocratic amateurs who may have been among his intended audience. The wealthy amateur makes a brief appearance in Vitruvius's Preface to Book 6, which deals particularly with private buildings. With so many incompetent architects about, Vitruvius says, "I cannot but praise the heads of households who, trusting in their own reading, build for themselves in the belief that, if they must entrust a commission to amateurs, they themselves are more worthy of the expenditure, which will be according to their own wishes rather than those of others."[35] Notably, Vitruvius mentions these admirable heads of households in a section of the *Libri decem* where his goal closely resembles Wotton's; at least in part, he seems to be giving aristocratic patrons a reason to read his treatise. Wotton would have been familiar with aristocratic amateurs, who were among his circle of acquaintances. In relation to Wotton's description of the architect quoted above, for instance, Timothy Mowl notes that Wotton might well have had in mind Robert Cecil, the coordinator of his own building works at Hatfield House.[36] In 1609, Cecil had appointed Wotton to order and then transport the elaborate mosaic representing his father, William Cecil, which is still on display at the house.[37] Cecil had also employed and supervised a number of English workmen at Hatfield: Robert Lyming built the north front and the window grid; Inigo Jones, according to some architectural historians, was responsible for a wing of the south front; John Bucke designed much of the impressive interior woodwork; Maxmilian Colt (famous as the sculptor of Queen Elizabeth's tomb) made the chimneypieces; Richard Buckett provided painted decoration; and the firm of Bentham, Dauphen and Butler produced the stained glass.[38] Similar building schemes had recently been undertaken by George Villiers, Duke of Buckingham, another patron, to whom Wotton would send architectural books and plans in 1624.[39] In 1620–1621, Buckingham had pulled down the first house on his estate at Burley-on-the-Hill and had a new one built. It was in this second house that he had received King James in August 1621.[40] In 1622, Buckingham had purchased the sixteenth-century palace New Hall, in Essex, and reportedly employed Inigo Jones to alter it "according to the modern fashion."[41] A glorification of the aristocratic amateur would have been more appealing to Wotton's desired audience than a promotion of the unfamiliar and largely unavailable professional architect.[42]

Seventeenth-century conceptions of the country house, then, were patterned on contemporary patronage models and on practices of land surveying, which focused on architecture's relationship to landscape and on the historically grounded obligations that governed the social and political relations of the estate. Architecture, loosely defined as the practice of building, was thus intimately tied to both mapping and history. Before describing the hierarchy of architect and superintendent discussed above, Wotton has already located both parties in the midst of an estate where an owner's possessions are continually and pleasantly revealed to him. Like Vitruvius and Alberti, Wotton runs through a number of considerations relevant to the choice of a "seat," including the quality of the air and soil, a pleasant degree of sun and wind, and the absence of malign astrological influences.[43] Most expansive, though, is Wotton's description of the ideal view, and this seems to constitute a version of the estate survey. In choosing a site, he writes, some factors "may bee said to bee *Optical*."

> Such I meane as concerne the *Properties* of a well chosen *Prospect*: which I will call the *Royaltie* of *Sight*. For as there is a *Lordship* (as it were) of the *Feete*, wherein the Master doth much joy when he walketh about the *Line* of his owne *Possessions*: So there is a *Lordship* likewise of the *Eye* which being a raunging, and Imperious, and (I might say) an *usurping Sence*; can indure no narrow *circumscription*; but must be fedde, both with extent and varietie. Yet on the other side, I finde vaste and indefinite viewes which drowne all apprehension of the uttermost *Objects*, condemned, by good *Authors*. (4–5)

The heavy political significance with which Wotton invests this particular point is characteristic of the surveying treatise, with its emphasis on landlord-tenant power relations, but it is absent from Wotton's classical and Continental sources.[44] Alberti, the "good Author" on whom Wotton mainly relies here, merely remarks that the private house should have "a view of some city, town, stretch of coast, or plain, or it should have within sight the peaks of some notable hills or mountains, delightful gardens, and attractive haunts for fishing and hunting."[45] Alberti is frequently explicit about the relationship between architecture and the display of power, but here, his remarks remain couched in the language of beauty and pleasure, in contrast to Wotton's invocation of "Royaltie," "Lordship," and "usurp[ation]." It may be opportunistic that Wotton invokes two aspects of the land survey in this passage. The first, the "*Royaltie* of *Sight*," seems to emerge from advances that had recently been made in estate mapping that allowed for the visual estimation and quantification of land. The second, the "*Lordship* . . . of the *Feete*" may refer to the older practice of surveying land by walking the boundaries. McRae writes that, while this tradition was originally associated with Catholic rogation ceremonies, it was "subsequently embraced by the Elizabethan establishment . . . for its practical function of confirming property and parish boundaries."[46]

Wotton differs from Alberti in his description of the ideal country seat, but he departs still more sharply from Vitruvius, whose most detailed instructions about the selection of a site are not centered on an individual owner at all but concern the location of whole towns. When it comes to private buildings, Vitruvius does speak of what he calls "optics," but Wotton has wrenched the word into a new context, indeed into an entirely new perspective. Vitruvius applies the term to the activity of looking at houses, not looking out from them, and this area of expertise is assigned to "the special skill of a gifted architect to provide for the nature of the site, the building's appearance, or its function, and make adjustments by subtractions or additions." "Optics," in Vitruvius, thus consists of "the impact of images on our vision."[47] In the *Elements*, optics has more to do with the experience of the owner than with the skill of the architect, and it is grounded in ownership rather than images, in the practice of the surveyor rather than in the design of the architect. "Lastly," Wotton adds, "I remember a private *Caution*, which I know not well how to sort, unlesse I should call it *Political*. By no means, to build too neere a great *Neighbour*; which were in truth to bee as unfortunately seated on the earth, as *Mercurie* is in the Heavens, for the most part, ever in *combustion*, or *obscuritie*, under brighter beames then his owne" (5). Wotton is not borrowing this idea; it seems to be "private" in that it is his own. The country house, then, in Wotton's description following the surveying tradition, is transformed from the classical object of vision to the occasion for the contemplation of the surrounding landscape. As Norden had imagined in *The Surveyors Dialogue*, the patron is to see his estate, and to see his own prerogative reflected in it, as the house becomes a topographical landmark that reveals the expanses and lineaments of his own sprawling possessions.

Because Wotton was interested in the topic of country houses in general, not just a single estate, his architectural treatise does not include the kind of local and specific histories that characterized the work of antiquarians and estate surveyors. These details, however, appear abundantly in another seventeenth-century genre permeated by the practices of antiquarian chorography and estate mapping, the country house poem. It is customary to think of country house poems as historical in the sense that they are conservative and nostalgic, extolling the traditional values of local hospitality and family-oriented rural retirement.[48] Wotton himself provides a similar interpretation of the country estate, calling "Every Mans proper *Mansion* House and *Home* ... the *Theater* of his *Hospitality*," and noting that English floor plans ought to differ from Italian ones, because "by the naturall *Hospitalitie* of *England*, the *Buttrie* must be more visible, and wee neede perchance for our *Raunges*, a more spacious and luminous *Kitchin*" (82, 70–71). These social ideals have been well explored in recent criticism and situated in the political and social contexts of Jacobean England.[49] It is not my goal to rehearse these arguments here. Instead, I build on these observations to show how the representation of these ideals is indebted to—and enabled by—markedly antiquarian ways of thinking about architecture's relationship to both landscape and human history.

A handful of country house poems pointedly set this historical mode of interpretation against visual and spatial experiences of architecture, which form the basis of classical and Continental aesthetic descriptions. Whatever its strategic modifications, the *Elements* was in part intended to educate English readers in a foreign architectural language, by explaining how to look at and judge a building in a particular and systematic way. The poems I consider here, however, consciously reject these modes of understanding and talking about architecture as irrelevant and even obtrusive, insisting instead that their readers rely on an alternative form of architectural literacy. According to Jonson, Carew, and Marvell, the virtues of an estate become visible only in the retelling of stories.

Country house poets are generally said to have found their source material in classical pastoral and georgic; their debt to English antiquarian texts has been little recognized.[50] The *Britannia* is almost never named as a source for this genre, yet interspersed among its prose descriptions, Camden's compilation offers the reader some of the earliest English country house poems (which are written in Latin).[51] In a description of Greenwich, for instance, Camden inserts a verse by Leland, whom he names the "*Antiquarian* Poet." The Latin precedes the following translation by Philemon Holland:

> How glittereth now this place of great request,
> Like to the seat of heavenly welkin hie?
> With gallant tops, with windowes of the best.
> What towres that reach even to the starry skie:
> What Orchards greene, what springs ay-running by.
> Faire *Flora* heere that in this creeke doth dwell,
> Bestowes on it the flowre of garden gay;
> To judge no doubt of things he knew ful well,
> Who gave this banke thus pleasant every way,
> So fit a name, as did the thing bewray.[52]

Similar descriptions integrating architecture with both topography and political preeminence are invoked at both Windsor and Hampton Court, regarding which Camden quoted from his own long Latin chorographic poem "The Marriage of

Tame and *Isis*."[53] In turn, as John M. Adrian has written, country house poems describe estates in ways that recall the *Britannia* and similar works. Adrian points out that in "To Penshurst," "that quintessential English country house poem, the estate is imagined in terms of the same categories of local definition that chorography helped to establish."[54]

In appropriating these antiquarian approaches to architecture, country house poems pose a different set of critical questions than those asked by architectural historians interested in questions of period and style. In the examples examined here—"To Penshurst," "To My Friend G.N., from Wrest," and "Upon Appleton House"—the question is not whether English architectural style is superior to Italian or French architectural style; it is whether architectural style, at least insofar as it characterizes the appearance of a building, is a significant criterion for the judgment of architecture at all. The poems thus proceed from a dichotomy of deliberately incommensurate terms, replacing the visually perceptible features of a building with stories of local and human history, or, we might say, replacing the art of the architect with that of the surveyor and antiquarian chorographer.

"To Penshurst" famously begins by comparing the house to some unidentified competitor:

> Thou art not, Penshurst, built to envious show
>   Of touch or marble, nor canst boast a row
> Of polished pillars, or a roof of gold;
>   Thou hast no lantern whereof tales are told,
> Of stair, or courts; but stand'st an ancient pile,
>   And these grudged at, art reverenced the while.[55]

The lines seem at first to describe Penshurst through the use of contrast; more accurate would be to say that Jonson declines to describe the house, at least in visual terms. Jonson himself would have been familiar with the kind of foreign sources Wotton attempted to import; his acrimonious relationship to Inigo Jones in the creation of court masques would have exposed him to numerous representations of cupolas and polished pillars, and his own annotated copy of Vitruvius survives.[56] Armed with these tools for describing architectural appearances, however, Jonson begins by laying them aside. The only possibly physical quality we are provided is that Penshurst is "ancient," and this descriptor has as much to do with time as with appearance; at least, there are any number of ways in which a house could look old. Modern scholars sometimes classify Penshurst, with its crenellated battlements and central oak-beamed hall, as medieval or Neo-Gothic in style, but Jonson is never that specific.[57] In the poem, Penshurst does not appear one way or another. Looking at the house is not the right way to understand Penshurst at all.

In these opening lines, the place name Penshurst clearly refers to the house, but as the poem continues, the term expands silently to include the estate as well. By looking immediately outward from the house, rather than at it, the poem performs a perspectival reorientation that is similar to Wotton's adaptation of Vitruvius's discussion of optics. Jonson's description, like Wotton's, reflects the practices of the estate surveyor or antiquarian. The virtues of Penshurst become accessible through the notation of other features than marble and gold, as Jonson reconstitutes the aesthetics of the estate: "Thou joy'st in better marks, of soil, of air, / Of wood, of water; therein thou art fair" (7–8). Here, Jonson applies the term "fair" to "marks" which are either invisible ("air") or simply not pretty or artful in the same way as pillars and lanterns.

Frustrating the reader's expectation, and rejecting a particular kind of description, Jonson reveals the human histories and local associations of the house. His interests become antiquarian and aetiological. Historical memory is shallow but insistent in the poem. Describing an oak that was said to have been planted at the birth of Robert Sidney's illustrious (and already deceased) brother Philip, for instance, Jonson writes:

> That taller tree, which of a nut was set
>   At his great birth, where all the muses met.
> There, in the writhèd bark, are cut the names
>   Of many a sylvan; taken with his flames. (13–16)

That Philip was a sibling rather than an ancestor of Robert highlights one of Jonson's challenges in the poem. Penshurst was an old estate, but the Sidneys had only recently acquired it, a fact that they themselves attempted to disguise by bribing a herald to create a fake "twelfth century" deed, granting Penshurst to an invented ancestor.[58] Newly rich off the spoils of Reformation politics, they had actually owned the estate only since 1552, when Robert's grandfather William Sidney was rewarded for his service to Edward VI.[59] Like Camden, who had deftly transferred the title "*de Penhurst*" from Stephen de Penhurst "a famous Warden of the Cinque ports" to Robert Sidney, "Baron *Sidney of Pensherst*," Jonson manufactures an antiquarian reading of the estate, streamlining the complications of history toward culmination in the stability of the present landowner.[60]

In "writhèd bark," Penshurst is literally inscribed with traces of the family's history. Similarly, the following lines point to the history of another family member, more contemporary with the poem:

> And thence the ruddy satyrs oft provoke
>   The lighter fauns to reach thy lady's oak.
> Thy copse, too, named of Gamage, thou hast there,
>   That never fails to serve thee seasoned deer. (17–20)

The names of both the oak tree and the copse refer to Robert Sidney's wife, Barbara Gamage, who was said to have been taken with labor pains under the tree in question and to have enjoyed feeding deer in the copse.[61] In such instances, Jonson creates from the materials of the present an elegant fiction of historical depth.

Jonson's marked interest in landlord-tenant relationships also reflects the historiographic aspects of the estate surveyor's profession, and it has little to do with the aesthetic emphases of classical and Continental treatises. In a less aggressive way than Fitzherbert or Norden's surveyor, Jonson documents the system of obligation that binds the landowner to inhabitants of the land, although we might see here a similar sensitivity to the tension between paternalistic and economically articulated conceptions of estate management. The building itself is partly understood through the history of these relationships: "And though thy walls be of the country stone, / They're reared with no man's ruin, no man's groan" (45–46). The pun on "ruin" here contextualizes the material building in the historically established harmony between Sidney and his tenants: Sidney hasn't raised the money for his house by exploiting his tenants to the point of their ruin, and the house hasn't been built with materials pillaged from other structures, resulting in the ruin of preexistent buildings. Architectural and human history converge as the "country stone" reifies the virtues and traditions that historically characterize the country estate. The building process is imagined as the joint production of the estate's material and historical resources, both its "country stone" and the history of harmonious coexistence that characterizes its social ties.

By Jonson's account, the landlord-tenant relationships at Penshurst are uncontentious, charitable, reverential, and mutually respectful, but they are not confined to spontaneous expressions of hospitality and good will. They are grounded in the exchange of real, material goods which might constitute, in part, the practical manifestations of a tenant's obligation. The rustics of Penshurst are not skeptical of being cheated or exploited, as the farmers of *The Surveyors Dialogue* are; this harmony between landlord and tenant emerges from the mutual agreement that they owe something. Robert Sidney welcomes the lowlier members of the local community—"the farmer, and the clown," along with "their ripe daughters"—but they do not arrive "empty-handed":

> Some bring a capon, some a rural cake,
>   Some nuts, some apples; some that think they make
> The better cheeses, bring 'em. (48, 49, 54, 51–53)

In addition, the phrase "ripe daughters" intermixes the human and natural resources of the estate by transposing an epithet generally applied to fruit to another kind of offspring altogether. Don Wayne has amply explored the politics of class and labor in such passages; here, I would point out that Jonson's sustained attention to the legal and historical interests of the estate survey make the house an occasion for narrative, and thus further guide the reader away from the visual architectural splendor, toward which the opening lines gesture, putting forth in its place an alternative way of understanding and talking about the estate.[62]

Structurally, the center of the poem lies in the rooms of the house itself, not in their symmetrical disposition or well proportioned floor plans but in the exceptional hospitality and economy that the poet is experiencing there. While the core of the poem teaches the reader about the virtues of the house and its inhabitants, the closing lines return to the broader question of how houses ought to be judged. Adequately prepared, the reader is at last able to compare Penshurst to other houses on the basis of what it is rather than what it is not.

> Now, Penshurst, they that will proportion thee
>   With other edifices, when they see
> Those proud, ambitious heaps, and nothing else,
>   May say, their lords have built, but thy lord dwells. (99–102)

Having read the poem ("Now"), the reader sees architectural proportion differently; no longer attached to visual symmetries or physical size, the notion of proportion is redefined in incommensurate terms as the reader is engaged in an act of deliberation which depends on the perception of less tangible virtues and, significantly, on temporal or narrative distinctions. The tense shift of the final line insists that the house be measured, or proportioned, according to its human history rather than by its physical dimensions; and by this measurement, Penshurst extends further than its competitors, by reaching the present moment. Properly interpreted, visual perception dissolves into moral judgment and a historical sense of architecture's value. The "proud, ambitious heaps" are found empty and wanting. It's not that there is nothing to see in them, but there is *only* something to see "and nothing else." Historically speaking, the "ambitious heaps" are limited, for their vitality falls short, quarantined to a past moment by Jonson's use of the perfect tense. Rather than applying the visual and spatial aesthetics of a foreign treatise, then, Jonson echoes both estate survey and antiquarian chorography, implicating description of architecture with description of landscape and tying both to the retelling of human stories.

It is not surprising that no professional architects are mentioned in "To Penshurst"; such a figure—who might have been dismissed as a builder who does not dwell in or inhabit the house—is simply irrelevant to Jonson's praise of the estate. Later in the century, however, Thomas Carew would present a pointed denunciation of the Vitruvian-style architect, along with the visual aesthetics his designs were meant to comprise. "To My Friend G.N., from Wrest," first published in Carew's *Poems* of 1640, describes Wrest Park, the Bedfordshire home of Henry Grey, eighth Earl of Kent.[63] Carew's description presents a lesson in architectural connoisseurship that directly opposes the kind of precepts that Wotton borrows from his sources. While Wotton had directed that the censurer proceed by "runn[ing] backewardes . . . from the *Ornaments* (which first allure the *Eye*) to the more essentiall *Members*" and Alberti had called sight "the keenest of all the senses" for judging "what is right or wrong in the execution and design of a work," Carew renders both ornament and visual allurement as detractive and misleading.[64] Instead, the virtues of Wrest are seen precisely because it fails to "allure the *Eye*" at all. The beginning of Carew's poem inverts the structure of "To Penshurst," by beginning with a description of the estate and then applying the estate's native and natural ornaments to the house. Both country house poems, however, resemble the antiquarian chorography or estate survey in that the house is understood through its relationship to a topographical context, and in both, beauty is derived from what Jonson called the "better marks" of the property.

At Wrest, as at Penshurst, authenticity is constituted through the absence of expenditure and art. As "the pregnant Earth / Sends from her teeming womb a flowery birth," "native aromatics" obviate the need for extravagant imported plantings:

> No foreign gums, nor essence fetched from far,
> No volatile spirits, nor compounds that are
> Adulterate, but Nature's cheap expense
> With far more genuine sweets refresh the sense.[65]

Applying these criteria to the judgment of the house, Carew declares: "Such pure and uncompounded beauties bless / This mansion with an useful comeliness" (19–20). It is easy to imagine how a gum or spirit could be "uncompounded"; it is more difficult to imagine how a house, which could only be successfully assembled with a certain degree of deliberation and intervention, could be so. But in the following lines, we learn that the house is "uncompounded" because it remains untainted by a particular kind of architectural aesthetics. The house is

> Devoid of art; for here the architect
> Did not with curious skill a pile erect
> Of carvèd marble, touch, or porphyry,
> But built a house for hospitality. (21–24)

The architect's sufficiency, strangely, rests in a lack of skill, in his capacity not to exercise art or to obtrude the traces of his influence between the qualities of the estate owner and the qualities of the house. For a professional architect of the Vitruvian school, the work of "curious skill" would be precisely to integrate the artful and the useful, not separate them from one another, to make "carvèd marble, touch, or porphyry" serve the interests and needs of the patron.[66] Visual design and "use" would ideally be mutually constitutive. But for Carew, the visual and the functional counteract, rather than reinforcing, one another.

> No sumptuous chimney-piece of shining stone
> Invites the stranger's eye to gaze upon,
> And coldly entertains his sight, but clear
> And cheerful flames cherish and warm him here. (25–28)

Like Penshurst, Wrest has been stacked against some unnamed competitors. As scholars, including Alastair Fowler, Christy Anderson, and Anthony Wells-Cole, have pointed out, many "ambitious" houses boasted spectacular carved chimneypieces whose designs were often derived from foreign pattern books.[67] Wotton dedicated a subsection of the *Elements* to the subject of chimneys, which suggests that he thought the subject would be of interest to English patrons (or perhaps that they might see their own houses mirrored there), and his introduction to the topic implies that it was a point in which English houses might particularly exceed their foreign competitors. "*Italians,*" he observes, "who make very frugal fires, are perchance not the best Counsellers"; still, one might learn from them "how to raise faire *Mantels* within the roomes" (59–60). Whether or not Carew intended an implicit comparison, his statements explicitly contrast modes of sensory perception, not fireplaces. A coldness of sight, they imply, somehow prevents the perception of invisible warmth.

Throughout Carew's poem, architectural description turns on an imagined animosity between that which "entertains" one's "sight" and that which is for "use." He continues:

> Nor think, because our pyramids and high
> Exalted turrets threaten not the sky,
> That therefore Wrest of narrowness complains,
> Or straitened walls; for she more numerous trains
> Of noble guests daily receives, and those
> Can with far more conveniency dispose
> Than prouder piles, where the vain builder spent
> More cost in outward gay embellishment
> Than real use; which was the sole design
> Of our contriver, who made things not fine,
> But fit for service. (47–57)

The ostentation of "prouder piles" is replaced by "conveniency," and "embellishment" by "real use," while "design" is desirable only where it is indistinguishable from "service." The acts of contriving and designing which in the architectural profession would culminate in visual and material realization here lead only to a visual void. We are never told what Wrest looks like, because we are not supposed to be looking at it. The only description is negative, as the reader learns simply that Wrest is "not fine."

Like Jonson, Carew had a well-developed notion of what he was rejecting, and the contrasts through which he describes Wrest appear to reflect his own experience and resultant fluency in two architectural languages. In common with Jonson, Carew would have known many of the terms and aesthetic effects of foreign architectural treatises through his involvement in the creation of court masques performed against the elaborate theatrical sets of Inigo Jones.[68] Carew's own masque, *Coelum Britannicum* (1634), first performed in 1633, begins with a detailed "Description of the Scaene," which provides clear evidence of both the degree to which the scenery was structured around the display of architectural elements and of the writer's extensive and sophisticated vocabulary for describing these elements: "[T]he Scaene, representing old Arches, old Palaces, decayed walls, parts of Temples, Theaters, Basilica's and Therme, with confused heaps of broken Columnes, Bases, Coronices and Statues, lying as underground, and altogether resembling the ruines of some great City of the ancient Romans, or civiliz'd Brittaines."[69] In contrast to a house such as Wrest, stage sets would have been designed only to entertain the eye, having no real "use" as buildings at all. The printed version of *Coelum Britannicum* begins, "The first thing that presented it selfe to the sight, was a rich Ornament, that enclosed the Scaene; in the upper part of which, were great branches of Foliage growing out of leaves and huskes, with a Coronice at the top."[70] This is exactly the kind of lifeless presentation that is absent from Wrest, where

> No Doric, nor Corinthian pillars grace
> With imagery this structure's naked face:
> The lord and lady of this place delight
> Rather to be in act, than seem in sight. (29–32)

Grey's hospitality, moreover, creates real, living versions of Amalthea and Bacchus, who are not represented "in effigy" or on "a marble tun" (58, 63). Wrest "offer[s] not in emblems to the eyes, / But to the taste, those useful deities" (65–66). Unlike the performance of a masque, "acting" is being and not seeming, and architecture itself follows suit as the house is rendered not as an artful and ornamented façade but as a "naked face." In contrast to Wotton, then, who had imagined the architectural ornaments of a country house as a kind of stage set in the "*Theater*" of the owner's "*Hospitality*," where visual decorum and the actions of a noble character converged, Carew refuses to reconcile the two.

In the opening lines of "Upon Appleton House," probably written in the early 1650s, Marvell's critique of the architectural profession is more specifically leveled at the intrusive figure of the architect himself. While Carew excluded "foreign gums" from the natural gifts of Grey's estate, in Marvell's poem, it is the architect who is foreign, not because he hails from another country, but because he interrupts the mutually productive identity of estate owner and estate and is alien to the history that truly defines the house's character. The poem begins

> Within this sober frame expect
> Work of no foreign architect,
> That unto caves the quarries drew,
> And forests did to pastures hew,
> Who of his great design in pain
> Did for a model vault his brain,
> Whose columns should so high be raised
> To arch the brows that on them gazed.

2
Why should of all things man unruled
Such unproportioned dwellings build?[71]

Scholars have speculated about which "foreign architect" Marvell might have had in mind, but the description is hardly specific to an individual.[72] Each line of the first stanza alludes to and then dismisses some part of the Vitruvian-style architectural treatise and, by inference, all architects trained in that tradition. Marvell's list of topics here—the quarrying of stone, acquisition of timber, the conception of a "design" for the whole work, the construction of a model, and the optical analysis of the façade—could all have been culled from almost any of the architect-authors from whom Wotton had "gather[ed]" his "stuffe." Where Wotton had marginalized the role of the architect in order to centralize the influence of the patron, "Upon Appleton House" expunges the work of the architect altogether.

Marvell does his own gathering of stuff from foreign treatises, but rather than adapting his terms strategically, he radically redefines them. With his charge that grander works of architecture are "unproportioned," Marvell twists another common principle of the classical and Continental treatise: architectural symmetries mirror the natural symmetries of the human body. For Vitruvius, the success of a design is determined by its relationship to the harmoniously proportioned whole: "Just as in the human body there is a harmonious quality of shapeliness expressed in terms of the cubit, foot, palm, digit, and other small units, so it is in completing works of architecture."[73] Alberti uses a similar analogy as a basis for "judgments on beauty." Like a well-composed building, "every body consists entirely of parts that are fixed and individual; if these are removed, enlarged, reduced, or transferred somewhere inappropriate, the very composition will be spoiled that gives the body its seemly appearance."[74] Wotton adopts this precept, although he claims to have thought of it himself through rational contemplation: "I will propound a Rule of mine owne Collection.... [W]hat are the most judicious *Artisans* but the *Mimiques* of *Nature*? This led me to contemplate the Fabrique of our owne Bodies, wherein the *High Architect* of the world, had displaied such skill, as did stupefie, all humane reason" (6–7). By claiming that the rules of a specialized aesthetic system are apparent in nature, Wotton, like Marvell, minimizes the influence of the architect (here called an "Artisan"), who is ideally not an original designer or creator, but a mimic of patterns that are readily available to all pious and rational men.

But Marvell's revisions go further. Appleton House is indeed proportioned according to human characteristics, but not the anonymous ideal physical specimen that Vitruvius had in mind. Instead, the country house follows nature because it reflects the individual character of its inhabitant. "The beasts," Marvell continues, "are by their dens expressed.... No creature loves an empty space; / Their bodies measure out their place" (11, 15–16). Man, by contrast,

>   superfluously spread,
> Demands more room alive than dead;
> And in his hollow palace goes
> Where winds (as he) themselves may lose;
> What need of all this marble crust
> T'impark the wanton mote of dust,
> That thinks by breadth the world t'unite
> Though the first builders failed in height? (17–24)

But Appleton House is no such "hollow palace":

> But all things are composed here
> Like Nature, orderly and near:
> In which we the dimensions find
> Of that more sober age and mind,
> When larger-sized men did stoop
> To enter at a narrow loop;
> As practising, in doors so strait,
> To strain themselves through heaven's gate. (25–32)

To be properly "composed" is thus to embody "dimensions" that follow the character of the patron rather than a foreign "palace" conceived in the mind of the architect. Its "dimensions" are those of the "sober ... mind" (echoing the "sober frame" of line 1) rather than those of a "larger-sized" body. By the exclusion of the architect—because "Humility alone designs / Those short but admirable lines"—Appleton House truly reflects nature, and its "holy mathematics can / In every figure equal man" (41–42, 47–48).

As Fowler has pointed out, little is known about the appearance of the house at the time Marvell wrote, and the poem does not give us much information.[75] Instead, both architectural features and architectural history dissolve into stories of the estate's human history and human virtue, of the dwelling, Jonson might say, rather than the building. Like so many country houses in the *Britannia*, Appleton House had been a monastic house, and it seems to have been physically converted in stages over the century following the Reformation. And Marvell's vocabulary for describing the house, like the estate surveyor's or antiquarian topographer's, is as much historical as visual. A perusal of Appleton House's "fragrant gardens, shady woods, / Deep meadows, and transparent floods" (79–80) becomes the opportunity for an account of its past:

> While with slow eyes we these survey,
> And on each pleasant footstep stay,
> We opportunely may relate
> The progress of this house's fate.
> A nunnery first gave it birth
> (For virgin buildings oft brought forth);
> And all the neighbour-ruin shows
> The quarries whence this dwelling rose. (81–88)

Unlike Penshurst, the walls of Appleton House have been raised with someone else's ruin, productively reappropriating the materials of a Catholic past instead of violently scarring the earth, as is suggested by line 3 ("that unto caves the quarries drew"). The reason Appleton House became Protestant is, of course, that England did, a national shift at which Marvell only glances, by noting that Fairfax acquired the property "at the demolishing" (273). In the poem, this national transition is overshadowed by a long story of religious conversion—looking forward to the house's architectural conversion—that precedes it. In twenty-four stanzas, Marvell recounts Isabella Thwaites's seduction by salacious lesbian nuns, who are "dispossessed" of their charge only when Sir William Fairfax "through the wall does rise" to find Isabella weeping at the altar (272, 258). When Appleton House does change hands, the language—"escheat" and "willed"—picks up the legal overtones of "dispossessed" and hints at the kind of legal records and documents that enabled the historical dimensions of the land survey and of antiquarian chorography (274, 275). In the opening sections of "Upon Appleton House," Marvell replaces the aesthetic standards of classical and Continental treatises with another—and perhaps more familiar—way of understanding architecture. The house becomes meaningful in relation to the estate and to features comprehensible only in human and historical terms. It is thus a particular and strategically applied mode of architectural literacy that transforms Fairfax's estate to "paradise's only map" (768).

In *The Surveyors Dialogue*, Norden imagines a conversation between the surveyor and a bailiff. Drawing within sight of a country house, the baliff observes confidently that "a stately house it is indede." The surveyor is slower to draw a conclusion:

> It seemes to be a large and loftie cage, if the Bird be answerable.... I mean, that a *Titmus* may harbour in a *Peacockes* cage, and yet the cage maketh her not a *Peacocke*, but will be a *Titmus*, notwithstanding the greatnes of the cage: So this loftie Pyle bee not equalized by the estate and revenewes of the builder, it is as if *Paules steeple* should serve *Pancras* Church for a Belfrey.[76]

Architectural correctness is a not a matter of proportion among the respective parts of a finished building; St. Paul's and St. Pancras are offered mainly as the vehicle of a simile. The real proportional harmony is to exist among the credentials of house, owner, and estate: "Now, if upon view of the demeines," the surveyor concludes, "and the rest of the parts, it be not found like unto a child borne in Cheshire, with a head bigger then the bodie, I shall like it well."[77] Here, Norden resorts to the conventional connection between correct architectural proportion and the human body, but the body imagined can be pleasing only if the architecture resides in a suitably "answerable" network of historical, topographical, and human relationships that extends beyond the house itself.

Norden's treatise, *The Elements of Architecture*, and the seventeenth-century country house poems help us to understand the traditional social and intellectual networks in which early modern English architecture was implicated. In sixteenth- and seventeenth-century England, architectural writing already constituted a different genre from the Continental architectural treatise; it was carried out in different terms and it relied on different conventions. The country house poems discussed here reveal the ways in which this genre's ideas were seen to exclude—even to be threatened by—the precepts of foreign treatises that centralized the architect and the visual experience of materials and space. England's architectural writing at this point owed more to the historical estate survey and to antiquarian chorography than to the elements of classical design that were trickling slowly into the country. Wotton strove not to violate traditional models, even as he sought to introduce a new set of architectural standards and to imagine the professional architect on the English country estate. As a result, the *Elements* is less successful as a building manual or a systematic guide to connoisseurship than it is as a strategic balance between two forms of architectural literacy. While Wotton's treatise differs in form from the country house poems, it is indebted to the principles they expound. In the end, Wotton understood that the historical dimensions of a house were as important as its spatial and material qualities and that the splendid lines of an Italian villa must not erase the human stories that attached to the English country estate. Taken together, Wotton's treatise and the country house poems allow us to see the architecture and architectural writing of early modern England differently: not as a failed or half-hearted imitation of the Italian Renaissance, but as a part of the nation's historiographic and antiquarian traditions; not as a fractured reflection of classicism, but as a sophisticated and ingeniously adapted art.

CHAPTER THREE

Strange Anthologies

The Alchemist *in the London of John Stow*

Moving from the genres and settings of the country house poem and county chorography, with which the first two chapters have been primarily concerned, we now consider the distinctive architecture of early modern London in two roughly contemporary texts that are rarely paired: John Stow's *Survey of London* (1598) and Ben Jonson's *The Alchemist* (1610).[1] Different as Stow's meticulous history is from Jonson's raucous comedy, the two texts help to illuminate aspects of each other and of early modern London architecture. First, each text relies on a historical sense of architecture's value, and taken together, the two allow us to see the particular challenges that the architecture of early modern London presented to the antiquarian modes of architectural interpretation exemplified in the *Britannia* and, very soon afterward, in Jonson's early country house poem "To Penshurst" (c. 1612). In the country house narrative, architecture is frequently used to generate stories of ancestral continuity and social stability, culminating in the celebration of an aristocratic or genteel owner's identity and legitimacy. Translated to the architecture of the early modern capitol, however, this historical approach to architectural writing produces a very different effect. Narratives of London architecture result in a sense of what Andrew Griffin has called "diachronic fragmentation."[2] Continually disrupted, dismantled, and reassembled, these stories point far more consistently toward change and instability than toward continuity or order. Stow discovered in the disordered cityscape the materials for a work that has often been called nostalgic or elegiac.[3] For Jonson, the incongruity and volatility of his urban setting produced comic possibilities. In this way, architecture can be seen as contributing to an effect Jean E.

Howard describes as the "intimate synergy... operating between London and the early modern commercial theater."[4]

Second, Stow's *Survey* enables a new way of understanding Jonson's architectural setting. Critics have frequently noted that in *The Alchemist* location is everything, and Lovewit's house has been admired as both a virtuoso imposition of the neo-Aristotelian unities and a reflection of the theater that housed this imagined space.[5] The house is twice referred to as being located in the "Friars": once in the opening quarrel between Subtle and Face and again in Act 4, when Sir Epicure Mammon laments that a wealthy and beautiful gentlewoman (humorously played by Doll Common) should occupy an obscure "nook... of the Friars."[6] Among others, F. H. Mares, R. L. Smallwood, and Ian Donaldson have pointed out Jonson's cleverness in these allusions; Blackfriars was the name of both the theater and the neighborhood where the play was probably first performed, increasing, in Smallwood's words, "the audience's sense of involvement and immediacy."[7] At the same time, critics note, the suggested identity of house with theater infuses the setting with the capacity for wild transformation.[8] Donaldson goes so far as to characterize the house as "magic"; it is "capable of being whatever people most want it to be."[9]

I argue that we might equally see Lovewit's house as a representative London building of circa 1610. Unexpected similarities between the *Survey* and *The Alchemist* reveal that as much as "To Penshurst" is a country house poem, *The Alchemist* is a city house play. As the setting for a play performed in a theater that was itself a converted monastery, Lovewit's house is not only a meta-theatrical or dramaturgic device but a conscious appropriation of London's material architectural features in the post-Reformation period. It is this appropriation that Stow helps us to perceive. Reaching back to the models of Leland and Camden, the *Survey* describes architecture in a way that expounds its connections to human history and social legitimacy.[10] In addition to telling us what London buildings looked like then, Stow demonstrates the breakdown of traditional formulations of identity, as constituted at the intersection of architecture, history, and land.[11]

In *The Alchemist*, this disintegration of the association between person and place produces new ways of imagining legitimacy and identity. As Lovewit retreats to the margins of the play, so does the social order that depended on his presence. The house is no longer an occasion for the celebration of stable tenure and genteel identity, and Lovewit no longer provides a human culmination for architectural history. As antiquarian narratives fall apart, the genteel household is replaced by the alchemical laboratory, and ancestral histories are supplanted, in part, by alchemy itself. The product, as well, of strategic distillation and successive stages of generation, the alchemical process promises a new culmination, which, if realized, would enable the legitimization of an entirely new social hierarchy.[12] Presumably, if the tricksters actually succeeded in creating the philosopher's stone, they would no longer need to fear Lovewit's return.

While critics have often noted Jonson's pervasive interest in architecture, they have found it difficult to reconcile its manifestation in "To Penshurst" with the architectural setting of *The Alchemist*; and despite the two works' proximate dates of composition and the fact that both were dedicated to members of the Sidney family, few studies have considered the two works side by side.[13] Stow's *Survey* evinces an antiquarian influence on *The Alchemist* that resembles the influence of antiquarian architectural interpretation on the country house poem. Also, the *Survey* helps to explain how a common view of architecture can contribute to two such different works. Each work appropriates features of its setting, but "To Penshurst" affirms and exploits the conventions of country house historiography while *The Alchemist*, like London architecture itself, exposes that historiography's failures and limitations.

Many recent studies of early modern London have amply described the dramatic social, demographic, and topographical changes in the city during this period. John Schofield, in particular, has extensively investigated the impact of the dissolution and the resultant land sales on the built environment. In the Priory of Christ Church, Aldgate, Schofield sees an especially memorable example. Following the monastery's dissolution in 1531, the property was sold to Sir Thomas Audley, who tore down much of the old church and sold off the stone at very cheap rates. The property then passed, through marriage, to Audley's son-in-law, Thomas Howard, Duke of Norfolk, who converted the remaining buildings piecemeal to his own "mansions and . . . outbuildings," along with a separate house "called the Ivy Chamber" and an assortment of "smaller tenements," accompanied by "fireplaces, ovens, and privies." This new growth was all "grafted" onto the architecture of the old building, with parts of the nave, choir, walls, arches, and windows visibly remaining. "Here," Schofield speculates, "perhaps . . . John Stow, who lived nearby, looked in as he collected material for his *Survey of London*."[14] Medieval skeletons were thus incongruously fleshed out with the projects of enterprising new owners.

Schofield's investigations suggest that this transformative effect of the Reformation was particularly visible in London architecture, with its more compressed and numerous population and proximate mixture of social classes.[15] As Vanessa Harding has shown, population growth exerted its own pressures on London's built environment, producing other forms of haphazard and unsystematic architectural clutter, as it manifested itself in "divided houses, higher buildings, and the building-over of back plots." Further, "in the immediate fringe beyond the walls, development took the form of closes, narrow, blind alleys onto which a dozen or more dwellings opened."[16] This seems to be the sort of disorder King James sought to remedy in proclamations of 1605 and 1611, which commanded that all new buildings be constructed of brick or stone, because of their superior fire resistance and the attractive front they presented to the street.[17] The proclamations express special regret over the lack of "Uniformitie" in "the foreparts and forefronts of the houses, standing and looking towards the Streets."[18]

These peculiar qualities of London architecture also affected its capacity to represent the social and individual identities of its human inhabitants in the way that country house literature imagined houses to do. In his 1587 *Description of England*, William Harrison rather proudly noted, claiming it as a particularly English quality, a certain architectural deceptiveness to the fronts of London's houses: "many of our greatest houses have outwardly been very simple and plain to sight, which inwardly have been able to receive a duke with his whole train and lodge them at their ease." In addition, the *Description* continues, "the fronts of many of our streets have not been so uniform and orderly builded as in foreign cities."[19] In opaque and crowded street fronts, writes Harding, "the simple relationship between house and householder ... was undermined." London's architectural arrangements made it "more difficult to perceive the human community, since the spatial obscurity of such dwellings also obscured the identity of the inhabitants."[20] Ian Archer adds that "the degree of population turnover weakened the associations between people and place," while Henry S. Turner posits that "the process of urbanization was in many ways a process of interiorization, as the subjects of the city withdrew indoors into private rooms, to be glimpsed partially through windows and doorways or over a garden wall."[21] This social and demographic instability also made its mark on the writing that emerged about London. In both Stow's *Survey* and *The Alchemist*, strategically composed narratives like the county chorographies attached to the country house failed to cohere; they were not easily deduced from buildings that had, themselves, been so visibly and rapidly fragmented and transformed. As Archer points out, the *Survey* "could not perform the same functions as the county chorographies (to which it owed a lot), for which a degree of dynastic continuity among local gentry families provided a more stable 'textual community.'"[22]

Much has been made of the nostalgia displayed by Stow in the *Survey*. This disposition is generally seen as the product of Stow's own experience and personality. Born in 1525, he might well have lamented the loss of the medieval city;

as Patrick Collinson opines, "Old men hate change."[23] But Stow's elegiac strains are not entirely the result of geriatric yearning; he also inherited certain genres and conventions from the *Britannia* and other county chorographies. To see how Stow's models failed, or at least changed, as he translated them to London architecture, we return briefly to the *Britannia*. Camden's description of Hexham, Northumberland, treats a type of site Stow would have known well, the converted monastery. Camden used the histories and idealized virtues of genteel families effectively to produce threads of continuity, subsuming architectural and religious change under the names of past and present patrons:

> But now all the glory that it hath, is in that ancient Abbay, a part whereof is converted into a faire dwelling house, belonging to Sir *John Foster* Knight. As for the Church, it standeth whole and sound, save that the West end onely thereof is pulled downe: and ... within the quire whereof, is to be seene an ancient tombe of a noble man, of that warlike family of the *Vmfranvills*, as appeereth by his Escutcheon of Armes, lying with his legges a crosse. After which fashion in those daies were they onely enterred ... who tooke upon them the crosse, and were marked with the badge of the crosse for sacred warfare, to recover the *Holy land* from the Mahometanes and Turkes.[24]

Camden's architectural description does indeed enfold the history of the dissolution. What was once an abbey has become "a faire dwelling house," and the church has been partly pulled down. Still, Camden emphasizes survival, rather than loss. The present participle "dwelling" records the building's continued occupation and use. "Dwelling house" is a common phrase in the *Britannia*, and we might perhaps hear its echo in Jonson's "To Penshurst," where the closing line—"thy Lord dwells"—is used to sum up the present tense vitality of Sidney's historical and social connections to his estate.[25] Camden marks the landscape with the identity of Sir John Foster, whose name absorbed the former "glory" of the "ancient Abbay." Although the history is not Foster's own, his name and tenure provide an ostensibly stable endpoint to the history of the place. Despite its partial demolition, the church "standeth whole and sound"; and its architecture is materially inscribed with the history of the Umfranvills, as heraldic representation tags it with visually encoded narratives of ancestry. Further, in the text of the *Britannia*, the effigy of the "noble man" is both literally and figuratively positioned with respect to its history. Both the attitude of the crossed legs and Camden's verbal explanation of this detail trace the family's origins at least as far back as the Crusades. Although he acknowledges religious and architectural conversion at Hexham, Camden keeps his usual narrative threads and themes intact.

Stow's description of the former Augustinian monastery in Broadstreet Ward engages several of the same themes: architecture, ancestry, history, and aristocratic identity. Here, though, the effect is very different, as these elements of the story reflect the architectural incoherence of the building's elements. In London, buildings' history could no longer be accurately subsumed under the names of families or institutions, as architectural structures themselves had become strange anthologies that were difficult to synthesize or accurately name. In Camden's account of Hexham, one structure neatly supersedes the other. In Stow's narrative of the former Augustine Friars' monastery, by contrast, the progression from one period of the building's history to the next is far less tidy, and there is no stable culmination to its story. Jonathan Gil Harris has argued that "the polychronic elements of Stow's London do not always resolve themselves into a temporality of supercession.... The past is less canceled by the present than set to work in and against it."[26] Less than working directly "against" the present in this case, however, the past provides a set of strangely aligned foundations—an anthology of incongruous texts—on which the conditions of Stow's topography rest.

This Augustinian monastery, founded in 1253, had been "surrendred" to Henry VIII in 1538, at which time it was valued at fifty-seven pounds. At least part of the complex had then been sold to the Lord Treasurer, William Powlet, who, along with his son, made disturbing modifications. The Powlet house, says Stow,

> was builded by the said Lord Treasurer in place of *Augustine* Friers house, cloyster, and gardens, &c. The Friers Church he pulled not downe, but the West end thereof inclosed from the steeple, and Quier, was in the yeare 1550. graunted to the Dutch Nation in London, to be their preaching place: the other part, namely the steeple, Quier and side Isles to the Quier adjoyning, he reserved to householde uses, as for stowage of corne, coale, and other things, his sonne and heyre Marques of Winchester sold the Monuments of noble men there buried in great number, the paving stone, and whatsoever (which cost many thousands) for one hundred pound, and in place thereof made fayre stabling for horses. He caused the Leade to be taken from the roofes, and laid tile in place, which exchange prooved not so profitable as he looked for, but rather to his disadvauntage. (1.176–177)

Here, Stow does describe architecture in terms of its owners or patrons, and even of ancestry and inheritance, but the building's history is not distilled to any simple endpoint such as the "faire dwelling house" of Sir John Foster, even though Powlet apparently inhabited part of the old monastery. In fact, the transference of property from father to son occasions only the record of another dissolution, this time that of the building itself. Rather than documenting a mutually definitive and continuous connection between family and place, place itself becomes unstable, literally fragmented. Camden cites modifications to the church at Hexham but points out that it remained essentially "whole and sound." At the former Augustinian monastery, Stow mentions that the church has not been entirely pulled down, only to begin a list of the many new (and relatively undignified) things it has become. While the church at Hexham encloses the arms and monumental effigy of the noble soldier, the church of the Augustine Friars is gutted of its noble names and monuments. What was once easily subjugated to the ownership of the Friars (their "house, cloyster, and gardens") has become difficult to name at all, at least with any noun that would succinctly describe it: it is not only a dwelling house, nor is it only a church, storehouse, or stable.

In the *Britannia*, architecture is often understood as a form of historical record that might solidify aristocratic identity by inscribing ancestry. In this passage from the *Survey*, it is the aristocrat himself who foils such antiquarian interests. As the marquis sells off the traces of history, out of acquisitiveness rather than iconoclastic furor, the landowner actively violates the very connections that antiquarian methodology exploits.[27] Stow's condemnation of both iconoclasm and avarice has often been noted, and his judgments seem to apply here.[28] The marquis is as offensive to Stow's antiquarian as to his religious and moral sensibilities. It is not only that the heir cares more for revenue than for religion. He also displays no regard for architecture's commemorative significance, and his inaccurate valuation of the church's architectural materials—its monuments and paving stone—seems to reflect a low valuation of its historical worth, as well. While Stow, like Camden, sought to write about architecture by translating it into human history, the marquis's enthusiasm for conversion and innovation precludes this possibility and breaks down such narratives.

In the *Survey*, what newly acquired buildings seem to represent to new owners is not identity or historical legitimization but fluid sources of wealth. Stow accordingly renders the marquis's mild punishment in financial rather than moral terms: selling the lead from the roof, presumably in hope of monetary gain, "prooved not so profitable as he looked for, but rather to his disadvauntage." From the dissolution onwards in the *Survey*, monasteries are often the objects of monetary transactions, with specific sums and assessments scrupulously recorded, as they are here. The Minories, for instance, which had housed the austere order of St. Clare from 1293, "was valued to dispend 418. pounds, 8.s. 5.d. yearely, and was surrendered by Dame *Elizabeth Salvage*, the last Abbeyes there, unto king *Henry* the 8. in the 30. of his raigne, in the yeare of Christ 1539," after which it was converted to "storehouses, for armour, and habiliments of warre, with diverse worke houses serving to the same purpose" (1.126). And the Whitefriars priory was replaced by "many fayre houses ... lodgings for Noble men and others," after being "valued at 62. li. 7.s. 3.d. and ... surrendred the tenth of November, the 30. of *Henrie* the eight" (2.47). The frequent obtrusion of these cash values and assessments also dissolves historical associations between person and place. A fungible and anonymous mediator, money preserves the specific identities of neither the people who trade it nor the buildings for which it is traded. These transactions tack together a kind of incongruous architectural genealogy or disjointed lineage by marking the points at which a property moves between entirely new owners or uses—from Dame Elizabeth Salvage to the Crown and from nunnery to powder house, for instance—as opposed to being passed down within a family or retained by successive generations of a religious order.

In the *Survey*, it is not only former monastic properties that challenge or disrupt narratives that had traditionally relied on close connections among landowner, architecture, land, and tenants. Just after his account of the former Augustine Friars' house, Stow provides the history of a building in nearby Throgmorton Street, a "very large and spacious" house. It had been built by the late Thomas Cromwell, who experienced a rapid rise in status, having been "Maister of the kinges Jewell house, after that Maister of the Rols, then Lord *Cromwell* knight, Lord privie seale, Vicker Generall, Earle of Essex, high Chamberlaine of England, &c." The story of his building projects reveals ruptures in the conventional political and social relationships relied on by Camden and the country house poems. "This house being finished, and having some reasonable plot of ground left for a Garden, hee caused the pales of the Gardens adjoyning to the northe parte thereof on a sodaine to bee taken downe, 22. foot to bee measured forth right into the north of every mans ground, a line there to bee drawne, a trench to be cast, a foundation laid, and a high bricke Wall to bee builded" (1.179). Despite its association with an illustrious figure, in Stow's text, this house functions as a distorted echo of the country house narrative, which appears here in an inverted and thwarted form. Social and moral conceptions of nobility are separated from each other and, rather than casting the house as stabilizing and legitimizing aristocratic identity through the reification of ancestral history, he describes it in terms of its newness. Further, this new architecture erases and overwrites traces of the past as Cromwell removes the "pales of the Gardens adjoyning" and scores the property with the "trench" of a new foundation, enforcing this new property line with a "high bricke Wall." His goal is not to recuperate history in a serviceable way, as a country house poet or owner might, but to deny it completely.

Stow continues by returning to the concern with just and harmonious landlord-tenant relations that characterizes both the work of the land surveyor and some country house poems, including "To Penshurst." It was a personal concern to him, for his own father was affected by Cromwell's redefinition of the property lines, which apparently encroached upon the holdings of multiple tenants ("every mans ground").

> My Father had a Garden there, and an house standing close to his south pale, this house they lowsed from the ground, & bare upon Rowlers into my Fathers Garden 22. foot, ere my Father heard thereof, no warning was given him, nor other answere when hee spake to the surveyers of that worke, but that their Mayster sir *Thomas* commaunded them so to doe, no man durst go to argue the matter, but each man lost his land, and my Father payde his whole rent, which was vi.s. viii.d. the yeare, for that halfe which was left. (1.179)

In "To Penshurst," Jonson would point out that the walls of Penshurst were "reared with no man's ruin, no man's groan" (46). These garden walls, by contrast, appear to have been raised accompanied by the groaning of many men, Stow's father among them. While the walls of Sidney's estate are presented as representations of the stable and harmonious social relationships that the poem goes on to celebrate, Cromwell's house literally and unjustly destroys such relationships: "each man lost his land, and my Father payde his whole rent ... for that halfe which was left." As opposed to the cheerful and forthcoming peasants who would appear in "To Penshurst," these tenants are frustrated by the oppressive power dynamics that structure landlord-tenant relationships: "no man durst go to argue the matter." In this case, the history being collected remains contested, instead of being channeled toward the celebration of a family or individual. Thomas Cromwell's status and authority supply Stow's themes, but his presence creates resentment and disorder. Both are reflected in the narrative itself, which, in Stow's view, lacks a satisfactory resolution. Even though "no man durst go to argue the matter," in the pages of Stow's record the matter continues to be argued. Further, this scene represents Cromwell's falling away from the ideals that Jonson later would celebrate in Sidney's welcoming house; Cromwell is previously cited in the *Survey* as an example of public charity.[29] Stow recalls having seen at Cromwell's gate "more then two hundered persons served twise every day with bread, meate, and drinke sufficient, for hee observed that auncient and charitable custome as all prelates, noble men, or men of honour and worship... had done before him" (1.89).

The moral with which Stow finishes Cromwell's story fittingly charges the statesman with ignoring historical authority and violating its continuity. Perhaps because of the immediacy of its characters (Stow's own father), this story is capped with an unusually explicit judgment: "Thus much of mine owne knowledge have I thought good to note, that the suddaine rising of some men, causeth them to forget themselves" (1.179). Like his less explicit judgment of the marquis, the observation reflects Stow's antiquarian interests; Cromwell's crime is not one of greed, but one of forgetting. In a way that parallels the marquis's sale of ancient funeral monuments, Cromwell's approach to architecture manifests his own disregard for the very stories that, from an antiquarian perspective, made architecture valuable. To the antiquarian or surveyor, architecture in part became legible through the lens of historical documents, the "rentes / fees, customes, & services, the lorde oughte to have of his tenaunts" described by Fitzherbert (see Chapter 2) or the "old Rowle[s], and Evidence[s]" Camden claims to have consulted.[30] Cromwell, however, uses architecture to render precisely such documents impotent and meaningless, as their set rents and measurements no longer correspond to set measures of land. In this case, an antiquarian's historical evidence undercuts the legitimacy of a landlord's connection to the land, so that instead of providing a felicitous confluence of virtue and social prominence or a stable culmination to Stow's narrative, the landlord initiates ruptures in this network of relationships.

Moreover, Cromwell's acquisition of his land did not result from lineal inheritance but from the events of his "suddaine rising." As the house of Stow's father is lifted on rollers and deposited elsewhere in his garden, architecture maps the displacements and discontinuities of history in a surprisingly literal way. The final lines of the building's story indicate an equally abrupt disjuncture; the building passes not from Cromwell to an heir but to the Company of Drapers, for use as their "common Hall," readers learn in the subsequent paragraph (1.180). Stow leaves one part of Cromwell's own history unspoken, although he might well have expected readers to remember it: in 1540, Cromwell, having fallen out of favor, was executed by, as the historian Edward Hall put it, "a ragged and Boocherly miser, whiche very ungoodly perfourmed the Office."[31] While Stow's version of the story does not include Cromwell's literal decapitation, his narrative is itself truncated and ruptured, its loose ends suddenly redirected towards a new and incongruous end. While a traditional country house narrative might have ended by celebrating a nobleman's titles and authority, Cromwell is stripped of both, displaced by the Drapers and a "common Hall." Punished for the crime of forgetting himself, in Stow's architectural history, Cromwell fails to achieve the final word.

Stow thus reminds us that by the early seventeenth century, London already resembled a map that had had its city pulled out from under it, in which both place names and architectural places presented historical riddles, rather than a stable association between person and place, or name and thing. Stow's account of the former Blackfriars monastery—for Jonson, the Blackfriars theater—reminds us, as well, that the real architectural setting toward which Jonson so pointedly gestures was equally a product of conversion and change. In 1610, Jonson's choice of topographical label ("Friars") was conspicuously both accurate and inaccurate, evoking at once the theater itself and an order of monks who no longer lived there. Stow's *Survey* records that from 1276 until 1538, the site had been occupied by the powerful Dominican order and had included "a large church, and richly furnished with Ornaments: wherein diverse parliaments and other great meetings hath beene holden." Some of these convocations were medieval, but the monastery had also witnessed important religious and political fluctuations in the past century of London's history. In 1529, "Cardinall *Campeius* the Legat, with Cardinal *Woolsey* sate at the said blacke friers, where before them as Legats & Judges, was brought in question the kings marriage with Queene *Katherin* as to be unlawfull, before whom the king and Queene were cited and summoned to appeare" (1.339). Before the year was out, however, the tide had turned: "The same yeare in the Moneth of October began a parliament in the Blacke Friers, in the which Cardinall *Woolsey* was condemned... this house valued at 104.li. 15.s. 5.d. was surrendred the xii. of November the 30. of *Henrie* the eight" (1.340). The land was sold to Sir Thomas Cawarden, Master of the King's Revels, who soon pulled down some of the complex, including the Blackfriars church. In Jonson's day, though, some of the original buildings remained, and it was one of these, the monastery's large medieval hall, that James Burbage purchased for use as the Second Blackfriars theater in 1596.[32]

If Jonson's reference to the "Friars" suggests similarities between the activities of the actors and those of the tricksters in *The Alchemist*, it also points to other correspondences between the play's imagined setting and the theater in which early performances took place. For Jonson, architecture was inherently historical, and Lovewit's house, like the theater building itself, documents stories of instability and change, of the dissociation between person and location. A reading of Stow thus illuminates the historical dimensions of Jonson's setting and, by extension, helps to explain some of the ways social identity is constructed in the play. Both the *Survey* and *The Alchemist* place us among the ruins of a particular kind of architectural narrative. In *The Alchemist*, the breakdown of conventional connections among architecture, topography, and authority allows new formulations of social prominence and identity to emerge.

Transported to an urban environment, the narrative threads that structure the accounts of country houses in antiquarian chorographies and land surveys, and that would soon structure Jonson's own "To Penshurst," are evident mainly in their acknowledged absence. In the play's first scene, questions of ownership, habitation, history, lineage, and ordered, hierarchical social relations are all raised only to be dismantled or dismissed. Most obviously, Lovewit, the current genteel owner, who would provide the culmination of a conventional country house description, is absent as long as "there dies one a week / O' the plague," and it is this very absence that sponsors the action of the play (1.1.182–183). Far from exemplifying husbandry and household economy, and in contrast to the lord who "dwells" in "To Penshurst," Lovewit is totally unaware of the ways in which his servant is behaving and his house is being used. Face assures Subtle and Doll, "O, fear not him ... he's safe from thinking toward London.... If he do, / He'll send such word, for airing of the house, / As you shall have sufficient time, to quit it" (1.1.182, 183, 185–188). Moreover, we learn that Lovewit's wife has recently died; instead of her presence keeping the house in order, her permanent disappearance has "broke [it] up" (1.1.58). Subtle's reference to human mortality introduces another disruption to any traditional order, and the mistress's death precludes the establishment of a stable lineage through the production of heirs, in contrast, for instance, to the "noble, fruitful" and "chaste" mistress of "To Penshurst" (90). More important, though, her absence opens a space for a new succession of mistresses—first Doll Common and then Dame Pliant—who each reflect and shape the new characteristics of the household. Thus, if the presence of Lovewit and his wife would have supplied the capstones of a country house story, the story of this house has become indeterminate and decidedly uncapped.

In a vitriolic quarrel, Face imagines himself as a kind of replacement for his absent master, and the play's first scene consists largely of Subtle's attempts to undercut that image. Face presents himself to Subtle as a version of the genteel householder, in a position either to dole out charity or to rent out space, playing at once the householder and the charitable benefactor:

> I ga' you count'nance, credit for your coals,
> Your stills, your glasses, your materials,

> Built you a furnace, drew you customers,
> Advanc'd all your black arts; lent you, beside
> A house to practise in. (1.1.43–47)

Constructing a scenario in which Subtle has violated both social order and harmonious landlord-tenant relations, Face accuses Subtle of failing to show either deference or gratitude, or to acknowledge his obligation to Face. To take Subtle in, according to Face, was less a promising investment than it was an act of charitable pity, as he reminds Subtle of their first meeting:

> at Pie Corner,
> Taking your meal of steam in, from cooks' stalls,
> Where, like the father of hunger, you did walk
> Piteously costive. (1.1.25–28)

Perversely enabled by Face's generosity, Subtle's arrogance, according to Face, is completely unfounded; it is his access to "The place" which Face has afforded him that has "made [Subtle] valiant" (1.1.63). Despite Face's attempts to escape the social hierarchy in which he was a servant, he re-imagines himself in a way that mimics its principles. In Face's view, priority remains closely connected to the control of "place."[33]

Subtle's response is to claim that rather than acting as a stable and legitimate head to the household, Face is only a parody of that figure, failing to fill the role on all counts, including moral character, social status, and historical authority. Face's representation of himself as a charitable landlord is delusional, Subtle points out, both because he is not charitable and because he is not a landlord. When Face asserts that he has "lent" Subtle "a house to practise in," Subtle reminds him that it is not his house at all. "Your master's house?" he retorts, and produces the same answer to Face's accusation that Subtle has misused his new accommodation by "stud[ying] the more thriving skill / Of bawdry, since": "Yes, in your master's house. / You, and the rats, here kept possession" (1.1.47, 49–50). Subtle thus reasserts Lovewit's prerogative as a way of preventing Face's assumption of the master's role. He also counters Face's pretensions to magnanimity and charity by claiming that he has failed to maintain even the barest hospitality toward the poor; he has instead kept "the butt'ry-hatch still lock'd, and save[d] the chippings" as well as selling "the dole beer to aqua-vitae men" (1.1.52–53). Moreover, unlike a true genteel landowner, Face's "possession" of the house is not supported by historical tradition:

You were once (time's not long past) the good,
Honest, plain, livery-three-pound-thrum; that kept
Your master's worship's house, here, in the Friars,
For the vacations. (1.1.15–17)

Resorting to a conventional way of telling time in antiquarian texts, Subtle argues that, "Within man's memory," Face has been promoted from this servitude by his means (1.1.20). While the names and arms of noble families might organize history in a country house narrative, Face possesses no similar social credentials: "Slave," Subtle goes on to accuse him, "thou hadst no name" (1.1.81).

While Subtle is proving that Face is a poor shadow of the legitimate genteel householder, Doll Common emerges as an equally perverted replacement for the household's deceased mistress. Doll imposes uneasy order on her colleagues by ending the quarrel, persuading them to "work close, and friendly"; but it is an order characterized specifically by its lack of regard for history, traditional virtue, or hierarchical social relations (1.1.161). In these respects, the household mirrors the character of Doll herself. No lofty example of virtue, chastity, or lineage, Doll, as a professed prostitute, confronts the audience with an obvious inversion of these qualities. As she recalls with a pun on her name—"Have yet some care of me, o' your republic"—Doll is herself a *res publica* or common thing, the undifferentiated property of many men and not, through chastity, the progenitor of a stable family line (1.1.110).[34] In fact, instead of representing the triumphant culmination of an ancestral history, Doll constantly works in this scene to erase the past, pleading with Subtle and Face to forget the former distinctions and liabilities they insistently dredge up. The "venture tripartite," according to Doll, is a "work . . . begun out of equality" with "All things in common" (1.1.133–136). She thus argues for a system of social relationships that is not historically established but is newly begun and that would allow the tricksters to collaborate "Without priority" (1.1.136). Grudgingly prodded back into a state of peace, Face and Subtle celebrate Doll as the house's new and comically distorted mistress:

at supper, thou shalt sit in triumph,
And not be styl'd Doll Common, but Doll Proper,
Doll Singular: the longest cut, at night,
Shall draw thee for his Doll Particular. (1.1.176–179)

In Face's description, Doll resembles the equitable household she imagines: she is distinguished by her lack of distinction. The final line of Face's tribute, which names Doll "Particular" is also the scene's most explicit reference to her undiscerning promiscuity and her failure to assume a stable social identity as one man's wife. She thus becomes "Singular" and "Particular" only by virtue of the behavior that makes her "Common."

Like the country house narrative, then, *The Alchemist* is in part about the formation and legitimization of social identities. Here, however, as the conventional ingredients of social status are pointedly shown to be lacking, new possibilities are introduced. During this expository squabble, it becomes apparent that there is more at stake for the tricksters than either vanity or the finite sums of money they will fleece from their willing gulls. They seem to have begun by seeking a more permanent social transformation that is not contingent on Lovewit's absence. While critical interpretations of *The Alchemist* have tended to focus on the tricksters' theatrical talents and ingenious deceptions, the first and final acts of the play, in particular, suggest that their enterprises are anchored in a sincere hope of achieving the philosopher's stone.[35] The sincerity of their belief raises the stakes of the tricksters' activities and changes our sense of what will be lost if Lovewit returns too soon. New possibilities emerge as serious competition for the traditional order that originally structured Lovewit's household, and the alchemical process itself presents an alternative to the social hierarchies and ancestral histories we see celebrated in narratives about the country house. Calling Subtle and Face "Sovereign" and "General" respectively in the fifth line of the play, Doll demonstrates that the "venture tripartite" is not only a business venture aimed at financial returns; it is also an investment in the transcendence of previous social limitations, in the making of new credentials and new titles.

In addition to deflating Face's representation of himself as a genteel replacement for Lovewit, Subtle in another way undermines the hierarchy that formerly ordered the household, by advancing an alternative form of authority. In Subtle's view, status depends not on ancestry, ownership, or a sense of *noblesse oblige* (all of which, he says, Face lacks), but on acquisition of the alchemical arts, which produce the possibility of more sudden transformations, both material and social.[36] It might be accurate to say that Face was originally Subtle's gull. Claiming to have given Subtle "credit for [his] coals," Face suggests that he has advanced to his unsuccessful colleague both money and belief, and when he speaks of purchasing "Your stills, your glasses, your materials" and having "Built you a furnace," he seems to be speaking literally; his original investment was in Subtle the alchemist, not Subtle the trickster. Despite his easy transition from alchemist to bawd, though, Subtle appears to believe in his own abilities, and his excuse for not having fulfilled his promises echoes one that actually appeared in contemporary alchemical treatises: he hasn't yet had time. In a new edition of George

Ripley's *Compound of Alchymy* (1591), Ralph Rabards bitterly complains, "if I had bin so fortunate as to have spent these seaven yeares past in one of your MAJESTIES manifold fruitlesse still-houses: I durst before this time have presumed to have promised more of my selfe than I will speak of."[37] Instead, Subtle says, he has been forced to waste time effecting another projection: that of Face himself, by imparting to Face the secrets of his own "great art." "[H]ave I," Subtle asks,

> Sublim'd thee, and exalted thee, and fix'd thee
> I' the third region, call'd our state of grace?
> Wrought thee to spirit, to quintessence, with pains
> Would twice have won me the philosopher's work?
> Put thee in words and fashion? Made thee fit
> For more than ordinary fellowships?
> Giv'n thee thy oaths, thy quarrelling dimensions?
> Thy rules, to cheat at horse-race, cock-pit, cards,
> Dice, or whatever gallant tincture else?
> Made thee a second in mine own great art? (1.1.68–77)

Given the list of dissolute misdemeanors that immediately precedes it—quarreling, gambling, and cheating—the phrase "great art" might seem to refer mainly to Subtle's "bawdry," but it can equally refer to alchemy itself, and in the coming acts it becomes apparent that Face has indeed been extensively schooled in the obtuse and coded language of alchemical treatises.[38] Subtle also seems serious in his threats to Face:

> I'll thunder you in pieces. I will teach you
> How to beware to tempt a Fury again,
> That carries tempest in his hand and voice. (1.1.60–62)

While the lines are a credible extension of Subtle's volatile personality, he thinks he is master of something more. In keeping with the aims of the "venture tripartite," Subtle's assertion that he has put Face "in words and fashion" and made him "fit / For more than ordinary fellowships" casts both of his areas of expertise—deception and distillation—as alternative forms of social advancement and legitimization, in place of the attributes—name, property, and historically established authority—he has proven Face not to possess.

As the play continues, the alchemical process itself emerges as an analogy, or even substitute, for the components of genteel or aristocratic identity. Through the comically cryptic language that veils alchemical mysteries, the laboratory becomes a site for the manipulation of time and generation. Performing for Sir

Epicure Mammon and Surly, Face describes the stages of alchemy as a genealogy or ancestry:

> It turns to sulphur, or to quicksilver,
> Who are the parents of all other metals.
> Nor can this remote matter, suddenly,
> Progress so from extreme unto extreme,
> As grow to gold, and leap o'er all the means.
> Nature doth, first, beget th' imperfect; then
> Proceeds she to the perfect. Of that airy,
> And oily water, mercury is engender'd;
> Sulphur o' the fat and earthy part: the one
> (Which is the last) supplying the place of male,
> The other of the female, in all metals. (2.3.153–163)

These metallic "parents," according to Subtle, "can produce the species of each metal / More perfect thence, than nature doth in earth" (2.3.169–170). The alchemical breeding process thus replicates the more commonly observable phenomenon of spontaneous generation: "Art can beget bees, hornets, beetles, wasps, / Out of the carcasses, and dung of creatures" (2.3.172–173). This effusion is, of course, intended to confirm Mammon's optimism; and, significantly, Subtle turns to the language of parentage and pedigree when he seeks to assert the legitimacy of his art.

Subtle thus presents himself as the manipulator of a history that resembles many aristocratic pedigrees: it is part nature and part art, part conscious invention and part earnest belief. The alchemist's goal, as Subtle represents it, is to improve on what happens naturally, or at least to speed it up, proceeding more rapidly from the "imperfect" to the "perfect." Alchemy allows metals to pass through the generations of this pedigree in record time and to arrive more quickly at its stable endpoint, the gold that, Subtle says, all metals would "be ... if they had time" (2.3.136). Anticipating the arrival of Sir Epicure Mammon, Subtle says, "He [Mammon] will make / Nature asham'd of her long sleep: when art, / Who's but a step-dame, shall do more than she" (1.4.106–107). The alchemist thus intervenes as a "step-dame" in a natural process, here figured in the terms of biological lineage. As Subtle continues, he imagines alchemy as creating an accelerated series of generations, which, repeated again and again, is as productive as nature: "For look, how oft I iterate the work, / So many times, I add unto his [the stone's] virtue," ultimately producing a result "As good as any of the natural mine" (2.3.106–107, 114). While the ancestral narratives of the *Britannia* and the country house poems practice a kind of narrative distillation by filtering and shaping history so that all stories point toward the stable and legitimate tenure of the current landowner, the alchemist practices his own distillation, holding forth the possibility of an alternative endpoint in the form of the philosopher's stone and the gold it will produce.

The play's opening scene lays out two temporal trajectories—Lovewit's return and the success of alchemy—and the former comes to fruition at the expense of the latter. Still, the play's final scene confronts both gulls and audience with the material evidence of the tricksters' endeavors; it appears that some sort of chemical experiment has actually been taking place. Lovewit describes the interior of his house to the disgruntled gulls:

> Here, I find
> The empty walls, worse than I left 'em, smok'd,
> A few crack'd pots, and glasses, and a furnace,
> The ceiling fill'd with poesies of the candle. (5.5.41–44)

Traces of the alchemical process are here viewed from a different temporal perspective, evoking memories, rather than sparking hopes. There is something wistful about these abandoned material fragments and the "poesies" written by a light now extinguished. As Anne Barton writes, "this final description of the house always comes as a shock. . . . It becomes plain that Mammon, Tribulation and the rest are not the only ones who have been fooled by art."[39] The remnants of Subtle's apparatus point again toward alchemy's competing history, toward the generative process that would produce an alternative ending to the landowner's authority.

Throughout, *The Alchemist* is threaded with elements of the country house narrative—ancestry, land ownership, inheritance, and hospitality—but they are disrupted and comically modified. Lovewit's house (transformed to the alchemical laboratory) is repeatedly presented as a place where characters seek to transcend the limitations of their own identities by reformulating traditional sources of social status. Unable to produce the felicitous familiar they have promised Dapper, for instance—which, Face tells Kastril, "will win . . . / By unresistible luck, within this fortnight, / Enough to buy a barony"—the tricksters temporarily gratify their victim by inventing for him a more illustrious ancestry (3.4.58–60). Rather than being "a special gentle, / That is the heir to forty marks a year,"—"which I count nothing," Face will later say—and "the sole hope of his old grandmother," Dapper becomes the nephew of the Queen of Fairy (1.2.50–51, 3.4.57, 1.2.53). Doll pretends that this invented relative "may chance / To leave him three or four hundred chests of treasure, / And some twelve thousand acres of Fairyland" (5.4.53–55). Although this region remains impenetrable to the general public, Dapper's benevolent supernatural aunt resembles nothing so much as a wealthy, childless dowager looking for somewhere to bestow her wealth, over which, as a "lone woman" she has total control (1.2.155). Like a country house, Lovewit's house becomes a site for the staging of hospitality, here represented as not generous and bountiful but capricious and disgusting. Dapper (in preparation for a long wait in the "privy lodgings") is sent "a dead mouse, / And a piece of gingerbread, to be merry withal," reportedly taken from her Grace's "own private trencher" (3.5.79, 65–66). The offering anticipates, in comically diminished form, the "liberal board" and "lord's own meat" which Jonson would praise in "To Penshurst" (59, 62), as Dapper eagerly believes he will ascend from his station as a clerk to that of a genteel landowner, the heir to a formerly unknown country estate ("some twelve thousand acres"). Dapper believes that the limitations of ancestry and social station may be erased by Subtle's art and replaced with the promise of a new, more lucrative and expedited inheritance, whose fulfillment feels more imminent, even as it is perpetually deferred.

In contrast to Dapper, who imagines alchemy as a way of making substitutions within the conventional components of social status and legitimacy—inheritance, landownership, and ancestry—Sir Epicure Mammon believes it will allow him to transcend these requirements altogether. Enjoying a social status higher than any other character in the play, Mammon might reasonably rely most heavily on the possession of these attributes. Instead, he sees them not as advantages but as constraints to his desire. Rather than invoking idealized connections between landowner and land, identity and ancestral history, or social status and moral character, Mammon looks to alchemy as a way of severing these ties and escaping the limitations they define. Like the Marquis of Winchester as he appears in Stow's *Survey*, the acquisitive Mammon displays no regard for the historical and topographical associations from which he might be expected to benefit.[40] It is not only that Mammon hopes to dismantle buildings so that he can transmute base metals purchased from various sites around London. ("Buy / The coverings off o' churches.... Let 'em stand bare, as do their auditory. / Or cap 'em new, with shingles," Face says when Mammon wonders where he "will get stuff enough ... to project on" [2.2.13, 15–16, 12]). Mammon also believes he will need to transmute the insufficient features of the landscape itself in order to make it commensurate with his desires. His first lines in the play imaginatively transform Lovewit's house into an idealized new world. "Come on, sir. Now, you set your foot on shore / In *novo orbe*," he gushes to Surly, "here's the rich Peru" (2.1.1–2). Clearly figurative in this case, this transformative projection becomes more literal as he imagines mining the resources of the English countryside, with the purpose of transmuting it entirely: "I'll purchase Devonshire, and Cornwall, / And make them perfect Indies!" (2.1.35–36). Instead of establishing familial and historical ties to a local geographic place in England, as a county chorography would do, Mammon appropriates the imagery of a vaster empire. The nation, apparently, is not enough world for him, and all nearly available places are inadequate indicators of his new identity.

In his courtship of the disguised Doll Common, Mammon rejects the notion that topographical names and regions are sufficient to contain or describe the status he plans to achieve. The narratives of the country house poems and of chorographies such as the *Britannia* are firmly pinned to the landscape; their logic depends upon securing a mutually definitive relationship between person and place. But for Mammon, this specificity is only confining. Having already told Doll that he would "spend half [his] land" (4.1.104) to rescue her from her current social invisibility, Mammon goes on to imagine a new, exalted status through increasingly transcendent and unnamable ideas of the places they will inhabit:

> I am pleas'd the glory of her sex should know,
> This nook, here, of the Friars, is no climate
> For her, to live obscurely in, to learn
> Physic, and surgery, for the Constable's wife
> Of some odd hundred in Essex; but come forth,
> And taste the air of palaces
> . . . .
>   when the jewels
> Of twenty states adorn thee, and the light
> Strikes out the stars; that, when thy name is mention'd,
> Queens may look pale. (4.1.130–135; 141–144)

Mammon's assumption is that Doll's status is defined—and here circumscribed—by the places she knows or inhabits. Her coming forth, then, is reflected in Mammon's progress from confined to unconfined conceptions of place, from "the Friars" or "some odd hundred in Essex" to dislocated "palaces" and wealth that is boundless, being made up of "the jewels / Of twenty states." Mammon imagines Doll's preeminence as being greater than any conferred by the sovereignty of a nation; it is not only a "nook" or neighborhoods or counties but countries that become insufficient markers of identity. Far from feeling that he or Doll will be elevated through association with some named and demarcated area of land, Mammon feels that they would actually be diminished by it.

Mammon's treatment of history and ancestry resembles his treatment of place. Rather than seeking to inscribe his relationship to a particular family or past, Mammon seeks to supplant the necessity of either. At first, his interest in Doll seems to emerge from a fixation on the qualities most celebrated in the country house poem: titles, lineage, and inherited wealth. Face claims that he has, at Mammon's request, prepared Doll for her new suitor by advancing his status as a "noble fellow" and "told her such brave things o' you, / Touching your bounty and your noble spirit" (2.3.318, 4.1.6–7). According to Face, similar themes should supply Mammon's conversation as he first accosts her: "And you must praise her house, remember that, / And her nobility" (4.1.19–20). "Let me, alone," Mammon replies. "No herald, no nor antiquary, Lungs, / Shall do it better. Go" (4.1.20–21). Face's recommendations are no doubt intended to make Mammon additionally ridiculous as he heaps traditional moral and social values on a woman whom we know to possess none of them. But in the end, Mammon invokes these qualities only to reject them emphatically. Once he has acquired the stone, Mammon believes, neither his past nor Doll's will make any difference, since he will have the power to invent them both anew. Calling Doll the "Daughter of honour," he tells her: "I will rear this beauty / Above all styles" (4.1.116, 117–118). Rather than encapsulating or expressing status, "styles," or titles, like set measures of land, signal only limitation.

Throughout, Mammon's fantasies diminish the significance of lineage and generation celebrated in the country house narrative, where both marriage and parentage are constitutive of identity. At first, he asserts gold's potential to supersede familial relationships, as he envisions purchasing sex with the "sublim'd pure wife" of a "wealthy citizen, or rich lawyer" ("unto that fellow / I'll send a thousand pound, to be my cuckold"), or employing "fathers and mothers" as his "bawds" (2.2.54–56, 57–58). Later, in his courtship of Doll, Mammon produces an odd adaptation of the Danaë myth, in which gold becomes less a vehicle for divine insemination than a strange sexual proxy for Mammon himself:

> Think therefore, thy first wish, now; let me hear it:
> And it shall rain into thy lap, no shower,
> But floods of gold, whole cataracts, a deluge,
> To get a nation on thee! (4.1.125–28)

Here, wealth and status are no longer compounded in the propagation of a noble line through the union of two aristocratic families, a method that Mammon seems at first to pursue when he hears of Doll's fortune. Instead, Mammon invents a new concept of nationhood in which a population is begotten in an orgiastic fornication with gold itself. Social identity is no longer tied to biological parentage, history, titles, or places, as these concepts are all superseded by the seminal agency of the philosopher's stone and the gold it will produce. We might think here of Jonson's reassuring address to Penshurst: "His children thy great lord may call his own, / A fortune in this age but rarely known" (91–92). Mammon's children, the "nation" with which he identifies, are decidedly not his own, as gold erases the significance of biological ancestry and replaces it with an alternative pedigree. Mammon's actual reproductive utility, his most basic involvement in the formation of familial relationships, is made obsolete by a shower of gold. Mammon seems to envision this scenario as a way of overcoming the practical limitations of human reproduction, which make even the most fruitful marriage unlikely to produce a nation; but ironically, unlike Sir Robert Sidney's influence and identity, Mammon's are effaced rather than iterated or reinscribed, through the sexual consummation of his union with Doll.

Mammon's disdain for historical markers of identity is fittingly accompanied by a generally garbled sense of antiquity, and when he attempts to invoke history as a way of legitimizing alchemy, he is patently unconvincing to anyone but himself. "Will you believe in antiquity? Records?" he demands of Surly, then goes on to mix periods, places, and locations in a ridiculous way:

> I'll shew you a book where Moses and his sister,
> And Solomon have written, of the art;
> Ay, and a treatise penned by Adam—
> . . . .
> O' the philosopher's stone, and in High Dutch
> . . . .
> Which proves it was the primitive tongue. (2.1.80–83, 84, 86)

Whatever he believes about alchemy's "antiquity," Mammon's insertion of "High Dutch" into biblical history certainly proves that he is no antiquarian, as his citation of documentary evidence is incompetent. His sloppy and opportunistic invocation of these specious historical "Records" points not only to Mammon's gullibility but to his characteristic orientation toward history. Mammon thinks seriously only about future "projections," and despite his eagerness to legitimize alchemy, "antiquity" is not what he cares about at all. It is perhaps in response to Mammon's perspective that the tricksters invent Doll's particular brand of madness:

> She falls into her fit, and will discourse
> So learnedly of genealogies,
> As you would run mad, too, to hear her, sir. (2.3.240–242)

Doll's purported antiquarianism is, in this house, a form of insanity, not learning, and once Mammon accidentally sets her off, her "discourse" becomes one more tirade in a general cacophony, reduced from narrative to indistinct noise.

In Mammon's view, this capacity to erase or supersede history will also make alchemy the means by which social and moral nobility might be alienated from one another, upsetting the supposed harmony between status and character that legitimizes authority in country house narratives. Surly interrupts Mammon's fantasy of taffeta shirts and perfumed, bird-skin gloves with the objection that even if Mammon is stupid enough to take alchemy on its own terms, he ought to acknowledge that character does matter, because the success of the alchemical enterprise is determined by the nature of the stone's owner:

> Why, I have heard, he must be *homo frugi*,
> A pious, holy and religious man,
> One free from mortal sin, a very virgin. (2.2.97–99)

Mammon protests, however, that his own character is irrelevant, because the philosopher's stone is transferrable from person to person through the mediation of cash: "That makes it, sir, he is so," Mammon replies; "But I buy it. / My venture brings it me" (2.2.100–101). In Mammon's view, "venture" is as good as virtue, and as a result, his fantasies are also devoid of virtue, economy, or piety. Once again, attributes that might be used to naturalize and legitimize genteel or aristocratic status appear to Mammon only constraints.

As Subtle and Mammon address each other, they construct between them the fiction of an inheritance, forged by the exchange of money rather than by a shared bloodline. Subtle repeatedly addresses Mammon as "son" and pretends that he expects him to perpetuate his own virtuous character as he inherits the stone. "Son," he says, "I doubt / Y' are covetous" (2.3.4–5), and later,

> If you, my son, should now prevaricate,
> And to your own particular lusts employ
> So great and catholic a bliss, be sure,
> A curse will follow. (2.3.19–22)

The scene is strewn with similar warnings: "Yes, son, were I assur'd / Your piety were firm," and "Son, be not hasty" (2.3.102, 55–56). Mammon responds in kind, purchasing Subtle as the ancestor from whom his own new inheritance will flow: "Well said, Father!" he tells Subtle after a particularly long dissertation on the stages of the alchemical process (2.3.176). In this perverse genealogy, Mammon constructs a lineage whose ligaments are monetary rather than biological, and he divorces social from moral conceptions of nobility by suggesting that one need not accompany the other, and that either, in the end, might be effectively replaced by "venture" or wealth. In "To Penshurst," Jonson would commend the Sidneys for passing on to their offspring "their virtuous parents' noble parts," which include "religion" and "innocence" as well as "The mysteries of manners, arms and arts" (97, 93, 94, 98). In Mammon's formulation, "venture" replaces both nature and nurture, obviating the need for any such moral education or inheritance.

Fired by his overactive imagination, Mammon chafes eagerly against the limitations of traditional markers of genteel or aristocratic identity—landownership, ancestry, and noble character—and thinks with pleasure of the life he would lead were he able to leave them behind. By contrast, Kastril, a young "gentleman, newly warm in his land," lacks such imagination; and it is through Face's intervention that he is brought to feel dissatisfaction, which gnaws away at conventional constructions of identity by dissolving Kastril's regard for connections between person and place, or a landowner, his name, and his land (2.6.57). However despicable Kastril's aspirations—"To learn to quarrel," Drugger reports, "and to live by his wits"—his sense of identity is originally grounded in these associations; when he arrives in London, he seems proud of his status, and he means, Drugger reveals, to "die i' the country" (2.6.61, 62). Kastril confirms that once he has acquired the behavioral accouterments of his genteel status, he hopes to "go down / And practise i' the country" (3.4.24–25). For Kastril, wealth is inseparable from lineage; were he not, he says "the best o' the Kastrils, I'd be sorry else, / By fifteen hundred, a year" (3.4.14–15). As he begins to teach Kastril to quarrel, Subtle addresses him in a way that both mocks and flatters his genteel inheritance:

> Come near, my worshipful boy, my *terrae fili*,
> That is, my boy of land; make thy approaches:
> Welcome, I know thy lusts, and thy desires,
> And I will serve, and satisfy 'em. (4.2.13–16)

As Mares notes, the phrase "*terrae fili*" is a euphemism for "bastard," and Subtle's translation, "boy of land," is comic because it manages to be both literal and inaccurate, reversing the insult entirely to pinpoint what Kastril believes to be an impressive social advantage.

But the country house gentleman is ill-equipped to function in this city house play. Face quickly dismantles Kastril's smug opinion of himself, and his land and income are transformed from points of pride to liabilities as Face persuades him that he could make more money gambling:

> It will repair you, when you are spent.
> How do they live by their wits, there, that have vented
> Six times your fortunes? (3.4.51–53)

Kastril's disbelief indicates that he has never before thought of such wealth, let alone dreamed of possessing it: "What, three thousand a year! . . . Are there such?" (3.4.53–54). Moreover, Face says, Subtle will introduce him to more lucrative sources of income "when your land is gone / (As men of spirit hate to keep earth long)" (3.4.83–84). Face's parenthetical remark plays on the supposed elemental baseness of earth, but to Kastril, the lines seem to mean that town gallants are eager to obtain the "excellent fashion" Face describes, by selling off their land (3.4.81). Kastril is a quick study in dissolution and stupidity, and traditional components of genteel and aristocratic identity suddenly pale. The narratives that order accounts of the country house fail when transported to this city house, outstripped and undone by the promises of the alchemist's art.

In several of its strands, then, this story of Lovewit's London house places us among narratives that dismantle the conceptions of genteel and aristocratic identity constructed by the narratives in the *Britannia* and, later, country house poems. These narratives resemble the disordered and truncated architectural stories of Stow's *Survey*, in which stable relationships among architecture, history, ancestry, and topography also fall into ruin. *The Alchemist*, however, may appear to depart from such accounts in its conclusion, which, on the surface, seems to place a stable capstone on this household's story with the return of the actual householder.[41] Face's early predictions about Lovewit's homecoming are prematurely fulfilled at the end of Act 4, displacing the operations of the alchemist's lab by physically displacing the alchemist himself. Face's identity suddenly reverts to the one Subtle insultingly recalled in the first scene: "I'll into mine old shape again, and meet him, / Of Jeremy, the butler" (4.7.120–121). Along with the hopes of the other gulls, Mammon's "*novo orbe*" and "rich Peru" vanish. As the house becomes Lovewit's once again, Face's pert question about whether the outraged Mammon intends to enter "Another man's house" reminds us that this has been "Another man's house" all along (5.3.11).

But this new household is not exactly a return to the old one, and it is fitting that Dame Pliant should become not only the house's new mistress, but the means through which Lovewit's house is, in some version, reestablished. "Give me but leave, to make the best of my fortune," Face says to Lovewit,

> And only pardon me th' abuse of your house:
> It's all I beg. I'll help you to a widow,

In recompense, that you shall gi' me thanks for,
Will make you seven years younger, and a rich one. (5.3.82–86)

Replacing Lovewit's deceased wife and the sexually undiscriminating Doll Common, Dame Pliant also defines and reflects qualities of the household. If the death of Lovewit's wife marked the end of a period when Face knew his place, and Doll represented the attempted foundation of a new "republic," Lovewit's marriage to Dame Pliant signals the inauguration of another new household, this one based on compromise and negotiation. As Lovewit prepares to don the Spanish cloak and boldly go where many men have attempted to go before by marrying this nineteen-year-old widow, he restores, in an oddly modified version, the traditional correspondence between a house and the history of its owner. Although Dame Pliant is not exactly the house's owner, she is in many ways the truest reflection of its recent past: she too bears the name of an absent master, and she too has been reappropriated following a fruitless union irreparably disrupted by death. She is not quite a replacement for the house's former mistress, as this new household is not quite a replacement for the one remembered at the beginning of the play. Both mistress and household bear traces or reminders of a recent and more unstable history.

As this dealing between Lovewit and Face (as Jeremy) indicates, Lovewit's return is not so much the appearance of a *deus ex machina* as it is the initiation of a multistage renegotiation, in which Face becomes something slightly more than a servant and Lovewit acts as something less than the definitive master of the house. As Brian Gibbons points out, "Lovewit . . . can do no more than acknowledge the skill and wit of Face."[42] The first and last scenes of the play complement each other, not only through a process of prediction and fulfillment, but through their recollection and imperfect recuperation of traditional architectural narratives about the relationship between landowner and land, householder and house, and person and place. It is true that Face is forced to resign his role as "Captain," to answer to "Jeremy" once again, and to dissolve the "venture tripartite" that had enabled him to hope he might shed that servile identity forever. When Lovewit first returns, however, he is no more able to reoccupy his own house than the indignant gulls are able to enter it. In this sense, he has less authority than the humble smith who offers to fetch a crowbar and pry open the door (5.1.45). Only once Face has dispatched with Dapper and reassessed his own bargaining chips does Lovewit reenter the house, because, as Face says, "here's no place to talk on't i' the street" (5.3.81). In addition, Face has not entirely changed his ways; the promise he makes to Lovewit regarding Dame

Pliant echoes the extravagant and supernatural returns he promised his earlier investors: "I'll help you to a widow... Will make you seven years younger, and a rich one."

Face's station in this household is partly new and partly old, partly remembered and partly achieved through Lovewit's own pliancy and Face's continued ingenious negotiations. Satisfied with the widow, Lovewit acknowledges his debt to his servant, promising, "I will be rul'd by thee in anything, Jeremy," and confessing to the audience his satisfaction at having "receiv'd such happiness by a servant, / In such a widow, and with so much wealth" (5.5.143, 147–148). And in the final lines of the play, it is Face, rather than Lovewit, who speaks in the language of the hospitable, genteel householder, as he turns to the audience and, instead of making a plea for kindness, once again lays a deal on the table: "this pelf, / Which I have got, if you do quit me, rests, / To feast you often, and invite new guests" (5.5.163–165). Face's "pelf" seems to consist of both his pardon and the new respect with which Lovewit regards him; if he hasn't exactly gained the upper hand, he has gained some control over his master. Lovewit himself admits that to accept Face's terms is "some small strain / Of his own candour" (5.5.151–152). In fact, Lovewit has bargained away more than his "candour"; he has also traded part of his identity as master of the house. Most obviously, the feasting and entertainment promised in these final lines refer to the possibilities of the theater itself, as a venue for new plays and new audiences. We might also perceive a similarity, however, to Penshurst's "liberal board" and to the hospitable contract the poem describes between landlord and guest. Face's new and unconventional station in the household—the "pelf" that he has "got"—is incongruously encased in the language of conventional hospitality that Jonson would revisit in his treatment of Sidney's country house. Face has the final word; although Lovewit returns as predicted, his presence no longer completely defines the order of the household or provides the stable endpoint to the story of his house.

Perhaps surprisingly, it is this fragmented, unstable, and disorienting sense of place that locates Lovewit's house most firmly in the cityscape of John Stow. In *The Alchemist*, as in Stow's *Survey*, architectural setting reveals history's contingencies and disruptions rather than a streamlined and idealized lineage in which status, landownership, and virtue neatly converge. In both works, these traditional narratives break down, appearing in partial and broken form as faint echoes of a genre based on stable associations among architecture, topography, and genteel or aristocratic identity. In the absence of the landlord, *The Alchemist*'s architectural setting lacks the order that characterizes antiquarian accounts of the country house, and it therefore becomes susceptible to appropriation into other kinds of stories. Both the tricksters and the gulls, like Thomas Cromwell, could be charged with forgetting themselves as they imagine the swell of a "suddaine rising." And, like the former monastery of the Augustine Friars—transmuted to stable, church, and storehouse—Lovewit's house succumbs to negotiation and acquisitiveness, becoming a site where identity and history might be erased and re-created as much as commemorated or confirmed.

Differences between the architectural narratives of the *Britannia* and those of Stow's *Survey* parallel the differences between the architectural settings of "To Penshurst" and *The Alchemist*. Like the chorographies of Camden and Stow, the two Jonson works are united by a historical view of architecture, but the application of this perspective leads to different ends in each case. As Archer has pointed out, the topography of early modern London presented special challenges to the writer of antiquarian history; and as I have shown, the fragmentation and dismantling of London's material architecture resulted in the fragmentation and disruption of the stories associated with it. The synthetic historical threads of the *Britannia* and "To Penshurst" elucidate what is lacking in Lovewit's unconventional household: not history, but a stable culmination to the stories of the past. Stow's *Survey* roots this instability and indeterminacy in the features of post-Reformation London itself and reveals that, just as "To Penshurst" gestures toward a real building that existed outside its pages, Lovewit's house is inseparable from the particular architectural features of the city to which it belongs.

CHAPTER FOUR

Restoring "The Church-porch"

George Herbert's Architectural History

The monasteries and churches of William Camden's *Britannia* (see Chapter 1) exemplified how religious architecture might carry associations for the early modern reader or viewer that had nothing to do with its Calvinist, Catholic, or Laudian allegiances. Camden often valued such buildings as repositories of local history, and they served as occasions for stories that, like the country house narratives, represent the characters, desires, interests, expenditures, failures, and virtues of individuals' lives. This chapter offers a specific example in the architectural setting of George Herbert's poem "The Church-porch." As a community center where important social events and rituals were supervised and recorded, the parish church porch provided Herbert with a way of addressing both the history and the character of his imagined auditor's life. The relationship between church architecture and the details of human history inspired the poem's didactic content and shaped its proverbial style. This reading of "The Church-porch" supports my argument that architecture—even church architecture—might be viewed from local and historical, rather than doctrinal, perspectives. In fact, as traditional centers of local history, religious buildings were particularly susceptible to this sort of interpretation.

While many of the devotional lyrics in George Herbert's *The Temple* have attracted sustained critical attention over the past several decades, "The Church-porch" has lain in comparative neglect for at least a century. At 462 lines, this is by far the longest poem in the collection, and it is the one Herbert chose to introduce the book, yet it would be difficult to collect 462 lines from anywhere in "The Church" that have been so resolutely ignored by modern scholars. In recent years, the poem's few sympathetic readers have been far outnumbered by those who dash quickly over it or skip it entirely; in many major studies of Herbert's poetry, "The Church-porch" barely earns a mention in the index.[1] Other critics have condemned the poem or apologized for it, admitting either that they themselves do not like it very much or that they do not expect readers to do so.[2] Compared to the intense personal agony and original introspection of Herbert's shorter devotional lyrics, the proverbial sentiments and smug didacticism of "The Church-porch" present readers with a stylistic challenge delightfully described by Joseph Summers, who imagines the poem "lying like a large and worldly dragon before the portals" of "The Church."[3] In Summers's opinion, though, it is not worldliness but inculcation that turns modern readers away. He posits that "most of us today are initially suspicious of any overtly didactic discourse," because we assume it to be manipulative and insincere.[4]

Summers is probably not off the mark, but the modern critical aversion to "The Church-porch" is not simply a result of our unwillingness to hear Herbert preach. Our difficulties with this poem arise from significant limitations in the way current literary studies contextualize the post-Reformation English church. Strangely, it is the poem's lack of obvious difficulty—its lack of contradiction and tension—which has made it difficult for modern scholars. It has by now become almost automatic for critics to set any literary reference to church architecture in post-Reformation England against a background of Reformation controversy, plotting its author on a spectrum from Puritan iconoclasm to Laudian uniformity. Following influential readings by such scholars as Louis Martz, Barbara Lewalski, and Richard Strier, recent readers of Herbert have turned for context to pamphlets, sermons, ideological treatises and theological debates.[5] Less consciously, I think, criticism has relied on categories and search terms generated by these polemical works. The result is that we have come to view post-Reformation churches through a fractured lens, their architecture crazed and battered by contested relationships between visible and invisible conceptions of the church or between private and public forms of worship.[6] These approaches have often been fruitful; doctrinal controversy provides plentiful evidence about how early modern viewers interpreted altar railings, statues of saints, and church ornament.[7] Concerning the church porch, however, it provides almost none. Viewed through a polemical lens, the church porch becomes invisible—not in the controversial sense that distinguishes visible and material church architecture from the invisible church of the heart, but in the sense that it simply does not appear in this literature at all. It makes sense, then, that readers steeped in Reformation doctrinal debate would choose to circumvent "The Church-porch" altogether and throw themselves directly on "The Altar," or enter "The Church" through "The Windows."

What all these approaches overlook is a historical environment for "The Church-porch" that has been hiding in plain sight: the parish church porch itself. A feature of nearly every English parish church, this local and familiar structure would surely have provided the poem's first association for Herbert's contemporaries. "The Church-porch" was Herbert's most-cited poem through the end of the seventeenth century, suggesting that early readers did not find it as unwelcoming as modern scholars have; and despite its near invisibility in polemical literature, the church porch would not have been at all invisible to seventeenth-century parishioners.[8] As ecclesiologist Stephen Friar writes "there are many instances of porches which appear to be far too large for the churches to which they are attached. But their very size is indicative of their importance as centres of community life."[9] Indeed, the first sentence might describe literary scholars' general opinion of Herbert's poem. N. J. G. Pounds confirms Friar's impression, calling the tower and the porch "the most visible parts of the fabric of the church."[10] In order to restore "The Church-porch" to our critical consciousness, we must restore the history of the parish church porch.[11] Herbert writes in a style appropriate to the place. The language and content of the poem are shaped by the architecture that frames them; moreover, the location inspires the poem's didacticism, suggesting a practice of reading which the speaker both teaches and demands of his readers. In this communal site, language functions differently than it does in the intimate scope of individual devotion, and the poem's familiar adages are valuable precisely because they are not the original coinages of a unique mind. Instead, they represent the commonly valued currency of a community. Historically, the church porch was not just an entryway. It was also a site for meetings and exchanges and the place where bonds and contracts were formed between individual and community, between parishioners, and between the religious and secular worlds.

Rather than ignoring a poem that does not present church architecture in the anxious way controversial literature has conditioned us to expect, we may attend to its differences. Whether or not "The Church-porch" speaks to modern readers as poetry, it might speak to us quite eloquently in other ways. To explore the past of the parish church porch is to rediscover a strain of religious history that literary scholars have often forgotten. The porch's former religious and secular functions—which continued through the seventeenth century and often long afterward—have been well studied and documented, but not by literary historians. Because its uses were more parochial than polemical, the church porch has remained an object of interest to ecclesiologists—such as Friar and Pounds—and local historians, while to most Herbert scholars in the academy, it has faded from view. When we turn from theology to ecclesiology, however, from academic theorists and critics to the works of church historians and local history societies, and from ideological categories to the details of parochial life, the desolate proverbs of "The Church-porch" appear suddenly to be set in populous and vibrant surroundings. Relocated to this original architectural setting, the poem also provides a way of reading church architecture that persists quietly outside the contested ground of Reformation polemic. Here, the material and spiritual dimensions of the church exist in intimate conspiracy, not constant antagonism. Like the historical functions of the church porch, "The Church-porch" does not depend on a progression from material to spiritual, nor does it assume any opposition between the two. Rather, it teaches the reader that these categories are inseparable; one folds perpetually back into the other, and expanses of eternity are woven through the histories of daily life.

While the porch remains a common feature of the English parish church, the structure no longer fulfills the broad range of religious and secular needs that it once did, with the result that Herbert's poem gestures beyond itself to a setting of which many modern readers have only the barest sense. To perceive the art of Herbert's "Church-porch," then, requires that we linger, with some care and curiosity, in the parish church porch itself, taking time to observe its crucial position between sanctuary and community, to search out its histories, and to rediscover the remnants of its past. The size of the church porch and, consequently, the extent of its customary functions varied from community to community, and it is certainly not my contention that the tiny porch of Herbert's church at Bemerton served all of these purposes. Even if, as Amy Charles postulates, Herbert wrote "The Church-porch" in 1614 with his younger brother Henry in mind, the poem addresses a wider elite male audience, giving instructions for several duties and occupations.[12] The poem need not have been written to correspond with a single church any more than with a single reader, and in examples drawn from throughout England we are able to trace clear patterns and to arrive at a detailed picture of the associations the church porch would have had for a seventeenth-century reader.

From at least the thirteenth century, the porch had several ritualized liturgical functions, and although some were abandoned at the Reformation, modified versions and evocative material evidence of these ceremonies lasted well beyond the seventeenth century.[13] Originally, the opening parts of the baptismal and marriage ceremonies took place in the church porch. Francis Bond discovered cases in which the porch was actually identified by its role in these events: In 1527, William Webster of Northampton "left his body 'to be buried in ye churchyarde of Sainte peter *before ye crystynynge dore*'." A fifteenth-century testator from Hull also wished to be buried in the porch, but "Latin fails when he comes to translate 'wedding porch.'; 'corpus meum ad speliendum infra *wedding porch.*' "[14] As the "sprinkling" of Herbert's "Superliminare" recalls, the baptismal font was usually placed just inside the church door, to complete a ceremony begun in the porch and to reflect the principle that baptism itself is a symbolic entry. The Edward VI Prayer Book was the last to direct that the candidate for baptism be received "at the church door," but royal proclamations and episcopal directions through the seventeenth century commanded that the font not be desecrated, sold, or used for baptizing livestock.[15]

In the medieval church, the legally binding part of the marriage ceremony, including the exchange of rings, also took place in the church porch. Bond located this detail in the official records of aristocratic marriages, and church historians are fond of quoting the boast of Chaucer's Wife of Bath: "Housbondes at chirche dore I have had fyve."[16] In the porch of Brigham Church, Cumberland, Isaac Fletcher discerned in 1880 a curious weathered finial whose genealogy was chronicled in the memory of the parish clerk: it represented "a male and a female kneeling and holding hands," and had been carved to commemorate an important aristocratic marriage of c. 1390.[17] In Herbert's day, even after the main ceremony was moved inside the church, the custom of a prenuptial blessing in the church porch remained. J. Charles Wall quotes as evidence a short poem from Robert Herrick's *Hesperides* (1648), "The Entertainment: or, *Porch-verse* at the Marriage of Mr. *Hen. Northly* and the most witty Mrs. *Lettice Yard.*"[18]

Before the Reformation, other forms of ritual blessing and induction might also have taken place in the church porch. In many churches, the holy water stoup was on the porch, where entrants would sign their bodies with a cross "as an act of self-consecration and spiritual cleansing."[19] In some porches, these reminders of pre-Reformation practice were still visible centuries later. More recent churchgoers might find directives for more practical forms of reverential cleanliness in the porch. Wall found at Stoke Albany the following inscription, representative of similar ones remembered by nineteenth- and twentieth-century churchgoers: "TAKE NOTICE, MEN ARE DESIRED TO SCRAPE THEIR / SHOES & THE WOMEN TO TAKE OFF THEIR PATTENS / BEFORE THEY ENTER THIS PORCH."[20] And where parishioners had been blessed, baptized, and married, they might at last return, for the church porch was not an uncommon place to be buried. Numerous wills specify this final resting place, and often, sepulchral slabs remain.

Bond notes that gravestones are sometimes found on the thresholds of church or porch doors, in "a possible reference to the text, 'I had rather be a doorkeeper in the house of my God than to dwell in the tents of ungodliness'" (Psalms 84:10).[21]

While most of the formal liturgical functions of the church porch were suppressed at the Reformation, the performative and socially binding nature of such rituals as baptism and marriage characterized many secular uses of the porch, which were little affected by shifts in England's national religious identity. Like baptismal and marriage ceremonies, these uses had to do with moral or practical education, social surveillance, and the preservation of parochial histories. For instance, it was usual for debts, bequests, and dowries to be paid in the porch, where the event could easily be witnessed. Records of this custom are numerous, with many dating from the seventeenth century. F. Thistleton Dyer records a Lancashire deed of 1641 in which "Alice Sidgreaves agrees to relinquish of James Sidgreaves certain lands on condition that he pays £130 on a certain day 'att or within the south porch of the p'ishe church or chappell of Goosnargh.'"[22] A letter to *Notes & Queries* mentions "a deed relating to land at Cottesbrook [Northamptonshire] and granted to Oliver Cromwell, 9 Feb., 1633, when it was agreed that the rent charge should be paid 'in the porch of the parish church of Cottesbrook twice yearly, Michaelmas and March.'"[23] Examples are noted through the eighteenth century.[24] Bond reports that in 1712, a testator in the Diocese of St. Asaph, Denbighshire, left "the interest of £5 ... for the purchase of flannel for four old men and women, who were to draw lots or throw dice for it in the church porch."[25] In the south porch of St. Peter and St. Paul in Eye, Suffolk, Henry Creed notes the presence of a "dole table," at which debts, tithes, and church dues would have been paid.[26]

Porches were also used for public displays of charity; there are numerous records of the indigent, homeless, and sick being allowed to shelter there. As late as 1854, the rector of West Tofts, Norfolk, reported that "a poor woman ... came the other day to ask whether I, as a magistrate, could render her any assistance" after "she and her family had become houseless, and were obliged to take up their abode in the church porch."[27] When a man was outlawed, the initial decrees were promulgated by the sheriff in the church porch. In some cases, the porch was also a site of public penance, and Bond recounts a representative instance from 1593 in which a woman was forced to appear in the church porch on three separate Sundays "clothed in a white sheet down to the ground, and having a white wand in her hand ... beseeching the people that pass into the church to pray to God for her and to forgive her."[28] Anderson describes a frightening instrument chained to the wall in Wateringbury, Kent, which had "a spike on one end and a ring at the other and was carried by the head man of a tithing . . . when empowered by the Court Leet to search for goods unlawfully concealed." According to Anderson, the mace was in use until 1748.[29]

By the early sixteenth century, many porches had grown to two or even three stories. Before the Reformation, some of these upper chambers evidently served as chapels, and Alec Clifton-Taylor notes that in a few cases they were used for the exhibition of relics.[30] Other uses persisted well beyond Herbert's day.[31] In some cases, surviving fireplaces and furniture seem to indicate that they provided living quarters for a priest, churchwarden, or sacristan.[32] It was common for village children to be taught their first lessons in the church porch. The seventeenth-century diarist John Evelyn remembers: "I was not initiated into any rudiments till neere 4 yeares of age; and then one Frier taught us at the Church-porch of Wotton."[33] Schools are recorded in the porch chambers of St. Sepulchre's, London, in 1592, at Colyton in Devonshire in 1660, and at Malmesbury in Norfolk as late as 1879.[34] It is perhaps this practice, as much as the epigrammatic and morally instructive nature of Herbert's poem, which accounts for its popularity through the seventeenth century and beyond in children's books. Raymond Anselment uncovers unmistakable borrowings from the poem in a seventeenth-century primer, and in a 1932 issue of *Notes and Queries*, Professor G. H. Palmer wistfully seeks an edition of "The Church-porch" by E. C. Lowe, who, years earlier as headmaster of Hurstpierpoint School, had required all entering pupils to memorize the entire thing.[35] "It was a rich endowment," Palmer says, "equipping a youth in all points of good morals and manners."[36]

In addition, these upper chambers could provide secure repositories for the common property and public records of the parish. There are reports of standard weights and measures being kept there, and they were frequently used as armories, muniment rooms, treasuries, or libraries.[37] R. J. Brown explains that "in most cases, the church would have been the only substantial building in the village. . . . It seems probable that valuables were kept in these upper chambers, for it is not uncommon for the door to be completely iron-clad."[38] Literary scholars might remember that in the upper chamber of the north porch of St. Mary Redcliffe (Bristol) the young Thomas Chatterton discovered a cache of medieval manuscripts that inspired his elaborate forgery of the works of Thomas Rowley.[39] In the church porch, then, the life of the parishioner was recorded in its particularity, even as it joined with other stories and other lives to form the longer and more enduring history of the parish.

Turning back to "The Church-porch" with the church porch in mind, I will argue that history and ecclesiology, more than theology, illuminate the poem's

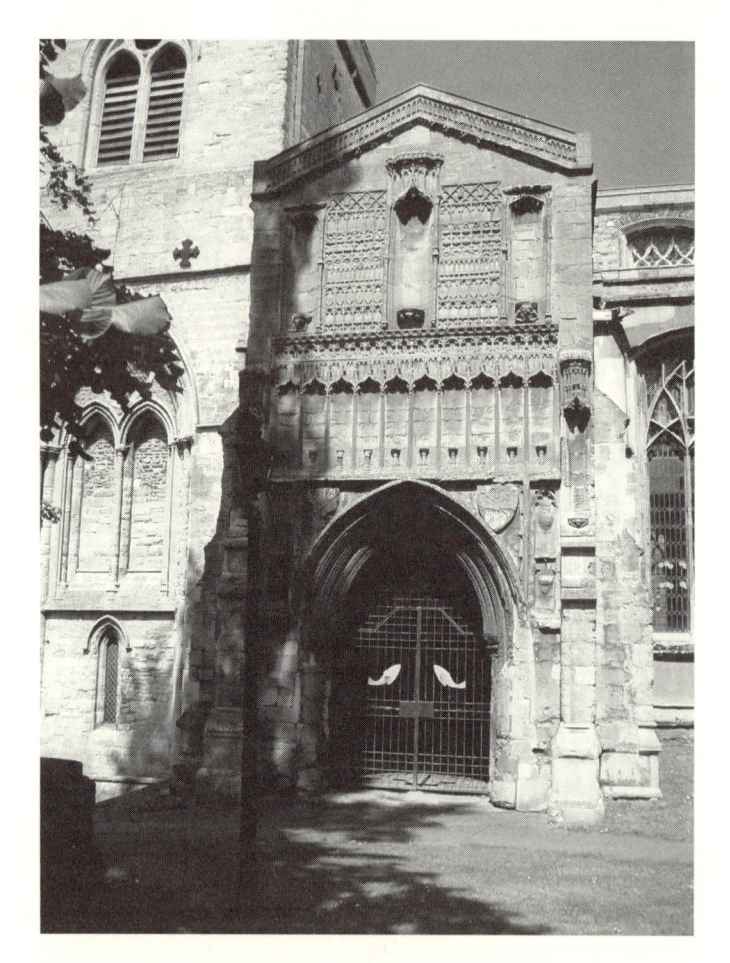

Two-story porch at St. Nicholas, King's Lynn, Norfolk

structural integrity; its organizational patterns, along with its content, style, and imagery, are inspired by the historic location and functions of the architectural setting itself.[40] Recent critics have tended to imagine "The Church-porch" as merely preliminary, a unidirectional passage from common ground to sacred space.[41] But this progress is not accomplished without what Martz describes as "some eddying and repetition," and to look in only one direction—toward the sanctuary—is to read against the grain of the poem, sixty-six of the seventy-seven stanzas of which are dedicated to aspects of parish life that take place outside the church.[42] John M. Adrian has noted of *The Country Parson* that, in contrast to Laudian strictures for uniformity in worship, "Herbert's communal bonds... derive more from human interactions, and often take place outside of church."[43]

Three-story porch at St. John the Baptist, Cirencester, Gloucestershire

This statement might also be made of "The Church-porch," and this initial outward focus also reflects the position of most porches, which had as much to do with the community as with the church. While porches most often appear at the south doors of churches, because that side provided the best protection from the weather, there are many exceptions to this pattern, and the chief consideration in the placement of a porch seems to have been that it face the village and manor it served.[44] In the pattern of Sundays and weekdays, in the progress from baptism to marriage to burial, and in the days appointed for annual payments or the fulfillment of contracts, the church porch was worn by generations of footsteps and repeated return. "The Church-porch," like its eponym, is not structured by progression from one space to another; it centers on the threshold itself. The poem looks outward first, then in toward the sanctuary; but worldly and otherworldly concerns are never separated from one another, and that is the point. The poem, indeed, suspends us in an eddy, where the current swirls constantly back into itself, mixing the divine with the secular and the secular with the divine.

North porch at St. Mary Redcliffe, Bristol, Gloucestershire

The most direct connections between poem and porch are established by Herbert's repeated references to events that would have taken place in the church porch. As a group, these events enfold moral and spiritual significance into the course of a parishioner's life; they have to do with the affirmation of religious responsibility or the inculcation and surveillance of socially useful virtues such as charity, thrift, and truthfulness. In the first line, the address to the "sweet youth" suggests the education of children, and this theme reappears in lines 97 through 99, which lament the "education" provided by those who "till their ground, but let weeds choke their sonne" or "mark a partridge, never their childes fashion."[45] The second and third stanzas look backward and forward in the life of the youth to baptism— "Beware of lust: it doth pollute and foul / Whom God in Baptisme washt with his own blood" (7–8)—and to marriage—"Abstain wholly, or wed" (13)—and line 33 imagines the man who, in unfettered drunken violence, "Is outlawed by himself." Many of the precepts are concerned with financial transactions of the sort that might have been executed in the church porch, lending, as

Bond puts it, "greater sanctity as well as publicity to a bargain or agreement."[46] Lines 103 through 114 relate the development of "a mast'ring minde" (104) to the prudent distribution of allowances and estates; line 119 exhorts the listener to honor promises and bonds: "who breaks his own bond, forfeiteth himself"; and lines 175 through 180 warn against debts that cannot be repaid: "By no means runne in debt: take thine own measure." Later stanzas cast friendship and kinship in terms of debts and bequests: "Thy friend put in thy bosome.... If cause require, thou art his sacrifice" (271–273) is followed by "Yet be not surety, if thou be a father. / Love is a personall debt. I cannot give / My childrens right, nor ought he take it" (277–279). Further on, Herbert deals with the generous yet prudent distribution of alms—"In Almes regard thy means, and others merit" (373)—and the ungrudging payment of tithes—"Restore to God his due in tithe and time: / A tithe purloin'd cankers the whole estate" (385–386). Finally, after sixty-six stanzas, the Verser prepares the reader to enter the church by removing not pattens but hat: "When once thy foot enters the church, be bare" (403).

This list by no means accounts for all of the topics covered in the poem, many of which—drinking, dressing, and dining, for instance—do not seem to have any connection to the place. And yet, the matter and style of these sections are equally shaped by the poem's architectural site and the concepts of liminality and exchange that it suggests. Critics have aptly described the style of the poem as proverbial, and its similarity to biblical Proverbs, to Jewish Wisdom literature, and to Herbert's own collection *Outlandish Proverbs* (1640) has been well noted.[47] However elevated their ancestry, though, the proverbial qualities of "The Church-porch" are precisely what have caused it to fall short in the estimation of modern readers. Summers, for instance, suggests that the poem's pat instruction "violates many popular modern notions concerning both poetry and religion," while James Boyd White describes its sentiments as "all too true, and boring."[48] What these remarks reveal is an inherent incompatibility of much poetry with proverbial wisdom. While most poetry, no matter how devout or deferential, displays the original talents of an individual writer, the proverb ideally appears to have no author, to be so worn and sensible and common that it cannot be limited to the description of one person's experience. As Chana Bloch notes, "The very form—terse, rhythmic, with the ring of long-acknowledged truths, of wisdom passed down from generation to generation—carries a certain authority, and does part of the work of persuasion."[49] But it is architectural setting, more than textual inheritance, which explains why Herbert might choose this uncharacteristic style for this particular poem. In its commonness, availability, and resilience, the proverb is not what we expect from the language of poetry, but it does resemble the language exchanged in the ceremonies, contracts, and promises that took place in the church porch. It is not only that the words of social contract and direction—the marriage ceremony, the bequest, the first lessons of a child—*need* not be original or verbally intricate; it is that they *must* not be. In such circumstances, words are valuable insofar as they are repeated and repeatable, mutually recognized, agreed upon, and understood. As in the fulfillment of a social or legal contract, words are binding, and originality is less important than the capacity to come true. Thus, if "too true, and boring" is a damning charge when leveled at a poem, it might favorably describe the language of proverbs, contracts, and bonds.

To compare the sentiments of "The Church-porch" to proverbs is to describe them in general terms. Really, many of Herbert's adages belong to distinct subsets of this group, sharing characteristics that are not intrinsic to the genre itself. As Summers, Bloch, and Jeffrey Powers-Beck have noticed, the poem as a whole is set in "a dense and particularized social world."[50] For a seventeenth-century reader, then, "The Church-porch" would have attached common sense and common values to immediate and recognizable surroundings. Ronald W. Cooley has explored Herbert's social commentary in the sixteenth stanza (91–96), which refers to enclosure and the wool trade, and subsequent stanzas re-imagine other popular proverbial topics in circumstances which would have been close to home.[51] Line 43 depicts the reader among drunken "Gallants"; later, he is exposed to the wisdom of "Old courtiers" (185). Lines 99 and 100 decry excessive devotion to partridge shooting and lament the practice of educating children by "ship[ping] them over." Inside the church, the reader finds the arms (perhaps his own) of the local parish gentry in a stained-glass window (197–198), along with the pins and silk stockings of parishioners' Sunday best: "Kneeling ne're spoil'd silk stocking: quit thy state" (407) is followed by "O be drest; / Stay not for th'other pin" (410–411).[52] And he is warned to leave his weekday occupations at the door: "Bring not thy plough, thy plots, thy pleasures thither" (422). Thus, like Herbert's direct references to the functions of the church porch, these sentiments tie the poem to the world of the seventeenth-century parish; they are commonplaces attached to a common place.

Yet it is not the social particularity of Herbert's proverbs that has made the poem inhospitable to modern readers of Herbert's poetry. It is their refusal to be metaphors. Some proverbs speak in terms entirely figurative. Proverb 693 of the *Outlandish Proverbs*—"It's a bold mouse that nestles in the catts eare"—is not actually a warning to mice, and some of the aphorisms of "The Church-porch" follow this pattern: "He pares his apple, that will cleanly feed" (64) is not a direction for food sanitation but a metaphor for cleaning up dirty or profane jokes before telling them again.[53] But throughout the poem, many of Herbert's proverbs remain anchored to their own literal referents—the "third glasse" (25), the debt paid (175), the pin abandoned (411)—and admirers of the virtuosic conceits in such poems as "The Flower," and "The Pulley" have found themselves unequipped to deal with words that really do mean what they say. In "The Church-porch" they often do: don't drink too much, pay your debts, come to church on time. Without ever abandoning the world of the quotidian, however, the objects and transactions of the poem constantly point toward more abstract and less quantifiable ideas and truths: they both really are and aren't really about pounds or pins or payments. Appropriate to their architectural setting, then, these proverbs are themselves a liminal kind of utterance. Standing between the particular and the ostensibly universal, they join the world of ordinary things to otherworldly consequences, and their effect is to locate the threshold to eternity in the details of daily life.

For some readers, the poem's attachment to common language, mundane objects, and practical affairs—what Arnold Stein has characterized as its "coarse or flat colloquialism"—has seemed to limit its scope and its complexity.[54] To equate familiarity with flatness, however, or commonness with simplicity is exactly to fail at the interpretive activity that the poem both teaches and asks of its reader. As much as it limits the figurative possibilities of language by tying its precepts to the local and physical world, the poem unfolds the significance of daily commerce and common things. For the successful reader of "The Church-porch," eternity is accessible through the quotidian, and enduring consequences of daily conduct are always present, always found. This process of discovery is not always reassuring; often it is startling and abrupt. In lines 25 through 48, for instance, to drink the third glass of liquor becomes an act of desecration: "The drunkard forfets Man, and doth devest / All worldly right, save what he hath by beast" (35–36). Thus, to refuse the "third glasse" (25) is to see man in God's image: "Stay at the third cup, or forgo the place. / Wine above all things doth Gods stamp deface" (47–48). In lines 79 through 84, idleness becomes a form of spiritual blindness:

> Flie idlenesse, which yet thou canst not flie
> By dressing, mistressing, and complement.
> If those take up thy day, the sunne will crie
> Against thee: for his light was onely lent.
>   God gave thy soul brave wings; put not those feathers
>   Into a bed, to sleep out all ill weathers.

The familiar pun on "sunne" here turns daylight to Christ's light—both are given and used, but never possessed—and the contemplation of common frivolities mirrors the interpretation of the pun itself: there is always a double meaning. To squander time on women, fashion, or sniveling will indeed wear out the light of day, but to indulge in these activities is also to waste, even deny, the light of Christ by failing to perceive or acknowledge it. And the couplet discovers in the soft feathers beneath a supine body the intangible wings of a rising soul. In lines 169 through 174, the money uncounted by avarice opens onto a view of uncountable stars:

> What skills it, if a bag of stones or gold
> About thy neck do drown thee? raise thy head;
> Take starres for money; starres not to be told
> By any art, yet to be purchased.
>   None is so wastefull as the scraping dame.
>   She loseth three for one; her soul, rest, fame.

Later, deference to the sins of "great persons" (253) in hope of social advancement makes the reader accomplice in a greater fall: "Feed no man in his sinnes: for adulation / Doth make thee parcell-devil in damnation" (257–258). Throughout, the poem reviews the daily affairs of the parish in a way that simultaneously increases and depreciates their value. The reader reaches the rewards of the soul, not by looking down on the things of this world or even by looking past them; instead, he must learn to look through them. Viewed in this way, common words and objects come to resemble the church porch itself as they stand at the limit of secular and religious meaning. And like the doors at each end of the porch, they give access to both at once.

By framing the poem in the church porch, Herbert reminds the reader that common use and availability have at least as much capacity to re-create meaning and value as to fix them. Historically, the church porch staged acts of transfer and agreement. While sums or names might vary from record to record, the church porch solemnized the moments at which things or words were traded, when money or promises or vows were passed between one person and another. And it is in these repeated moments of negotiation and reinvestment that things and words might express new intentions and desires; they might be put to new uses or traded with the expectation of different returns. As a result, the poem's many financial transactions—which have seemed to some critics out of place in a volume of religious poetry—become opportunities for complex interpretation and instruction.[55] Herbert is able to explicate money as one might a poem or biblical verse; placing it at the boundary of concrete and abstract significance, he expounds the kinds of value which are created and discovered in the practice of giving and taking, carefully parsing the moments in which old words and trite currency become the perceptible expressions of a living heart. For instance, he writes:

> Play not for gain, but sport. Who playes for more,
> Then he can lose with pleasure, stakes his heart;
> Perhaps his wives too, and whom she hath bore;
> Servants and churches also play their part.
>   Only a herauld, who that way doth passe,
>   Findes his crackt name at length in the church-glasse. (193–198)

In replacing the monetary tokens of the wager with the gamester's heart, Herbert signals the interdependence of financial and moral stakes, of legal tender and human tenderness. Here, the bet measures not only the gambler's commitment to a game but his lack of commitment to family and church. Herbert also unfolds the imprudent moment temporally, making it the intersection of past and future. As the cracked arms in the church window record the gambler's present short-sightedness, they also recall a virtuous, respectable ancestry and inscribe a future of social and spiritual disintegration.

Similarly, lines 373 through 384 represent almsgiving, not as a price tag for heaven, but as an index of the parishioner himself. At the alms table, the reader makes both financial and spiritual investments:

> In Almes regard thy means, and others merit.
> Think heav'n a better bargain, then to give
> Onely thy single market-money for it.
> Joyn hands with God to make a man to live. (373–376)

Summers worries that in such passages "the appeal to self-interest is so nakedly direct that a reader may misunderstand," and he clarifies that Herbert "does not mean to imply that *he* thinks salvation is something we can 'purchase,' bargain or not."[56] The following lines ought to assuage this anxiety though. They reveal that alms are valuable insofar as they indicate the absence of financial self-interest and produce a sympathetic disavowal of the self. Strier writes that, in this stanza and the next, "alms open heaven's gate. . . . There is no subtlety or irony to be missed."[57] Already, though, the lines gesture toward the complexity of this "bargain." As the hand that is conventionally clasped to seal a financial deal is replaced with the hand of God, the "man" of the last line acquires a double meaning: he might be either the recipient or the giver of the alms, depending upon whether we understand "live" as referring to bodily or spiritual welfare. The couplet completes the erasure of social and financial difference between benefactor and beneficiary: "Give to all something; to a good poore man, / Till thou change names, and be where he began" (377–378). This odd biography effaces its subject only to clear the slate for the following stanza, where the "poore man"—now either the giver or the recipient—is stamped with a new identity: "Man is Gods image; but a poore man is / Christs stamp to boot: both images regard" (379–380). The value of a coin laid on the alms table is here displaced onto parishioners themselves. By embodying the values of humility and charity in the conditions of human existence, alms reflect Christ's own humanity, laying a path toward the spiritual consequences which, in the poem, suddenly ensue:

> God reckons for him, counts the favour his:
> Write, So much giv'n to God; thou shalt be heard.
> Let thy almes go before, and keep heav'ns gate
>   Open for thee; or both may come too late. (381–384)

It is not exactly, as Strier says, that "alms open heaven's gate"; at least, it is not that simple. Rather, they indicate an understanding of earthly life which would have led there anyway. From the alms table, then, the pupil glimpses another threshold. Alms "go before" to stand at a "gate" from which the giver can review both financial and spiritual accounts, as well as the present and future states of his soul. Alms acquire a double nature that reflects both the church porch and the embodied divinity of Christ; they function at once in both earthly and eternal lives.

Even in transactions that might, on the surface, seem less morally charged than gambling or almsgiving, the poem assigns intangible and spiritual gains and losses to the transfer or exchange of material wealth. More than once, Herbert insists that the value of money rests not in itself but in its capacity to be exchanged. In lines 151 through 156, we read:

> Be thriftie, but not covetous: therefore give
> Thy need, thine honour, and thy friend his due.
> Never was scraper brave man. Get to live;
> Then live, and use it: els, it is not true
> That thou hast gotten. Surely use alone
>   Makes money not a contemptible stone.

"Use"—a surprising reversal of the way the word is generally used in connection to money—is the way that money accrues significant value in moral and human terms. Here use is tied to vitality itself—"then live, and use it"—as it is diverted into multiple channels of human community and experience: "thy need, thine honour, and thy friend."[58] Lines 165 through 168 also warn against accruing money, this time with stronger threats:

> Wealth is the conjurers devil;
> Whom when he thinks he hath, the devil hath him.
> Gold thou mayst safely touch; but if it stick
> Unto thy hands, it woundeth to the quick.

Wealth cannot be possessed; it can only be touched as it passes from one hand to another, and the poem gives many examples in which the value of money is determined by the particular ways in which it might be given and received. In lines 103 through 108, for example, Herbert writes:

> Some great estates provide, but doe not breed
> A mast'ring minde; so both are lost thereby:
> Or els they breed them tender, make them need
> All that they leave: this is flat povertie.
> For he, that needs five thousand pound to live,
> Is full as poore as he, that needs but five.

The following stanza continues in this vein: "The way to make thy sonne rich, is to fill / His minde with rest, before his trunk with riches,"(109–110) for "if thy sonne can make ten pound his measure, / Then all thou addest may be call'd his treasure" (113–114). Later, all sums become equally worthless to the "curious unthrift": "Who cannot live on twentie pound a yeare, / Cannot on fourtie" (176–177). In such examples, sums of money are reassessed—small amounts are suddenly worth more, and apparent wealth turns to poverty—based upon the understanding of the people who give and receive them.

A similar logic, in which value or meaning is determined through the process of use and exchange, extends beyond the financial advice of the poem and structures Herbert's view of parish life more broadly. Forms of the word "give" appear sixteen times, and the number increases if we account for synonyms or variations such as "lent" (82), "provide" (103), "leave" (106), "fill" (109), "addest," (114), and "restore" (385). Forms of "take" occur ten times, not including roughly synonymous terms such as "pick out" (235, 430), "embrace" (363), and "counts" (in the sense of "accepts," 381). "Get" (nine uses) and "gain" (six uses) are also common, as are words relating to purchase and payment. And spiritual and material acquisition are always balanced by the consequences of foolish or selfish investment: forms of the word "lose" appear at least twenty times. In lines 355 through 358, Herbert sums up much of the poem's advice:

> All forrain wisdome doth amount to this,
> To take all that is given; whether wealth,
> Or love, or language; nothing comes amisse:
> A good digestion turneth all to health.

The lovely parallelism of wealth, love, and language is so fluid that it is easy to miss, or to dismiss as a casual linking of incongruous terms; but once again, the poem's architectural location helps us to discover its integrity: what wealth, love, and language have in common is that all are traded, forming bonds and relationships as they are taken and given between one parishioner and another. Further, the phrase "forrain wisdome" anticipates Herbert's own title *Outlandish Proverbs*, perhaps specifying the sort of commonplace, proverbial knowledge the poem itself offers. In their very disparity, wealth, love, and language reflect the varied transactions of the church porch itself. The exchange of marriage vows or blessings, the payment of a debt, and the witnessing of a contract are accomplished through different means and with different ends in mind; yet all of these exchanges, like the poem's financial transactions, express intent and commitment. The value of words and of love, like that of money, is created and re-created in the process of trade. For instance, in lines 205 through 210, words traded in conversation are meaningful only to the degree that they truly represent the qualities of the speaker:

> In conversation boldnesse now bears sway.
> But know, that nothing can so foolish be,
> As empty boldnesse: therefore first assay
> To stuffe thy mind with solid braverie;
>> Then march on gallant: get substantiall worth.
>> Boldnesse guilds finely, and will set it forth.

Subsequent stanzas deal with uses and abuses of wit, which depend equally on the intent of the speaker, the discretion of the recipient, and the object of the jest. The reader is told that "the wittie man laughs least: / For wit is newes onely to ignorance" (229–230) and "Make not thy sport, abuses: for the fly / That feeds on dung, is coloured thereby" (233–234). The next stanza warns against "Profanenesse, filthinesse, abusivenesse," which are "The scumme, with which course wits abound: / The fine may spare these well, yet not go lesse" (236–238). Then, indiscriminate wit becomes tasteless and dangerous: "Wit's an unruly engine, wildly striking / Sometimes a friend, sometimes the engineer" (241-242). Later, in lines 289 through 306, conversation is benevolently tailored for the benefit of the listener: in "discourse" (289) the reader is told to "draw the card; / That suites him best, of whom thy speech is heard" (293-294). The topic continues in the succeeding stanza, which begins, "Entice all neatly to what they know best; / For so thou dost thy self and him a pleasure" (295-296). Finally, dominating a conversation becomes a violent form of excess: "If thou be Master-gunner, spend not all / That thou canst speak, at once; but husband it" (301-302).

Throughout the poem, however, it often turns out that neither financial success nor artful conversation is entirely the point; the Verser seeks, by perusing these topics, to cultivate the ability to discover and exchange love, which is described as being given and taken the way wealth and words are. In lines 307 through 312, words traded in argument are valued according not to their persuasiveness but to the sympathy and motives of the disputant:

> Be calm in arguing: for fiercenesse makes
> Errour a fault, and truth discourtesie.
> Why should I feel another mans mistakes
> More, then his sicknesses or povertie?
>   In love I should: but anger is not love,
>   Nor wisdome neither: therefore gently move.

In lines 283 and 284 we read, "If thou be single, all thy goods and ground / Submit to love." Lines 328 through 330 impress on the reader the rewards of active kindness:

>   Finde out mens wants and will,
> And meet them there. All worldly joyes go lesse
> To the one joy of doing kindnesses.

Soon after, we are told, "Slight not the smallest losse, whether it be / In love or honour: take account of all" (343-344), and then, "Scorn no mans love, though of a mean degree; / (Love is a present for a mightie king)" (349-350).

Once we become attuned to the ways in which value is both constantly reassessed and actively re-created in the course of human communication and exchange, it is easier to perceive the poem's pedagogic goals. Strier has argued that "'The Church-porch' does not aim to transform its audience," and here I would agree.[59] If the poem transforms the reader, it is by teaching him to find and transform the value of the life he is already living, in the world that already exists around him. It is not only the Verser who—as the etymology of his name suggests—exchanges one kind of value for another, or "turn[s] delight into a sacrifice" (6). To begin with, it is indeed the verse which "finde[s]" the pupil who has flown from the sermon to the pleasures of secular life (5). Ideally, however, the pupil himself learns to find moral and spiritual value outside the sanctuary and to turn the common words and material objects of parish life to sacred kinds of currency. Forms of the word "turn" appear only twice after the first stanza, and in both cases it is the listener who is instructed to perform the action: once in line 358, quoted earlier—"a good digestion turneth all to health"—and once in line 441—"Then turn thy faults and his into confession." Forms of the word "make," in the sense of "render" or "transform," however, appear far more often, at least twenty-nine times in all. At first, it is the Verser who will "make a bait of pleasure," but as the poem continues, it is repeatedly the listener who is either to bring about or prevent the change (4): In lines 49 and 50 he is told, "Yet, if thou sinne in wine or wantonnesse, / Boast not thereof; nor make thy shame thy glorie"; in lines 119 and 120, "Who breaks his own bond, forfeiteth himself: / What nature made a ship, he makes a shelf"; in lines 211–212, "Be sweet to all. Is thy complexion sowre? / Then keep such companie; make them thy allay"; in lines 259 and 260, "Envie not greatnesse: for thou mak'st thereby / Thy self the worse, and so the distance greater"; and in lines 287 and 288, "God made me one man; love makes me no more, / Till labour come, and make my weaknesse score." Without re-creating himself or the world, the successful reader of "The Churchporch" learns to change and create the spiritual value of his own secular affairs.

It is thus not a willingness to reject the world but a readiness to understand it which prepares the reader to enter the sanctuary. In lines 397 through 450, the Verser at last turns his attention to the interior of the church, mirroring spatially the turns between secular and religious that structure the earlier part of the poem. To the limited understanding, we discover, the sanctuary is no more religious than the secular world. Once the reader has learned to see everywhere the convergence of earthly and spiritual values, it ought not surprise him that the transition from social to sacred space is characterized more by continuity than difference. Sundays, like the weekday world, require the reader's interpretation; even in the sanctuary, he must actively perceive in the conditions of mortal life the conditions of eternity. Throughout this section, the familiar ideas of gaining and losing, making and turning, reappear. In line 411, quoted earlier, he is warned against tardiness: "Stay not for th'other pin: why thou hast lost / A joy for it worth worlds . . . Thy clothes being fast, but thy soul loose about thee" (411–414). Similarly, if he ogles the finery of other parishioners, he "Makes all their beautie his deformitie" (420). Instructions for listening to the sermon also clearly recall earlier sections of the poem: it turns out that interpreting the Word is not very different from interpreting words. In lines 427 through 432, the reader is told:

> Judge not the preacher; for he is thy Judge:
> If thou mislike him, thou conceiv'st him not.
> God calleth preaching folly. Do not grudge
> To pick out treasures from an earthen pot.
>   The worst speak something good: if all want sense,
>   God takes a text, and preacheth patience.

This stanza echoes line 63, which is about hearing and telling jokes ("Pick out of tales the mirth, but not the sinne"), and lines 235 through 240, also quoted earlier:

> Pick out of mirth, like stones out of thy ground,
> Profanenesse, filthinesse, abusivenesse.
> These are the scumme, with which course wits abound:
> The fine may spare these well, yet not go lesse.
>   All things are bigge with jest: nothing that's plain,
>   But may be wittie, if thou hast the vein.

In each case, it is not the quality of the verbal material, but the quality of the reader that makes the difference, and to hear either a joke or a sermon properly might demand the ability to turn something base and "earthen" into something rarer. Lines 439 through 444 convey a similar message, this time about mocking the preacher:

> Jest not at preachers language, or expression:
> How know'st thou, but thy sinnes made him miscarrie?
> Then turn thy faults and his into confession:
> God sent him, whatsoe're he be: O tarry,
>   And love him for his Master: his condition,
>   Though it be ill, makes him no ill Physician.

The topic of uncharitable jesting recalls lines 233–234, ("Make not thy sport, abuses: for the fly / That feeds on dung, is coloured thereby"), while the word "turn" and the images of bodily health might remind us of line 358: "A good digestion turneth all to health." The startling statement in line 429, "God calleth preaching folly" seems to refer to 1 Corinthians 1:18: "For the preaching of the cross is to them that perish foolishness; but unto us which are saved it is the power of God," or perhaps 1 Corinthians 1:21: "it pleased God by the foolishness of preaching to save them that believe," and the allusion reappears in line 449: "The Jews refused thunder; and we, folly." Both instances raise the stakes of the interpretive practices the poem has been teaching all along: the ability to draw spiritual benefit from the flawed materials of earthly life is no longer the means of differentiating wit from foolishness, but of sorting the saved from the damned.

In the final two stanzas, the interpretive lessons of the sanctuary lap gently back over the business of everyday existence, and scrutiny of the sermon is replaced with self-scrutiny as the poem draws to a close:

> Summe up at night, what thou hast done by day;
> And in the morning, what thou hast to do.
> Dresse and undresse thy soul: mark the decay
> And growth of it: if with thy watch, that too
>   Be down, then winde up both; since we shall be
>   Most surely judg'd, make thy accounts agree.

It is now the life of the reader, not the world of the parish, which mediates between secular and religious forms of meaning. Cristina Malcolmson has argued that this stanza completes the poem's earlier sartorial instructions by concluding that in the end "the secular... is defined as a kind of clothing that needs to be removed so that the soul can be spiritually 'dressed'."[60] I would argue that while this is the conclusion we might expect from a religious poem, it is not the one we get. The action of the final stanzas is to interfuse matters of body and soul, not to strip them away from each other. These lines describe a life which mirrors the church porch itself: it is lived at the threshold of material and spiritual experience, of earthly and eschatological time. From this point of view, the values of this life and the next are indistinguishable; they are possessed and perceived simultaneously. In the end of a day lies the End of Days, the watch becomes both the object that marks the minutes of the day and the vigilant mind that marks in those minutes the approach of God's judgment, and to dress and undress the body is to bare and equip the soul. In the familiar financial language of the final line—"make thy accounts"—the reader does not "make" one thing into another, nor is there any longer an explicit distinction between spiritual and monetary kinds of accountancy. But the poem has taught us that one does not preclude the other; in fact, both are inevitably present.

In the final stanza, the reader surveys a life lived in hours and minutes, in investments and payments, in friendship and charity—the life which the poem so attentively describes—all the while perceiving himself at the edge of a life everlasting:

> In brief, acquit thee bravely; play the man.
> Look not on pleasures as they come, but go.
> Deferre not the least vertue: lifes poore span
> Make not an ell, by trifling in thy wo.

The stanza begins by distinguishing mortal from eternal time; "In brief" refers at once to the summation of the poem and to the moments in which one "play[s] the man." The lesson here is familiar. Once again, the reader is warned against misestimating the value of the world; he must not "make" a "poore span" into a seeming eternity by "trifling in [his] wo." The couplet, however, does not provide the consolation we might anticipate: the "poore span" is not replaced with eternal paradise, and there is no palliative promise of escape:

> If thou do ill; the joy fades, not the pains:
> If well; the pain doth fade, the joy remains.

In "The Church-porch," the spirit is never released from the material world. These final lines thread the fate of the soul back through the sinews of the body as they register eternity in the language of mortal sensation. Summers points out that this sentiment is borrowed from the Stoic orator Cato the Censor, marking this conclusion as somehow "pre-Christian."[61] If the Verser has succeeded in his instruction, however, the reader will perceive both immediate and everlasting joys and pains here, and they are felt at once. Technically, as well, the couplet contains two kinds of time. In the repetition of sonorants and diphthongs, the words strain against their own terse expression. Counted like the minutes on a watch, the syllables are perfectly regular; in a less quantifiable way, they last and feel longer.[62]

Before leaving "The Church-porch" behind, I would like to step, for a moment, back into the parish church porch and reflect again on the connection between poem and place. Inscriptions in porches are common, and in some ways, the precepts of "The Church-porch" are more at home among these architectural records than they are among discussions of Herbert's lyric poetry. Frequently, the porch was inscribed not with polemical or even liturgical significance, but with lives of the individual parishioners who, in the course of their spiritual and practical affairs, crossed its threshold many times. For instance, the construction and maintenance of the porch were often accomplished through parishioners' donations, and the arms or names of benefactors were recorded in its fabric, commemorating, like the poem, financial benevolence and social responsibility, even as they anticipate eternity. In the porch of St. Nicholas, Addlethorpe, for example, Wall found the following inscription:

THE CRYST THAT SUFFERED
GRETTE PANYS AND HARD
HAFE MERCY ON THE SOWLE
OF JOHN GODARD
THAT THYS PORCHE MADE
AND MANY ODER THYNGES DEDE
THEN FOR THEE CRYST
GRAUNT HYM HYS MEDE[63]

Likewise, it was common to remember the dedication and service of churchwardens, as in the church of All Saints, Harthill, Cheshire, where the arms of the local gentry are surmounted by the inscriptions "Rondcull Prickett, Churchwarden ever since 1606 until 1611" and "John Webster, George Drake, Ch. 1779."[64] Reflections on the relationship of earthly and eternal time, as well as financial and spiritual accounts, also resemble the lessons of the poem. In the porch of St. Bartholomew, Churchdown, Gloucester, for instance, Frederick Smithe observed in 1888 "a gaunt emblem of Death, having the long hair and breasts of a woman; the fleshless arms are extended, holding in one hand an hour-glass to denote the brief span of man's life, and in the other hand, to signify the grave, is an asperge."[65] In 1883, the vicar of Thornbury Church, Bristol, noted an inscription beneath the sundial in the upper chamber of the south porch: "'Pereunt et imputantur'—'the hours pass away and are reckoned to our account.'"[66] The sentiments and the imagery of such inscriptions recall the final stanzas of "The Church-porch."

At last, I return to the dole table in the porch of St. Peter and St. Paul, Eye, Suffolk, above which several observers have remarked a more lengthy inscription, dated 1601. These brief verses seal the connection between Herbert's poem and its architectural setting:

> Seale not to soone lest thou repent to late,
> Yet help thy frend, but hinder not thy state.
> If ought thou lende or borrow, truly pay
> Ne give, ne take advantage, though thou may,
> Let conscience be thy guide; so helpe thy frend,
> With loving peace and concord make thy end.[67]

As poetry, these lines are neither original or arresting. To readers of "The Church-porch," however, their content and aphoristic style ought to sound familiar. Here, as in the poem, financial, social, and spiritual debts and invest-

Porch at St. Peter and St. Paul, Eye, Suffolk

Dole table in the porch of St. Peter and St. Paul, Eye, Suffolk. The inscription on the plaque above is still faintly legible (transcribed in text opposite).

ments intermingle. To ecclesiologists, the inscription obviously refers to the practical functions of the porch: on the dole table, contracts were settled, and debts, bequests, tithes, and church dues might all have been paid. To settle one's accounts, or "truly pay" does more, however, than secure "loving peace and concord" among "frend[s]." In the final lines of the inscription, as in the final stanzas of the poem, "peace and concord" steal quietly from the fulfillment of a contract over the "end" or fulfillment of life itself. The dole table, like the porch, mediates between contract and Covenant: the parishioner who enters into social and financial bonds prudently and honors them conscientiously does not regret rash investments or decisions, and he also does not, in a more important sense, "repent to late." Together, these inscriptions remind us that, unlike the introspective struggles of spiritual biography, the story of the church porch is not a univocal narrative; it is composed in the formulaic language of proverbs and common sense, of wills and contracts, of annual tithes, of marriages, baptisms, and epitaphs. It traces the histories of individuals within the history of a community, and it is not limited to the mind, or the life, of a single author. The histories recorded by the church porch, are, like Herbert's poem, difficult to integrate with the strands of Reformation polemic, because they do not take positions. Nevertheless, as both poem and inscriptions remember, through days and years and generations, they quietly take place. Adam Smyth, for instance, has recently identified relationships between the entries in parish registers and biographical and autobiographical writing of the period, noting instances in which the former bleed into the latter, demonstrating the role of parish church records in the preservation of parish lives.[68]

If this chapter has not succeeded in persuading the reader to like "The Church-porch," I hope at least it has shown that the poem has much to offer. "The Church-porch" is about church architecture, yet it does not treat the visible and the invisible or the internal and the external as though they were irreconcilable categories, nor does it seem to anticipate a reader who will view them that way. The world of the poem is not merely material, nor is its matter indifferent. Instead, by explicating the proverbial pounds, payments, and promises of parish life, the poem surprisingly expatiates the significance of common things. "The Church-porch" provides access to a form of reading we have neglected and a strand of religious history we have too often ignored. Through sustained and respectful attention to the local and particular, to the worn words and necessary objects of ordinary lives, we might learn to see doctrine in a glass pushed away, in a pin abandoned before church, in the sum of five thousand pounds weighed against five.

In 1930, ecclesiologist A. R. Powys lamented that churches had lost many of the practical and communal functions which were once "so intermixed" with their religious significance that it was "difficult to say, of many—'This is of the church, this of the manor.'" Continuing, he speculates, "It may well be, that it is this material separation of the things pertaining to our daily bread from those pertaining to the soul's welfare that now gives to some persons a sense of unreality and of an emphasis on a worship unrelated to life when they visit churches, and especially those which have no long parochial history."[69] Powys's overt religious investment in his subject may set him apart from many contemporary literary critics. Nonetheless, his concept of "material separation" identifies a real divergence in the study of religious history, a separation which has, in turn, affected our study of literature. In the academy, ecclesiology has so often been pared away from theology, and the local details of a "long parochial history" from the history of ideas, that our reconstructions of historical context have in fact stripped churches of their own inveterate pasts. By writing *The Temple* into the history of the Reformation, we have erased it from the plain and familiar view of seventeenth-century life. In "The Church-porch," Herbert resists the "material separation" between church and manor, spiritual and practical, insisting instead on the material and linguistic integration of secular with sacred and quotidian with divine. Rather than ignoring "The Church-porch," then, or apologizing for its defects, we ought to approach it as a poem which requires—and teaches—its own interpretive logic.

In the local historians and ecclesiologists who have continued to study the church porch (and from whom I have gathered much of my information) we might see the direct descendents of early itinerant antiquarians such as John Leland, William Camden, and John Stow. In fact, a recent collection entitled *The Changing Face of English Local History* begins with chapters on Camden's *Britannia* and Stow's *Survey of London*.[70] As much as he differs from these early chorographers, and from their modern successors, Herbert also looks at church architecture with an antiquarian's eyes. For him, the church porch told the stories of a local community, and in its attention to the parochial and particular, "The Church-porch" fits more comfortably among these historical texts than it does among the pages of doctrinal controversy. As the histories of the church porch are recovered, "The Church-porch" also becomes more accessible to us. We might now appreciate its remarkable features and come to admit that we have, all along, been in too great a hurry to enter "The Church."

CHAPTER FIVE

Construction Sites

The Architecture of Anne Clifford's Diaries

As critics have noted, the late diaries and the architectural projects of Lady Anne Clifford (1590–1676) were both parts of an elaborate plan to prove that she had been wronged more than forty years earlier. In 1605 her father, George Clifford, died, leaving his lands and titles to his brother and his brother's heirs, rather than to Anne, his only daughter; for years, she and her mother attempted without success to prove his bequest illegal. Only in 1643, when her cousin died without issue did she finally inherit the property. Taking this "[d]eliverance" as evidence that her cause was "visibly susteyned by a Divine favour from above," Clifford spent the rest of her life compiling proof that her father's lands and castles should have been hers all along.[1] The portion of the late diaries that is now published, covering the years 1650–1676, represents less than 10 percent of a much larger body of work intended to establish historical and legal precedent for this claim.[2] This compilation, known as the Great Books of Record, fills three thick folio volumes and approximately one thousand pages. It was not the private confessional suggested by the title "Diaries," a label modern editors have grafted onto her published work. Far from stashing her writings away or encoding them in Pepysian shorthand, Clifford employed professional scribes to make three almost identical copies of the series to be preserved for the use and edification of her posterity. The Great Books trace the history of her ancestors from the time of King John, conveyed mainly in the form of deeds, wills, post mortem inquisitions, and family trees. These are interspersed with Clifford's own summaries and marginalia explaining how the documents support her right to her family's lands in Cumberland, Westmorland, and the West Riding of Yorkshire. The Great Books have received significant critical attention in recent years, particularly since all three copies are now publically available in the Cumbria County Archive, and critics have realized that the diaries look quite different in the context of these legally motivated volumes. The diaries appear less personal than political, less private than public, and less emotionally frank than strategically self-fashioned.[3] Clifford scholars have begun comparative studies of the three versions; because the Great Books seem not to have been produced concurrently, Clifford's own marginalia and successive changes provide traces of her own habits of reading, revision, and interpretation.[4]

Rewarding as such analysis may be, I follow a different path by arguing that the Great Books should prompt us to place the diaries within still broader contexts, to look outward from their pages even as we search more deeply into the archive. Clifford's diaries and her architectural works were interdependent projects. The diaries were shaped by their inclusion in the Great Books, but they were also formed by their direct reference to Clifford's architectural projects; books and buildings point reciprocally to each other. We can look to the deeds, wills, and inquisitions which originally preceded the diaries not only for ancestral and legal context but for an interpretive method. Such documents are influenced by the motives and interests of their original owners, but they are not meant to be emotionally revealing. Moreover, they are not meant to stand on their own. Instead, they point beyond themselves to physical places, objects, and people known to the author and, presumably, the reader. Without this correspondence between the text and identifiable physical referents, they are emptied—at least in part—of their significance and effectiveness. Clifford perceived this connection between a legal document and a piece of physical property, and she relied upon and exploited it to create a record of legal ownership which was not entirely recorded in either documents or properties. As we have seen in many other architectural descriptions of the seventeenth century, the relationship between text and building is one of contingency and mutual influence rather than analogy or simile. Books and buildings require each other to complete their meanings.

Like the Great Books, Clifford's architectural works are both extensive and legally motivated. She transformed the castles at Skipton, Appleby, Brough, Brougham, and Pendragon into powerful statements of her own entitlement to those properties. They were in varying states of decay when they reverted to her possession, and in 1649, shortly before the death of her second husband, she traveled north and instigated an aggressive program of architectural repair for both the castles and the local churches, supplying each with a triumphant inscription that proclaimed her inherited titles, her ownership of the land, and her role in their reconstruction. Architectural historians have speculated about why her architectural choices give no evidence of her experience at the Jacobean Court, which must have led her into contact with the Palladian tastes of Inigo Jones.[5] Clifford applied a very different method of understanding architecture—the one with which this book has been mainly concerned—in which history was a more relevant category than aesthetics. In their evident antiquity, her buildings resembled legal documents because they established historical precedent, and in undertaking restoration rather than innovation, Clifford literalized the goals of her legal project; like her castles, her rights had been restored.

Recognizing this contingent and mutually constitutive connection between text and architecture allows us to see Clifford in a new light with regard to her contemporaries. In the context of seventeenth-century diarists, or even just other women writers, Clifford's writings appear largely idiosyncratic. As a seventeenth-century antiquarian enterprise, however, they appear much less so. So far, antiquarianism of this period has been treated by critics as an isolated tradition and one confined entirely to male scholars and writers. This view is understandable, as seventeenth-century female antiquarians are difficult to find, at least in the published record. But Clifford's activities as both builder and writer rupture this homogeneity. In fact, we might consider Clifford among the earliest female antiquarians, perhaps even the first of her kind. The very form and content of the Great Books invite us to place them among seventeenth-century antiquarian works with which we know Clifford to have been familiar. Her relationships with prominent antiquarian writers and thinkers have also been well documented. Clifford's approach to both writing and building thus implicates her in broader intellectual networks of seventeenth-century thought, causing her to appear both more innovative and less isolated in the strategies she deployed than she has been given credit for being.

Appreciating Clifford's reliance on antiquarian traditions illuminates the logic of both diaries and architecture and reveals the ways in which she turned those traditions to her own particular ends. Her works display their derivation from—and dependence on—a form of antiquarian historiography that was carried out partly through observation of the built environment and partly through the production of texts. Clifford, however, enjoyed privileges that most antiquarians did not: she was writing her own ancestral history, not that of other people; and while she shared the antiquarian sense that the architectural record might vanish, she was in the unusual position of being able to restore it physically, even as she recorded its existence in writing. In Clifford's case, as in the case of earlier writers, such as Stow, Camden, and Weever, and of her contemporaries, such as William Dugdale and Roger Dodsworth, the built architectural record shaped and produced a particular kind of written historical evidence. In Clifford's projects of repair and inscription, she produced an architectural record that was clearly informed by a textual tradition. Moreover, she enlisted all of these materials in the creation of her own public identity: in the tactics and practice of antiquarian historiography, she discovered a way of telling her own story. These antiquarian influences reveal that, if we are to understand Clifford's works as some form of autobiography, we must abandon the notion that autobiography is solely a textual genre. Clifford developed a kind of life writing that could not be entirely contained in a text; it was composed of the calculated collection of built and documentary resources she assembled around and outside of herself.

To begin with, Clifford's reliance on the correspondence between text and architecture helps to elucidate long stretches of the published diary that, despite their first person narration, are strangely barren of personal, psychological, or even causal significance. In 1655, for instance, she wrote:

> The eighteenth day of September following I removed again with my family out of Applebie Castle in Westmerland towards Skipton Castle in Craven (lyeing all night by the Way at Kirkby Lonsdale) and came safe thither the nineteenth; I having not bin in this Castle of Skipton since the seconde day of August was a twelve month, till now. So I lay then in my said Castle of Skipton till the first day of August next following, which was about ten months and tenne daies over, at which time I removed the said 1st April 1656 out of the said Castle of Skipton towards Brougham Castle in Westmerland to lye there in it for a while, lyeing all night by the Way at the Inne at Kirkby Lonsdale.
>
> So as I continewed to live in my said Castle of Brougham till the second of October following at which time I, with my family removed to Appleby Castle in Westmerland. (*Diaries*, 129)

The purpose of this information, which has no explicit impact on either Clifford's emotions or her legal fortunes, is not immediately evident, and yet writing of this sort is extremely common in Clifford's diaries. Many critics have understandably found such passages inhospitable to interpretation, and indeed after reading a year or two of the late diary it is difficult not to skip over them in search of something more sensational, or at least less soporific.[6] The passage certainly lacks stylistic flair, and its emphasis is so clear that it becomes tiresome. Clifford notes the geographical location of each castle far more often than is necessary for purposes of clarification. The location of Appleby in Westmorland has already been mentioned two paragraphs earlier, and it is mentioned twice in this passage. The names of the castles are also repeated far more often than they need to be; the name of Skipton Castle is repeated four times in two sentences. Furthermore, the reader who began the late diary in 1650 could already have passed a quiz on the castles' locations and would probably have bet money that Clifford would spend the night in Kirkby Lonsdale. Unenlightening and uninteresting as this repetition may appear, Clifford is in fact offering us a way of understanding her work: as we read the diary, we are to consider her buildings.

Only in redirecting our attention from autobiographical to architectural landmarks can we begin to perceive the purpose of this meticulous monotony. The narrative makes a legally significant assertion about the castles by documenting a continuous pattern of occupation; Clifford means to support the written record of her ownership with the incontrovertible fact of her frequent physical presence. In her family's squabbling over estates, physical occupation had been an important and effective means of asserting ownership of a building. The Cliffords' disputes had not taken place in writing alone. Following the death of Margaret Clifford in 1616, Anne's husband, Dorset, recognizing the northern lands as a potential source of income, sent servants to occupy Brougham Castle, where the countess had died. In June of that year Clifford wrote that Dorset "had sent a letter down into Westmoreland to my Lady's [Margaret Clifford's] Servants and Tenants to keep possession for him & me, which ... gave me much contentment for I thought my Lord of Cumberland [Anne's uncle] had taken possession of the Jointure quietly" (*Diaries*, 38). Later, after Clifford herself had arrived at Brougham, her servants came to blows with her uncle's as she tried to direct the activities of the household. In 1645 Clifford successfully occupied and appropriated Barden Tower, which, even her most sympathetic biographers agree, belonged legally to her cousin, the Countess of Cork. Richard Spence records that "the Corks' names on court rolls for 2 October 1644 were crossed out and Anne's inserted, as daughter and heir to Earl George."[7] Physical occupation of the castle became an effective way of revising the written record, which supported her cousin's claim. Reading the condensed account of her successive habitations in the diary, we get the sense that if Clifford could have lived in all of the castles at once, she would have. Compressing them into a few consecutive paragraphs creates a spatial and narrative proximity that transcends the temporal lapses during which each castle stands empty. Though many months may separate her visits to a particular castle, many words do not.

Clifford's architectural structures thus inform the narrative structures of the diary. The diary does relate sequences of events, but they are often not organized, as we might expect, according to the chronology of Clifford's experience of them. Instead, they are clustered conceptually around objects and places that exist outside the text. After the passage quoted above, for instance, she returns to October, then to April, then to July, then to October again to recount significant events, such as births, deaths, and the commencement of building projects. And in each case, she restates her location: "when I now lay in this Appleby Castle" or "when I lay now in my house here at Skipton" (*Diaries*, 130, 131). Her narrative patterns are not illogical, but they are sometimes confusing, because their organizational landmarks, the foci of their narrative concerns, are not located within them but are scattered over the landscape of Cumberland, Westmorland, and Yorkshire.

In this way, Clifford organizes events according to a logic that might better fit the history of a building than that of a person. In 1650 she wrote: "I came hither [Skipton] and continewed to ly in my said Castle for a whole yeare together. And that was the first time I came to Skipton where I was borne; when I was the second time a Widdow (I being then Countesse Dowager of Pembroke and Montgomerie) as well as Countess Dowager of Dorset" (*Diaries*, 112). We note her customary painstaking documentation, but this is not solely a record of occupation; biographical events and declarations of rank obtrude. The passage's subordination of chronology to geography also defies our expectations for an autobiographical account. But our confusion results mostly from context. When very similar text appears in an architectural inscription, we understand that, while Clifford is telling her own story, she is also filtering it through a locative lens; we are ostensibly reading the story of the building. This plaque on Barden Tower represents the style and content of many of Clifford's inscriptions:

THIS BARDEN TOWER WAS REPAYRED
BY THE LADIE ANNE CLIFFORD COVNTE
SSE DOWAGER OF PEMBROOKEE DORSETT
AND MONTGOMERY BARONNESSE CLIFFORD
WESTMERLAND AND VESSEIE LADY OF THE
HONOR OF SKIPTON IN CRAVEN AND HIGH
SHERIFFESSE BY INHERITANCE OF THE
COVNTIE OF WESTMERLAND IN THE YEARES
1658 AND 1659 AFTER ITT HAD LAYNE
RVINOVS EVER SINCE ABOVT 1589 WHEN
HER MOTHER THEN LAY IN ITT, AND WAS
GREATE WITH CHILD WITH HER TILL

NOWE THAT ITT WAS REPAYRED BY
THE SAYD LADY ISA. CHAP. 58 VER. 12[8]

The similarity of the diary passage to the public inscription on the castle encourages us to read autobiographical and architectural history simultaneously by collapsing the formal distinctions between the two. Although the wording is not particularly succinct, both diary and inscription compress time frames and characters into a small space. The rectangular text block of the architectural inscription reminds us of its spatial constraints. Clifford's architectural inscriptions often appear to strain against their boundaries; in line two of the Barden Tower inscription, one of her titles is split between two lines as it overflows its spatial limits, and in many inscriptions her titles, nearly always written out in full, run on for several lines, as though they might press the end of the building's story off the bottom of the slab. On the Chapel at Mallerstang, her plaque gives a detailed account of a financial transaction involved in the structure's funding, including the exact amount Clifford paid for the lands, and the corners of the rectangular slab almost press up against the slanted eaves that frame them.

If the succinct compression of architectural inscription finds its way into the diary, the diary also explicates these tightly bordered texts, unfolding them both spatially and temporally. The similarity of the diary passage and inscription both quoted above may make them appear parallel, rather than complementary, two different vehicles for conveying the same information. The diary account and inscription of Brougham Castle, though, provide an example in which Clifford uses the formal differences of the diary to unpack the implications of this encapsulated information. Here, a shared biblical allusion explains both the historical depth and the practical purpose of the stories Clifford hoped her castles would tell. On the castle a stone panel once read:

THIS BROVGHAM CASTLE WAS REPAIRED
BY THE LADIE ANNE CLIFFORD
. . . .
IN THE YEARES OF 1651
AND 1652 AFTER IT HAD LAYEN RVINOVS
EVER SINCE ABOVT AVGVST 1617 WHEN
KING IAMES LAY IN IT FOR A TIME IN
HIS IOVRNIE OVT OF SKOTLAND
TOWARDS LONDON VNTIL THIS TIME.
ISA. CHAP 58 VERSE 12
GODS NAME BE PRAISED.[9]

Inscription by Anne Clifford on porch of Mallerstang Chapel, Cumbria

In the diary entry of 1653 the same biblical reference appears in this context: "And for repayring of this Brougham Castle which had layne so itt were, ruinous and desolate ever since King James, his lying in itt in 1617, till I made itt lately habitable, caused me againe to apply that Saying to my selfe: Isaiah 58:2–12" (*Diaries*, 125). The scripture passage cited concludes: "And they that shall be of thee shall build the old waste places: thou shalt raise up the foundations of many generations; and thou shalt be called, The repairer of the breach, The restorer of paths to dwell in."[10]

This quotation appears in many of Clifford's architectural inscriptions, and perhaps she liked it not only because it added a biblical title—"repairer of the breach"—to her political honors, but because it unfolds from the present moment a seamless narrative of multiple time frames. Like the narratives of the country house poem, which enumerate both ancestry and progeny, this passage from Isaiah locates Clifford's buildings in a history that cannot be contained by the past tense. It provides a model for interpreting the temporal valences of the compact architectural inscriptions, most succinctly and powerfully expressed in the family motto Clifford had cut into the battlements of Skipton Castle: "Desormais," "Henceforth." The word is a complicated compression of past, present, and future. Tradition held that the Cliffords had adopted this motto following the attainder and restitution of their lands. "If this tradition was based on fact," writes Spence in his biography of Anne's father, "there are three possibilities" for the date of this restitution, "1234, 1327 and 1485."[11] In Volume 2 of the Great Books, dating the event in 1486, Clifford explains, "[w]hich Restauration was the chiefe grownd of the Lady Anne Clifford now countess Dowager of Pembrook her tytle to the Landes of her Inheritance, which by gods Blessing, shee now enjoys both in Westmorland, and in Craven."[12] The motto itself thus serves as a kind of historical property deed, while simultaneously insisting that the future always unfolds from the present moment. Isaiah's promises pay off not in salvation but in reputation, not in heavenly preferment but in earthly presence.

In the case of Brougham Castle, Clifford's diary gives an example of how to apply Isaiah's model to the building and to the writing on it. Her use of Isaiah's prophecy, in the joint context of diary and inscription, shows that Clifford understood the architectural breaches on her properties as the literalization of a temporal one. In the diary as on the castle, the quotation refers principally to the architectural restoration. The diary entry about Brougham Castle quoted above, however, is preceded by a paragraph that conceptualizes the "repayring" differently:

> And I had not layne in this Brougham Castle in Thirty Seaven yeares till now. For ye month of December in One Thousand sixe hundred and sixtene (when I was

Clifford family motto ("Henceforth") on gatehouse of Skipton Castle, Yorkshire married to Richard, Earle of Dorset) I went out of itt upp towards London to him, and never lay in itt till this night. In which long time I past through many strange and hard fortunes in the Sea of this World. Soe as I may well apply that Saying to myself: Ps. 107 & Ps. 109.27. (*Diaries*, 124)

The architectural repair of Brougham Castle, following as it does this account of Clifford's past alienation from her lands, becomes the expression for a project of historical, geographical, and legal repair. Predictably, Psalm 107, cited at the end of the passage, enlists the hand of the Lord in some satisfying retributive smiting, but its themes also interweave it with the verse from Isaiah. Psalm 107 reads: "And [the Lord has] gathered them out of the lands, from the east, and from the west, from the north, and from the south. They wandered in the wilderness in a solitary way; they found no city to dwell in."[13] The last verse looks forward to the restoration of the "paths to dwell in" described by Isaiah. The similarity of these two scripture passages suggests that Clifford perceived her return to Brougham Castle and her architectural restoration of it as related achievements. The Brougham Castle restoration responds to and repairs a historical rupture, defined in the diary as the period of Clifford's dispossession.

We can use the Isaiah quotation as a model for explaining many of Clifford's inscriptions, as well as the short inscription-like passages of the diary, for it seems to have provided a template for Clifford as she fabricated her histories along with her castles. Clifford wanted to write the past and the future, but, again following the model of Isaiah's prophecy, she wanted to spin both out of her own physical and historical presence. Identifying herself with Isaiah's "repairer of the breach" allowed her to resolve two otherwise contradictory ways of asserting her authority. On the one hand, she wanted to separate herself from past and future, to isolate her individual importance as a commemorator of the family's past and a progenitor of its continuation. Simultaneously, though, her writing submerges her identity as an individual in a consistently powerful and unbroken historical tradition in which she figures as her father's legitimate daughter and the mother of two equally legitimate heirs.

Clifford understood her buildings as resembling Isaiah's addressee: architecture is rendered in temporal and narrative terms as it becomes an important intersection of past, present, and future. For instance, looking back to the diary passage about Skipton Castle and the inscription on Barden Tower, both quoted above, we see that the events of both texts are chosen not nostalgically but strategically; the building becomes at once a historical and a geographical marker. The inscriptions connect the castles to a socially important past through the mention of Anne's dead mother and the spectral presence of her dead husbands, conjured up by her notations of marriage and widowhood. The castles are also made endpoints, sites of completion, by Anne's triumphant return and successful repair of Barden Tower's ruins. Both, though, are associated with Anne's birth; they signal a beginning as well as an end. The castles, then, are inhabited by both the dead and the living; as both gravestones and birthplaces, they not only solidify past events but generate their own futures.

The rich relevance of the prophecy Clifford had carved on so many of her buildings ought also to suggest to us that the insistent repetitions in her diary are not insane or inept but selective and deliberate. The ritualistic repetition of both content and phrasing is a rhetorical strategy that Clifford extended across years. Again, the correspondence of written text to architectural inscription helps to explain this interesting and tedious feature as a process of verbal chiseling. Critics have tended to ignore this aspect of the diary by selecting and compiling details according to the particular narrative they are trying to construct, thus wrenching these details out of context in the service of psychological profiling or narrative efficiency. Spence, for instance, in his attempt to prove Clifford's affection for her father, writes, "She often referred to his birth in Brougham Castle."[14] But this fact turns from a touching detail to a kind of official designation if we take into account that she refers to his birth there at least twelve times in the late diary, almost always as part of a set phrase used to document her habitation of a certain room. The entry of 1 April 1656, for example, records: "And so thatt evening from thence [Melkinthorpe] I came into my said Castle of Brougham, where I lay in the Chamber which my Noble father was borne in and in which my Blessed Mother dyed, for some sixe monthes" (*Diaries*, 132–133). The organization of this small narrative gestures formally towards the architectural inscription, because it attaches to a place, not a person. In addition, the reader who has Isaiah's prophecy or Clifford's architectural inscriptions in mind will immediately recognize its pattern: the room is both a gravestone and a birthplace. Furthermore, the tag describing this room maintains not only its narrative form but its phrasing in successive recurrences. The wording varies only slightly from year to year, and it always includes exactly the same epithet for each parent. It finally becomes much less personal in the last entry of her journal, where it appears word for word in the hand of an unknown author who added her death to the list of significant events that had occurred in the room: "[S]he, with much cheerfulness, in her own chamber in Brougham Castle, wherein her noble father was born and her blessed mother died, yielded up her precious soul into the hands of her merciful Redeemer" (*Diaries*, 281).[15] In this case, the phrase has effectively become an inscription for the room, displaced from the realm of Clifford's own psychology onto the physical space itself. Its status as such is only realized through the persistent and exact repetitions that metaphorically set it in stone.

Once we stop trying to sift through Clifford's repetitiveness and allow it to focus our attention rather than hinder our searches for fresh autobiographical matter, we become attuned to particular repetitive rituals. The room of her father's birth and her mother's death is not the only object of this verbal strategy. Clifford names "the Chamber" in Skipton Castle "wherein I was borne into the World" (*Diaries*, 165), repeating the phrase at least nine times; and she frequently assaults the reader with slight variations on the phrase "the Landes of myne Inheritance" (see, for instance, *Diaries*, 114, 126). In 1669 she began detailing the staged, ceremonially repetitive routes by which she entered and left her castles, documenting both their structural features and her own presence in each room. "[C]oming out of my owne chamber [in Appleby Castle]" she writes that year, "I pass'd through the great chamber and went into the Chappell and through the Hall," and "took my Litter at the Hall Doore in the Court" (*Diaries*, 206, see also 212, 217). As Elizabeth Chew has argued, Clifford uses architectural description to inscribe her own history in the scope of a longer ancestry, making the house "a vessel of the past that connected her to present and future."[16]

These inscriptive phrases also appear on the multiple funeral monuments Clifford commissioned. Once established in the north, at the same time she began keeping her yearly accounts, she erected monuments to her tutor Samuel Daniel (Beckington, 1654), to her father (Holy Trinity Church, Skipton, 1654), and to herself (St. Lawrence's Church, Appleby, 1655). Biographers have often considered these monuments as the products of either individual aesthetic taste or private emotion.[17] The moment she chose for commissioning these tombs, however, suggests that, for her, they were conceptually linked to her architectural and written projects rather than to strong personal feelings about the events they commemorated. Wordsworth perhaps sums up our modern sentimental expectations about the composition of epitaphs when he describes the epitaph as a "delineation ... performed by the side of the Grave."[18] But when Clifford constructed her father's monument, she had long been away from the side of the grave and had had forty-nine years to recover from any spontaneous overflow of powerful feeling. When she wrote her own epitaph, she would not be buried beneath it for another twenty-one years. Both her father's monument and her own are called funeral monuments, but neither marked a funeral. Both, though, were exactly contemporary with Clifford's late diary and her flurry of architectural projects. We can read these monuments as expressions of the same motivations that drove the repetitions in her diaries and inscriptions: a desire to locate herself in both history and geographical space, crucially positioned at the intersection of past, present, and future stories. Ultimately, Clifford fashioned and inscribed these monuments to perpetually reproduce the bodies of the past and her own living presence.

Clifford's epitaphs, like her other architectural inscriptions and her diary, again follow the model of her favorite verse from Isaiah, constantly explicating complex temporal intersections. They distinguish and illuminate the layers of social, historical, and legal meaning that are collapsed on the body of a dead aristocrat. By identifying herself with Isaiah's "repairer of the breach," Clifford made both herself and her buildings important hinges in an ancestral story; the epitaphs she wrote also depict human bodies as vital confluences of past, present, and future meanings. Her mother's tomb—commissioned immediately after the countess's death in 1616—describes the piety of Margaret's character and life, but it also identifies the tomb's subject as "COUNTESS DOWAGER OF CUMBERLAND, YOUNGEST CHILD TO FRANCIS RUSSELL, SECOND EARL OF BEDFORD," mentions her twenty-nine-year marriage to the third Earl of Cumberland, and names Anne as her sole daughter and the patron of her monument.[19] The countess, like Isaiah's addressee, is poised at the juncture of multiple time frames, as well as social and spiritual forms of immortality. In *The Ancient Funerall Monuments* (1631), John Weever refers to the tradition of placing tombs by the roadside, where they could directly address travelers "to put passengers in minde, that they were like those so interred, mortall."[20] When Clifford imperiously addresses the passenger, however, it is to ensure the survival of social distinction, not to level it: "BVT PASSENGER / KNOW, HEAVEN AND FAME CONTAYNES THE BEST OF HER."[21] Rather than recalling the brevity of earthly existence, the inscription conjoins heaven and fame in a way that makes the reputation as enduring as the soul.

The inscription on the tomb of Clifford's father likewise makes him the product of "a long continued descent of ancestors," as well as "one of the noblest personages of England in his time," the husband of "the blessed and virtuous Lady the Lady MARGARET RUSSELL," and the father of "but one legitimate child . . . his daughter and sole heir the Lady ANNE CLIFFORD."[22] Anne's own inscription also characterizes her in terms of her parentage, her marriages, and her progeny, as "HAVINGE BEFORE HER DEATH SEEN A PLENTIFUL ISSUE BY HER TWO DAUGHTERS OF THIRTEEN GRANDCHILDREN." The married identities of Clifford's two daughters are recorded in the arms that flank her own on the reredos, and the epitaph projects her ancestral identity into the future by describing them and their many

Inscription on Anne Clifford's tomb, St. Lawrence Church, Appleby, Cumbria

children as having survived her.[23] This assertion of ancestral continuity is weakened slightly by a poignant reminder of disruptive mortality; Isabella, Anne's younger daughter, did not outlive her mother. She died in 1661, between the time the tomb was commissioned in 1655 and Anne's own death in 1676.

These epitaphs not only reproduce the identities of the deceased but perpetually create Clifford's own. Even her monument to Daniel defines him in terms of herself as her intellectual ancestor; about thirty-four of the inscription's words are about the poet, while approximately forty-five are about Clifford herself.[24] In the case of her parents, the ancestry required two bodies, and she seems to have been uncomfortably aware that she was unable to use a tomb with side-by-side recumbent effigies of man and wife. Her parents are not even buried in the same church. When Margaret died in 1616, her uncle controlled Skipton Castle and would not allow Anne to bury her mother there, and Margaret's will at first specified that she wished to be buried next to her brother at Alnwick. A codicil left the choice up to Anne, who had her mother interred at Appleby, the place she specified for her own funeral monument.[25] The countess's original decision, however, might remind us that if Clifford's parents were not spending eternity together, they had not spent a great deal of their lives that way either. The earl had carried on a very public affair, apparently at times to his wife's humiliation. In their epitaphs, Clifford strains to pull together the edges of both the spatial and the marital distance; each parent's epitaph produces the presence of the other. Both epitaphs refer to their marriage, and her father's records his spouse's death and place of burial. While she was not able to locate their bodies physically in the same place, she used inscriptions to unite them in Brougham Castle. Her mother's inscription records that she died there, and her father's inscription repeats this information after noting that he had been born in the castle. Clifford's pointed remark in her father's epitaph—that she was Lord George's only "legitimate child"—indicates her awareness of the potential legal difficulties presented by publicly known extramarital affairs. Her earlier diaries confirm her legally motivated discomfort over her parents' eternal separation. Immediately following her mother's death in 1616, Clifford wrote, "[W]hen I consider'd her Body should be carried away & not interr'd at Skipton ... I took that as a sign that I should be dispossessed of the Inheritance of my Forefathers" (*Diaries*, 37). Her mother's exclusion from the church at Skipton becomes a concrete representation of her own exclusion from an inheritance diverted to her uncle and his male heirs.

Clifford's monuments were constructed without the aid of a funeral; in her contemporaneous diary, she realized that she did not really require a funeral monument either. The problem with true funeral monuments is that there can only be one per person. Each individual can have only one epitaph that truthfully begins "Here lies." Clifford disseminated her own presence by asserting in the diary that she "lay" in each of her castles in rapid succession. In their studies of funeral monuments, Camden and Weever had responded to the problem of a tomb's uniqueness by recording epitaphs in books, which were both portable and reproducible.[26] Clifford's diary is not a collection of epitaphs, but she, too, is reproducing bodies in writing. Through the use of repetition, she is continually being born in Skipton Castle and stamping her presence on the lands she had finally inherited. Her compressed narrative tag for her room in Brougham Castle—"the Chamber in which my Noble father was borne in and in which my Blessed Mother dyed" (*Diaries*, 133)—echoes both her parents' epitaphs. This compact little story reenacts the function of the epitaphs as it repeatedly reproduces Clifford herself by placing her parents side-by-side in a space they probably rarely shared in life.

It was not only the specific information inscribed on Clifford's buildings and monuments but the practices of building and inscribing themselves that were meant to engage both past and future, locating Clifford herself at the auspicious apex of an inveterate and enduring lineage that was expressed architecturally as much as in written texts. In the context of the Great Books, Clifford's activities as a builder and repairer clearly position her as the heiress of a long ancestral tradition. Clifford's marginalia carefully document the physical condition of each castle at different points in time—"this shewes that Skipton Castle did want great reparations," she notes in the margin of a fourteenth-century property deed (2.75)—and summaries of her ancestors' lives conflate building and biography in a way that makes one emblematic of the other. She often describes her ancestors as builders and encapsulates their lives through an account of the castles, churches, and funeral monuments they commissioned or restored. Of Robert Lord Clifford (1305–1344), for instance, she writes, "It is belevied by tradition That hee did build some parte of Skipton Castle, for it was much repaired in the beginning of Edward the thirds time, When hee was Lord of it" (2.200). Another ancestor, Roger Lord Clifford (1333–1389), is described as "a great Builder, and repayrer of his Castles and howses in the North, So as hee built the greatest part of Browham Castle in Westmorland" (2.263).[27]

The records are sometimes much more detailed. Of her fifteenth-century ancestor John de Clifford she notes:

> much of his tyme was spent in the Warres in France, Yet was hee a Builder both in Westmorland and Craven as apeares by some old Wryteings that are now almost consumed with tyme.
>
> It is certaine hee built the strong and fine arteficiall Gatehowse at Appleby Castle in Westmorland of stone all Arched overhead. Wherein is ingraven his Armes of the Veteriponts and Clifford and his Wyves Armes of the Percyes joined together....
>
> And as this John Lord Clifford did build that Gatehouse there, So his sonne Thomas Lord Clifford did build a great part of the said Castle of Apleby in Westmorland that stands Eastward, as the hall, the chappell, and great Chamber, whych were then fallen into great decay, though it had bene a Castle of note ever since William the Conquerers tyme, and before. (2.362)

And in "A Sumarie of the Records of Roger Lo: Clifford who married Isabella de Verteripont," biographical and architectural history are made to converge on— and unfold from—the same three-word inscription, a version of which remains above the gate of the ruined castle today:

> And certaine it is That this Roger de Clifford the younger after hee was married to Isabella de Veteripont and was possessed, as in her Right of Browgham Castle.

Did build & repaire much of the said Castle So as Hee caused a stone to be sett in the Wall thereof over the Doore of the Inward gate. Wherein is ingraven theis woords following, as they thus stand:

This

made

Roger

Which words are severally interpreted for some think Hee meant it Because Hee built that, and a great part of the said Castle, and also repaired the greatest Tower there, called the Pagan tower.

And some think he meant it, Because hee was made in his fortune by marriage with Isabella de Veteripont, By whome hee became possessor of this Castle, and much other Landes & Castles in the said County in severall places of it. (2.40)

Clifford's interpretation of the inscription may be a borrowing from Camden, who, in his account of Windsor in *Britannia*, tells the story of William Wickham, Bishop of Winchester. Wickham was made overseer of the construction of a tower at the castle. "Some report," recounts Camden, "that the said Wickham, after hee had built and furnished this Tower, in a certaine inner wall, engraved these

Plaque above the gatehouse of Brougham Castle, Cumbria ("thys made roger")

words, *This made Wickham* which maner of speech in the English tongue, that seldome maketh distinction of cases, carrieth such a doubtfull construction, that uncertaine it is, whether he made these buildings, or the buildings made him." Having fallen into displeasure with the king for claiming such credit, Wickham defended himself. Camden wrote that he claimed, "[t]hat he had not arrogated, and ascribed to himselfe the praise of so sumptuous, and princely an aedifice, but accounted this building, and peece of work to have been the meanes of all his dignities and preferments: neither have I (quoth he) made this castle, but this castle hath made me."[28] While Clifford's perception of the phrase's ambiguity may have derived originally from her reading of Camden, here she presses the potential double significance into quite different service: the confluence of the two meanings reflects the marriage they might commemorate and, rather than pulling against one another, both seem, in Clifford's account, to be applicable at once. The failure of English to distinguish between subject and object perfectly encapsulates Clifford's biographical method. As a life is recorded in the making of buildings, the architectural history becomes a way of producing a narrative, of making, in one sense, a life.

As this possible adaptation from Camden suggests, both Clifford's diaries and her architectural works are in part derived and adapted from antiquarian textual practices that were, by the last years of Clifford's life, well established in English historiography. There is ample evidence that Clifford knew some of the major works and key figures that emerged from this tradition. In the Great Books, Clifford mentions both Stow's *Chronicles* and Camden's *Britannia*, and the latter volume is visible behind her on the shelves of books in the Appleby Triptych (1647).[29] Through analysis of her own and her scribes' marginalia, Stephen Orgel has shown how Clifford mined the enlarged 1609–1610 edition of William Baldwin's *Mirror for Magistrates* for useful moral sentiments and salutary bits of family history.[30] Georgianna Ziegler has similarly described a recent acquisition of the Folger Shakespeare Library, a copy of John Selden's *Titles of Honor* (1631) owned by Clifford and annotated in her own hand and probably those of her personal scribes. As Ziegler notes, "John Selden's exact relationship to Lady Anne Clifford is a little obscure," but, as she points out, there were a number of mutual acquaintances through whom they could have known each other, and Spence records a letter of February 1650 to Elizabeth Grey, Countess of Kent, in which Anne asks the countess "to remember my love and service to worthy Mr Selden."[31]

Certainly immediate to Clifford's own experience were the antiquarians Roger Dodsworth and William Dugdale, authors of the 1655 *Monasticon Anglicanum*, an extensive history of England's former religious houses. Clifford employed Dodsworth to collect and copy many of the documents included in the Great Books: to these volumes, writes Spence, "as with the *Monasticon*, Dodsworth's was a great though virtually anonymous contribution."[32] Dugdale was also her personal acquaintance, and Spence records his staying with Clifford at Brougham Castle in March 1665.[33] While Clifford herself could not have read the *Monasticon* because she did not read Latin, the physical and formal similarities between this work and the Great Books betray the influence of such antiquarian writing.[34] Both works consist of three massive folio volumes and, more important, both are composed in part of legal documents—copied in full—relating to various land grants and properties.

Another striking correspondence between Clifford's activities and the goals of the *Monasticon* lies in their originators' desire to preserve the architectural record. It would not have been practical, of course, for Dodsworth or Dugdale to maintain or rebuild monastic remains; nonetheless, the *Monasticon* is remarkable for its many engraved plates, created by Daniel King and Wenceslaus Hollar, which Dugdale commissioned from aristocratic and genteel patrons at £5 a piece.[35] The plates depict views of both extant cathedrals and monastic ruins, and, not unlike Clifford's buildings, each plate bears an inscription. These brief sentiments in Latin invariably record the name and titles of the illustration's sponsor. Some of these mottos differ in tone from Clifford's architectural inscriptions in their pessimism. As Graham Parry says, "almost all these inscriptions are elegiac, lamenting the ruin of the church they depict."[36] Also common, however, as Parry notes, are inscriptions that proclaim the donor's hope that the engraving will preserve the building, in some form at least, for posterity. Next to a view of the north front of Canterbury Cathedral, for instance, a cartouche reads, "Posteritati sacrum impensis Edoardi Darrel" ("Sacred to posterity at the expense of Edward Darrel").[37] A view of the north front of Westminster Abbey sponsored by William Bromley reads simply, "Contra injuriam temporum" ("Against the injury of the times").[38] And a plate of the west front of Sherborne Cathedral paid for by William Cole reads, "Resurgat Ecclesia, et resplendescat in eternum" ("Let the church rise again, and increasingly shine for eternity").[39] For Dugdale's sponsors, the special urgency of preservation resulted from the Reformation and, more immediately, the historical and religious ruptures of the Civil Wars; for Clifford, it resulted from the period of her disinheritance; but in each case, architecture is seen as a compression of multiple time frames: it is part of the historical record, it is an important way of commemorating a present individual's identity, and it is meant to overcome temporal gaps and speak, in a way, to the future.

Nor were the fields of monastic history and aristocratic legal prerogative perceived as being unrelated in the seventeenth century. Spence provides a detailed account of the monastic records Dodsworth used in preparing the Clifford evidences, and these survive among the 161 volumes of Dodsworth's manuscripts that are now deposited in the Bodleian Library.[40] In his *Church History* (1656), Thomas Fuller argued, "Although many Modern Families have been great Gainers by the destruction of the Monasteries, yet the Antient Nobility (when casting up their *Audits*) found themselves much impaired thereby both in power and profit, commodity and command."[41] "It cannot be denied," Thomas Tanner wrote in an abridged translation of the *Monasticon* of 1695, "but that our Historians and Lawyers must have constant recourse to [the monasteries'] Annals."[42]

There are many other similarities between Clifford's works and contemporary antiquarian texts. Her record of her own movements and her locative methods of organization resemble the antiquarian itinerary, and both reflect a distinctly antiquarian approach to understanding and interpreting architecture. In her texts and inscriptions, as in the antiquarian itinerary, buildings gain their significance from their association with the particular human stories they preserve and inspire. It is not simply that Clifford's castles displayed wealth and land ownership in general terms; they were made to retell a specific history which Clifford feared was in danger of being lost. Just as John Stow deplored the dismantling of funeral monuments in exchange for anonymous sums of cash, Clifford rejected the compromise by which King James had compensated her for the loss of her lands with a cash sum of £20,000. Clifford's steadfastness in this position caused a long conflict with her first husband, the Earl of Dorset "about the desire hee had, to make mee sell my righte in the Landes of my auntientt Inheritance, for Money, which I never did, nor ever would Consent unto" (3.205).[43]

Furthermore, like Leland and Stow, Clifford styled herself a seeker and collector of manuscripts. "By the time Dorset died [1624]," Spence writes, "Anne ... was the owner of a collection [of manuscripts] of which many an antiquary would have been proud."[44] She also shared the antiquary's fear that, if unrecovered, the manuscript record might disintegrate. In the account of John de Clifford's building at Appleby Castle, quoted above, she speaks of "some old Wryteings that are now almost consumed with tyme," and next to a fourteenth-century property deed appears the marginal note, "This Deed is torne and scarce legeable" (2.277). The title page of each volume of the *Monasticon Anglicanum* lists the libraries from which documents were drawn to be sorted ("digesti") by Dodsworth and Dugdale;[45] Clifford's title pages document the research activities of her mother and herself: "The chiefe of ... Recordes in this sayd Booke was By the Care &

Painfull Industry of that Excellent Lady Margaret Russell Countes Dowager of Cumberland Gotten out of Severall offices & courts of this Kingdom," the title page of Volume 2 reads, continuing "which Booke was compiled many yeares after By the care and Industrie of the sayd Lady Ann Clifford." And marginal notes record and summarize the means by which she acquired specific manuscripts. Next to a deed concerning the ownership of Skipton Castle, for instance, a note adds, "This Record being a breife of a Scire Facias was copied out of the Originall by the appointment of Margaret Countess Dowager of Cumberland for the good & behafe of her sole daughter & heire the Lady Anne Clifford / 1606," and elsewhere, "the Coppy of this was sent me by Sir Thomas Witherington July 1648" (2.231, 2.161). In a summary concerning the will of her thirteenth-century ancestor Agnes de Condy, she notes that it is "said to bee one of the auntiest willes now extant, The originall whereof remayneth now in the Custody of Sir Symon de Ewes" (1.176). Such remarks show not only Clifford's concern with the preservation of documents but her active participation in networks of antiquarian sociability and exchange. Despite the narrower focus of her interests, Clifford's antiquarian activities seem to have placed her on a level with some of the period's leading collectors and historians, though she has rarely been considered among their ranks.

Whether or not Clifford's interpretation of the plaque on Brougham Castle—"This made Roger"—was inspired by the *Britannia*, the Great Books demonstrate that she had attended to the architectural descriptions included in that work. Volume 1 includes notes from the *Britannia*, such as "fol. 618.6 touching the building of Clifford Castle," while next to a deed for the "Manor of Corsham" Clifford's marginal note reads, "The right name of this Castle is Corvisham, as appears by Mr. Cambdens Description of Shropshire in his Britannia" (1.161, 1.188). Even if Clifford's exposure to antiquarians and antiquarian texts was not clearly documented, the similarity of her descriptive methods suggests a conscious imitation of these predecessors and contemporaries. Take, for instance, Camden's account of the former Woodford Castle, Dorsetshire: "Where in old time *Guy Brient* a Baron and renowned warriour had a little Castle of his owne: which afterward was the habitation of *Hugh Stafford* of *Suthwick*; by one of whose daughters Inheretrices, it came as I have heard to *Thomas Strangewaies*, who being borne in Lancashire and brought hither by the first Marques *Dorset* obtained a great and rich inheritance in these parts, and his issue built a very faire house at *Milbery*."[46] Camden's concatenation of biographies is less focused than Clifford's, since the *Britannia* is not centered on a single family or human subject, but it demonstrates similar concerns: the distinctions of a "renowned warriour"—John de Clifford spent much of his time "in the Warres in France"—the enumeration of names and titles, the recording of inheritances, and the establishment of parentage and progeny. In addition, such descriptions reflect the same kind of research which produced the Great Books; it was based at once in both the observation of physical places and the synthesis of documents that recorded the transfer of property.

Clifford's strategic use of these antiquarian practices helps to explain the inspiration for habits of hers which biographers have found compulsive, egocentric, and bizarre: distributing paintings and commemorative medals of herself, bestowing upon her friends large stock locks with her initials on them, and scattering her name and initials liberally over the castles, churches, and funeral monuments she built and repaired. Speculating an explanation, Henry Summerson writes, "Much in her which her contemporaries must have found strange... should doubtless be attributed to the advance of old age."[47] But it was not just in her last years that Clifford engaged in these actions. While Clifford was not in a position to strike her own coin, John Charlton has suggested that she might have liked to do so, and she did enlist medals as a way of ensuring the survival of her unique identity.[48] Leland and his successor John Bale had argued that the contents of monastic libraries must be preserved through replication made possible by printing; in the dissemination of commemorative medals adorned with her portrait, Clifford found yet another way of copying and preserving herself.[49]

Aware of what antiquarians extracted from epitaphs, initials, arms, and inscriptions, Clifford scattered them about her buildings and churches. She also used such evidence to piece together the history of her ancestors. Of Thomas Lord Clifford (1414–1455), for instance, she writes: "This Thomas Lord Clifford was buryed with his Unckle Henery Percy second Earle of Northumberland then also slayne in the Abbey church of Saynt Albanes in the County of Hartford, as apeares by the Legior Book of that Abbey And also by a Monument of these two Lordes which was standing there within our fathers, and our Memoryes" (2.397). Readers of antiquarian texts since Leland recognize the phrase "within our fathers, and our Memoryes" as a familiar way of recording time.[50] As we have seen, the same Thomas had been a "great Builder" at Appleby Castle, where, in the windows of hall and chapel, she records, were

> sett up in the Glass The Armes of the Vyponts, and the Cliffords,/And also the Dacres Armes, which was his Wyves Armes joyned with the Cliffords./
> And in the Glass wyndowes of the said Chappell is sett up the Armes of his then new borne Grande child after Henerey Lord Cliffford, which was the Clif-

ford and Bromeflette Coates... And in the bottom of the said Chappell wyndow is thus written./
This chappell was built by Thomas Lord Clifford Anno Domini
one Thowsand fower hundred fiftie fower. (2.400)

Anne Clifford followed suit in all these forms of architectural record keeping. In Holy Trinity Church, Skipton, the initials A.P. (she acquired the name Pembroke from her second husband) appear in the windows, and they can also be found on a cartouche in the chancel at St. Michael, Bongate, on the great gateway of Skipton Castle, and on the reredos at St. Ninian's Church in Ninekirks. A rafter in the Church of St. Lawrence, Appleby, reads "[A]NN CONNTESSE OF PEMBROKE IN AN⁰ / [16]55 REPAIRED ALL THIS BVILDING," and her arms and initials also appear at various locations around the main courtyard of Skipton Castle, along with the date 1659, the year in which she carried out major repairs.[51]

In keeping with her favorite passage from Isaiah, Clifford's antiquarianism looked forward even as it looked back to the practices of her ancestors. Equipped with the unusual privilege of building and restoring the architectural record to place alongside the documentary evidence, Clifford created a history for present and future antiquarians to discover and record. There was abundant testament to their interest in this architectural documentation. In 1620, her own future employee Dodsworth had made notes of arms and monument inscriptions in thirty-eight Yorkshire churches, concentrating on the West Riding, where Clifford's own Yorkshire properties were located.[52] The *Britannia* indicates that finding such markings was to be expected. At Silcester, for instance, Camden describes "a pretty Church... in which, while I searched for ancient inscriptions, I found nothing, but onely in the windowes certaine armes," which he goes on to describe in detail.[53] Weever's *Ancient Funerall Monuments* was written with the aid of evidence collected largely, Weever would claim, from firsthand observation: "with painefull expences... I travailed over the most parts of England, and some part of Scotland; I collected the Funerall Inscriptions of all the Cathedrall Churches of the one, and in some of the other, and ever by the way gathered such as I found in Parochiall Churches."[54] And Dugdale's *History of St. Paul's Cathedral* (1658) combines records "[e]xtracted out of originall Charters, Records, Leiger Books, and other Manuscripts" with "sundry Prospects of the Church, Figures of Tombes, and Monuments."[55] In her extensive use of inscriptions, Clifford appears not only to have been promoting her own influence but ensuring that no future antiquarian would ever, like Camden, report that he had "found nothing." She was assuring that her buildings would be included in this specific kind of textual history. In Clifford's hands, architectural inscription becomes a way of regenerating and perpetuating a textual tradition, as she made certain that her physical buildings would someday find a place among the stories of some family history or antiquarian work.

In Clifford's case, architecture both provided a way of writing her life and produced an earthly afterlife. When Edward Rainbow, Bishop of Carlisle, preached Clifford's funeral sermon in 1676, he confronted a brief form of the task Clifford had set for herself: to remember a life, to construct an identity, and to imagine what she had left to the future. Rainbow, closer than modern readers are to both her life and her landscape, recognized the connections among identity, architecture, and afterlife. His composition is not particularly subtle, but the sermon methodology, which parses both the literal and the metaphorical meanings of the chosen text, led him to this kind of synthesis. Rainbow's text was Proverbs 14:1, which reads, "Every Wise woman buildeth her House." In his introduction, the bishop says that he will take the words of the verse "as they stand in their Natural and Proper, together with their Parabolical and Figurative sense" as "the Clew which shall lead me through all the *Labyrinths* and Passages and Rooms of this great *House*."[56]

By trading on the literal and metaphorical meanings enabled by joint consideration of her person, her text, and her architecture, the sermon re-performs important functions of the diary and the architectural projects. It connects the buildings very specifically to Clifford's physical body, making them manifestations of her presence there. Rainbow says that "her Body [was] Durable and Healthful" and that, "although nature framed her but as the Subject of this Text, a *Woman*; yet she [had] a Body... well ordered, as well as built."[57] The words "Durable," "framed," and "built," mix body and architecture so that the reader cannot help but perceive both at once, making her the timeless occupant of many architectural spaces. The sermon also echoes Clifford's architectural inscriptions by comprehending the narrative trajectory that launches her public image into the future, for the afterlife he promises is not solely spiritual. "The monuments which she had built in the Hearts of all that knew her," he says, "shall speak loud in the ears of a profligate Generation; and tell, that in this general Corruption, lapsed times decay, and downfal of Vertue, the thrice Illustrious *Anne* Countess of *Pembroke, Dorset,* and *Montgomery,* stood immovable in her Integrity of Manners, Vertue, and Religion."[58] The surprising grammatical parallelism of social and religious qualities indicates Rainbow's perception, or at least flattering commemoration, of Anne as a socially and publicly important presence; even her religious qualities are not here listed as proof of her eligibility for heaven but of her strong, even obtrusive place on earth.

As Clifford did in her diary, Rainbow relied on the capacity of his text to inscribe her presence and character on physical spaces that existed beyond the words themselves. He says of Clifford that "she would frequently bring out from the rich Store-house of her Memory, *things new and old*, Sentences, or Sayings of remark, which she had read or learned out of Authors, and with these her Walls, her Bed, her Hangings and Furniture must be adorned; causing her Servants to write them in Papers; and her Maids to pin them up."[59] If this anecdote is true, Clifford herself was practicing literal inscription by posting a visible and deliberately constructed account of her thoughts on her physical surroundings. But the historical truth of the story is irrelevant, for the moment Rainbow lifts it into his sermon, her room is inscribed with a monumental identity that outlives the physical presence and mental functioning of Clifford herself. It was in this room that Virginia Woolf, 255 years later, imagined Clifford: "Words from great writers nailed to the walls of the room in which she sat, eternally transacting business, surrounded her as she worked, as they surrounded Montaigne in his tower in Burgundy."[60]

Given her own ways of imagining her identity, Clifford would probably have liked Rainbow's funeral sermon a great deal. I would offer as evidence what we might see as Clifford's final utterance on the relationship among bodily presence, architecture, and text. In her will, Clifford ordered that her body be "wrapt only in seare cloth and leade, with an inscription on the breast whose body it is."[61] The inscription reads:

> The body of ye most noble
> vertuos & religious Lady Anne
> COUNTESS DOWAGER OF PEMBROKE
> Dorset & MONTGOMERY DAUGHTER AND
> sole HEIR to ye late RIGHT HONO[ble]
> George Clifford Earl of CUMBERLAND
> BARONESS Clifford WESTMERLAND
> & VESCY Lady of ye honour of
> Skipton in CRAVEN & high
> SHERIFESS by inheritance of ye
> County of WESTMERLAND who
> departed THIS life in HER Castle
> of BROUGHAM in ye COVNTY ye 22nd
> MARCH 1675 [/6] HAVIN ATTAINED ye
> age of 86 years the 30th of JANUARY
> before.[62]

Here we step back into the familiar formal constraints of architectural inscription and see the sermon performed in miniature. She connects her body to her buildings, locating her death in Brougham Castle, of all her properties the one most heavily laden with ancestral identities by both her inscriptions and her diary. The familiar litany of her titles and ancestry ensures that her presence will resonate widely by tying her remains to all the buildings that bear this list and to the diary that repeats again and again her possession of these lands. Her body itself thus becomes a site of antiquarian interest, as it coordinates and conjoins diverse historical materials. After writing so many times, in ink and stone, these claims of ancestry and social rank, her final move was to anchor them in her own physical presence, creating a kind of permanent cross-reference among her body, her writing, her political identity, and the local landscape of Cumberland and Westmorland.

As Bishop Rainbow offered a commemorative statement of the connection between autobiography and architecture at the end of Clifford's life, we can turn to her earlier years for what might—we can only speculate—have been a formative connection. In 1611, Anne's tutor Samuel Daniel introduced his own book of poetry thus:

> And howsoever be it well or ill
> What I have done, it is mine owne I may
> Do whatsoever therewithall I wil.
>   I may pull downe, raise, and reedifie
> It is the building of my life the fee
> Of Nature, all th'inheritance that I
> Shall leave to those which must come after me.[63]

For Daniel, as for Clifford, both building and book are means of reconstructing the past in the service of an enduring public image, and he emphasizes not historical accuracy but authorial agency. Both building and text are edited by the author's freely exercised discretion: "What I have done, it is mine owne I may / Do whatsoever therewithall I wil." And if he is not locating himself in any particular geographical location, Daniel, too, is practicing a kind of transcendent postmortem occupation by asserting his perpetual presence in the pages of his book. Calling his book "all th'inheritance that I / Shall leave to those which must come after me," he expresses both charming humility and absolute authority. He indeed calls attention to his own lack of material property, but he also exercises complete control over the image that will survive him. The book and the building together become an authorized biography in a literal sense.

Decades after her education with Daniel, Clifford would adapt the same poetic trope—in which literature and architecture are both imagined as postmortem monuments—in a way appropriate to her own sense of history and identity. Around the battlements of Skipton Castle, beneath the family motto "Desormais," appears a roughly quoted passage from Horace, turned to the purpose of commemorating Anne Clifford's father:

GEORGII. MERITVM. MARM. PERENNIVS

REGALIQVE. SITV. PYRAMIDVM. ALTIVS. QVOD. NON. IMBER. EDAX.

NON AQVILO. IMPOTENS. POSSIT. DIRVERE.

AVT INNVMERABILIS ANNORVM SERIES. ET FVGA TEMPORVM.[64]

Spence quotes a translation by the Reverend John Ward: "George's merit is more enduring than marble, and higher than the royal elevation of pyramids, a merit which the corroding rain and the furious north wind cannot overthrow, nor a countless series of years, nor the flight of time."[65] George Williamson notes that "this is a very free adaptation of the words of Horace in the last ode of the third book and intended to read as praise of George, third Earl, her father."[66] The quotation, however, is bizarrely misapplied. In the Ode, Horace makes a claim similar to Daniel's: his poetry will serve as his monument, and, he adds, this fame will outlive even the greatest architectural tributes. It is appropriate, as it was for Daniel, that Horace should make this claim in a poem, the very artifact he feels will ensure his immortality. It is far less logical, however, to place the claim that a person's fame will outlive architectural monuments *on* an architectural monument. Clifford thus conflates two forms of commemoration that, for Daniel and Horace, were quite separate. For Clifford, identity was not constructed independently of ancestry or architecture; at the same time, architecture depended on a textual record of human history to acquire its meaning. Text and architecture rely continually on each other to create a form of biography that is not entirely contained in either.

The contrast between Daniel's figurative verbal architecture and Clifford's concrete architectural monuments alerts us to the insufficiency of reading the diary as though it were a literary artifact or autobiographical narrative meant to stand on its own. We must understand the materials of her autobiography more broadly. They comprise not only the written record of a unique life but the diverse sources of antiquarian historiography: the documentary evidence of the Great Books, and the architectural evidence of her castles, churches, and funeral monuments. Daniel's desired public image would be based in his intellectual merits; it could be completely and very aptly expressed in the lines of a literary work. Clifford's final verbal gesture, however, was to locate her own significance outside of herself, in ancestral history, in progeny, and in the physical features of a real built environment. In the materials of antiquarian historiography, Clifford discovered a way of fashioning her buildings, her story, and, finally, herself. And this is why some passages of the diary, when read as autobiographical narrative, are so strangely empty. Biographers have sought Clifford's identity in her writing alone, but she continually informs them that they will not find it there. In order to read the diary, we must look beyond its pages, and the better we understand what it does not contain, the more it finally reveals.

CHAPTER SIX

Recollections

John Evelyn and the Histories of Restoration Architecture

In the history of English architecture, John Evelyn is almost important. Howard Colvin includes him in the *Biographical Dictionary of English Architects* as "a virtuoso whose theoretical knowledge of architecture was probably as considerable as that of Roger North or Roger Pratt, but who (unlike them) appears rarely to have put it to practical use."[1] Viewed retrospectively, Evelyn's contribution to Restoration building has generally paled beside the accomplishments of such professionals as North and Pratt, along with John Webb, Hugh May, and, most prominently, Christopher Wren. Following the Great Fire of 1666, Evelyn missed being the first to present plans for the rebuilding of London by only two days, by which time, he would write to Samuel Tuke, "Dr. Wren had got the start of me."[2] Aside from these plans, and the scattered observations of his journals, Evelyn's only writing on the subject of architecture is not mainly original, consisting mostly of a very direct translation of Roland Fréart's *Parallèle de l'architecture antique avec la moderne* (Paris, 1650). Reframed with new prefatory material and an appended essay by Evelyn himself and dedicated to England's new monarch, King Charles II, the work was published in 1664 as *A Parallel of the Antient Architecture with the Modern*. In the history of English architectural taste, Evelyn's emphases seem slightly askew; in particular, as Edward Chaney points out, Evelyn failed in both treatise and diary to recognize the prominence of Palladio, the most influential figure for both Inigo Jones, who flourished a generation before Evelyn, and for many who would come a generation after.[3] Other scholars have commented on the incipient and rudimentary nature of Evelyn's architectural knowledge. Li Shiqiao notes that Evelyn failed to make distinctions between classical and baroque styles that would appear important to later architectural historians and theorists; Alice T. Friedman characterizes him as being "overwhelm[ed]" in his attempts to "make sense" of classical and Renaissance architectural forms; and Kerry Downes points out that, when it comes to detailed architectural description, "words often failed Evelyn."[4] John Bowle, as well, sees the significance of Evelyn's *Parallel* as mainly preliminary, "prepar[ing] public opinion to give Wren a free hand when the chance came."[5]

This sense of Evelyn's architectural knowledge, however, emerges largely from scholars' tendency to consider only the novel aspects of his work. That is to say, Evelyn is most often viewed through the lens of future developments in English architectural history rather than in terms of previous architectural conventions and traditions in English architectural writing. The *Parallel* looks back as well as forward, and it evinces delicate negotiations between tradition and innovation, the weaving of older historical strands into a new kind of history. It also shows a keen sensitivity to the intensely political and historical nature of architectural history and aesthetics. In keeping with the central concerns of this book, I am here less interested in Evelyn's contribution to English building—the application of his knowledge to "practical use"—than in his selection and reframing of Fréart's treatise, both of which reveal his understanding of English architectural literacy during this period. Fréart's, and by extension Evelyn's, interpretation and representation of architecture strike chords that earlier writers have made familiar to us, at the same time that both writers adapt architectural historiography to the peculiarities of their own historical moments.

As with so many of Evelyn's writings, we might wish that Evelyn himself were a little more present in the pages of the *Parallel*, a little more visible behind the trappings of translation and panegyric. Nonetheless, Evelyn's English publication of the *Parallel* reveals much about his perception of Restoration politics, architectural aesthetics, and the relationship between the two. In particular, the *Parallel* evinces unexpected continuities between pre- and post-Restoration views of architecture, even as it reflects on moments of political rupture and aesthetic novelty. Evelyn's choice of material, along with his own supplementary matter, indicates that, even after the Restoration, historical and antiquarian modes of architectural interpretation had not become obsolete. As he attempted to introduce aesthetic standards that would have appeared new to many English readers and viewers, Evelyn recollected and relied on earlier assumptions about the relationship between architecture and history. As a result, we can read the *Parallel* as a work of English historiography as much as an innovative introduction of Continental architectural styles. In selecting and repackaging a Continental architectural treatise for an English audience, Evelyn's task both resembled and differed from that of the authors discussed in previous chapters. Like Camden, Wotton, Jonson, and Clifford, Evelyn saw architecture as a way of celebrating a powerful patron, but rather than exploiting a historical association among landowner, architecture, and local topography, Evelyn confronted and recorded a history of dislocation, fragmentation, and restoration. As John Miller notes, in 1660 Charles II "was a stranger to his kingdom, with little first-hand knowledge of its institutions, of his leading subjects and of the relative strengths of the political and religious groups which had fought it out since 1640."[6] Likewise, N. H. Keeble remarks that Charles was "not in the least implicated in recent history," a detachment that one contemporary writer attempted to turn to a strength by speaking of "those great opportunities which he hath had, by his so long being abroad, of diving in to the great Councels of Forrein Princes and States."[7] In recollecting and representing the artifacts of a foreign Renaissance, Evelyn both told the story of a kingless past and celebrated the authority of a new English king. Evelyn's selection and translation of the *Parallel*, therefore, becomes remarkable as a complex positioning of Restoration architecture at the confluence of historical and aesthetic modes of literacy and perception.

Perhaps surprisingly, the structure of the *Parallel* corresponds less directly to Evelyn's activities as a builder, which, as Colvin establishes, were limited, than it does to his activities as a virtuoso, or connoisseur and collector. Evelyn's diaries frequently record the natural, aesthetic, and antique curiosities he amassed while traveling on the Continent. To take only a few examples, at Puzzolo in 1645 he purchased "divers Medailes & other curiosities, Antiquities &c of the Country people, who daily find such things amongst the very old ruines of those places," and from Venice in 1646, he came away with "purchases of *Books, Pictures, G<l>asses, Treacle, &c.*"[8] In 1667, he visited Arundel House, where he found the Arundel marbles "neglected, & scattred up & downe about the Gardens & other places" and persuaded Henry Howard to donate them to the University of Oxford where, after being "removed & piled together," they would be rearranged and preserved in an orderly way.[9] In 1689, he wrote to Samuel Pepys a long letter on the art of collecting medals, coins, prints, and books, with particular instructions that the integrity of the collection be protected (presumably following Pepys's death) "from the sad dispersions many noble libraries and cabinets have suffered in these late times: one auction, I may call it diminution, of a day or two, having scattered what has been gathering many years."[10] And the diary is itself a collection, or rather a recollection, not only of personal experience, but of terms and descriptions drawn from the books and guides of earlier English and European travelers.[11] This chapter, accordingly, examines the ways in which Evelyn enlisted the ideas of collection, fragmentation, and recollection in his interpretation of architecture, which was in turn enlisted in the service of his own reconstruction of English history and his own political panegyric. In viewing the *Parallel* as a calculated assemblage of the extant architectural artifacts of a fragmented past, we tread, in a new way, in the footsteps of John Leland and William Camden, traveling not the physical landscape of England but the uneven ground of English history nonetheless.

As its title suggests, Fréart's *Parallèle* aligned ancient with modern examples, focusing on constructions of the five orders, or types of classical columns. Fréart gathers his evidence for classical building practice mainly from drawings of extant fragments of classical buildings, such as the Baths of Diocletian and the Theater of Marcellus at Rome.[12] The treatise is a collection itself, anthologizing and comparing what Evelyn calls "the *marrow* and very *substance* of no less than *ten* judicious *Authors*" (a 4 r–v). These include eight fifteenth- and sixteenth-century Italians and two sixteenth-century Frenchmen.[13] In the *Parallèle*, they are compared to each other as well as to antique examples, and Fréart reliably backs the ancients, holding them up as the standards to which all subsequent architects ought to aspire. Fréart's collection is introduced by an epistle to his brothers, Paul and Jean Fréart, which consists largely of a tribute to his deceased patron, Sublet de Noyers, and a preface addressed to the reader. The treatise concludes with a brief glossary of terms. Evelyn's translation retains Fréart's front matter and is supplemented by two of his own dedications, one to the newly restored Charles II and another to Sir John Denham, who was at that time Surveyor of the King's Works. Evelyn also appended an original essay "Account of Architects and Architecture," which, in the 1664 edition, consists mainly of a lexicon of architectural terms. In 1707, another edition appeared with the same opening dedications. The "Account," however, had been enlarged with a more extensive condemnation of Gothic architecture, and to this portion Evelyn added a dedication to Denham's successor, Christopher Wren. In Fréart's alignments of ancient and modern examples, Evelyn would also have seen a parallel between the French author and himself. The treatise itself was a collection, and Fréart was a collector. The treatise and its front matter showcase his activities as an acquirer of architectural artifacts, books, and drawings. Like Evelyn, and unlike most of the architect-authors the *Parallèle* abstracts and anthologizes, he was not a practicing architect.[14] In its combination of antique and modern aesthetic artifacts, the book recalls the sort of collections Evelyn had seen and assembled while abroad. By appropriating and translating Fréart's treatise, then, Evelyn presents himself as a recollector of both architectural books and historical fragments, not the physical fragments of buildings, exactly, but their representations.

More important to the concerns of this book, however, Evelyn became a collector and rearranger of both foreign and English modes of understanding architecture. To Evelyn, Fréart offered the opportunity to return to and redeploy earlier English traditions that saw architecture as a record of history and architectural writing as a way of recounting human stories. At the same time, however, the *Parallel* allowed Evelyn to renovate and adapt older traditions. The terms and standards of classical aesthetics, as Friedman has pointed out, would have been unfamiliar to most English viewers of this period.[15] In the *Parallel*, as in the virtuoso's collection, history and novelty are allowed to coexist as antiquity lends its authority to what appears curious or strange. Like the country house poems and county chorographies of previous decades, the *Parallel* is as much about history as it is about building, and as much about patrons as it is about architects. These traditions, however, appear in fragmented and modified form; no longer are they contingent upon topographical, historical, or institutional continuities, nor do they rely on architecture's connection to the land. Instead, architecture is subjected to the historiography of the virtuoso, which allows for fracture, disintegration, renewal, and migration. And in the broadly construed timeline of classical exempla, Gothic barbarity, and Renaissance revival, Evelyn saw another correspondence between architectural and political history: a parallel to England's recent progression from monarchy to interregnum to Restoration. As a result, talking about architecture became for Evelyn a way of representing his royal dedicatee, of seeing, in foreign aesthetic histories, the portrait of an English king.

Evelyn's translation of the *Parallèle* is quite literal and direct. His additions and framing apparatus, however, mark it distinctly as a work of the English Restoration; and as it reconciles classicism with antiquarianism, or old and new models of architectural interpretation, the treatise, like the Restoration itself, looks back in order to look forward, or, as Evelyn would put it, repairs in order to build. In his dedication to Charles, Evelyn speaks of the king's recent building works: "It would be no *Paradox*, but a *Truth*, to affirme, that Your *Majesty* has already *Built* and *Repair'd* more in *three* or *four* Years . . . than all Your *Enemies* have *destroy'd* in *Twenty*; nay then all Your *Majesties* Predecessors have *advanc'd* in an Hundred" (a2v). Evelyn borrows the phrase almost exactly from Fréart's praise of his patron, changing the number of years to correspond with Charles's political career, but the notion of "paradox" is his own introduction. Most obviously, it refers to the apparent improbability that more could be accomplished in four years than in a hundred, but it also conveys something of the way both architectural and political history work in the treatise; it is a process of both innovation and renovation, in which the present is imagined through the recollection of a fragmented past.

Evelyn's perception of architecture thus relies on a connection between political historiography and contemporary antiquarian practice. By the second half of the seventeenth century, both local history and curatorial strands of antiquarian thought had become ingrained and self-conscious enough to anticipate themselves; and, as Anne Clifford did at about the same time, Evelyn crafted his own brand of forward-looking antiquarianism. Fragmentation and incompletion called out for the hand of a new collector, a new virtuoso to engage in the processes of extraction, recollection, and rearrangement. Alienated and disarticulated, antique and modern fragments offered themselves for enlistment in new historical narratives as they were managed, ordered, and repossessed. Through the arrangement and narration of architectural stories, the virtuoso becomes a curator of history; and for Evelyn, it was the very brokenness of that history that transformed it from a prospect of irretrievable loss to a renewable project of recollection.

In the *Parallèle*, it is impossible not to see architecture as being located in history. Illustrating aesthetics in a way that is distinctly diachronic, Fréart's *Parallèle* implies a complicated sense of time. Architecture is framed chronologically and historically, and for Fréart, aesthetic progression is a backward-looking enterprise, in which the present only becomes accessible through the lens of the past. The book is divided up order by order, and each is illustrated through the depiction of ancient examples followed by a comparative assessment of their modern interpretations. In his discussion of the Doric order, for instance, the plates proceed from "A Particular remarkable in the *Profile*, drawn from the *Theater* of *Marcellus*" to "Another *Profile* taken from the *fragments* of the *Dioclesian Bathes* at Rome" to "Another very antient *Profile* after the *Grand Maniere* elevated in *Perspective*, and now extant at *Albano* near Rome" to "*Palladio* and *Scamozzi* upon the *Dorique Order*," to Serlio and Vignola on the same subject, to Alberti and Viola, and finally to Bullant and de l'Orme. At last, Fréart returns to "A very antient *Sepulchre* to be seen near *Terracina*, at the side of the high way leading towards *Naples*" (16, 18, 20, 34). Ancient and modern are successively visible in the description of each order, as are multiple renderings and interpretations of the order's proportions and ornament. Fréart thus differs from a writer such as Palladio, who, as a practicing architect, saw his task as constructive and synthetic rather than analytic. Palladio dedicated, by his account, "long hours of immense

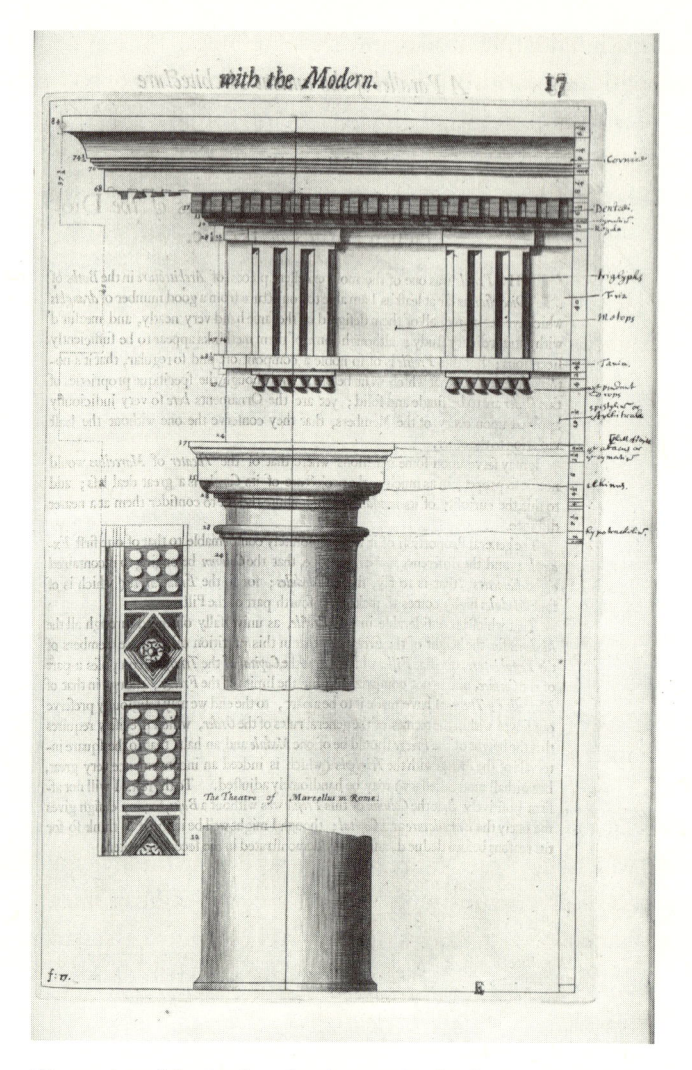

Illustration of the Doric order, from Roland Fréart, *Parallel of the Antient Architecture with the Modern*

effort, to organizing the remaining fragments of ancient buildings" so that the reader might learn by "measuring and observing whole buildings and all their details on a sheet of paper."[16] While Palladio sought to bring the artifacts of the past into a restored representation of their original contexts, Fréart often left them in pieces to bear physical evidence of the passage of time.

Fréart's history of architecture, presented as a quarrel between the ancients and the moderns in which the ancients continually reemerge as superior ex-

Illustration of the Doric order on the sepulcher near Terracina, from Roland Fréart, *Parallel of the Antient Architecture with the Modern*

amples, unfolds as a story of decline and aesthetic divagation. Modern practitioners of architecture have "wander'd" so far from the *"Principles"* of the ancients that "they are become degenerate, and scarce cognoscible to their very *Authors*"; ancient remnants are often used to illuminate the failings of the present (2–3). Fréart uses the sepulcher at Terracina at the end of his discussion of the Doric order, for instance, to alight with satisfaction on the topic of degeneration and error: "I was extremely glad to encounter an example so express and convincing against the abuse of the Moderns, who have very inconsiderably introduc'd *Bases* to the *Columns* of this *Order*" (34). Moreover, the modern Italian writers are not arranged in chronological order, as one might expect in a history of architecture or of architectural writing, but are roughly ranked in descending degrees of excellence, with excellence being determined by their approximation of classical models. The first is Palladio (whose *I Quattro Libri* Fréart himself translated into French in 1651), "without any contest ... to whom we are oblig'd for a very rare Collection of antique *Plans* and *Profiles* of all sorts of Buildings" (22). Scamozzi shares the same page but follows at some distance in quality as "a much inferiour workman," while Serlio and Vignola "hold of the second *Class*" (22). He then proceeds to enumerate the relative strengths of other pairs, ending his list with Alberti ("the most *Antient*") and his *"Corrival"* Viola ("the most *Modern*"), at which point the reader has descended from Palladio to a writer who, Fréart opines "is of the *Categorie* of those which the *Italians* call *Cicaloni*, eternal Talkers to no purpose" (23). Rather than adhering to the subject of architecture, Viola "amuses himself, poor man, in telling stories; so that in stead of a Book of *Architecture*, he has made (ere he was aware) a Book of *Metamorphoses*" (23). The Frenchmen de l'Orme and Bullant, whom Fréart explains he has separated out because French architects are so much less numerous in this collection, follow. By beginning the list with Palladio, "a Sectator of these great *Masters* of *Antiquity*" and, surprisingly, "even a Competitor with them, and emulous of their glory," Fréart physically replicates the writers' aesthetic closeness to classical models in the book (22). Palladio is not chronologically nearest to the ancients, but Fréart makes him nearer in another way, their "Sectator" literally as well as conceptually. In Fréart's account, to survey modern architectural history is to be led through a process of decline. Modern architecture emerges as inherently flawed and belated, with the final return to antiquity (the sepulcher at Terracina) indicating not proximity to, but distance from the ideals of the past.

This impression of general decline, of a progressive falling away from the past, is overlaid on a pattern of renaissance and revival, in which the greatest Italian and French masters have partly recuperated classical forms from the obscurity of their own ruins. As ancient examples demonstrate the failings of the present, their recovery also speaks of their own revival and possible reconstruction, however partial and incomplete. The illustration of the sepulcher at Terracina, for instance, has been re-imagined through a draft of its *"Vestigia* and footsteps," which are "yet extant," and which have been "discovered and (as one may say) disinterr'd ... (for 'twas almost buried amongst the brambles of a wild and uncultivated place" by the mid sixteenth-century architect and draftsman Pirro Ligorio (34). Here, architecture has been imaginatively resurrected in modern times from the obscurity of "a wild and uncultivated place," which, as we will see, Fréart imagined as representing a wild and uncultivated period in history. This word play on the etymological meaning of "vestiges," (footprints) along with the imagery of loss and disinterment recalls Fréart's epistle to the reader, where he claims that his *"Canons and Rules"* are drawn from "instances ... among the *Vestigia*'s and footsteps of the most flourishing ages" (5). Here, as well, these "instances" speak simultaneously of a wild and uncultivated historical interlude: "so many ages of ignorance have pass'd over us, especially in the Arts of *Architecture*, and *Painting*, which the Warr, and frequent inundations of *Barbarians* had almost extinguish'd in the very Country of their *Originals*" (2). Yet the subsequent insistence on their recent recovery resists Fréart's pervasive emphasis on their modern devolution. These arts, he says, "were in a manner new born again but a few years since, when those great Modern *Masters, Michael Angelo*, and *Raphael*, did as it were raise them from the Sepulchers of their antient ruins, under which, these poor *sciences* lay buri'd" (2).

For Fréart, as later for Evelyn, architectural history writes political history; and this double sense of time, of revival and decay, reflects Fréart's assessment of his nation's historical moment and of his own lamentable patronless state. Architectural history both generates and is generated by a history of political ruptures. In Fréart's view, these ruptures had yet to be repaired. Fréart's work promotes architecture's monumental function, understanding it in terms both aesthetic and antiquarian, by claiming that it preserves the human stories of rulers, benefactors, and events. Trajan's Column, for example, "one of the most superb remainders of the *Roman* magnificence ... has more immortaliz'd the Emperour *Trajan* then all the *Penns* of *Historians*." In this artifact, "[i]t was *Architecture* her self which was ... the *Historiograph* ... and who since it was to celebrate a *Roman*, chose none of the *Greek Orders*" (88).

Fréart's treatise mimics the monumental function of architecture itself: it is presented as a memorial to a patron who had recently died, Fréart's own cousin, Sublet de Noyers. In addition, shortly before his death, de Noyers had lost his political influence and retired from public life due to the death of Cardinal Richelieu in 1640. The dedicatory epistle of the *Parallèle* is largely a biography of de Noyers, which focuses especially on his public works and, as is appropriate to the subject of the treatise, extensively on his patronage of architecture. For instance, Fréart attributes to him the "conservation ... and absolute restauration" of the Louvre and the Palace of Fountainebleau, which "but for him ... had been ... but one vast ruine, a very Carkass of building, desolate, and uninhabitable" (A 3 r). In addition to being associated with other magnificent structures ("The Castles of *S. Germains* and *Versailles*") he is praised for his skill in military architecture: "All our *Frontiers* are full of his Works" (A 3 r). Even the church where he is buried is a visible byproduct of his character: "his body being transported to the *Church* of the *Noviciat* ... which he had built in honour of St. *Xavieris*, and destin'd for his *Sepulchre*. This *Church* is look'd upon as the most regular piece of *Architecture* in *Paris*" (A 4 v). De Noyers's political fall and death are equally legible in architectural terms:

> But during all these mighty *Projects*, there happen'd a strange revolution which in less then six Monehts changed the whole face of the *State*, by the death of that superlative *Minister* the great *Cardinal de Richelieu*, the very *Column* and Ornament of *Monarchy* ... by the *Recess* of *Monseigneur de Noyers* ... We then presently beheld the work of the *Louvre* abandoned, the finishing of the great *Gallery* to cease; and generally all the *Fortifications* in *France*, without hopes of seeing the Work reassumed and taken in hand again of a long time. (A 4 r)

Fréart's description of Richelieu as "the very *Column* and Ornament of *Monarchy*" mixes architectural and political terminology; the state is represented as an architectural construction, supported by the very structural element (the column) with which Fréart's treatise is wholly concerned. Fréart thus generates both biography and political history through an assessment of France's architecture, with the features of one both revealing and creating the features of the other.

For Fréart, the Renaissance both had and hadn't already happened. Moments of both aesthetic and political recovery are wistfully distanced from the stagnation of the present moment, either remembered as part of an idealized history or projected into a conditional future. On the one hand, Fréart credits Raphael and Michelangelo with raising the arts "from the Sepulchers of their antient ruins" and claims, "We have had fresh experience of this under the *Reign* of *Francis* the first" (3). On the other hand, when Fréart was writing, Raphael, Michelangelo, and Francis I had all been dead for approximately a century. As we might expect, given Fréart's emphasis on architecture as a product of patronage, revival might be achieved only through the agency of the present French aristocrats who were poor replacements for de Noyers and his contemporaries, at least in their appreciation of architecture and aesthetics. Could French "*Grandees*... devest themselves of... prejudice and disdain" towards the arts in general and architecture in particular, "there would be great hopes we should yet see them reflourish, and be born again as 'twere from *New* to *Antique* (3). It is characteristic of Fréart's sense of time that progress is a process of return and building a process of repairing what has been lost. Architecture can only move forward by moving back, in his view, and its history is created by being undone: "born again as 'twere from *New to Antique*." The traces of antiquity are faint but legible, relinquished but partly recovered. Progress is a process of regression, and the future becomes accessible by treading exactly in the footsteps of the past.

In his own dedicatory material, and in his "Account of Architects and Architecture," Evelyn adopts Fréart's sense of an architectural history that plays out in contrapuntal strains of construction and decay, as well as the idea that architectural history is a means of recounting human and political history. Evelyn, however, reorients Fréart's timeline; far from being cordoned off from Restoration England, the Renaissance is in the process of happening, and it is representative of the Restoration in multiple ways. To repair is also to build, as the dilapidated remnants of pre-interregnum England are rescued from the ruins of England's own recent wild and uncultivated age. Many of the buildings Evelyn lists as examples of Charles's works resemble the Renaissance examples of Fréart's treatise in that they carry connotations of both newness and antiquity, emblemizing both the king's commitment to progress and his connection to an ancestral and national past: "what Your *Majesty* has so magnificently design'd and carried on at that Your antient *Honour* of *Green-wich* . . . those Splendid *Apartments*, and other useful Reformations for *security* and *delight*, about your *Majesties* Palace at *White-Hall*," along with the "care, and preparation for Saint *Paul's*, by the impiety and iniquity of the late confusions almost *Dilapidated*" (a 3 r).

Among these many achievements, however, remain corruptions and obscurities that have yet to be corrected, and, as at the sepulcher near Terracina, part of the work of the translation will be to demonstrate the failings of the present. Like Fréart, Evelyn projects the possibilities of a conditional future, but for him, it will be built upon a moment that has already begun. Moreover, Evelyn's view of architectural progress is actually progressive, a rebirth from antique to new rather than new to antique: "You well know," he writes in the dedication to Sir John Denham, "that all the mischiefs and absurdities in our modern *Structures* proceed chiefly from our busie and *Gotic* triflings in the *Compositions* of the *Five Orders*," a fault that the treatise will make apparent: "from the noblest *Remaines* of *Antiquity* accurately *Measur'd*, and perspicuously *Demonstrated*, the *Rules* are lay'd down; and from a solid, judicious, and mature comparison of *modern Examples*, their *Errours* are detected" (*b v). Similarly, in the "Account," Evelyn expresses a conservative view, introducing architecture as a "useful *Art*," which, "having been first deriv'd to us from the *Greeks*, we should not without infinite ingratitude either slight, or innovate those *Tearms* which it has pleased them to impose upon the particular *Members* and *Ornaments* belonging to the several *Orders*" (115). This passage sounds like a return to Fréart, who claims in his epistle to the reader that he will not "broach *Novelties*" but rather "would (were it possible) ascend even to the very sourse of the *Orders* themselves" (2). Not surprisingly, for Fréart, renewal does not involve newness at all, and this ascension is underwritten by the fantasy—"were it possible"—of regressing in time. But as the "Account" goes on, Evelyn transforms the orders from the inaccessible origins of what will never be perfectly recovered to the accessible origins of what might be swiftly achieved. He calls for some "industrious Person" to "oblige the *Nation* with a through examination of what has already been written . . . and in what shall be found most beneficial for our *Climat* . . . and advance upon the *Principles* already establish'd, and not so acquiesce in them as if there were a *Non Ultra* Engraven upon our *Columns* like those of *Hercules*, after which there remained no more to be discovered" (118–119). Fréart specifically disparages such excuses for change, dismissing as "vain and frivolous reasonings" the arguments that "*Art* is an infinite thing, growing every day to more perfection, and suiting it self to the humor of the several *Ages*, and *Nations*" (2). For Evelyn, however, the orders are allowed to become what they never were before, not isolated relics that gesture to the wholeness of an idealized past, but the boundary where innovation will meet history. They point at once toward the classical world (the columns of Hercules) and to new, foreign worlds in which they will continue to arrive.

In appropriating these assumptions, Evelyn himself imports the foreign novelties of a recent French treatise, but he also recuperates and recollects earlier English approaches to architectural writing. There are, of course, significant differences between Evelyn and the earlier writers: for Leland and Camden, the urgency of attending to architecture was produced in part by the recognition that it might disappear, and neither of these writers idealized the ages of Romans or monasteries in the same way that Fréart longed for inaccessible ancients or the more recent tenure of Sublet de Noyers. Still, in its emphasis on the authority of architectural fragments as a means of reconstructing historical narrative, the *Parallèle* mirrors antiquarian interest in England's architectural remains. A closer connection between the English writers and Fréart occurs in the idea that architectural history is a history of patronage—in the forms of expenditure and ownership—and that it records the stories of builders—in the sense of owners and patrons—at least as effectively as it preserves the traces of designers and architects. Just as items in a virtuoso's collection might reconcile antiquity and novelty by placing old artifacts or fragments in new physical and functional contexts, Evelyn's translation reconciles history with newness, enlisting older modes of English architectural literacy in the service of promoting an aesthetic system that, despite its antiquity, would have appeared new to many English viewers. And because it relies on the connection between architectural and human history, Evelyn's translation of the *Parallèle* becomes a piece of Restoration political historiography, reflecting the simultaneous process of building and repairing that underwrote the very notion that a Restoration was possible at all.

Like Renaissance aesthetic styles, the monarchy itself was both new and old in 1664, and Evelyn discerns in the progression from classical to Gothic to Renaissance aesthetic styles an analogy for England's own recent architectural history, and, by extension and implication, its political history. The aesthetic time line put forward in Fréart's treatise is thus resettled over a new set of architectural examples, which, in turn, are read as reflections of a new set of political conditions. England's arts, Evelyn could reasonably claim, had, within his generation's memory, suffered at the hands of England's own barbarians, who are invoked several times in his dedication to the king and are distilled in his argument that Charles "*Built* and *Repair'd* more in *three* or *four* Years . . . than all Your *Enemies* have destroy'd in *Twenty*," and that his "care" of St. Paul's would correct the "impiety and iniquity of the late confusions" (a 2 v – a 3 r). Later, he commends the king for having "so prosperously guided this giddy *Bark* through such a *Storm*," like "those glorious *Hero's* of old, who first brought Men out of *Wildernesses*" (a 3 v, a 4 r). And yet, both political and architectural histories are also stories of return. It is to this "chas[ing]" of "*Barbarity*" that "*Architecture* . . . ows her *renascency* amongst *Us* . . . and to as many of those *Illustrious* Persons as by their large and magnificent *Structures* transcribe your Royal *Example*" (a 4 r). In the dedication to Sir John Denham, Evelyn similarly views architecture as a reflection of government, and he describes both as being in a period of renaissance and renewal. In the very process of emerging from a historical and cultural wilderness, London recalls ancient Rome: "They were not a foolish or impolitick *People*, who from the very *Principles* of *humanitie*, destin'd for the ease of their *Subjects*, so many spacious *Waies*, cool *Fountains*, shady *Walks*, refreshing *Gardens*, and places of publick *Recreation*, as well as stately *Temples*, and *Courts* of *Justice*, that *Religion* and the *Laws* might be published with the more *pomp* and *veneration*" (*b 2 r). This past-tense description of a vanished city is quickly reoriented to point toward the present, as Evelyn collapses ancient Rome under contemporary London, reattributing the architectural and civic machinery of a past cultural moment to his own surroundings and his own royal dedicatee: "And if his *Majesty* . . . hath contributed to *something* of *all* this, it is *that* for which the whole *Nation* becomes obliged; as the promoting of such *publick* and *useful* Works (and especially that of *Building*) a certain Indication of a *prudent Government*, of a *flourishing* and *happy People*" (*b 2 r–v).

This constant balance of return and progression, of loss and recuperation, directly reflects aspects of Restoration political thought. As George Southcombe and Grant Tapsell point out, early legislation conceived of the Restoration in ways that relied on both memory and a willingness to forget, a sense that the reign of Charles II was both completely contiguous with pre-interregnum history and rested on a correction of the traumatic political disruptions that had immediately preceded it. On the one hand, Southcombe and Tapsell write, "it was to be as if the civil war and interregnum had never happened"; on the other "minds were not wiped blank.... The past indelibly affected the present: the major political issues, the political languages used; and the political and religious decisions taken; all of these things bore the marks of the experiences that had preceded 1660."[17] In 1660, the Act of Oblivion was passed, "to bury all Seedes of future Discordes and remembrance ... as well in His [Charles II's] owne Breast as in the Breasts of His Subjects one towardes another."[18] In the same year however, an act was passed with the purpose of enshrining the king's return—and, by extension, the memory of his absence—in public consciousness; it demanded that subjects celebrate "his Majestyes late most wonderfull glorious peaceable and joyfull Restauration to the actuall possession and exercise of his undoubted hereditary Soveraigne Regall Authority over them" annually in "some usuall Church Chappell or place where such publique thankgivings and praises to Godes most Divine Majesty shall be rendered." The proclamation figures the king's return as a kind of political renaissance, because the celebration and thanksgivings are to take place on May 29 "the most memorable Birth day not onely of his Majesty both as a man and Prince but likewise as an actual King, and of this and other His Majesties Kingdomes all in a great measure new borne and raised from the dead."[19]

Like Evelyn himself, then, political language imagined the Restoration as a project of both building—a new order raised on the foundations of oblivion—and repairing—a project of remembering and re-assembling historical fragments to restore a government that could be described as being born and reborn, something constructed from the strategic and ordered recreation of public memory. In the *Declaration at Breda*, addressed by Charles to the House of Peers in 1660, the king represented himself as a "healer," to use Keeble's term: "If the generall Distraction and Confusion which is spread over the whole Kingdome, doth not awaken all men to a desire and longing, that those wounds which have so many yeers together been kept bleeding, may be bound up, all We can say will be to no purpose."[20] His choice of figure, a binder of open wounds, corresponds obliquely to the *Parallel*'s representation of architectural progress as a process of realignment, a redressing of historical ruptures and the reassembly of a broken body of work. But both architectural treatise and contemporary political language rely on a worrying of those wounds through their constant recourse to memories of brokenness, their emphases on temporal, political, or material fragmentation. We cannot help but feel that, for both Evelyn and Charles II, whatever the efficacy of healing a wound, there remained an important commemorative value in the scar.

On a more practical level, Fréart's method of writing architectural history as a history of politics and patronage helped Evelyn to accomplish two goals. First, it allowed him to call for new patrons of the architectural styles Fréart's treatise promoted. Second, it provided a solution to an older problem in the history of English architectural writing, that of the "foreign architect" (to use Marvell's phrase), who interfered with the close identification among architecture, landowner, and land (see Chapter 2).[21] Put simply, in a historiographic and descriptive tradition that proceeded primarily through the articulation of these relationships, there was no room for the role of the professional architect. Buildings were legible as historical and ancestral documents, not as statements of an architect's technical or professional skill. This problem of the professional architect had equally confronted Henry Wotton when he wrote *The Elements of Architecture* forty years earlier (see Chapter 2). Wotton had negotiated the difficulty by conflating the figures of patron and architect, allowing the gentleman amateur to occupy the place of the practically and theoretically skilled professional. This maneuver seems to have served Wotton's purposes by helping to secure the aristocratic patronage that would soon gain him the lucrative provostship of Eton College. To a certain extent, Evelyn took the same tack. When he referred to Charles as a "builder," for instance, he was using conventional language that applied this term to the person who commissioned and paid for a building, rather than to the person who designed it or to those who actually built it.

Evelyn's goals, however, were far broader than Wotton's, and they forced the development of a different strategy, an elevation of the architectural profession that would somehow not impinge on the status of the patrons he hoped also to attract. In the front matter of the *Parallel* as well as in his later plans for the rebuilding of London, he displays an interest in civic improvement, urban planning, and public works of a sort that seems never to have crossed Wotton's mind.[22] As Surveyor of the King's Works, Denham may have exemplified for Evelyn the gentleman amateur's limitations in accomplishing such projects. According to Colvin,

Denham's appointment to the office of Surveyor "can only be explained in terms of personal favour to a deserving Royalist" who "had given many proofs of his loyalty since the day in 1642 when, as sheriff of Surrey, he had rashly but gallantly attempted to hold Farnham Castle against Waller." Nevertheless, Denham had been preferred over Jones's assistant John Webb, "by far the most experienced architect then to be found in England."[23] In 1661, Evelyn disagreed with Denham over the siting of the new royal palace at Greenwich and "came away, knowing Sir John to be a better *Poet* than *Architect*, though he had Mr. Webb (*Inigo Jone's* Man) to assist him."[24] In his dedication to Denham, Evelyn does admire Denham's work in paving "the ruggedness" of London's "unequal *Streets*," an act which, he rather desperately extrapolates, contributed to the "*beauty* of the *Object*, the *ease* of the *Infirme*, the *preserving* of both the *Mother* and the *Babe*; so many of the *fair-Sex* and their *Off-spring* having *perish'd* by *mischances*" (*b 2 r). However public spirited Denham might have been, Evelyn's praises do not really seem to fit the subject matter of the treatise itself, so wide is the gap between the practical action of paving streets and the sophisticated appreciation of the aesthetic principles that Fréart's assembled columns are intended to convey.

Undeniably, the kind of aesthetic innovations promoted in Evelyn's "Account" were not derived from the work of civic minded amateurs such as Denham but from that of professional architects whose names were then—and are now—often known. Indeed, to readers of the earlier architectural literature discussed in this book—the *Britannia*, the country house poems, and *The Elements of Architecture*, for instance—one of the most striking features of both Evelyn's diary and the *Parallel* is that they are studded with names, not only those of aristocratic owners or dedicatees, but of painters, sculptors, and architects. In the expanded 1707 edition of the "Account," he mentions in particular "the *Banqueting-House* built at *White-Hall* by *Inego Jones* after the Antient manner; or . . . what his *Majesties* present *Surveyor* Sir *Christopher Wren* has lately advanc'd at St. *Paul's*."[25] Fréart's treatise provided a logical ground for the celebration of such important figures and works, because it illustrates the aesthetic and intellectual underpinnings of their art. Fréart extols the skill of architects in the front matter of the work, lamenting a general aristocratic "disdain" for the "*Arts*, and . . . those who apply themselves unto them" (3). Moreover, most of the authors he abstracts and catalogs were practicing architects.

Both Fréart and Evelyn, however, constantly walk the line between promoting the architectural profession and subverting its utility to the authority of aristocratic patrons. In part, Fréart accomplishes this by decrying modern abuses; it is not the nature of the architectural profession itself but the shortcomings of its current practitioners which demote its status: "have we at this present any reason in the World to call those *three* by the name of *Orders*, viz. *Dorique, Ionique,* and *Corinthian*, which we daily behold so disfigur'd, and ill treated, by the *Workmen* of this age?" (3). In the "Account," Evelyn takes a less derogatory approach, building a balance between architect and patron into the very definition of his terms. Wotton diverted the role of the architect toward the glorification of the patron by collapsing the terms of architect and patron, creating one less position in Vitruvius's three-part hierarchy of patron, architect, and superintendent; and in his dedication to Charles, Evelyn uses the same strategy when he insists that Charles is himself a skilled "*Builder*," who can not only "pertinently... *discourse* of the *Art*, but judiciously... *contrive*" (a 2 r, a 3 v). In the "Account," by contrast, he splits the position of the architect into two roles that, he says, share equally in the creation of a building. One, the "*Architectus Ingenio*" or "*Superintendent*" is a practically and intellectually skilled professional who brings to the project both a "judicious *head*" and a "skilful *hand*," and who is responsible for attending to the "three *transcendencies*" of building: strength, utility, and beauty (117). Evelyn borrows his account of the architect's training (like his list of the "three *transcendencies*") from Vitruvius, enumerating the same impressive list of accomplishments that ought to contribute to his education.[26] The architect must be "*docil* and *ingenious*," "*literate*," "Skilful in *designing* and *drawing*," as well as in geometry, optics, arithmetic, history, philosophy, medicine, law, and astrology (116). The architect, he insists, is no "commonly illiterate *Mechanick*... but the Person who *Superintends* and *Presides* over him with so many advantages" (117). Even in placing the architect at the nexus of the design and construction processes, however, Evelyn is careful not to obscure the patron's role. To the figure of the *Architectus Ingenio* he adds the "*Architectus Sumptuarius*," the person with "a full and overflowing *Purse*: Since he who bears *this* may justly also be styled a *Builder*, and that a *master one* too." It is *this* architect for whom, if not by whom, a building is constructed, "indeed the *primum mobile* which both begins and consummates all designs of this nature," and whom the finished building will emblemize (117). Despite Evelyn's reversion to Latin, *Architectus Sumptuarius* is not one of Vitruvius's terms. Vitruvius customarily refers to the patron as the lord or *dominus*, a word which does not, in itself, suggest the same sort of parallel between architect and patron as creators of a building.[27]

In the "Account," then, what begins as Evelyn's discussion and definition of the professional architect once again returns to an emphasis on the role of the patron. Even rhetorically, the architect does not eclipse his employer; he is only a means. Just as histories of the country house were pared down by Camden and the country house poets and strategically directed toward praise of the current landowner, Evelyn repeatedly drifts back toward stabilizing the authority of aristocratic "builders." In the subsequent paragraph of the "Account," for instance, he begins by suggesting that universities make room for architecture among the liberal arts, and he ends by explaining the benefits such educated professionals would offer the state, and the king as their patron. Evelyn imagines the king as an alternative form of superintendent, the employer and gatherer—even, perhaps, the collector—of artists and architects who will all, in their various media, "celebrate his *Majesty* by their works to posterity" (118). "[I]t is to be hoped," he writes, "that when his *Mojesty* [sic] shall perfect his Royal *Palace* of *White-Hall* . . . he will . . . destine some *Apartiments* for the ease and encouragement of the ablest Workmen in *this*, as in all other *useful, Princely,* and *Sumptuous* Arts . . . *Printers, Painters, Sculptors, Architects,* &c." In this project of aesthetic recruitment, the king would align himself with great European patrons: "*Francis the First, Henry the Fourth, Cosimo de Medices,* the *Dukes* of *Urbin,*" and Cardinal Richelieu, as well as with Augustus himself (118). Evelyn thus presents a model of patronage that allows for the production, employment, and appreciation of educated professionals but which absorbs their significance into the eminence of the patron. In this list, as elsewhere in the treatise, it is the names of rulers, not of architects, that buildings preserve.

In a treatise dedicated to a recently exiled and newly restored monarch, however, the traditional connections between architecture and aristocracy, or between building and patronage, required modification and adaptation to a new set of circumstances. Earlier English perceptions of architecture were heavily influenced by the chorographic history or estate survey and tended to unite architecture with human history by attaching them to a single place. As Marjorie Swann points out, these ties were weakened by the second half of the seventeenth century; "the cultural understanding of the English countryside as a site of hereditary landholding had decisively eroded, giving way to a new landscape of possessive individualism constituted by objects and their owners."[28] In an early manifestation of this problem, in John Stow's *Survey of London*, impressions of disorder and indeterminacy emerge as Stow confronts a post-Reformation cityscape where ownership, use, and financial control had, within Stow's own memory, rapidly changed. But the problems of geographical and historical disorder and disconnection were even more pressing in a narrative constructed around Restoration history, and for a writer praising the new reign of a recently exiled monarch who, within nearly everyone's memory, had been dispossessed of his own land. This disarticulation of land ownership and hereditary privilege had only been exacerbated by the interregnum. As Gary S. de Krey writes, "Sorting out the proper ownership of lands that had been confiscated or sold under duress during the civil wars and the Interregnum was [a] . . . troublesome issue for the Convention and for thousands of landed and tenant families. . . . More land had changed hands than at any time since the dissolution of the monasteries in the reign of Henry VIII."[29] In Fréart's *Parallèle*, as in Evelyn's additions to the treatise, topography no longer provides continuous narrative threads among patron, land, and architecture; and if Evelyn was to preserve or recollect the connection between architecture and history, he had to account for the breakdown of traditional associations and for the foreignness of the king's recent past. It is not coincidental, then, that the aesthetic styles the treatise promotes were themselves foreign. Softly trailing their classical histories behind them, they had been "transplant[ed]," as Fréart says "into a strange soile": first into the new historical framework of the Renaissance, and then, at Evelyn's hands, into the land of an English king (2). In the architectural forms of the Renaissance Evelyn discovered a parallel for his royal dedicatee. Both were supported by the authority of their lineage, but neither had entirely English roots.

In carrying Fréart's connections among architecture, Renaissance aesthetic styles, and enlightened patronage into his own dedicatory epistles and applying them to English architectural and political matter, Evelyn again threads the new through the old, arriving at an understanding of English architecture that might be called both antiquarian and classical, or both historical and aesthetic. It depended, at once, on storytelling and visual design, on building and repairing, and on reassembling the fragments of architectural and political history into a new—and orderly—unity. In the 1707 expansion of the "Account," Evelyn decried Gothic architecture as "*Monkish*" and "full of *Fret* and lamentable *Imagry*"; and in the dedication to Denham, he argued that England's current architectural irregularities revealed human flaws: "It is from the *asymmetrie* of our *Buildings*, . . . want of *decorum* and proportion in our *Houses*, that the irregularity of our *humors* and *affections* may be shrewdly discern'd" (*b 1 v).[30] Both observations rest on the assumption that architecture writes human history and character, but in the *Parallel* they are marshaled into the promotion of classical aesthetics, as reflected in the terms "*decorum*" "proportion," and "irregularity." It is this last move that turns what might have seemed a familiar antiquarian sensibility to a new end. But, in reading aesthetic qualities as the products of cultural history, in the first case, and of a nation's human characteristics, in the second, Evelyn also exploits the antiquarian possibilities of classical aesthetics.

Evelyn borrowed this intermingling of human and aesthetic stories from Fréart's own account of architectural history. The treatise's illustrations reflect a similar interpenetration of classical aesthetics and the antiquarian fragment. Part Palladian treatise and part virtuoso's cabinet, the *Parallèle* lays the process of construction over the representation of material fragmentation, and the effect is that the ideas and visual representation of order, decorum, and proportion are imperfectly accomplished through the reassembly of history's broken pieces. Building is once again understood as the strategic reparation of disorder. For Fréart, architectural history was visually recorded as a collection of foreign fragments, disarticulated from their original places and historical moments by time in general and by periods of political decline and disruption in particular. They were, he wrote, "almost extinguish'd in the very Country of their *Originals*" by "the Warr, and frequent inundations of *Barbarians*" (2). Derived from the dim embers of these "almost extinguish'd" classical examples, Renaissance interpretations of the orders are, in Fréart's view, anchored in antiquarian artifacts which point toward the absence of their own original sites. Fréart's illustration headings describe many of his antique examples as having been "drawn" from or "taken" (*tirés*) from structures that were already themselves in pieces. Like the English "draw," the French *tirer* carries both the senses of "to illustrate" and "to pull from." A few of the illustrations, like the sepulcher near Terracina, are reconstructions of complete structures. More often, though, the pictures preserve a sense of brokenness and incompleteness. As an example of the Ionic order, "The *Perspective* Elevation of a *Profile* drawn from the *Baths* of *Dioclesian* at *Rome*" is shown; and although Fréart's explication claims that the illustration is meant to "represent the *Idea* of an *Order*, and the effect which it produces being put in *Work*," this "*angle* or *coinage* of a return of a Wall" has been abstracted and apparently broken off from any complete idea of the building it once helped to support (42–43). Illustrations are further broken and interrupted by the interposition of Fréart's labels. The illustration of Trajan's column provides a similar example, as the column itself, along with the history its bas-relief figures represent, is broken in the middle by Fréart's identifier (93). Fréart doubtless broke up the columns for practical reasons, to enlarge the details and ornament of both capitals and bases. Nevertheless, this breakage, sometimes enhanced by the representation of cracks or slightly rough edges, also contributes to the sense of a history written through the realignment of fragments. Placed in the retrospectively arranged sequence of a newly recovered history and bounded by the neat edges of the boxes that frame them, the fragments are only partly reassembled to evoke a new "*Idea*" of what they had formerly been.

Fréart's illustration of modern authors gives a similar sense of fragmentation

Illustration of the Ionic order, taken from the Baths of Diocletian, from Roland Fréart, *Parallel of the Antient Architecture with the Modern*

and imperfect realignment that pulls against the simultaneous effects of symmetry, order, measure, and visual integrity. Each ancient artifact is allotted its own plate, but this is not true for Fréart's modern subjects. Instead, as visual accompaniments to his own comparative judgments, these illustrations literally measure one author's work up against another, as columns are sliced down the middle and placed beside mismatched halves, creating an imperfect mirror

Illustration of Trajan's Column, from Roland Fréart, *Parallel of the Antient Architecture with the Modern*

image. Columns are again broken in the middle and labels identifying their authors obtrude between capital and base. Ornamentation (or its absence) also differs from one side to another, as do the numbers that measure the proportion of each component. In some cases, the two halves appear nearly to complement each other, as with Palladio and Scamozzi on the Ionic, where "there is so great a resemblance 'twixt the *mouldings* and the *measures* of these two *Profiles*, that the difference is hardly considerable" (44). In others, they are more grossly mismatched, as in the subsequent illustration of Serlio and Vignola on the same order, where "the inequality of these two *Profiles* is so wide, that 'tis almost impossible to approve of them both" (46). Fréart's comparative illustrations thus do not make much sense if we attempt to imagine them as the structural elements of complete buildings. Nonetheless, these fragments of columns, neatly incised down the center, lined up against each other, measured, labeled, and framed, are arranged according to the aesthetic principles of symmetry, order, decorum, and proportion which they are meant, as a group, to teach. As a whole, then, the *Parallèle* assembles its sense of classical aesthetics from the wreckage of previous unities and presents the practice of building itself as a form of recollective historiography. To design is to remember, as much as to plan, to select, excise, reorder, and reassess, the traces of other architects and other historical moments. The treatise's aesthetic principles emerge from a species of antiquarian practice, from an understanding of architecture as judiciously constructed from the fragments of the past.

Like many of the collections Evelyn had viewed while abroad, and like those he himself assembled, Fréart's treatise compiles, or at least illustrates, a diverse set of antique and modern objects: drawings, books, material fragments. In many ways, the treatise recalls Swann's account of the seventeenth-century catalogue, a printed taxonomy of the items a collection contained. As much as the collection of material objects, the catalogue becomes a means of imagining the collector's identity through a constellation of objects, histories, and people.[31] Fréart's treatise likewise commemorates his relationship to influential political figures and documents his own activities and judgments as a collector. These emerge in his epistle to his brothers, where he reports exercising "great diligence to get made, and collect together . . . the most excellent *Antiquities*, as well in *Architecture* as *Sculpture*; the chief pieces whereof were two huge *Capitals*, the one of a *Column*, and the other of an angular *Pilaster* from within the *Rotunda*," along with "threescore and ten *Bas-reliefs* moulded from *Trajans Column*, and several other of particular *Histories*" (A 3 v). Evidence of his acquisitions is also shown, in the descriptions that accompany his illustrations. The Doric profile from the Baths of Diocletian, for instance, is said to have been selected from among "a good number of *draughts* which lye yet by me, all of them design'd in the same hand very neatly"; and later he wrote, "I have made a very curious and rare Collection of a certain Ornament which they call the *Fret*" (18, 110). The treatise is itself a collection of authors and examples, but it is also presented as a kind of catalogue, a direct product of the kind of collecting with which Evelyn would have been familiar.

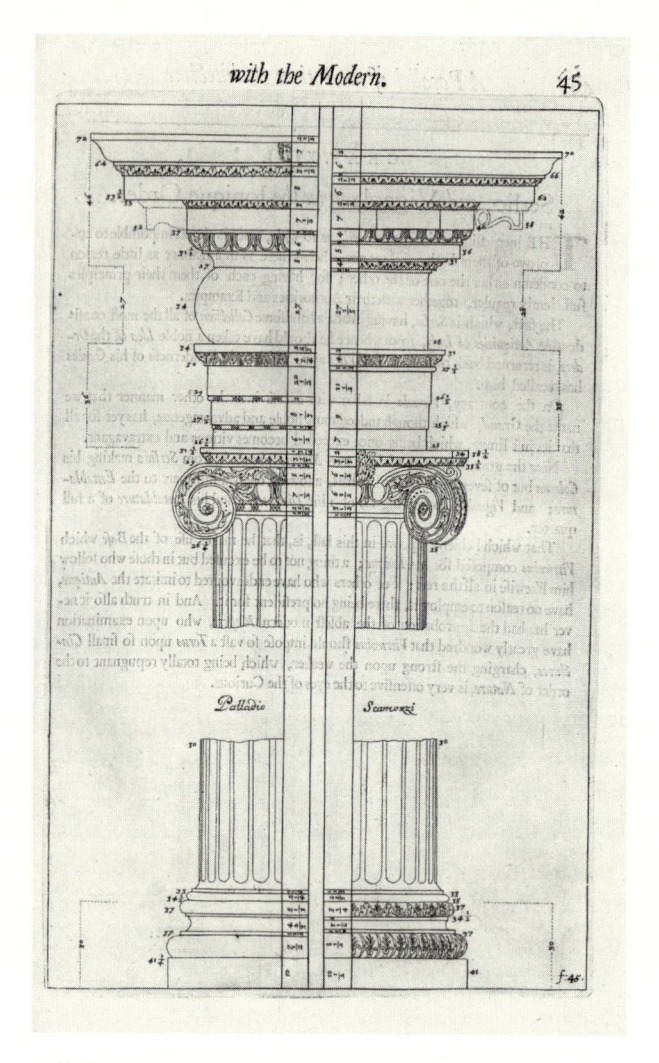

Palladio and Scamozzi on the Ionic order, from Roland Fréart, *Parallel of the Antient Architecture with the Modern*

The treatise foregrounds Fréart's own judgment and aesthetic refinement and anticipates those of his ideal reader; it is in the context of his commentary and discriminating assessments, rather than in the context of three dimensional structures, that the split columns of his comparative illustrations make sense. It is Fréart's arrangement that brings these mismatched halves into some kind of alignment. For instance, of Serlio and Vignola on the Ionic order, he says that, despite their "wide" differences, "there is . . . as little reason to condemn either one

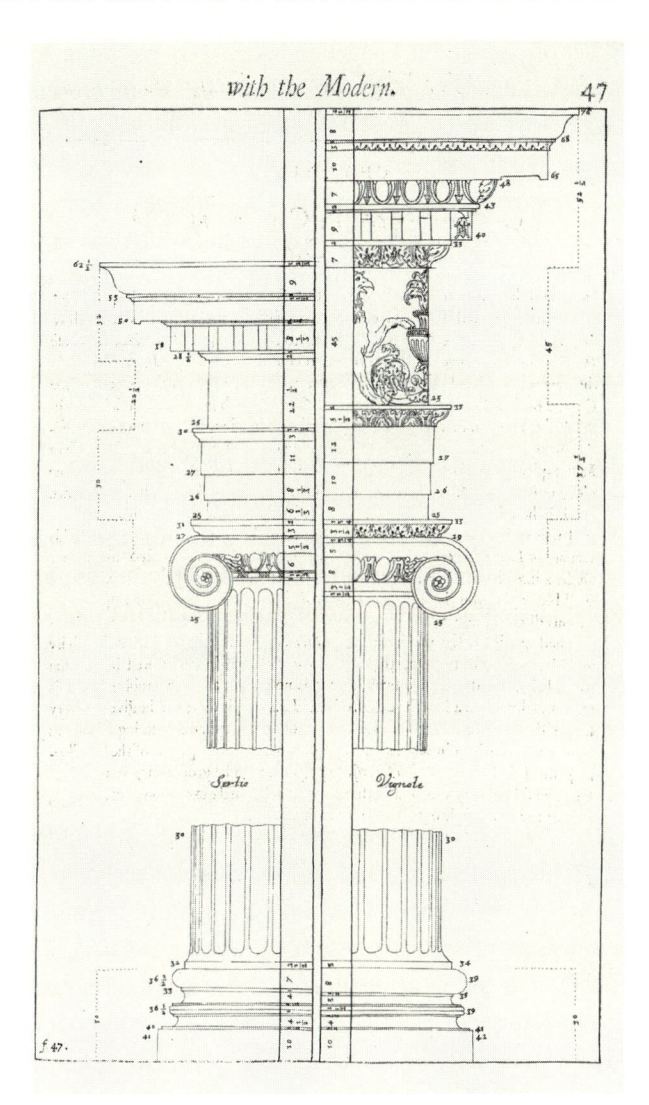

Serlio and Vignola on the Ionic order, from Roland Fréart,
Parallel of the Antient Architecture with the Modern

or the other ... having each of them their principles sufficiently regular, together with their Authorities and Examples," which he proceeds to enumerate (46). In these commentaries, Fréart plays the role of the curator or scholar, providing what Susan Pearce has described as "a degree of explication" that is "fundamental to our enhanced understanding" of both collected objects and the narratives we associate with them. To explicate the objects in a collection is to engage in "a rhetorical act of persuasion," which helps viewers "to make some kind of sense" of their relationship to the object and to the past and present narratives it implies.[32] For Fréart, the interpretation of a collection was indeed a dynamic process that occurred at the intersection of object, curator, and viewer. His idea of beauty was derived from antique examples, but he believed that it became evident only through the intervention of his explication, which was written to guide the "Masterly Eye" of the ideal observer: "For in these particulars our eyes do see no further then our understanding purges them, nor do their admirable beauties reveal themselves at once, nor to all the World in general; They will be curiously observed and discovered with industry" (91–92). In arranging and curating the authors and antique objects of his collection, then, Fréart projects ideas of both himself as connoisseur and collector and of the ideal reader, who will, through his guidance, be capable of understanding their worth.

To Evelyn the collector, one remarkable thing about Fréart's treatise would have been that it made architecture collectible. Architecture was not, on the face of it, particularly susceptible to the kind of antiquarianism that focused on the acquisition, importation, and preservation of objects. As we see in the *Britannia* and *A Survey of London*, one of the most reliable qualities of architecture is its tendency to disappear over time. In 1697, Evelyn would implicitly address this problem for collectors in *Numismata*, claiming that one benefit of collecting coins and medals is that "[t]hey present us with the most magnificent and stately Buildings that ever stood upon the Face of the Earth" and "afford us the Prospect of . . . Triumphal Arches, *Obelisks, Pyramids, Colossus*'s, and other Royal and Magnificent Fabrics of venerable Antiquity, long since collapsed and buried in their own Ruines; but from out of which, by *Reverses* and *Medals*, have almost all the antient Orders and Ornaments of Architecture (well near lost or corrupted) been much revived, restored, and vindicated from *Gothick* Barbarity."[33] Here, Evelyn makes architecture available to the virtuoso by transposing it from buildings, which were never intended to circulate, to coins and medals, which were designed to do precisely that. Fréart's treatise accomplishes the same: it makes architecture circulate. Through the representation and visual realignment of fragments and pieces, Fréart displaces and acquires what had seemed to be rooted in foreign or ancient soil. Of course, books are not buildings, and they did not literally make architecture circulate any more than coins or medals did. Yet, visually and rhetorically, the treatise suggests that buildings, as much as coins or more portable curious objects, might offer themselves to the virtuoso, who could construct with them a new orderliness from the disordered pieces of the past. In a collection, as Susan Stewart has written, "objects are naturalized into the landscape of the collection itself."[34] Architecture thus becomes an importable curiosity, transplanted from the soil into which it was physically anchored to the landscape of a new country and the alien prospect of foreign and modern eyes.

The *Parallel* thus allowed Evelyn and Fréart to enact a kind of self-presentation, as architecture revealed the designing and discriminating hand of the collector as much as that of the architect. But, as we have seen, in the *Parallel*, architecture also inscribed a history of politics and patronage which extended beyond the circumscribed "landscape" of the collection itself. I argue that the historiography of the virtuoso's collection presented particular opportunities for a post-Restoration English writer. Maintaining the notion that architecture was legible as history, the collection was nonetheless a form of history that was enabled, rather than threatened, by fragmentation and disintegration, brokenness and migration. Significantly, Stewart's description of the collection as an assemblage of objects in a new "landscape" resembles Jonathan Scott's account of Restoration political ideologies: "Since the causes of the troubles, and the substance of the revolution lay ... in ideas, it is not surprising that this reconstruction of the institutional fabric of the old order did not end them. Instead, it created a new context for them."[35] As Stewart notes, the objects in a collection maintain something of their own histories, while allowing for a newly calculated representation of the past: "The collection does not displace attention to the past; rather, the past is at the service of the collection."[36] A similar statement might be made of the monarchy; as Steven Zwicker writes, "the politics of the restored monarchy was harbinger of the new and remnant of the old."[37] Like the virtuoso's collection, or Renaissance architecture itself, the Restoration was not exactly a reconstruction of the past, but it depended on the selective redeployment of the remnants thereof. And it was precisely the incompleteness of those remnants, their elegiac gestures toward what no longer existed, which required the hand of a new collector, a new connoisseur to place them in a new context and, through this process of acquisition and discretion, to use them to make sense of history. Lamenting the death of de Noyers, Fréart presents his treatise as an artifact damaged by the disruptions of both politics and mortality. His original and whole idea of the work does not survive, he says, "since I have been forc'd to alter, and even retrench divers particularities which were then very essential to my designe, but would now have been altogether useless and unseasonable" (A 4 v). In its insufficiency, though, the treatise offers itself up to reappropriation and requires the meaning that will be conferred by a new collector and a new context: "Receive then (my dear *Brothers*) this *Fragment* of a *Book*, so much at least as remains of it," in order to see "if there occurr any thing which may prove yet considerable in such clear and discerning eyes as yours are, and that my designs seem worthy of any place amongst your other *curiosities*" (A4v). What had seemed irrelevant, lost, untimely, and "altogether useless and unseasonable" is made "worthy" by the discernment of a potential collector. It was this call, perhaps, that Evelyn himself took up when the *Parallèle* came to the notice of his "discerning eyes"; and he himself collected it, translating, transporting, and repackaging his acquisition for the benefit of a new patron in the person of a new king.

Despite the fact that the *Parallel* is mainly a translation, Evelyn's reframing of Fréart's elegy to antiquity does achieve an important shift from the original; Evelyn, much more than Fréart, looks forward as well as back. From this curatorial strand of historiography, Evelyn crafted his own brand of forward-looking antiquarianism, one that imagined both present and future through strategic recollection of the past. Notably, multiple critics have discerned a similar strategy in Evelyn's 1666 plans for the rebuilding of London. Cynthia Wall, for instance, writes that "all of Evelyn's plans . . . reveal a symbolic (and for that matter literal) underground sense of recovery and preservation . . . which in its own way testifies to Evelyn's ambivalence about the powerful potential of the new space and the implications for shaping it."[38] Sydney Perks likewise notes that "Evelyn worked to improve the City for traffic and at the same time to preserve the ancient sites and all that was of interest to an antiquarian."[39]

Stewart writes, "Once the object is completely severed from its origin, it is possible to generate a new series, to start again within a context that is framed by the selectivity of the collector."[40] Evelyn, however, had chosen a treatise in which architecture, like the monarchy, was only imperfectly severed from its past. For both Evelyn and Fréart, a return to those origins was impossible; for Evelyn, it was not desirable either. Nevertheless, the reordering and rearticulation of the present—the "new series" and the "new context"—were paradoxically enabled by loss. In dedicating the 1707 "Account" to Wren, Evelyn would describe St. Paul's Cathedral as the recuperation of a fragmented architectural and political history and would remember its "*Dilapidations*" even before the "*Dreadful Conflagration*" of 1666, "after it had been made a *Stable* of *Horses,* and a *Den* of *Thieves.*"[41] For Evelyn, though, Wren's works would achieve their greatest glory not at the moment they were completed—which in 1707 was still to come—but at the moment they might be remembered, appearing as shining remnants in some once-again-darkened world: "if the whole *Art* of *Building* were lost," Evelyn wrote, "it might be *Recover'd* and *found* again in St. *Paul's,* the *Historical Pillar,* and those other Monuments of Your Happy Talent and extraordinary *Genius*."[42] As John Leland had done more than a century before and as Anne Clifford did, Evelyn imagined a path for the future observer of both architecture and history. By Evelyn's time, however, the "vestigia," or footsteps, had changed. Lifted from the ruins of a post-Reformation landscape and imprinted on the artifacts of a foreign antiquity, they nonetheless laid out a map for a new virtuoso, who, recollecting the fragments of a dilapidated history, would follow in the footsteps of Evelyn's own most flourishing age.

CODA

St. Helen's Bishopsgate

Antiquarianism and Aesthetics in Modern London

On April 10, 1992, the church of St. Helen's Bishopsgate in the City of London was severely damaged by an Irish Republican Army bomb. The incident seemed to end an extraordinary run of luck: the medieval church, which had its roots in a thirteenth-century nunnery, had "miraculously" survived both the Great Fire of 1666 and the bombing raids of the Second World War, in which many of its neighbors had suffered significant damage.[1] Choosing to see this misfortune as an opportunity, the parochial council commissioned architect Quinlan Terry not only to restore the church to a safe and serviceable state but to redesign its interior in a way that better suited the needs and style of worship of its current congregation. Terry's plans were decried by conservationists, including the Victorian Society, English Heritage, and the Society for the Preservation of Ancient Buildings, for introducing changes that were too radical; and the designs did call for major modifications to the floor and roof, as well as the creation of a new gallery and the repositioning of many important funeral monuments and much interior woodwork and furniture. A vitriolic controversy followed, culminating in a Consistory Court hearing of nine days' length during June 1993. With one or two minor alterations, however, Terry's plans were accepted, and the present church reflects a fairly complete realization of his vision. "If you knew the 'pre-bomb' St Helen's," the introduction to the current guidebook reads, "you will see a great difference."[2] The result of this controversial renovation is a surviving and very explicit body of evidence—in the written records of the court hearing and in the material fabric of the church itself—about the varying ways in which architecture might continue to be perceived and understood. It is with both the controversy surrounding these alterations and the design of the finished church that I am concerned here.

This Coda traces the persistence of an approach to interpreting architecture that we might call antiquarian or historical alongside methods that emphasize aesthetic concerns. As a group, the authors explored in this book raise questions about how a literary or historical text might be informed by its architectural setting and how architecture ought to be understood, evaluated, and designed. The story of St. Helen's demonstrates the continued relevance and urgency of these questions; the church is an example of their influence on modern perceptions and discussions of English architecture and, in this case, I argue, on its material fabric and design. As we have seen, these questions themselves have a long history. The debates over the new St. Helen's are embedded in the needs and priorities of a late-twentieth-century church and its congregation, but they might be positioned lineally, as much as laterally, and be read as a recent manifestation of a long historiographic and literary tradition. Contextualized in both contemporary and historical terms, the story of St. Helen's can provide a hinge between early modern subjects and ongoing scholarly conversations about architectural interpretation and historiography.

In 1993, Quinlan Terry was an established architect with strong convictions. Associated with the approach called New Classicism, he had publicly expressed his disdain for both Victorian and modernist architecture, vehemently preferring Georgian architecture instead.[3] His commitment to the style is not merely aesthetic; famously, he professes to believe that the proportions of the classical orders were communicated by God to Moses for use in the Tabernacle before being opportunistically hijacked by the pagan cultures of Greece and Rome: "the *visual form* of the building in which the one true God was to be worshipped, could not be left to the vain imagination of man; so a detailed description was given to Moses." The "appearance of Classical buildings," he writes, "*does something to people.*" He continues, "I can only explain the phenomenon of the Classical orders as a direct consequence of the fact that first and foremost they were ordained to contain the visible manifestation of human worship of the only true God."[4] For these beliefs, architectural critic Ian Martin has written, "Quinlan Terry is widely held to be barking mad."[5] It is not surprising, then, that the renovated St. Helen's Bishopsgate reflects elements of classical design. The interior is "wide open, light and airy," writes Claire Melhuish.[6] Funeral tablets accent white, lime-washed walls, and insofar as is possible, they are symmetrically and evenly arranged. White Doric pillars support the west gallery, and dark wooden beams accent a white plaster ceiling. Clear glass windows have replaced most

Redesigned interior of St. Helen's Bishopsgate, London, looking east along the north wall, with the altar and its reredos visible through the middle arch

of the medieval and Victorian stained glass that had been in the church, most of which had been damaged by the bomb.[7] While such elements as clear glass windows, white ceilings, Doric pillars, and lime-washed walls are not confined to classical or Georgian styles, it is plausible to suggest, in Terry's case, that a conscious reference to these models played some role in their selection.

Also, however, the new church is clearly influenced by the very historical concerns that opponents accused Terry of disregarding. Ashley Barker, an architect and expert consultant in the preservation of historic buildings, testified that the new church design retained many features that would be of interest and "delight to the historians and amateurs of architecture in subsequent years."[8] While detractors called the new scheme a "return to a notional architectural plan ... of the

Redesigned interior of St. Helen's Bishopsgate, London, showing the west gallery, Jacobean doorcase, and organ

early 18th century," Terry's designs place the historical features of the church on display.[9] "His approach," as Sheila Cameron, a lawyer specializing in ecclesiastical law, described it, was "to retain as many as possible of the internal features of the church, even though numerous items would be moved and repositioned elsewhere."[10] The result is that, like many old English churches, St. Helen's continues to present its viewer with a series of odd chronological juxtapositions: a fifteenth-century arcade, a thirteenth-century doorway, an early-sixteenth-century sepulcher which doubled as a nuns' squint (designed so that sick or occupied nuns could still see the elevation of the host, even when they could not attend the service), a seventeenth-century doorcase and pulpit, a modern immersion baptistery. The notable collection of funeral monuments—wall plaques, floor slabs, tomb chests, and a canopied sepulcher—represents the late fourteenth through the nineteenth centuries.[11] Barker summed up his testimony to the Consistory Court with the remark, "Mr Terry has demonstrated how the ancient and modern elements of the existing building [will] be preserved in the new design."[12]

In his own defense, Terry testified, "It is sometimes said that I specialise in Classical architecture to the exclusion of all other styles. This is not entirely true. ... I have always felt that the enduring character of English architecture is neither classic nor Gothic, but the combination of the two."[13] Terry's remark sug-

Northeast corner of redesigned interior of St. Helen's Bishopsgate, London, showing tomb chest of Sir Thomas Gresham, nuns' squint behind it, and wall plaques from several centuries

gests that the conflict over the new church design centered on incompatible aesthetic preferences, but this seems not entirely—or even mainly—to have been the case. In fact, it emerged from the incompatibility of two different modes of architectural literacy: one in which architecture was valued for its capacity to record history, and one in which it was perceived as a visual work of art designed and engineered through the skill of an architect. The historical approach to architecture, which Terry was accused of ignoring, is a direct descendent of post-Reformation antiquarian writing such as Camden's *Britannia* and John Stow's *Survey of London*. As we have seen, churches and funeral monuments were of special antiquarian interest, and George Herbert, in "The Church-porch," recognized the role of the parish church as a site that recorded and witnessed the human stories of a local community. In addition, as it did in the architectural

View of redesigned St. Helen's Bishopsgate, London, looking from the south transept toward the north wall, showing a nineteenth-century chancel screen, wall monuments from various periods, and a thirteenth-century doorway

works of Anne Clifford, antiquarianism seems to anticipate itself by becoming an actual principle for the design or modification of buildings. It was not simply that architectural evidence might sponsor and shape the historical narratives extracted by antiquarian writers or viewers; for Terry's detractors, as for Anne Clifford, such narratives provided a blueprint that ought to shape the production of the architecture itself.

Moreover, as I have shown, questions about the way architecture should be interpreted and understood—historically or visually—date back to the country house poems of the seventeenth century, and, in its balance of these perceptions and of classical aesthetics with antiquarian sensibilities, the St. Helen's project resembles that of John Evelyn, when he selected and translated the *Parallèle* of Roland Fréart. Visually, in fact, the church bears some loose resemblance to Fréart's illustrations, as architectural fragments with their own histories are collected, realigned, and neatly put on display within the church. Stemming from these conflicting modes of literacy, there emerged in the controversy over St. Helen's a similar anxiety or disagreement about the agency and obtrusion of the architect in the design of a building highly valued by some for the historical information it conveyed.

Terry's assertion of his interest in Gothic architecture as an aesthetic style did not quite address the objections of his opponents; it was not really Gothic style in itself that they seem to have been anxious about preserving, and the word "Gothic" rarely comes up in their testimony or written objections. Instead, their descriptions of the old church building as "accretive" or "historical" reveal the antiquarian underpinnings of their perspective; these are words that might be used to describe the perspective of antiquarian chorographers.[14] A church building, in this view, ought to be designed—or, more accurately, be allowed to develop—so that it can offer itself up to these methodologies, representing visually the interests and activities of an antiquarian viewer. These modern descriptions of the church remain rooted not in enthusiasm for a particular aesthetic style but in the history of the church's fabric itself and the stories it tells. In Stow's *Survey*, London architecture is seen to have disrupted and challenged a particular kind of antiquarian narrative that was threaded along continuous strands of ancestry, ownership, and occupation. By the late twentieth century, historians of London architecture registered such evidence of historical change as a distinctive virtue that enriched the value of this ancient City of London church. And it was this antiquarian approach, not Gothic style, against which Terry ultimately found himself arguing, complaining to the Consistory Court in his "Proof of Evidence," "There has been much criticism of the proposals from the narrow perspective of history. It is significant that there has been no criticism or reservations expressed on aesthetics."[15] In summation, he asserted that the two concerns are not necessarily at odds with each other, a point which he believed was proved by his design: "The rich palimpsest of history will remain and take its place in this new work."[16]

Terry's opponents implied that, as a "wholesale dispersal, reassembly and reordering of parts," the new church design disrupted a certain kind of integrity or wholeness; but the whole that was compromised was clearly historical, not visual or aesthetic.[17] Even before it was bombed, St. Helen's was a fragmented building. Not surprisingly for an ancient London structure, the pre-bomb church appears to have been its own strange anthology. Much like a page from Stow's *Survey*—and it does have a page there—the church preserved fragmented narratives from multiple periods, patrons, and occupants.[18] Because it had remained a church after the Reformation, St. Helen's recorded some degree of institutional continuity, but it also spoke of the changes within that institution. The church's distinctive double nave and chancel for instance—which remain today—are remnants of the nuns' quire, which was originally separated from the main sanctuary of the church, while the Jacobean pulpit reflected a new emphasis on preaching following the Reformation. Wooden chancel screens designed by the celebrated Victorian church restorer J. L. Pearson, along with a lowered and gradated floor creating a series of steps to the chancel and altar, were the visible byproducts of a nineteenth-century Tractarian style of worship that Terry and the church's rector, the Reverend Richard Lucas, found incompatible with the church's current emphasis on a "preaching ministry."[19]

At least one of Terry's supporters found this concatenation of periods and styles displeasing, but it was precisely this historical inclusiveness that preservationists would cite as the building's greatest virtue. "From the architectural point of view," correspondent John Norman wrote to Gordon Watkins, secretary of the Diocesan Advisory Council, "the present layout is lopsided and ugly and makes little visual sense. [Terry's] proposals ... would restore a feeling of spatial unity which is currently missing."[20] It was not spatial unity, though, with which detractors were concerned. During the Consistory Court hearings, architect John Russell Sell, a member of the Society for the Preservation of Ancient Buildings, argued, "The possible need for change has to be balanced against the undoubted importance of St Helen's as an historic building." At the same time, he asserted, "St Helen's is an example of a building whose character derives to a very large extent from change." Sell seems to have been urging that the process of change itself be visibly preserved, and in Terry's design, he argued, "the history of the building [was] denied and its accretive character destroyed by the damage scale and thorough-going nature of the proposed new interior."[21] Similarly, Terry opponent Sophie Andreae protested in a letter to Watkins that the church's "development over many centuries" had been "incremental." "Its unique qualities," she wrote, "derive to a very large extent precisely from its 'palimpsest' nature.... What is proposed now is not the addition of another layer but a stripping back of historic layers."[22] Andreae's implication that an ideal repair would constitute "the addition of another layer" suggests that for her, antiquarianism becomes not only a mode of interpretation but the basis of architectural practice. The architect's goal, in such a case, would be to preserve items of antiquarian interest and to anticipate this interest through "addition." Put differently, the architect should respect the accretion of historical narrative and add a new page to the story. In another letter to Watkins, Hermione Hobhouse expressed the opinion that the new design should not violate "the antiquarian demands of the opposition.... St Helen's is a major medieval monument with a number of important accretive changes of all periods. These record the history of both the City in which the church is set, and of the varying changes in worship of the Church of England."[23]

Hobhouse thus reads the architecture of St. Helen's in a way that is now familiar: it is a historical document or record, not only of its own development as a building, or even solely as a religious institution, but of a wide range of human stories that might be associated with it. Like the monasteries and churches of Camden's *Britannia*, or Herbert's church porch, St. Helen's was a religious artifact that recorded much more than religious history. Newspaper columnist A. N. Wilson, for example, lamented in the *Evening Standard* the bomb's destruction of a Victorian stained-glass window "depicting Shakespeare, who must have known the church." Calling Lucas a "vandal in a dog collar," Wilson saw the proposed renovations as little more than a continuation of the damage.[24] Like some of the correspondents of Gordon Watkins quoted above, Wilson values church architecture for its commemorative, in addition to its religious, qualities, for its possible (and in this case very tenuous) associations with both topography and human identity. In the summation to his testimony, Lucas charged preservationists with attempting to use "history ... as a straight jacket, an original text (if that could be found)," and even as he advanced an alternative view, his analogy between architectural fabric and "text" reveals his familiarity with an antiquarian mode of architectural literacy, in which buildings and texts might function in parallel and interdependent ways.[25]

As it had in seventeenth-century country house poems and in Wotton's *Elements of Architecture*, this historical understanding of architecture resulted in the marginalization of the architect as visual artist and controlling figure in a building's design. In these modern debates as well, the architect becomes an encroaching figure whose influence is perceived as "foreign" (to use Marvell's term) and even inimical to the histories a building might preserve.[26] Frequently, Terry and his supporters found themselves defending not only Terry's particular designs but his right to design at all. Terry contended that the elements of his proposal could not be adopted piecemeal because they constituted an integrated whole: "An architect must be given some freedom to use his skill; if this is denied he ceases to produce a consistent work of architecture, because he is forced to design against his better judgment."[27] Lucas declared, "I must . . . pay tribute to the knowledge and skill of our distinguished architect," and Cameron argued that "it is clearly right that an architect should be given scope for originality."[28] Andreae, however, disagreed with this deference to an architect's "skill," which she perceived as being opposed to the integrity of the building's historiographic meanings. Andreae denied that the church restoration represented "the creation of a work of art" that "should thus be allowed in its totality," feeling that this premise was not "an appropriate way to approach a historic interior of the intricacy and complexity of St Helen's."[29] In addition, Andreae's (above quoted) objection to Terry's design as "notional" echoes Marvell's critique in "Upon Appleton House" of theoretical or intellectual approaches to building, of the sort inspired by classical and Renaissance treatises. The detractors, agreeing with Marvell, thought that St. Helen's did not need an architect who "of his great design in pain" would "for a model vault his brain."[30]

Terry's supporters countered such objections by arguing that Terry had used his architectural skill not to erase the historical associations of the building but to integrate aesthetic and antiquarian concerns, thereby making the building legible on two registers at once. At the same time, their arguments implicitly acknowledge the tension between antiquarian and aesthetic interests, presenting one as a counterpoint to, rather than a reinforcement of, the other. Describing the pre-renovation church, Barker testified, "The interior of the church presents itself today more as an historic 'arena for worship' than as a highly integrated work of art or architecture. This observation is not intended to diminish its importance as an historic building, so much as to indicate that the interest is 'accretive' and to be seen in the layers of its history, rather than as a single work of architectural creation."[31] Barker's remarks indicate an essential incompatibility or tension between historical and aesthetic priorities. Despite his ostensible respect for the church's historical interest, his characterization of it as a "historic 'arena for worship'" seems intended as a critique that might potentially "diminish" preservationists' views. History is here imagined as undermining the achievement of "a highly integrated work of art or architecture." Further, Barker places "creation" in opposition to "accret[ion]" suggesting that the difference between historic and aesthetic values consists partly of the architect's intervention, the influence of a mind whose "creation" the building represents. Barker's analysis thus remains equivocal; while he does not "deny" the church's "importance as an historic building," he suggests that by overemphasizing this importance, detractors deny both the prerogative of the architect and the building's aesthetic potential.

Although Barker would finally argue that aesthetic "creation" and "historic" importance were reconciled in Terry's designs, in his view this reconciliation comprised the balancing of opposites. The design's integrity and symmetry would be constructed in part by the equal consideration of history and aesthetics and would be held in place by a kind of isometric tension between the two. "It is the intention of the parish and its architect that no items of architectural, artistic or historic value should be lost or taken from the church," he said, "rather that they should all play their part in a new architectural unity."[32] Architectural, artistic, and historic values are differentiated from one another, even as they are placed in parallel. "Unity" is here perceived as an architectural effect, to be imposed upon the miscellany of "items" with which preservationists were concerned. In summation, Barker testified, "In my opinion the proposals before the Court do make the 'best use' of the inheritance both as a church and as architecture."[33] His syntax ("both . . . and") again suggests both a symmetry and a tension between St. Helen's "as a church" and St. Helen's "as architecture." In context, the phrase "as a church" seems to refer most directly to the building's functional utility, but Barker's reference to the church's "inheritance" makes clear that history constitutes part of this ecclesiological value.

Terry's own testimony, as much as his design, is an exercise in balance. "My primary interest is not history," he said, "but architecture; the elements of which are (to quote Sir Henry Wotton) 'Firmness, Commodity and Delight'."[34] Superficially, Terry seems to use Wotton as a way of dismissing or demoting history, but the quotation is also a way of bolstering his own view with its historical ancestry. Moreover, the sentiment is not original to Wotton; it is a fairly direct translation of Vitruvius.[35] By choosing the English source, instead of the Roman one, Terry deemphasized both the foreignness of his view and its association with classical aesthetics, defending his work as being grounded in English history: the design is not only the product of individual aesthetic tastes but a sign of his connection to ancestry and part of his own "inheritance" as an English architect. Significantly, Terry returns to Wotton as he registers the tension between the agency of the architect's skill and a regard for architecture's historical meanings. As we saw in Chapter 2, Wotton's *Elements of Architecture* was also shaped by awareness of this problem. Although Wotton dealt with country houses rather than churches, he, like Terry, attempted to lay out elements derived from classical building design for an audience more invested in understanding architecture in historical terms.

Other supporters of the new church design also authorized their position by invoking history, pointing out that both some material aspects of the proposed design and the principles on which it was based were in fact older than the features that detractors were fighting to preserve. Proponents frequently argued, alongside Terry, that utility and function were more important than history, or, as he would say, that "history is not the first ingredient of architecture."[36] In this case, functionality involved the accommodation of the church's current style of worship, described by supporters as a "preaching ministry" and by opponents as "their ... horrible happy-clappy love-ins ... out of tune with the religion of their ancestors."[37] Yet supporters countered the charges of disregarding history with their own historical evidence. For instance, Terry grounded the parish's commitment to a "preaching ministry" in Reformation developments that predated the Tractarian style of worship reflected by the nineteenth-century arrangement of the church. The chancel screens and raised altar which preservationists wanted to protect were, in Terry's view, infelicitous innovations of a relatively recent historical moment when the "mind liberated by an understanding of the Bible at the Reformation, now turned back to the bondage of visual forms and spectacular ritual."[38] Dodging comparisons to Reformation iconoclasts, though, Lucas argued that this emphasis on preaching "was certainly a major concern before the Reformation, in late medieval times. For example, the City benefited enormously from ... the work of a preaching order like the Dominicans (the Black Friars)," who "had in mind, as Wren later ... the needs of worshippers."[39] The re-ordering of the church, then, would not ignore or erase history but use "history as a pointer to the times when faith was rediscovered and the churches built to meet the demands of a multitude of seekers after God."[40] Thus, while Terry criticized his opponents for the view that "anything that is old, whether good or bad, must not be disturbed *because* it is old," he and his supporters simultaneously exploited history to their own ends, balancing, once again, a notion of the church "as architecture" with an evident regard for its historical "inheritance."[41]

"The result," wrote the current rector, William Taylor, in his introduction to the church's present-day guidebook, "is that, today, St Helen's is coherent, comfortable and in a good state of repair. Its rich tapestry of history remains."[42] In this assessment, Terry's design succeeds in balancing aesthetics and utility, coherence and comfort, and opens up both synchronic and diachronic experiences of architecture. The church is poised at the intersection of visual and historical modes of architectural expression. Terry, like John Evelyn and Roland Fréart before him, worked as a collector of architectural fragments, and, more broadly speaking, his design collects multiple modes of architectural literacy. The first is based loosely in the principles of classical aesthetics and engages the viewer in a synchronic analysis of space, arrangement, and materials, expressing Terry's belief that the "appearance" of buildings is capable of "*do[ing] something* to people." The second is based in an antiquarian perspective and queries the particular histories of artifacts or items, moving backward and forward in time.

Given the methodological similarities between Terry's project and Evelyn's, it is perhaps not surprising that the finished church, like the treatise Evelyn chose to import, embodies principles of collecting. In relation to Fréart's treatise, I quoted Susan Stewart's observation that "the collection does not displace attention to the past; rather, the past is at the service of the collection."[43] A similar statement might be applied to Terry's design for St. Helen's. Stewart's point seems to express the logic underlying much of Barker's argument that "items of architectural, artistic, or historic value should . . . all play their part in a new architectural unity." Fréart's plates neatly broke down, rationalized, reordered, and realigned their visual pieces of evidence in a way that created order from evident disarticulation; in St. Helen's as well, the fragmentation and discontinuities of history are clearly visible. The bright white space of the lime-washed walls and white stone floor isolates monuments and items of church furniture from one another and creates an obvious visual contrast with earlier aesthetic preferences, as displayed in the heavy, dark wood of the elaborately carved Jacobean doorcase and pulpit, the tracery of the Victorian screens, the grey stone of the nuns' squint, the painted and carved figures of the Elizabethan wall monuments, the pale and worn effigies of a late-fourteenth-century tomb chest. Like the architectural fragments depicted in Fréart's treatise, each object arrives in a new context, visibly deracinated, while still trailing its history behind it. I have argued that John Evelyn seems to have seen in Fréart's *Parallèle* an analogy for the history of the Restoration itself and a representation of the restored monarch to whom he dedicated his translation. The disruption and recuperation of a fragmented past described the history of the English monarchy as much as the history of classical and Renaissance architecture. In St. Helen's as well, we might read this visually interrupted history as a reflection and partial consequence of the literal, material fragmentation caused by IRA bombs, a simultaneous recollection and reparation of the church's own recent past.

It might be said that many old London buildings are collections of fragments that represent the discontinuities of history. At St. Helen's, though, the ordering influence of classicism and the conscious arrangement of a collector are especially evident. In Fréart's treatise, bases and capitals are carefully excised, aligned, judged, measured, and framed. In St. Helen's, monuments and artifacts have obviously been rearranged rather than simply allowed to accrue. Wall monuments are spaced at even distances, while accommodating older architectural features, and overall, the ordered display of woodwork and wall plaques complements the symmetrical effect created by the double nave and chancel, which are still divided by a row of columns and pointed arches.

In the introduction to this study, I cited the work of recent architectural historians who have noted that the particular lenses through which we interpret architecture—as examples of an aesthetic period, as plot points in an architect's body of work, or as heritage from the past—are themselves historical acquisitions or cultural constructions, rather than inevitable outgrowths of buildings themselves. The design of the new St. Helen's and the debate surrounding it give evidence that these questions are not merely theoretical or academic; they play a practical role in the way buildings are created and perceived. These discussions have a long history. It is not only modern critical inquiry that has produced the awareness that buildings might be interpreted in both historical and visual terms, as the works of an architect or as the products of history. The debate over St. Helen's, and its current physical fabric, were shaped by antiquarian approaches to architecture that can be traced at least as far back as the mid-sixteenth century, while a sensitivity to the tension between antiquarian and visual modes is clearly evident in works of the early seventeenth. The recent history of St. Helen's can thus be read not only in the context of modern theoretical discussions but as a late chapter in the longer story this book tells.

Modern day viewers of St. Helen's might well find it comfortable and modern, and might also be impressed by its "distinguished, unaffected" design.[44] But they might equally be following in the footsteps of John Leland, who, in the mid-sixteenth century, toured England's landscape, spurred by the urgent desire of regathering its history. For Leland, buildings told stories that were not about architects or even architecture, presenting instead a much broader cast of characters and a wider range of subjects. Despite Terry's division between "architecture" and "history," his design demonstrates his awareness of the complicated interdependence that has been the main subject of this book. Architecture is understood not only through the spatial and visual effects it creates; it also continues to be read as a form of literature or history, indelibly inscribed with its human connections, and valued, still, for the stories it can tell.

Notes

INTRODUCTION: BUILDING STORIES: WRITING ABOUT ARCHITECTURE IN POST-REFORMATION ENGLAND

1. Leland and Bale, *The Laboryouse Journey and Serche of Johan Leylande, for Englandes Antiquitees Geven of Hym as a New Yeares Gyfte to King Henry the VIII*, A ii v. For use of the word "monument" in this sense, see OED 3.
2. Leland and Bale, *Laboryouse Journey*, B i r–v.
3. Leland and Bale, *Laboryouse Journey*, B ii r. Leland's *Itinerary* remained unpublished until 1710, but his notes were apparently available to subsequent scholars, and his ambitious (perhaps delusional) vision of mapping Britain topographically and historically would lay the groundwork for antiquarian projects over the course of the following century, informing such monumental productions as William Camden's *Britannia* (1586) and the *Monasticon Anglicanum* (1655) of Roger Dodsworth and William Dugdale.
4. Camden, *Britannia*, tr. Philemon Holland, 163. For a reading of Leland's sense of loss, see Schwyzer, *Literature, Nationalism and Memory in Early Modern England and Wales*, 61–66. For Leland's importance in the development of English architectural and topographical description, see Howard, *The Building of Elizabethan and Jacobean England*, 110. For comment on the connection between the dissolution and antiquarian interest in the preservation of manuscripts, see Watts, "English Place-Names in the Sixteenth Century," 42. For a detailed description of Leland's project, see Kendrick, *British Antiquity*, 45–56.
5. Güven, "Frontiers of Fear: Architectural History, the Anchor and the Sail," 76.
6. Arnold, "Preface" in *Rethinking Architectural Historiography*, xvii.
7. Evett, *Literature and the Visual Arts in Tudor England*, 79, 45.
8. Roston, *Renaissance Perspectives in Literature and the Visual Arts*, 6, 238.
9. Gent, *Picture and Poetry, 1560-1620*, 1.
10. Harris with Savage, *British Architectural Books and Writers, 1556–1785*, 513–514.
11. See Harris with Savage, 419; and Hind, *Engraving in England in the Sixteenth and Seventeenth Centuries*, 1.60.
12. Wells-Cole, *Art and Decoration in Elizabethan and Jacobean England*, 10–11.
13. Gent, "'The Rash Gazer': Economies of Vision in Britain, 1550–1660," 378.
14. Howard, *Building*, 9. See also chap. 3, "A Language for Architecture," 95–120.
15. Leland, *Leland's Journey through Wiltshire, A.D. 1540–42*, 7; Leland, *The Itinerary of John Leland the Antiquary*, 2.52–53.

16. Leland, *Itinerary*, 2.52.

17. Leland, *Itinerary*, 2.53.

18. Leland, *Itinerary*, 2.53.

19. Johnson, *Ben Jonson: Poetry and Architecture*; Eriksen, *The Building in the Text: Alberti to Shakespeare and Milton*, esp. p. xviii.

20. Donne, "The Canonization," line 32; Jonson, *Discoveries*, 591.

21. Yates, *The Art of Memory*, 129–159; 342–367; Carruthers, *The Book of Memory*, 71–79. Carruthers gives a useful account of the classical roots of the tradition in such texts as Cicero's *De Oratore* and *Rhetorica ad Herennium* and Quintillian's *Institutio*.

22. For a discussion of Leland's struggle with textual form, see Klein, *Maps and the Writing of Space in Early Modern England and Ireland*, 140–141.

23. Marchitello, *Narrative and Meaning in Early Modern England*, 77. See also Helgerson, *Forms of Nationhood: The Elizabethan Writing of England*, 105–148; and Swann, *Curiosities and Texts*, 100. For the tension between spatial and historical models for imagining the nation, see Klein, 137–170.

24. Leland and Bale, *Laboryouse Journey*, A ii v.

25. Leland and Bale, *Laboryouse Journey*, D v v.

26. Simpson, "Diachronic History and the Shortcomings of Medieval Studies," 29.

27. Summit, "Leland's *Itinerary* and the Remains of the Medieval Past," 161.

28. Camden, *Britannia*, tr. Holland, 242; Schwyzer, *Archaeologies of English Renaissance Literature*, 75.

29. Bryson, Holly, and Moxley, "Introduction," xvi.

30. Bryson, Holly, and Moxley, xvii.

31. Sherlock, *Monuments and Memory in Early Modern England*; Nigel Llewellyn, *Funeral Monuments in Post-Reformation England*.

32. Whinney, *Sculpture in Britain, 1530–1830*; Llewellyn, 20, 35. See also Cooper, who writes, "At the beginning of the [seventeenth] century, very few people would have had any idea of the notion of an architectural 'style'." *The Jacobean Country House*, 30.

33. See Weever, *Ancient Funerall Monuments*, Camden's *Reges, Reginae, Nobiles et Alij in Ecclesia Collegiata B. Petri Westmonasterij Sepulti*, and Browne's *Repertorium*.

34. See Hunneyball, *Architecture and Image Building in Seventeenth-Century Hertfordshire*. Hunneyball writes, "Even assuming that classical motifs were indeed being employed because patrons wished to allude to the glories of antiquity, it is still far from clear that most of them really appreciated the elements of classical design at a more than superficial level," 175.

35. Zevi, *Architecture as Space: How to Look at Architecture*, 22.

36. De Certeau, *The Practice of Everyday Life*, 122.

37. See, for instance, Orlin's "The Tudor Long Gallery in the History of Privacy," 284–298; "Women on the Threshold," 50–58; and *Locating Privacy in Tudor London*.

38. See, for instance, Schofield's diagrammatic reconstruction of the post-Reformation floor plan of the former Holy Trinity Priory, Aldgate, in *The Building of London from the Conquest to the Great Fire*, 148.

39. See, for instance, Fumerton, who calls study of the "everyday" a "new new historicism" that "focuses primarily on the common . . . in both a class and cultural sense" ("Introduction," 3).

40. See Treswell, *The London Surveys of Ralph Treswell*; Godfrey, *Wenceslaus Hollar: A Bohemian Artist in England*; Thorpe, "The Book of Architecture of John Thorpe"; Brown "Continuity and Change in the Urban House: Developments in Domestic Space Organisation in Seventeenth-Century London," 558–590; Maguire, "A Collection of Seventeenth-Century Architectural Plans," 140–182; Orlin, "Temporary Lives in London Lodgings," 219–242.

41. For the pervasive sense of change in Leland's work, see Scattergood, "John Leland's *Itinerary* and the Identity of England," 64–65.

42. For an account of the development of Palladian classicism in England, see Anderson, "Palladio in England: The Dominance of the Classical in a Foreign Land," 122–129.

43. Belsey, "Afterword: Classicism and Cultural Dissonance." 427.

44. Arnold, *Reading Architectural History*, 99.

45. See especially Summerson, *Inigo Jones*; Peacock, *The Stage Designs of Inigo Jones: The European Context*; and Anderson, *Inigo Jones and the Classical Tradition*. For Jones's precocious knowledge and adaptation of Palladio, see Burns, "Palladio and the Foundations of a New Architecture in the North," 16–55, esp. 19–35.

46. See, for instance, Schofield, who writes that Jones's masterworks of the 1620s and '30s would have remained "totally alien to the man in the London Street" until much later in the century (*Building of London*, 168).

47. Wilton-Ely, "The Rise of the Professional Architect in England," 183.

48. Peacock, 36.

49. Belsey, 428.

50. Arnold, *Reading Architectural History*, 42, 99, 183.

51. Summerson, *Georgian London* and *Architecture in Britain, 1530–1830*; Colvin, *A Biographical Dictionary of English Architects, 1660–1840*, 1st ed.

52. For consideration of patron-builder relationships, see Howard, *Building*, 121–164; Hunneyball, 57; Sutton, *Materializing Space at an Early Modern Prodigy House: The Cecils at Theobalds, 1564–1607*; Girouard, *Robert Smythson and the Elizabethan Country House*.

53. Camden, *Britannia*, tr. Holland, 251, 703, 200.

54. De Grazia, Quilligan, and Stallybrass, "Introduction," 5.

55. Clifford, Great Books of Record, 2.40. Quotations from the Great Books are reproduced by kind permission of the Cumbria Archive Centre, Kendal.

56. Gent, "'The Rash Gazer'," 379.

57. Sinfield, "*Poetaster*, the Author, and the Perils of Cultural Production," 75–76.

58. Harris, "Shakespeare's Hair: Staging the Object of Material Culture," 480.

59. Parry, *The Trophies of Time: English Antiquarians of the Seventeenth Century*, 30.

60. Yegül, "Hercules at the Roundabout: Multidisciplinary Choice in the History of Architecture," 63.

61. For an account of the historically "antagonistic" relationship between literary and archaeological methodologies, see Schwyzer, *Archaeologies of English Renaissance Literature*, 5–6.

62. This strict division between material and linguistic forms of evidence has been questioned by other scholars. See, for instance, Ekinci, "Reopening the Question of Document in Architectural History," 121–134.

63. Harris and Korda, "Introduction," 17.
64. Vine, *In Defiance of Time: Antiquarian Writing in Early Modern England*, 5.
65. Harris, *Untimely Matter in the Time of Shakespeare*, 11, 24. In conceptualizing "a temporality that is not one," Harris is drawing Biddick's *The Typological Imaginary: History, Technology, Circumcision*, 1.
66. Harris, *Untimely Matter*, 33. For the figure of the palimpsest, see pp. 1–5, 13–19.
67. Wotton, *The Elements of Architecture*, A 2 v.
68. See, for instance, Wilton-Ely, who writes that unlike the works of Inigo Jones, "Wren's direction of the Office of Works and the sheer range of buildings carried out under him had a lasting impact upon the status and responsibilities of the architect as well as upon the organization of the entire building industry.... Wren represents, as perhaps never again, the universal competence envisioned by Shute a century earlier," 185.

CHAPTER 1: LOSS AND FOUNDATIONS: CAMDEN'S *BRITANNIA* AND THE HISTORIES OF ENGLISH ARCHITECTURE

1. Shute, *The First and Chief Groundes of Architecture*; Blum, *The Booke of Five Collumnes of Architecture*; Serlio, *The Five Books of Architecture*; Wotton, *The Elements of Architecture*.
2. Wotton mentions the garden of Sir Henry Fanshaw at Ware Park (*Elements*, 110).
3. For comment on Camden's incipient empiricism, see Parry, *The Trophies of Time: English Antiquarians of the Seventeenth Century*, 30–31; Woolf, *The Social Circulation of the Past: English Historical Culture, 1500–1730*, 142–144, 152; Herendeen, "Wanton Discourse and the Engines of Time: William Camden—Historian among Poets-Historical," 150–151; Kendrick, *British Antiquity*, 150–155. For Camden's relationship to seventeenth-century practices of collecting, see Swann, *Curiosities and Texts*, 13–14, 98–100.
4. On Camden's use of oral tradition, see Woolf, *Social Circulation*, 359–360.
5. Vine, *In Defiance of Time: Antiquarian Writing in Early Modern England*, 18.
6. See Swann, 1–6 and chap. 1, "Cultures of Collecting." For essays on the history of collecting in England, see *The Evolution of English Collecting*, ed. Chaney.
7. On reactions to England's monastic ruins, see Schwyzer, "Dissolving Images: Monastic Ruins in Elizabethan Poetry," in *Archaeologies of English Renaissance Literature*, 72–107, esp. 72–74; McBride, *Country House Discourse in Early Modern England*, 17–46; Herendeen, *From Landscape to Literature: The River and the Myth of Geography*, 184; and Aston, "English Ruins and English History: The Dissolution and the Sense of the Past," in *Lollards and Reformers: Images and Literacy in Late Medieval Religion*, 313–338. For possible associations between architectural classicism and Catholicism or Protestantism, see Howard "The Treatise and Its Alternatives: Theory and Practice in Sixteenth-Century England," 141–153; Llewellyn, *Funeral Monuments in Post-Reformation England*, 28; Hart, "From Virgin to Courtesan in Early English Vitruvian Books," 312–318; Thomas, "English Protestantism and Classical Art," 221–238; Hart, "'A peece rather of good *Heraldry*, than of *Architecture*': Heraldry and the Orders of Architecture as Joint Emblems of Chivalry," 56–57. For the relationship between Puritanism and classicism, see Mowl and Earnshaw, *Architecture without Kings: The Rise of Puritan Classicism under Cromwell*, 2–7.

8. For an elegant summary of this argument, see Peacock, *The Stage Designs of Inigo Jones: The European Context*, 35–38.

9. For a comparison of the treatment of the English aristocracy in successive editions of the *Britannia*, see Rockett, "*Britannia*, Ralph Brooke, and the Representation of Privilege in Elizabethan England," 474–499.

10. For the publication history of these and other early architectural books, see Harris with Savage, *British Architectural Books and Writers, 1556–1785*.

11. Parry, 48. On the *Britannia*'s circulation and influence, see Woolf, *Social Circulation*, 152, 154, 253–255.

12. Ben Jonson, "Epigram 14," line 8.

13. For a list of the books included in the Great Picture and Appleby Triptych (of which it forms the center panel), see Spence, *Lady Anne Clifford*, 190–191. The Great Picture itself is reproduced on p. ii, and the left- and right-hand panels on pages 16 and 112, respectively. For Evelyn's contribution, see *The Diary of John Evelyn*, ed. de Beer, 5.206.

14. For a discussion of architecture's role in English folklore and antiquarianism more generally, see Woolf, *Social Circulation*, 310–315.

15. Piggott, "William Camden and the *Britannia*," 21. For broader views of chorography, see also Swann, 99–101, and McRae, *God Speed the Plough: The Representation of Agrarian England, 1500–1660*, 231–261.

16. Parry, 3.

17. On Camden's debt to Leland, see Kendrick, 147–149; Brooke, *A Discoverie of Certaine Errours Published in Print in the Much Commended* Britannia, *1594*. See also the anonymous poem "Leylands Supposed Ghost," bound with Brooke's *Discoverie* in the British Library copy (shelfmark 796.g.12).

18. Kendrick, 150.

19. Klein, "Imaginary Journeys: Spenser, Drayton, and the Poetics of National Space," 209.

20. Quotations from Camden, *Britannia*, tr. Philemon Holland, "The Author to the Reader," [7]. All subsequent quotations from this edition of *Britannia* are cited parenthetically by page number in the text.

21. Swann, 13; Parry, 30.

22. Solomon, *Objectivity in the Making: Francis Bacon and the Politics of Inquiry*, xix.

23. The problems of considering Camden's works a prototype of modern historical method are considered in detail by Collinson, "One of Us? William Camden and the Making of History," 139–164.

24. Levy, *Tudor Historical Thought*, 252–258.

25. The question of the *Britannia*'s genre has been most thoroughly treated by Herendeen. See *William Camden: A Life in Context*, 208–220, and "Wanton Discourse and the Engines of Time: William Camden—Historian among Poets-Historical," 142–156.

26. Summit, *Memory's Library: Medieval Books in Early Modern England*, 178, 176.

27. Herendeen, "Wanton Discourse and the Engines of Time," 152.

28. Woolf observes that in the early seventeenth century "objects were almost invariably situated within a knowledge field defined by literary texts" (*Social Circulation*, 313).

29. Vine, 10.

30. The Richborough Roman Fort and Amphitheatre are now an English Heritage site.

31. Leland and Bale, *The Laboryouse Journey and Serche of Johan Leyland, for Englandes Antiquitees, Geven of Hym as a Newe Years Gyfte to Kynge Henry the VIII*, B ii r.

32. Harris, *Untimely Matter in the Time of Shakespeare*, 103, 113.

33. For ancient coins, see Camden, 105. For reused building materials, see, for example, 569, 669, and 699.

34. Camden, *Britannia*, tr. Edmund Gibson et al., A 2 r.

35. Harris, "Shakespeare's Hair: Staging the Object of Material Culture," 480.

36. For Camden's relationship to Cotton and his extensive use of Cotton's library, see Summit, *Memory's Library*, 174–183.

37. Harris, *Untimely Matter in the Time of Shakespeare*, 95–101.

38. Klein, "Imaginary Journeys," 209.

39. This portion of the chapter builds on a significant body of scholarship surrounding the English country house. Other studies of the country house during this period include Cliffe's *The World of the Country House in Seventeenth-Century England*, Howard's *The Early Tudor Country House*, Girouard's *Life in the English Country House*, and *Robert Smythson and the Elizabethan Country House*. Studies of the country house in the literary tradition include McBride's *Country House Discourse in Early Modern England*, Fowler's *The Country House Poem: A Cabinet of Seventeenth-Century Estate Poems and Related Items*, McClung's *The Country House in English Renaissance Poetry*, and Hibbard's "The Country House Poem of the Seventeenth Century," 159–174.

40. See, for instance, Fowler, 7–8; Heal, *Hospitality in Early Modern England*, 112–113; McClung, 105–106.

41. Helgerson, *Forms of Nationhood: The Elizabethan Writing of England*, 105–148, esp. 108–124.

42. For detailed accounts of the Cecils as architectural patrons, see Sutton, *Materializing Space at an Early Modern Prodigy House: The Cecils at Theobalds, 1564–1607*; Croft, *Patronage, Culture, and Power: The Early Cecils*, 3–98.

43. For detailed accounts of the Sidneys at Penshurst, see Celovsky, "Ben Jonson and Sidneian Legacies of Hospitality," 178–206; Fowler, 53–62; Wayne, *Penshurst: The Semiotics of Place and the Poetics of History*.

44. Orlin, *Locating Privacy in Tudor London*, 13.

45. The tendency of literary studies to adopt this approach is discussed in more detail in Chapter 4, with particular reference to George Herbert. Influential historical studies for generating this framework include Duffy's *The Stripping of the Altars: Traditional Religion in England, c. 1400–c. 1580*, and Fincham and Tyacke's *The Altars Restored: The Changing Face of English Religious Worship, 1547–c. 1700*. My point here is not to invalidate these magisterial works but to suggest the persistence of an alternative way of thinking about religious architecture. For the assumed connection between church architecture and the visual arts more generally, see Peacock, 36.

46. Hunneyball, *Architecture and Image Building in Seventeenth-Century Hertfordshire*, 175; Llewellyn, 28.

47. Leland and Bale, *Laboryouse Journey*, A ii v.

48. Tanner, *Notitia Monastica, or a Short History of the Religious Houses in England and Wales*, b 8 r.

CHAPTER 2: ARISTOCRATS AND ARCHITECTS: HENRY WOTTON AND THE COUNTRY HOUSE POEM

1. See, for instance Wilton-Ely, "The Rise of the Professional Architect in England," 180–208. Wilton-Ely measures the architects of early modern England against what a previous chapter in the same collection calls "The New Professionalism in the Renaissance" (Wilkinson, 124–160).

2. See, for instance, Wells-Cole, *Art and Decoration in Elizabethan and Jacobean England: The Influence of Continental Prints, 1558–1625*, 15–22; Belsey, "Afterword: Classicism and Cultural Dissonance," 427–431; Evett, *Literature and the Visual Arts in Tudor England*, 55–57.

3. M. Vitruvius Pollio, *Ten Books on Architecture*, tr. Ingrid D. Rowland 1.1, p. 21. See also Kruft, who names the notebooks of the post-Restoration architect Roger Pratt (unpublished until 1928) as an early instance of an architectural writer's "attempting to systematise the process of perception, i.e. to plot how the observer's eyes roam over the building before him" (*A History of Architectural Theory from Vitruvius to the Present*, 233).

4. For comment on Jones's innovations, influence, and atypical career, see Anderson, *Inigo Jones and the Classical Tradition*, 1–6; Wilton-Ely, 182–185; Summerson, *Inigo Jones*, esp. 1–2; Wells-Cole, 11; Mowl, *Elizabethan and Jacobean Style*, 143. A different view of Jones's architectural career, emphasizing his early work on masque design is offered by Peacock, *The Stage Designs of Inigo Jones: The European Context*, 55–112.

5. See, for instance, Belsey, 429. Belsey contrasts the "the façades of Longleat, symmetrical and neoclassical in imitation of Renaissance Italy" with "the solid and traditional values of indigenous English architecture" praised by Ben Jonson in "To Penshurst."

6. For comment on the relationship between chorography and estate surveying during this period, see Swann, *Curiosities and Texts*, 100–101; McRae, *God Speed the Plough: The Representation of Agrarian England, 1500–1660*, 231–233.

7. For the relationship between architecture and surveying, see Wilton-Ely, 181–183, and Summerson, *Inigo Jones*, 15–16.

8. For the novelty of Wotton's work, see Gent, "'The Rash Gazer': Economies of Vision in Britain, 1550–1660," 388, and Harris with Savage, *British Architectural Books and Writers, 1556–1785*, 499.

9. McRae, 172–179.

10. Fitzherbert, *Surveyenge*, fol. 38 v–39 r. An earlier edition of the manual was published in 1523 under the title *Here Begynneth a Right Frutefull Mater: And Hath to Name the Boke of Surveyeng and Improvementes*.

11. For a detailed account of the surveyor's duties, see McRae, 169–197; Thompson, *Chartered Surveyors: The Growth of a Profession*, 1–29.

12. Norden, *The Surveyors Dialogue*, A 6 r.

13. Fitzherbert, fol. 16 r.

14. William Camden, *Britannia*, tr. Philemon Holland, 4–[5].

15. McRae, 231.

16. Leland and Bale, *The Laboryouse Journey and Serche of Johan Leylande, for Englandes Antiquitees*, D v v.

17. Norden, *Speculum Britanniae: The First Parte: An Historicall, and Chorographicall Discription of Middlesex*; *Speculi Britanniae Pars: The Description of Hartfordshire*.

18. Norden, *The Surveyors Dialogue*, 15.

19. Lucar, *Treatise Named Lucarsolace*, 50–52, quoted in McRae, 190.

20. Rivius [Walther Ryff] (c. 1500–after 1545) published a German translation of Vitruvius's *De architecttura libri decem* with commentary (Nuremburg, 1548). Philander's edition was published at Lyon in 1552. Baldi (1553–1617) published *De verborum vitruvianorum significationes* [On the meanings of Vitruvian words] (Augsburg, 1612).

21. Wotton, *The Elements of Architecture*, ¶ 3 r. All subsequent quotations are from this edition and are cited parenthetically in the text.

22. Vitruvius, *Ten Books*, 1.1, pp. 22, 23.

23. Alberti, *On the Art of Building in Ten Books*, Prologue, 3.

24. De l'Orme, *Architecture de Philibert de l'Orme*, 1.3, fol. 10–11.

25. Rykwert offers a brief biography of Alberti in his introduction to *On the Art of Building in Ten Books*, ix–xxi; Palladio's life is outlined by Tavernor in his introduction to *The Four Books on Architecture*, viii–xii.

26. A detailed biography of Wotton is given in Smith, *The Life and Letters of Sir Henry Wotton*, 1.1–226. This description of the volume is from Wotton's handwritten inscription to Prince Charles, to whom he sent a copy (Smith, 2.284).

27. Smith, 2.284.

28. Harris with Savage, 499.

29. Wotton bargained with Buckingham by allowing Buckingham to sell two less prestigious offices that were due to revert directly to Wotton himself. These were the Mastership of the Rolls and half of a Six Clerk's place in Chancery. For Wotton's shrewd management of these bargaining chips, as well as his appeals to other patrons, see Smith, 1.199–201.

30. Cleland, *The Institution of a Young Noble-Man*, 91–92.

31. Vitruvius, *Ten Books*, 6.8, p. 84. Latin quotations from Vitruvius are taken from *On Architecture*, ed. and tr. Granger, 2.56, 58.

32. Harris, 501.

33. Alberti, *Art of Building*, 9.11, p. 318.

34. De l'Orme, 1.3, fol. 10 r. The French reads "que sa liberté doit estre exempte de toute contrainte & subjection d'esprit."

35. Vitruvius, *Ten Books*, 6; Preface, p. 76.

36. For collaboration between patrons and craftsmen during this period, see Hunneyball, *Architecture and Image Building in Seventeenth-Century Hertfordshire*, 57.

37. Smith, 1.452, 460.

38. Mowl, 144. See also Gapper, Newman, and Ricketts, "Hatfield: A House for a Lord Treasurer," 67–98.

39. Smith, 2.287.

40. Fowler, *The Country House Poem*, 99.

41. Lockyer, *Buckingham: The Life and Political Career of George Villiers, First Duke of Buckingham, 1592–1628*, 120–121.

42. On the shortage of architects, see Aubrey's account of Wilton House in *The Natural History of Wiltshire*, compiled between 1656 and 1691. Aubrey claims that King Charles I, who "did love Wilton above all places... intended to have had it all designed by his own architect, Mr. Inigo Jones, who being at that time, about 1633, engaged in his Majesties buildings at Greenwich, could not attend to it; but he recommended it to an ingeniouse architect, Monsieur Solomon de Caus, a Gascoigne, who performed it very well; but not without the advice and approbation of Mr. Jones" (Aubrey, 83–84). Colvin has since proven that the architect of Wilton's famous south front was not Solomon de Caus but his son or nephew, Isaac ("The South Front of Wilton House," 136–157).

43. Vitruvius, *Ten Books*, 1.4, pp. 26–28; Alberti, *Art of Building*, 1.3–6, pp. 9–18; Wotton, 2–6.

44. For the supervisory role of the lord in the history of estate surveying, see McRae, 140–143, 192–194.

45. Alberti, *Art of Building*, 5.17, p. 145.

46. McRae, 180.

47. Vitruvius, *Ten Books*, 6.2, p. 78.

48. See, for instance, Fowler, 7–8; Heal, *Hospitality in Early Modern England*, 112–113; McClung, *The Country House in English Renaissance Poetry*, 105–106.

49. My readings of these poems, like this chapter as a whole, build on a significant body of scholarship surrounding the English country house. Other studies of the country house during this period include Cliffe's *The World of the Country House in Seventeenth-Century England*, Howard's *The Building of Elizabethan and Jacobean England* and *The Early Tudor Country House*, and Girouard's *Life in the English Country House* and *Robert Smythson and the Elizabethan Country House*. Studies that consider the country house in the literary tradition include McBride's *Country House Discourse in Early Modern England*, Fowler's *The Country House Poem*, McClung's *The Country House in English Renaissance Poetry*, and G. R. Hibbard's "The Country House Poem of the Seventeenth Century," 159–174.

50. See, for instance, McClung, 7–17; Fowler, 11–17.

51. For a rare and enlightening discussion of country house poetry's debt to chorography and to other English representations of landscape, see McRae, 285–297.

52. Camden, *Britannia*, tr. Holland, 327.

53. Camden, *Britannia*, tr. Holland, 289, 420.

54. Adrian, *Local Negotiations of English Nationhood, 1570–1680*, 154.

55. Ben Jonson, "To Penshurst," lines 1–6. Subsequent quotations are cited parenthetically by line number in the text.

56. See D. J. Gordon's influential essay "Poet and Architect: The Intellectual Setting of the Quarrel between Ben Jonson and Inigo Jones," 77–101. A. W. Johnson reproduces several pages of Jonson's Vitruvius, including Jonson's annotations in *Ben Jonson: Poetry and Architecture*, plates 1–7.

57. Fowler, 57.

58. This forgery is reproduced in the present day guidebook to the house and gardens, *Penshurst Place and Gardens*, 7.

59. Fowler, 57–58. On Robert Sidney's financial difficulties, which Jonson may be ignoring or covering up in the poem, see McBride, 66–69.

60. Camden, *Britannia*, tr. Holland, 329.

61. Fowler, 60.

62. Wayne, *Penshurst: The Semiotics of Place and the Poetics of History*, 126-128.

63. Fowler, 92

64. Wotton, 116; Alberti, *Art of Building*, 2.1, p. 33.

65. Carew, "To My Friend G.N. from Wrest," lines 9-10, 14-18. All subsequent quotations from the poem are cited parenthetically by line number in the text.

66. See, for instance, Vitruvius, Book 6, which discusses both the use and attractiveness of various elements of private buildings.

67. Fowler, 93; Anderson, "Learning to Read Architecture in the English Renaissance," 239-242. Wells-Cole offers many examples of chimneypieces. See, for instance, his illustration of the overmantel at Castle Ashby, Northamptonshire, dated 1599 (57).

68. See Orgel and Strong, *Inigo Jones: The Theatre of the Stuart Court*, 2.567-597.

69. Carew, *Coelum Britannicum*, 2.

70. Carew, *Coelum Britannicum*, 1.

71. Marvell, "Upon Appleton House," lines 1-10. All subsequent quotations from the poem are cited parenthetically by line number in the text.

72. Fowler, 296.

73. Vitruvius, *Ten Books*, 1.3, p. 25. For an intellectual history of this idea, see *Body and Building: Essays on the Changing Relationship of Body and Architecture*, ed. Dodds and Tavernor.

74. Alberti, *Art of Building*, 9.5, p. 302.

75. Fowler, 294-295.

76. Norden, *The Surveyors Dialogue*, 84.

77. Norden, *The Surveyors Dialogue*, 86.

CHAPTER 3: STRANGE ANTHOLOGIES:
THE ALCHEMIST IN THE LONDON OF JOHN STOW

1. It is not my contention that Jonson drew directly on the *Survey* in writing *The Alchemist*. He was, however, familiar with some of Stow's work. See his remark in the *Conversations with Drummond*: "John Stow had monstrous observations in his *Chronicle*, and was of his craft a tailor. 'He and I walking alone, he asked two cripples what they would have to take him to their order'," 608. Harry Levin discusses this remark at length in "Jonson, Stow, and Drummond," 167-169.

2. Griffin, "Preserving and Reserving the Past in Stow's *Survey of London*," 57.

3. For comment on Stow's nostalgia, see Griffin, 56-57; Howard, *Theater of a City*, 5-7; Lindley, *Tomb Destruction and Scholarship*, 75; Collinson, "John Stow and Nostalgic Antiquarianism," 27-51; and Archer, "The Nostalgia of John Stow," 17-34.

4. Howard, *Theater of a City*, 2.

5. For Jonson's use of neo-Aristotelian unities, see Mardock, *Our Scene Is London: Ben Jonson's City and the Space of the Author*, 87; Sterling, "Jonson and His Era: Overviews of Modern Research: Alchemist, The," 115; Donaldson, *Jonson's Magic Houses*, 90-91.

6. Jonson, *The Alchemist*, ed. F. H. Mares, 1.1.17, 4.1.131. All subsequent quotations from the play are cited parenthetically by act, scene, and line numbers in the text.

7. Mares, "Introduction," lxiii–lxv; Donaldson, 66–105; Smallwood, "'Here, in the Friars': Immediacy and Theatricality in *The Alchemist*," 149. For arguments that the play was first performed in the Globe, see Herford and Simpson's commentary in Jonson, *Works*, 9.223; and Gibbons, "The Question of Place," 35–36. Campbell raises the possibility that the play was first performed at the Globe but was intended to be performed at the Blackfriars ("Introduction," xvii).

8. Mardock extends the implications of the identity between house and theater to argue that "[t]he house in the 'Friars allows Jonson to make the claim that the dramatic spatial practices of the theater can affect not only the potential worlds inside the playhouse, but also the urban world outside it," 85. On the play's meta-theatricality, see McEvoy, *Ben Jonson: Renaissance Dramatist*, 104–105; Evans, *Habits of Mind: Evidence and Effects of Ben Jonson's Reading*, 149; Cave, *Ben Jonson*, 77–78; Riggs, *Ben Jonson: A Life*, 172.

9. Donaldson, 77. See also Barton, *Ben Jonson, Dramatist*, 143.

10. Stow apparently owned a copy of Leland's itineraries, in exchange for which Camden offered him an annuity of eight pounds. Herendeen, *From Landscape to Literature: The River and the Myth of Geography*, 198.

11. See McIntosh, who argues that in *The Alchemist*, "the city is integral to the ways in which its citizens imagine themselves and carry out their attempts to climb the social ladder" ("Space, Place and Transformation in *Eastward Ho!* and *The Alchemist*," 71).

12. Many critics have commented on the centrality of alchemy as the play's unifying metaphor. Knapp notes that "alchemy was a practice familiar enough to signify a range of personal and social desires and yet sufficiently mystified to dazzle" ("The Work of Alchemy," 576). See also Barton, 137; Flachmann, "Ben Jonson and the Alchemy of Satire," 260; and Gibbons, *Jacobean City Comedy*, 169–170.

13. *The Alchemist* is dedicated to Lady Mary Wroth, the eldest daughter of Sir Robert Sidney and wife of the landowner addressed in Jonson's estate poem "To Sir Robert Wroth" (Mares, 3–4). For Jonson's interest in architecture, see A. W. Johnson, *Ben Jonson: Poetry and Architecture*, 9–19; and Gail Kern Paster, "Ben Jonson and the Uses of Architecture," 306–320. See also Jonson's remark in *Discoveries*, which compares the structural decorum of a literary work to that of a well-proportioned house (591). Studies that do consider the two works together include Donaldson (67–88) and Jenkins, *Feigned Commonwealths: The Country House Poem and the Fashioning of the Ideal Community* (45).

14. Schofield, *The Building of London from the Conquest to the Great Fire*, 147–148. See also Schofield, "The Topography and Buildings of London, ca. 1600," 296–321. Stow also describes the fate of the priory, as well as its history in *A Survey of London*, 1.121–124. All quotations from Stow are hereafter cited parenthetically by volume and page numbers in the text.

15. For London's mixture of social classes, see Peck, "Building, Buying, and Collecting in London, 1600–1625," 277; and Schofield, "The Topography and Buildings of London," 297.

16. Harding, "City, Capitol, and Metropolis: The Changing Shape of Seventeenth-Century London," 127. For London's crowded conditions, see also Orlin, "Boundary Disputes in Early Modern London," 345–376. For the city's changing demographics, see Griffiths, Landers, Pelling, and Tyson, "Population and Disease, Estrangement and Belonging, 1540–1700," 2.195–233.

17. Hughes and Larkin, eds., *Stuart Royal Proclamations*, 1.111–112.

18. Hughes and Larkin, *Stuart Royal Proclamations*, 1.267. For a detailed and localized study of how such regulations were received and implemented, see Griffiths, "Politics Made Visible: Order, Residence and Uniformity in Cheapside, 1600–45," 176–196.

19. Harrison, *The Description of England*, 197.

20. Harding, 127.

21. Archer, "Discourses of History in London," 206; Turner, *The English Renaissance Stage: Geometry, Poetics, and the Practical Spatial Arts, 1580–1630*, 192.

22. Archer, "Discourses of History," 206.

23. Collinson, "John Stow," 34.

24. William Camden, *Britannia*, tr. Philemon Holland, 807–808.

25. Jonson, "To Penshurst," line 102. Quotations from "To Penshurst" are hereafter cited parenthetically by line number in the text.

26. Harris, *Untimely Matter in the Time of Shakespeare*, 96–97.

27. Herendeen posits, "With the willful destruction of history's treasures began a period of intense acquisitiveness" (*From Landscape to Literature*, 187).

28. Lindley, 75; Collinson, "John Stow," 36–37; Archer, "The Nostalgia of John Stow," 20–23.

29. For Stow's treatment of charity in the *Survey*, see Archer, "The Nostalgia of John Stow," 27–28.

30. Fitzherbert, *Surveyenge*, fol. 38 v–39 r. Camden, *Britannia*, tr. Holland, "The Author to the Reader," 4–[5].

31. Hall, *The Union of the Two Noble and Illustre Fameleis of Lancastre & Yorke*, SSS ii r.

32. Hosley, "The Second Blackfriars Playhouse," 3.197–205.

33. Mardock comments on the necessity of "exerting a tight control over *lieu*" in the play, 87.

34. Jenkins comments on the significance of gender in this scene: "It is . . . a *woman's* body rather than a man's, that maps the ideological boundaries of *The Alchemist*'s 'commonwealth' of knaves" (49).

35. See, for instance, Knapp, who feels that the play does not deal with "alchemists who are, or believe they are, carrying out the alchemical project" (578).

36. For extensive discussion of alchemy as a process that "affects not metals, but human beings," see Barton, 137–141.

37. Ripley, *Compound of Alchymy*, A 4 r.

38. For Jonson's familiarity with alchemical treatises and terminology, see Linden, "Ben Jonson and the Drama of Alchemy," in *Darke Hieroglipicks: Alchemy in English Literature from Chaucer to the Reformation*, 118–153; and Flachmann, 260.

39. Barton, 152.

40. On Jonson's "anti-acquisitive attitude" in the play, see Knights, *Drama and Society in the Age of Jonson*, 206–210.

41. For comment on Lovewit's imposition of order, see Barton, 150–151; and Gibbons, *Jacobean City Comedy*, 176.

42. Gibbons, *Jacobean City Comedy*, 178.

CHAPTER 4: RESTORING "THE CHURCH-PORCH":
GEORGE HERBERT'S ARCHITECTURAL HISTORY

1. Extended modern discussions dedicated specifically to "The Church-porch" are few. See Summers, "Introduction" in *Selected Poetry of George Herbert*, xiii–xxiii; Kessner, "Entering 'The Church-Porch': Herbert and Wisdom Poetry," 10–25; Hinman, "The 'Verser' at *The Temple* Door: Herbert's 'The Church-porch'," 55–75; Anselment, "Seventeenth-Century Adaptations of 'The Church-porch'," 63–69; and Powers-Beck, "'The Church-porch' and George Herbert's Family Advice" in *Writing the Flesh: The Herbert Family Dialogue*, 59–94. For briefer treatments see Strier, "George Herbert and the World," 225–232; Bloch, *Spelling the Word: George Herbert and the Bible*, 180–188; Singleton, *God's Courtier: Configuring a Different Grace in George Herbert's Temple*, 164–173; Shuger, *Habits of Thought in the English Renaissance*, 93–105; and Malcolmson, *Heart-work: George Herbert and the Protestant Ethic*, 70–81. Influential modern studies which do not treat the poem in depth include Rickey, *Utmost Art*; Vendler, *The Poetry of George Herbert*; Fish, *The Living Temple: George Herbert and Catechizing*; Strier, *Love Known: Theology and Experience in George Herbert's Poetry*; Schoenfeldt, *Prayer and Power: George Herbert and Renaissance Courtship*; Hodgkins, *Authority, Church, and Society in George Herbert: Return to the Middle Way*. In his recent study of the intrusive "untimely matter" of Herbert's poetry, Harris neglects "The Church-porch," which we might call the most emphatically material of Herbert's poems, despite the fact that its objects take on the sort of polychronic valences with which Harris is concerned in *Untimely Matter in the Time of Shakespeare*, 32–65.

2. Strier, comparing the poem to works by François de Sales and John Donne, describes "The Church-porch" as "the crudest and nastiest of the texts" and suggests that Herbert later came to feel "revulsion against the attitudes that he there expressed" ("Sanctifying the Aristocracy: 'Devout Humanism' in François de Sales, John Donne, and George Herbert," 38). James Boyd White describes the poem as "deeply flawed: by banality, by the emergence of destructive and selfish impulses, and by blindness to its own nature" (*"This Book of Starres": Learning to Read George Herbert*, 71). More mildly, Benet contrasts the poem with "Herbert's best poems," those which "praise God and instruct the reader without alienating by direct assaults" (*Secretary of Praise: The Poetic Vocation of George Herbert*, 36).

3. Summers, xiii.

4. Summers, xiv.

5. Martz, *The Poetry of Meditation*; Lewalski, "Artful Psalms from the Temple in the Heart" in *Protestant Poetics and the Seventeenth-Century Religious Lyric*, 283–316; and Strier, *Love Known*.

6. For instance, see readings of "The Altar" by Targoff and Guibbory. Targoff writes: "On the one hand, Herbert offers the equivalent of wordless sighs and groans; on the other hand, he proposes a formalized prayer composed in the shape of an altar" (*Common Prayer: The Language of Public Devotion in Early Modern England*, 101). Similarly, in a chapter entitled "Devotion in *The Temple* and the Art of Contradiction," Guibbory concludes: "Herbert shares [the] puritan fear of framing or fashioning an idol. Yet his suspicion of art and inven-

tion in worship is at odds with his hopes for the poem's legitimacy and his claims for its devotional function" (*Ceremony and Community from Herbert to Milton*, 48). See also Whalen, "George Herbert's Sacramental Puritanism," 1273-1307.

7. In addition to Guibbory and Targoff, see Davidson, "George Herbert and Stained Glass Windows," 29-39; Cunnar, "Herbert and the Visual Arts: Ut Pictura Poesis: An Opening in 'The Windows'," 101-138; and Johnson, "Recreating the Word: Typology in Herbert's 'The Altar'," 55-65.

8. Anselment, 63; Leach, "More Seventeenth-Century Admirers of Herbert," 62-63.

9. Friar, *The Sutton Companion to the English Parish Church*, 356.

10. Pounds, *A History of the English Parish: The Culture of Religion from Augustine to Victoria*, 373.

11. Malcolmson comments briefly on the historical uses of the porch, but beyond noting that the porch was sometimes also associated with childhood education, she does not reflect extensively on the connections between the poem and its architectural setting (*George Herbert: A Literary Life*, 58-59).

12. Charles, *A Life of George Herbert*, 78. See, for instance, lines 85-90, which address magistrates, students, and soldiers. The topics of gentility and social class in the poem have been usefully discussed at Summers, xv; Strier, "Sanctifying the Aristocracy," 44-58; Malcolmson, *George Herbert: A Literary Life*, 58-59; and Powers-Beck, 60-95.

13. Porches dating from before the thirteenth century are rare, but by the fourteenth century they were "regarded as a necessity" (Brown, *The English Village Church*, 113-114). For other summaries of the porch's development and historical functions, see Barr, *Anglican Church Architecture*, 32-33; Dyer, *Church-Lore Gleanings*, 39-52; Wall, *Porches and Fonts*, vii-174; Cox and Ford, *The Parish Churches of England*, 41-43, 71-72; Boyle, *Old Parish Churches and How to View Them*, 24-26, 78-79; Anderson, *Looking for History in British Churches*, 74-76; Betjeman, ed. *Collins Guide to English Parish Churches, Including the Isle of Man*, 25-26; and Clifton-Taylor, *English Parish Churches as Works of Art*, 121-122.

14. Bond, *An Introduction to English Church Architecture from the Eleventh to the Sixteenth Century*, 2.731, 733. Bond offers an exceptionally thorough history of church porches (2.718-734).

15. Wall, *Porches and Fonts*, 218, 223-225.

16. Chaucer, "The Wife of Bath's Prologue," line 5.

17. Fletcher, "Brigham Church," 161-162.

18. Wall, *Porches and Fonts*, 15. See also Herrick, "The Entertainment; or, *Porch Verse*," 124.

19. Friar, 241.

20. Wall, *Porches and Fonts*, 174. A conversation in *Notes and Queries* of 1908 indicates that directives about pattens (protective footwear) were not uncommon. See, for instance, Page, "Pattens in the Church Porch," 268. Betjeman, in deriding the work of Victorian church restorer J. P. St. Aubyn, remarks that he often "left his mark at the church porch in the form of a scraper [for boots and shoes] of his own design, as practical and unattractive as his work" (27).

21. See Bond, 2.733; Circket, ed. *English Wills, 1498-1526*, 15, 27, 65; Ware, "Notes upon the Parish Church of Kirkby Lonsdale," 198; and Richards, *Old Cheshire Churches*, 25.

22. Dyer, 39–40.
23. Paterson, "The Church Porch," 303.
24. See, for instance, Hailey, *Notes and Queries*, 284, who records a similar instance of 1751.
25. Bond, 2.734.
26. Creed, "The Church of St. Peter and St. Paul, Eye," 129.
27. A.S., *Notes and Queries*, 597. See also Bumpus, *London Churches, Ancient and Modern*, 1.232n.
28. Bond, 2.733.
29. Anderson, *Looking for History*, 76.
30. Clifton-Taylor, 122.
31. In some descriptions, the upper chamber of a porch is referred to as a parvise, but most ecclesiologists insist this term is not technically accurate. For the etymology and significance of the word, see Bond, 2.727–728n. For specific instances of porch chambers as chapels, see Bell, *Bedfordshire Wills, 1484–1533*, 31, 177; and Rodwell and Rouse, "The Anglo-Saxon Rood and Other Features in the South Porch of St. Mary's Church, Breamore, Hampshire," 298–325.
32. Clifton-Taylor, 122.
33. Evelyn, *Diary*, ed. Bédoyère, 21.
34. Price, "St. Sepulchre's, London: The Church Porch," 366–367; Rogers, "Keeping School in the Parvise over the Church Porch," 394; Dyer, 43.
35. Anselment, 63.
36. Palmer, "E.C. Lowe's Edition of George Herbert's 'Church Porch'," 442. Benet notes that John Ruskin enthusiastically planned a similar undertaking (35n6).
37. "Cheltenham Church," 65; Anderson, *Looking for History*, 76; Clifton-Taylor, 122; Cox and Ford, 43; Bumpus, 1.232.
38. Brown, *The English Village Church*, 117. See also Richards, who noted in the porch chamber of St. Mary, Astbury, "old vestment chests, the remains of a chained library, part of an early fifteenth-century screen, pewter flagons, old alms pans, and sections of a fourteenth-century pavement and many curious old items of long ago" (26).
39. For the Chatterton story, see Lewis, "St. Mary Redcliffe: A Life's Failure" in *Cathedrals, Abbeys and Churches of England and Wales*, 3.398–404; and Meyerstein, *A Life of Thomas Chatterton*, 104–128.
40. One complaint about the poem has been its seeming randomness. See, for instance, White, who writes, "The speaker meanders from topic to topic in a kind of random way" (71), while Summers suggests that the repetition may be partly attributed to Herbert's revisions and excuses it on the grounds that "seventy-seven stanzas of imperative moral advice are a large number for anyone to manage without repetition" (xv).
41. See, for instance, Walker, "The Architectonics of George Herbert's *The Temple*," 289–305; Kessner, "Entering 'The Church-porch': Herbert and Wisdom Poetry," 10–25; Malcolmson, *Heart-work*, 79–80; Dyck, "Locating the Word: The Textual Church and George Herbert's *Temple*," 228.
42. Martz, 291.
43. Adrian, *Local Negotiations of English Nationhood: 1570–1680*, 109.

44. See, for instance, Cautley, *Norfolk Churches*, 10; Boyle, 25; Brown, *The English Village Church*, 113.

45. Quotations from the poem are cited parenthetically by line number and are taken from *The English Poems of George Herbert*, ed. Wilcox.

46. Bond, 2.733.

47. See, for instance, Kessner, "Entering 'The Church-porch'"; Bloch, 176–189; and Summers, xvii.

48. Summers, xiii; White, 69.

49. Bloch, 185.

50. Summers, xiv.

51. Cooley, *'Full of All Knowledg': George Herbert's* Country Parson *and Early Modern Social Discourse*, 84–85, 96–97.

52. For the historical connections between heraldry and church architecture, see Poole, *A History of Ecclesiastical Architecture in England*, 209–210.

53. Herbert, *Outlandish Proverbs Selected by Mr. G.H.*

54. Stein writes that, in "The Church-porch," "we must not expect to find answers to any of our important questions. . . . The faults of dull rhythm and language and of strained wit are not instructive, nor do we need to study, in Herbert, examples of coarse or flat colloquialism in order to distinguish these from the superior precision of refined colloquialism" (*George Herbert's Lyrics*, 13–14).

55. See, for instance, Summers, xviii; and Strier, "Sanctifying the Aristocracy," 50–53.

56. Summers, xviii.

57. Strier, "Sanctifying the Aristocracy," 50.

58. I thus disagree strongly with Strier, who concludes from these passages: "With regard to social rather than strictly economic life, hoarding, calculation, and thrift are entirely approved in 'The Church-porch.' Individual survival and gain are the only concerns. The poem contains no vision of community" ("Sanctifying the Aristocracy," 52–53). Rather, I would argue, the poem teaches that social, economic, and communal behaviors are inseparable from one another.

59. Strier, "George Herbert and the World," 227.

60. For the poem's sartorial themes, see lines 80, 179–192, 371–372, 407–408, 410–414, and 419–420. I agree with Malcolmson's useful point that Herbert does not suggest that "aspects of gentry lifestyle are trivial or expendable," but our interpretations diverge in that Malcolmson sees the poem as being structured around a contrast or tension between the internal and external identities of the listener, where one must finally be shed in order to expose the other (*Heart-work*, 79). For a similar view of the relationship between social and sacred in the poem, see Singleton, 172–173.

61. Summers, xxii.

62. I would argue that in blending the introspection, experience, and emotion of the individual with his quotidian action in the external world, these final stanzas of the poem complicate readings that center on a tension between internal and external forms of religious experience or between social and interior constructions of the religious subject. In addition to Malcolmson, *Heart-work*, 70–83, and Singleton, 164–173, see Shuger, 93–105, where she posits the emergence of a "dual person" as we move from the "The Church-porch" to

"The Church" (105). I would not, of course, dispute Shuger's point that the latter is far less concerned with social behavior.

63. Wall, *Porches and Fonts*, 173. For more examples, see Wall, 172–174; Richards, 49, 331; Ware, 198; Creed, 127–29; and Smithe, "Notes on the Church of St. Bartholomew, Churchdown," 282-284. Gifts for the porch were apparently a very popular way to show devotion, because the porch was so publically visible. See Pounds, who writes: "In no aspect of the parish church were pride and emulation more visibly demonstrated than in the building of the tower and the porch. The tower had no liturgical significance, and the porch but little. Yet . . . in parish after parish, large sums were lavished on both," 373.

64. Richards, 181.

65. Smithe, 282.

66. Waters, "Thornbury Church," 86.

67. Creed, 129. The inscription is also recorded in Anderson, *Looking for History*, 75, and Cautley, *Suffolk Churches and Their Treasures*, 51.

68. Smyth, *Autobiography in Early Modern England*, 159–208.

69. Powys, *The English Parish Church*, 52–53, 54.

70. Richardson, *The Changing Face of English Local History*.

CHAPTER 5: CONSTRUCTION SITES:
THE ARCHITECTURE OF ANNE CLIFFORD'S DIARIES

1. Clifford, *The Diaries of Lady Anne Clifford*, ed. D. J. H. Clifford, 117. Hereafter cited parenthetically in the text as *Diaries*, with page numbers. The most thorough account of the legal proceedings is provided by Spence, *Lady Anne Clifford*, 40–58. For comment on the biographical and legal content of Clifford's writings and buildings, see, for instance Salzman, *Reading Early Modern Women's Writing*, 90–108; Seelig, *Autobiography and Gender in Early Modern Literature: Reading Women's Lives, 1660–1680*, 34–72; Wiseman, "Knowing Her Place: Anne Clifford and the Politics of Retreat," 199–213; Suzuki, "Anne Clifford and the Gendering of History," 195–229; Klein, "Lady Anne Clifford as Mother and Matriarch: Domestic and Dynastic Issues in Her Life and Writings," 18–38; O'Connor, "Representations of Intimacy in the Life-Writing of Anne Clifford and Anne Dormer," 79–96; Friedman, "Constructing an Identity in Prose, Plaster, and Paint: Lady Anne Clifford as Writer and Patron of the Arts," 359–376, and "Inside/Out: Women, Domesticity, and the Pleasures of the City," 229–250.

2. Both twentieth-century editions of the diaries—the first edited by Vita Sackville-West (*The Diary of the Lady Anne Clifford*) in 1924, the second by D. J. H. Clifford in 1990—include fragments of Clifford's much briefer early diaries, which cover four nonconsecutive years between 1603 and 1619. These have survived, separately from the Great Books, in two transcriptions, one of which is now in the Centre for Kentish Studies in Maidstone. The other remains in the collection of the Marquess of Bath. The diaries covering the years 1616–1619 have been published in a critical edition by Acheson, *The Diary of Anne Clifford, 1616–1619*.

3. See, for instance, Kunin, "From the Desk of Anne Clifford," 587–608; Salzman, 97; and Wiseman, 199.

4. See for instance, Spence, *Lady Anne*, 170–172.

5. See Chew, "A Mockery of the Surveyor's Style?: Alternatives to Inigo Jones in Seven-

teenth-Century Elite British Architecture," 57–95; McBride, *Country House Discourse in Early Modern England*, 77–78; Friedman, "Constructing an Identity," 369; Cocke, "Classical or Gothic?: Lady Anne Clifford Reconsidered," 324–326; and Henry Summerson, "The History of the Castle," 7–78, esp. 51–53.

6. On the impersonal nature of the diaries, see, for example, Salzman, 93–94; and Seelig, 57. Several critics have collected scattered details from throughout the diaries in order to analyze Clifford's treatment of particular themes. Lamb, for instance, notes the multiple instances in which the diary records the titles of books Clifford was reading; Lamb suggests possible motivations for Clifford's choices in "The Agency of the Split Subject: Lady Anne Clifford and the Uses of Reading," 347–368. Klein looks at Clifford's notations of children's births and deaths, and Suzuki considers how Clifford's portrayals of women in history respond to those of male historians, such as Samuel Daniel, who tutored Clifford when she was young.

7. Spence, *Lady Anne*, 108.

8. For a photograph of the inscription, see Spence, *Lady Anne*, 203.

9. Reproduced in Summerson, "History of the Castle," 52. The panel is now on display in the museum adjacent to the castle.

10. Isa. 58:12 (KJV).

11. Spence, *The Privateering Earl*, 7.

12. Clifford, Great Books of Record, 2.485. Subsequent references to unpublished material from the Great Books are to this record and are cited parenthetically by volume and page number in the text. Quotations are reproduced with the kind permission of the Cumbria Archive Centre, Kendal.

13. Ps. 107:3–4 (KJV).

14. Spence, *Lady Anne*, 6.

15. D. J. H. Clifford suggests that this was Edward Hassell, her private secretary and one of the four different scribes to whom she dictated her final entries.

16. Chew, "'Repaired by me to my exceeding great Cost and Charges': Anne Clifford and the Uses of Architecture," 111. For further discussion of this practice of repetition, see also Chew, "Si(gh)ting the Mistress of the House: Anne Clifford and Architectural Space," 167–182.

17. For an art-historical interpretation of Clifford's monuments, see Cocke, "Repairer of the Breach," 84–86. Spence notes that some biographers have read the monuments to her parents as barometers of her relative affection for each (*Lady Anne*, 224). Clifford had commissioned work on monuments twice before: a restoration of Edmund Spenser's monument in Westminster Abbey by the eminent mason Nicholas Stone in 1620, and a monument to her cousin Frances Bourchier in the Bedford Chapel at Chenies in 1615 (Spence, *Lady Anne*, 67, 68, 70).

18. Wordsworth, "Essay upon Epitaphs I," 2:58.

19. Williamson, *Lady Anne Clifford, Countess of Dorset, Pembroke and Montgomery, 1590–1676*, 408.

20. Weever, *Ancient Funerall Monuments*, 5.

21. Complete transcriptions of Anne's and Margaret's tombs are included in Bellasis, *Westmorland Church Notes*, 1.7, 24. They are here transcribed from a photograph by the author.

22. For a complete transcription of the epitaphs on the Clifford Tombs in Skipton, see Pyrah, *The Parish Church of the Holy Trinity Skipton: A History and Guide*, 10–14.

23. Williamson, 411.

24. For a photograph of the Daniel monument, see Spence, *Lady Anne*, 154.

25. See Spence, *Lady Anne*, 38. Margaret Clifford's will is compiled with other family documents in Clay, "The Clifford Family," 355–411.

26. In addition to Weever's *Ancient Funerall Monuments*, see Camden, *Reges, Reginae, Nobiles et Alij in Ecclesia Collegiata B. Petri Westmonasterij Sepulti*.

27. Dates of birth and death for Clifford's ancestors are taken from the genealogical table provided by D. J. H. Clifford in his edition of the *Diaries*, vi–vii.

28. Camden, *Britannia*, tr. Philemon Holland, 288.

29. Clifford, Great Books of Record, 1.106,161, 188. For a list of the books depicted in the Appleby Triptych, see Spence, *Lady Anne*, 190–191.

30. Orgel, "Marginal Maternity: Reading Lady Anne Clifford's *A Mirror for Magistrates*," 267–290.

31. Ziegler, "Lady Anne Clifford Reads John Selden," 3. Letter from Anne Clifford to Elizabeth Grey, February 10, 1650, BL, Harl. 7001, fol. 212, quoted in Spence, *Lady Anne*, 141.

32. Spence, *Lady Anne*, 167.

33. Spence, *Lady Anne*, 219–220. Clifford's contact with Dodsworth, Dugdale, and other antiquaries is described in detail on 165–172.

34. See Lewalski, *Writing Women in Jacobean England*, 137. In her assertion that Clifford could not read Latin, Lewalski refers to Clifford's own remark in her summary of her mother's life, as reprinted in Clifford, *Lives of Lady Anne Clifford and of Her Parents*, 28.

35. Parry, *The Trophies of Time: English Antiquarians of the Seventeenth Century*, 235.

36. Parry, 236.

37. Dodsworth and Dugdale, *Monasticon Anglicanum*, vol. 1, plate between pp. 18 and 19. Engraving by Daniel King.

38. Dodsworth and Dugdale, vol. 1, pl. between pp. 56 and 57. Engraving by Daniel King.

39. Dodsworth and Dugdale, vol. 1, pl. between pp. 62 and 63. Engraving by Daniel King.

40. Spence, *Lady Anne*, 168–169.

41. Fuller, *The Church-History of Britain from the Birth of Jesus Christ, Untill the Year M. DC. XLVIII*, book 6, p. 325.

42. Tanner, *Notitia Monastica, or a Short History of the Religious Houses in England and Wales*, a 3 r.

43. See, for instance, Stow's description of Austin Friars in *A Survey of London*, 1.176–177. For the details of the settlement, see Spence, *Lady Anne*, 57.

44. Spence, *Lady Anne*, 166.

45. Dodsworth and Dugdale, *Monasticon Anglicanum*.

46. Camden, *Britannia*, tr. Holland, 212.

47. Summerson, "History of the Castle," 54.

48. Charlton, "The Lady Anne Clifford," 310.

49. Leland and Bale, *The Laboryouse Journey and Serche of Johan Leylande, for Englandes Antiquitees*, B ii r.

50. See, for instance, my introduction, p. 14.

51. For a description of St. Michael, Bongate, see Pevsner, *The Buildings of England: Cumberland and Westmorland*, 218. For the gateway at Skipton Castle, see Charlton, 307. For the window at Holy Trinity Church, Skipton, see Cocke, "Classical or Gothic?" 326. For the church at Ninekirks, see Cocke, "Repairer of the Breach," 86. Inscriptions at Skipton and Appleby were observed by the author in August 2004, at which time the characters in brackets were no longer visible.

52. Dodsworth, *Yorkshire Church Notes, 1619–1631*. See also Hunter, "A Catalogue of the Manuscripts Written or Collected by that Eminent Antiquary Roger Dodsworth and Now Deposited in the Bodleian Library" in *Three Catalogues*, 69–72.

53. Camden, *Britannia*, tr. Holland, 271.

54. "Author to the Reader," in Weever, [2].

55. Dugdale, *The History of St. Paul's Cathedral in London*, title page.

56. Rainbow, *A Sermon Preached at the Funeral of the Right Honorable Anne, Countess of Pembroke, Dorset, and Montgomery*, 4, 15.

57. Rainbow, 16, 18.

58. Rainbow, 67–68.

59. Rainbow, 40.

60. Woolf, "Donne After Three Centuries," 34.

61. Clifford's will is transcribed in Clay, 401.

62. Williamson, 412.

63. Daniel, *Certaine Small Workes Heretofore Divulged by Samuel Daniel*, A 2 r. For Daniel's influence on Clifford's education, see Spence, *Lady Anne*, 12–17.

64. Reproduced in Williamson, 422.

65. Spence, *Lady Anne*, 129.

66. Williamson, 422.

CHAPTER 6: RECOLLECTIONS: JOHN EVELYN AND THE HISTORIES OF RESTORATION ARCHITECTURE

1. Colvin, *A Biographical Dictionary of English Architects, 1660–1840*, 3rd ed., 357–358.

2. Evelyn, *The Diary and Correspondence of John Evelyn, F.R.S.*, ed. Bray, 3.188. For Evelyn's plans for the rebuilding of London following the Great Fire, see Evelyn, *London Revived: Consideration for Its Rebuilding in 1666*.

3. Chaney, "Evelyn, Inigo Jones, and the Collector Earl of Arundel," 53.

4. Shiqiao, *Power and Virtue: Architecture and Intellectual Change in England, 1660–1730*, 33; Friedman, "John Evelyn and English Architecture," 157; Downes, "John Evelyn and Architecture: A First Inquiry," 32.

5. Bowle, *John Evelyn and His World: A Biography*, 128.

6. Miller, *The Restoration and the England of Charles II*, 14.

7. Keeble, *The Restoration: England in the 1660s*, 69; D. [Dauncey?], *The History of His Sacred Majesty Charles the II*, 21.

8. Evelyn, *The Diary of John Evelyn*, ed. de Beer, 2.343, 2.478. For comment on Evelyn's activities as a collector, see Chaney, "Evelyn, Inigo Jones, and the Collector Earl of Arundel," 37–60, and "The Italianate Evolution of English Collecting," 61. See also Hunter, "John

Evelyn in the 1650s: A Virtuoso in Quest of a Role," 79–106; and Friedman, "John Evelyn and English Architecture," 161.

9. Evelyn, *Diary of John Evelyn*, ed. de Beer, 3.495–496.

10. Evelyn, *Diary and Correspondence of John Evelyn, F.R.S.*, ed. Bray, 3.304.

11. De Beer concludes that the diary "becomes a contemporary document from about the beginning of 1684" (Evelyn, *Diary of John Evelyn*, 1.74). For Evelyn's use and borrowing of various source materials, see de Beer's detailed commentary on 1.85–105.

12. Fréart, *A Parallel of the Antient Architecture with the Modern*, tr. Evelyn, 17, 19. All subsequent references to this edition are cited parenthetically by page number in the text.

13. The modern Italian authors the *Parallèle* includes are Leon Battista Alberti (1404–1472), architect and author of *De re aedifactoria* (Florence, 1485); Sebastiano Serlio (1475–c. 1555), architect and author of *Tutte l'opere d'architettura* (Venice, 1584); Giacomo Barozzi da Vignola (1507–1573), architect and author of *La regola dell cinque ordini d'architettura* (Rome, 1652); Andrea Palladio (1508–1580), architect and author of *I Quattro libri de architettura* (Venice, 1570); Pietro Cataneo (b. c. 1510, d. after 1571), author of *I quattro primi libri de architecttura* (Venice, 1554) and *L'architettura de Pietro Cataneo* (Venice, 1567); Daniele Barbaro (1514–1570), translator of and commentator on Vitruvius, patron of Palladio, editor and translator of *I dieci libri dell'architettura de M. Vitruvio* (Venice, 1556); Vincenzo Scamozzi (1548–1616), architect and author of *L'idea dell'architettura universale* (Venice, 1615); and Giuseppi Viola Zanini (?1575–1631), architect and author of *Della architettura di Gioseffe Viola padovano pittore ed architetto* (Padua, 1629). The Frenchmen are Philibert de l'Orme (1514–1570), architect and author of *Nouvelles inventions pour bien bastir et à petits fraiz* (Paris, 1561), *Le premier tome de l'architecture* (Paris, 1567), and *Architecture de Philibert de l'Orme* (Rouen, 1648); and Jean Bullant (c. 1515–1578), architect and author of *Reigle générale d'architecture des cinq manières de colonnes à l'exemple d l'antique suivant les reigles et doctrine de Vitruve* (Paris, 1564).

14. Asfour and Bull, "Fréart," in *Grove Art Online. Oxford Art Online* (accessed July 14, 2009). For a more extensive analysis of Fréart as architectural theorist, see Lemerle-Pauwels and Stanic, "Introduction générale."

15. Friedman, "John Evelyn and English Architecture," 157.

16. Palladio, *The Four Books of Architecture*, 3.163.

17. Southcombe and Tapsell, *Restoration, Politics, Religion, and Culture*, 9, 10.

18. Great Britain, "An Act of Free and Generall Pardon Indempnity and Oblivion," 5.226.

19. Great Britain, "An Act for a Perpetuall Anniversary Thanksgiveing on the nine and twentieth day of May," 5.237.

20. Keeble, 69; Charles II, *His Majesties Gracious Letter and Declaration Sent to the House of Peers by Sir John Grenvil, K[t]. From Breda: And Read in the House the First of May*, 1660, 9.

21. Marvell, "Upon Appleton House," line 2.

22. For Evelyn's plans for the rebuilding of London, as well as his verbal commentary, see Evelyn, *London Revived*.

23. Colvin, *The History of the King's Works*, 5.5.

24. Evelyn, *Diary of John Evelyn*, ed. de Beer, 3.301.

25. Evelyn, "Account of Architects and Architecture," in Roland Fréart, *A Parallel of the Antient Architecture with the Modern*, tr. John Evelyn (1707), 10 of "Account."

26. See Vitruvius, *Ten Books on Architecture*, 1.1, pp. 21–24.

27. See Vitruvius, *On Architecture*, 6.9, pp. 56–59.

28. Swann, *Curiosities and Texts*, 99.

29. De Krey, *Restoration and Revolution in Britain: A Political History of the Era of Charles II and the Glorious Revolution*, 27.

30. Evelyn, "Account of Architects and Architecture," (1707), 9 of "Account."

31. Swann, 10.

32. Pearce, "Objects as Meaning; or Narrating the Past," 27, 28.

33. Evelyn, *Numismata*, 49.

34. Stewart, *On Longing*, 156.

35. Scott, *England's Troubles: Seventeenth-Century English Political Instability in European Context*, 162.

36. Stewart, 151.

37. Zwicker, "Irony, Modernity, and Miscellany: Politics and Aesthetics in the Stuart Restoration," 182.

38. Wall, *The Literary and Cultural Spaces of Restoration London*, 44.

39. Perks, *Essays on Old London*, 48.

40. Stewart, 152.

41. Evelyn, "To My Most Honoured Friend, Sir Christopher Wren, K^r," [2].

42. Evelyn, "To My Most Honoured Friend," [1].

CODA: ST. HELEN'S BISHOPSGATE: ANTIQUARIANISM AND AESTHETICS IN MODERN LONDON

1. Cameron, "In the Matter of the Petition of the Incumbent and Churchwardens of the Parish of St Helen Bishopsgate with St Andrew Undershaft and St Ethelburga Bishopsgate and St Martin Outwich and St Mary Axe Relating to the Church of St Helen Bishopsgate," 2. Records of the Consistory Court hearing, as well as Terry's proposals for the rebuilding, are preserved by the London Metropolitan Archives DL/A/C/MS30779/37. Quotations are reproduced by the kind permission of the London Metropolitan Archives and the Registrar of the Church of England Diocese of London.

2. *St Helen's Church*, [1].

3. See Terry, "The Authority for Architecture," 77–80, and "Architecture and Theology," 137. For accounts and illustrations of Terry's body of work and aesthetic convictions, see Watkin, *Radical Classicism: The Architecture of Quinlan Terry*; and Aslet, *Quinlan Terry: The Revival of Architecture*.

4. Terry, "Origins of the Orders," 29–33.

5. Martin, "News Week," 24.

6. Melhuish, "St Helen's Bishopsgate," 56.

7. For further description and illustration of the finished building, see *St Helen's Church*, and Watkin, 246–253.

8. Barker, "Proof of Evidence of Ashley Barker," 31. Among his many qualifications, Barker listed his status as a Fellow of the Royal Institute of British Architects, the Society of Antiquaries, and the Ancient Monuments Society; his former official employment as a spe-

cialist in historic buildings by the Greater London Council and English Heritage; and his former status as Surveyor of Historic Buildings for the Greater London Council and Head of the London Division of English Heritage (Barker, 1).

9. Andreae, Letter to the Reverend Gordon Watkins, [1].
10. Cameron, 3.
11. For a description of the major monuments of the church, see Barker, 14–16.
12. Barker, 32.
13. Terry, "Proof of Evidence of Quinlan Terry," 2.
14. Sell, "Proof of Evidence by John Russell Sell, RIBA, SPAB," 5; Hobhouse, Letter to Gordon Watkins, [2].
15. Terry, "Proof of Evidence," 15.
16. Terry, "Proof of Evidence," 41.
17. Andreae, [2].
18. Stow, *A Survey of London*, 1.171–174.
19. Terry, "Proof of Evidence," 22. For a history of alterations to the church from the thirteenth through the twentieth centuries, see Cameron, 15–23. For the emphasis on a "preaching ministry," see Lucas, "Testimony of the Revd Lucas," [7–9].
20. Norman, Letter to Gordon Watkins, [1].
21. Sell, 5.
22. Andreae, [1].
23. Hobhouse, [1–2].
24. Wilson, "Vandals in Dog Collars."
25. Lucas, [9].
26. Marvell, "Upon Appleton House," line 2.
27. Terry, "Proof of Evidence," 41.
28. Lucas, [11]; Cameron, 74.
29. Andreae, [1].
30. Marvell, lines 5, 6.
31. Barker, 5.
32. Barker, 30.
33. Barker, 32.
34. Terry, "Proof of Evidence," 21.
35. See Vitruvius, *On Architecture*, 1.3, pp. 34–35. Vitruvius's terms are "firmitas," "utilitas," and "venustas," translated by Granger as "strength," "utility," and "grace."
36. Terry, "Proof of Evidence," 21.
37. Piloti, "The Great Architect of the Universe Arrives."
38. Terry, quoted by Melhuish, 56.
39. Lucas, [8].
40. Lucas, [9].
41. Terry, "Proof of Evidence," 39.
42. *St Helen's Church*, [1].
43. Stewart, *On Longing*, 151.
44. Barker, 31.

Bibliography

Adrian, John M. *Local Negotiations of English Nationhood, 1570–1680*. Basingstoke: Palgrave, 2011.
Alberti, Leon Battista. *De re aedifactoria*. Florence, 1485.
———. *On the Art of Building in Ten Books*. Tr. Joseph Rykwert, Neil Leach, and Robert Tavernor. Cambridge, Massachusetts: MIT Press, 1988.
Anderson, Christy. *Inigo Jones and the Classical Tradition*. Cambridge: Cambridge UP, 2007.
———. "Learning to Read Architecture in the English Renaissance." In *Albion's Classicism: The Visual Arts in Britain, 1550–1660*. Ed. Lucy Gent. New Haven: Yale UP, 1995, 239–286.
———. "Palladio in England: The Dominance of the Classical in a Foreign Land." In *Palladio and Northern Europe: Books, Travellers, Architects*. Milan: Skira, 1999, 122–129.
Anderson, M. D. *Looking for History in British Churches*. New York: William Morrow, 1951.
Andreae, Sophie. Letter to the Reverend Gordon Watkins, January 27, 1993. London Metropolitan Archives. LMA MS DL/A/C/MS30779/37.
Anonymous. "Leylands Supposed Ghost." In Ralph Brooke. *A Discoverie of Certaine Errours Published in Print in the Much Commended* Britannia, *1594*. London, 1596. British Library, London, shelfmark 796.g12.
Anselment, Raymond, "Seventeenth-Century Adaptations of 'The Church-porch.'" *George Herbert Journal* 5 (1982): 63–69.
Archer, Ian. "Discourses of History in London." In *The Uses of History in Early Modern England*. Ed. Paulina Kewes. San Marino, California: Huntington Library, 2006.
———. "The Nostalgia of John Stow." In *The Theatrical City: Culture, Theatre and Politics in London, 1576–1649*. Ed. David L. Smith, Richard Strier, and David Bevington. Cambridge: Cambridge UP, 1995, 17–34.
Arnold, Dana. "Preface." In *Rethinking Architectural Historiography*. Ed. Dana Arnold, Elvan Altan Ergut, and Belgin Turan Özkaya. New York: Routledge, 2006, xv–xx.
———. *Reading Architectural History*. New York: Routledge, 2002.
Asfour, Amal, and Malcolm Bull. "Fréart." In *Grove Art Online: Oxford Art Online*. www.oxfordartonline.com/subscriber/article/grove/art/T029766pg1. Accessed July 14, 2009.
Aslet, Clive. *Quinlan Terry: The Revival of Architecture*. Harmondsworth: Viking, 1986.
Aston, Margaret. *Lollards and Reformers: Images and Literacy in Late Medieval Religion*. London: Hambledon Press, 1984.
Aubrey, John. *The Natural History of Wiltshire*. New York: Augustus M. Kelley, 1969.
Baldi, Barnardino. *De verborum vitruvianorum significationes*. Augsburg, 1612.

Barker, Ashley. "Proof of Evidence of Ashley Barker." June 1993. London Metropolitan Archives. LMA MS DL/A/C/MS30779/37.
Barr, James. *Anglican Church Architecture*. Oxford: J. H. Parker, 1842.
Barton, Anne. *Ben Jonson, Dramatist*. Cambridge: Cambridge UP, 1984.
Bell, Patricia, ed. *Bedfordshire Wills, 1484–1533. Publications of the Bedfordshire Historical Record Society* 76 (1997).
Bellasis, Edward. *Westmorland Church Notes*. 2 vols. Kendal: T. Wilson, 1888.
Belsey, Catherine. "Afterword: Classicism and Cultural Dissonance." In *Albion's Classicism: The Visual Arts in Britain, 1550–1660*. Ed. Lucy Gent. New Haven: Yale UP, 1995, 427–442.
Benet, Diana. *Secretary of Praise: The Poetic Vocation of George Herbert*. Columbia: U of Missouri P, 1984.
Betjeman, John, ed. *Collins Guide to English Parish Churches, Including the Isle of Man*. London: Collins, 1958.
Biddick, Kathleen. *The Typological Imaginary: History, Technology, Circumcision*. Philadelphia: U of Pennsylvania P, 2003.
Bloch, Chana. *Spelling the Word: George Herbert and the Bible*. Berkeley: U of California P, 1985.
Blum, Hans. *The Booke of Five Collumnes of Architecture*. London, 1608.
Bond, Francis. *An Introduction to English Church Architecture from the Eleventh to the Sixteenth Century*. 2 vols. London: H. Milford, Oxford UP, 1913.
Bowle, John. *John Evelyn and His World: A Biography*. London: Routledge and Kegan Paul, 1981.
Boyle, N. E. *Old Parish Churches and How to View Them*. London: Skeffington and Son, 1951.
Brooke, Ralph. *A Discoverie of Certaine Errours Published in Print in the Much Commended Britannia, 1594*. London, 1596.
Brown, Frank E. "Continuity and Change in the Urban House: Developments in Domestic Space Organisation in Seventeenth-Century London." *Comparative Studies in Society and History* 28 (1986): 558–590.
Brown, R. J. *The English Village Church*. London: Robert Hale, 1998.
Browne, Thomas. *Repertorium*. London, 1712.
Bryson, Norman, Michael Ann Holly, and Keith Moxley. "Introduction." In *Visual Culture: Images and Interpretations*. Ed. Norman Bryson, Michael Ann Holly, and Keith Moxley. Hanover, New Hampshire: Wesleyan UP, 1994, xv–xxix.
Bullant, Jean. *Reigle génèralle d'architecture des cinq manières de colonnes à l'exemple de l'antique suivant les reigles et doctrine de Vitruve*. Paris, 1564.
Bumpus, T. Francis. *London Churches, Ancient and Modern*. 2 vols. London: T. Werner Laurie [1908?].
Burns, Howard. "Palladio and the Foundations of a New Architecture in the North." In *Palladio in Northern Europe: Books, Travellers, Architects*. Milan: Skira, 1999, 16–55.
Camden, William. *Britannia*. Tr. Philemon Holland. London, 1610.
———. *Britannia*. Tr. Edmund Gibson et al. London, 1695.
———. *Reges, Reginae, Nobiles et Alij in Ecclesia Collegiata B. Petri Westmonasterij Sepulti*. London, 1600.
Cameron, Sheila. "In the Matter of the Petition of the Incumbent and Churchwardens of the

Parish of St Helen Bishopsgate with St Andrew Undershaft and St Ethelburga Bishopsgate and St Martin Outwich and St Mary Axe Relating to the Church of St Helen Bishopsgate." November 26, 1993. London Metropolitan Archives. LMA MS DL/A/C/MS30779/37.

Campbell, Gordon. "Introduction." In Ben Jonson. *The Alchemist and Other Plays*. Ed. Gordon Campbell. Oxford: Oxford UP, 1995, vii–xxi.

Carew, Thomas. *Coelum Britannicum*. London, 1634.

———. "To My Friend G.N., from Wrest." In Alastair Fowler. *The Country House Poem*. Edinburgh: Edinburgh UP, 1994.

Carruthers, Mary. *The Book of Memory*. Cambridge: Cambridge UP, 1990.

Cataneo, Pietro. *L'architettura de Pietro Cateneo*. Venice, 1567.

———. *I quattro primi libri de architettura*. Venice, 1554.

Cautley, H. Munro. *Norfolk Churches*. Ipswich: Norman Adlard, 1949.

———. *Suffolk Churches and Their Treasures*. London: B. T. Batsford, 1937.

Cave, Richard Allen. *Ben Jonson*. New York: St. Martin's, 1991.

Celovsky, Lisa. "Ben Jonson and Sidneian Legacies of Hospitality." *Studies in Philology* 106 (2009): 178–206.

Chaney, Edward. "Evelyn, Inigo Jones, and the Collector Earl of Arundel." In *John Evelyn and His Milieu*. Ed. Frances Harris and Michael Hunter. London: British Library, 2003, 37–60.

———, ed. *The Evolution of English Collecting*. New Haven: Yale UP, 2003.

———. "The Italianate Evolution of English Collecting." In *The Evolution of English Collecting*. New Haven: Yale UP, 2003, 1–124.

Charles, Amy. *A Life of George Herbert*. Ithaca: Cornell UP, 1977.

Charles II. *His Majesties Gracious Letter and Declaration Sent to the House of Peers by Sir John Grenvil, K^t, From Breda: And Read in the House the First of May, 1660*. London, 1660.

Charlton, John. "The Lady Anne Clifford." In *Ancient Monuments and Their Interpretations*. Ed. M. R. Apted, R. Gilyard-Beer, and A. D. Saunders. London: Phillimore, 1977, 303–314.

Chaucer, Geoffrey. "The Wife of Bath's Prologue." In *The Riverside Chaucer*. Ed. Larry D. Benson. Boston: Houghton Mifflin, 1987, 105–116.

"Cheltenham Church." *Transactions of the Bristol and Gloucestershire Archaeological Society* 4 (1879–80): 65.

Chew, Elizabeth V. "A Mockery of the Surveyor's Style?: Alternatives to Inigo Jones in Seventeenth-Century Elite British Architecture." In *Articulating British Classicism: New Approaches to Eighteenth-Century Architecture*. Ed. Barbara Arciszewska and Elizabeth McKellar. Aldershot: Ashgate, 2001, 57–95.

———. "'Repaired by me to my exceeding great Cost and Charges': Anne Clifford and the Uses of Architecture." In *Architecture and the Politics of Gender in Early Modern Europe*. Ed. Helen Hills. Aldershot: Ashgate, 2003, 99–114.

———. "Si(gh)ting the Mistress of the House: Anne Clifford and Architectural Space." In *Women as Sites of Culture: Women's Roles in Cultural Formation from the Renaissance to the Twentieth Century*. Ed. Susan Shifrin. Aldershot: Ashgate, 2002, 167–182.

Circket, A. F., ed. *English Wills 1498–1526. Publications of the Bedfordshire Historical Records Society* 37 (1957).

Clay, J. W. "The Clifford Family." *Yorkshire Archaeological Journal* 18 (1905): 355–411.

Cleland, James. *The Institution of a Young Noble-Man*. Oxford, 1607.

Cliffe, J. T. *The World of the Country House in Seventeenth-Century England*. New Haven: Yale UP, 1999.

Clifford, Anne. *The Diaries of Lady Anne Clifford*. Ed. D. J. H. Clifford. Stroud: Sutton Publishing, 1990.

———. *The Diary of Anne Clifford, 1616–1619*. Ed. Katherine O. Acheson. New York: Garland, 1995.

———. *The Diary of the Lady Anne Clifford*. Ed. Vita Sackville-West. New York: G. H. Doran, 1924.

———. Great Books of Record. 3 vols. Cumbria Archive Centre, Kendal. WD/HOTH/Acc 988/10.

———. *Lives of Lady Anne Clifford and of Her Parents*. Ed. J. P. Gilson. London: Roxburghe Club, 1916.

Clifton-Taylor, Alec. *English Parish Churches as Works of Art*. London: Batsford, 1974.

Cocke, Thomas. "Classical or Gothic?: Lady Anne Clifford Reconsidered." *Country Life* 167 (1980): 324–326.

———. "Repairer of the Breach." *Country Life* 184 (1990): 84–86.

Collinson, Patrick. "John Stow and Nostalgic Antiquarianism." In *Imagining Early Modern London: Perceptions and Portrayals of the City from Stow to Strype*. Ed. J. F. Merritt. Cambridge: Cambridge UP, 2001, 27–53.

———. "One of Us? William Camden and the Making of History." *Transactions of the Royal Historical Society* 8 (1998): 139–164.

Colvin, Howard. *A Biographical Dictionary of English Architects, 1660–1840*. 1st ed. London: John Murray, 1954.

———. *A Biographical Dictionary of English Architects, 1660–1840*. 3rd ed. New Haven: Yale UP, 1995.

———. *The History of the King's Works*, 6 vols. London: Her Majesty's Stationery Office, 1976.

———. "The South Front of Wilton House." In *Essays in English Architectural History*. New Haven: Yale UP, 1999.

Cooley, Ronald W. *'Full of All Knowledg': George Herbert's* Country Parson *and Early Modern Social Discourse*. Toronto: U of Toronto P, 2004.

Cooper, Nicholas. *The Jacobean Country House*. London: Aurum Press, 2006.

Cox, J. Charles, and Charles Bradley Ford. *The Parish Churches of England*. London: Batsford, 1935.

Creed, Henry. "The Church of St. Peter and St. Paul, Eye." *Proceedings of the Suffolk Institute of Archaeology and Natural History* 2 (1885): 125–148.

Croft, Pauline, ed. *Patronage, Culture, and Power: The Early Cecils*. New Haven: Yale UP, 2002, 3–98.

Cunnar, Eugene R. "Herbert and the Visual Arts: Ut Pictura Poesis: An Opening in 'The Windows'." In *'Like Season'd Timber': New Essays on George Herbert*. Ed. Edmund Miller and Robert DiYanni. New York: Peter Lang, 1987, 101–138.

Daniel, Samuel. *Certaine Small Workes Heretofore Divulged by Samuel Daniel*. London, 1611.

D., J. [John Dauncey?]. *The History of His Sacred Majesty Charles the II*. London, 1660.

Davidson, Clifford. "George Herbert and Stained Glass Windows." *George Herbert Journal* 12 (1988): 29–39.

de Certeau, Michel. *The Practice of Everyday Life*. Berkeley: U of California P, 1984.

de Grazia, Margreta, Maureen Quilligan, and Peter Stallybrass. "Introduction." In *Subject and Object in Renaissance Culture*. Ed. Margreta de Grazia, Maureen Quilligan, and Peter Stallybrass. Cambridge: Cambridge UP, 1994, 1–16.

de Krey, Gary S. *Restoration and Revolution in Britain: A Political History of the Era of Charles II and the Glorious Revolution*. Basingstoke: Palgrave, 2007.

de l'Orme, Philibert. *Architecture de Philibert de l'Orme*. Rouen, 1648. Repr., Ridgewood, New Jersey: Gregg Press, 1964.

———. *Le premier tome de l'architecture*. Paris, 1567.

———. *Nouvelles inventions pour bien bastir et à petits fraiz*. Paris, 1561.

Dodds, George, and Robert Tavernor, eds. *Body and Building: Essays on the Changing Relationship of Body and Architecture*. Cambridge, Massachusetts: MIT Press, 2002.

Dodsworth, Roger. *Yorkshire Church Notes, 1619–1631*. Yorkshire Archaeological Society Record Series 34 (1904).

Dodsworth, Roger, and William Dugdale. *Monasticon Anglicanum*. 3 vols. London, 1655.

Donaldson, Ian. *Jonson's Magic Houses*. Oxford: Clarendon, 1997.

Donne, John. "The Canonization." In *Seventeenth-Century British Poetry*. Ed. John P. Rumrich and Gregory Chaplin. New York: Norton, 2005.

Downes, Kerry. "John Evelyn and Architecture: A First Inquiry." In *Concerning Architecture: Essays on Architectural Writers and Writing Presented to Nikolaus Pevsner*. Ed. John Summerson. London: Penguin, 1968, 28–39.

Duffy, Eamon. *The Stripping of the Altars: Traditional Religion in England, c. 1400–c. 1580*. New Haven: Yale UP, 1992.

Dugdale, William. *The History of St. Paul's Cathedral in London*. London, 1658.

Dyck, Paul. "Locating the Word: The Textual Church and George Herbert's *Temple*." In *Centered on the Word: Literature, Scripture, and the Tudor-Stuart Middle Way*. Ed. Daniel W. Doerksen and Christopher Hodgkins. Newark: U of Delaware P, 2004.

Dyer, T. F. Thiselton. *Church-Lore Gleanings*. London: A. D. Innes and Co., 1892.

Ekinci, Sevil Enginsoy. "Reopening the Question of Document in Architectural History." In *Rethinking Architectural Historiography*. Ed. Dana Arnold, Elvan Altan Ergut, and Belgin Turan Özkaya. New York: Routledge, 2006, 121–134.

Eriksen, Roy. *The Building in the Text: Alberti to Shakespeare and Milton*. University Park, Pennsylvania: Penn State UP, 2001.

Evans, Robert C. *Habits of Mind: Evidence and Effects of Ben Jonson's Reading*. Lewisburg, Pennsylvania: Bucknell UP, 1995.

Evelyn, John. "Account of Architects and Architecture." In Roland Fréart. *A Parallel of the Antient Architecture with the Modern*. Tr. John Evelyn. London, 1664, 115–142.

———. "Account of Architects and Architecture." In Roland Fréart, *A Parallel of the Antient Architecture with the Modern*. Tr. John Evelyn. London, 1707, 1–57 of "Account."

———. *The Diary of John Evelyn*. 6 vols. Ed. E. S. de Beer. Oxford: Clarendon, 1955.

———. *Diary*. Ed. Guy de la Bédoyère. Woodbridge: Boydell Press, 1995.

———. *The Diary and Correspondence of John Evelyn, F.R.S.* 4 vols. Ed. William Bray. London: Henry Colburn, 1854.

———. *London Revived: Consideration for Its Rebuilding in 1666*. Ed. E. S. de Beer. Oxford: Clarendon, 1938.

———. *Numismata.* London, 1697.

———. "To My Most Honoured Friend, Sir Christopher Wren, K{{r}}." In Roland Fréart, *A Parallel of the Antient Architecture with the Modern.* Tr. John Evelyn. London, 1707, [1–2].

Evett, David. *Literature and the Visual Arts in Tudor England.* Athens: U of Georgia P, 1990.

Fincham, Kenneth, and Nicholas Tyacke. *The Altars Restored: The Changing Face of English Religious Worship 1547–c.1700.* Oxford: Oxford UP, 2007.

Fish, Stanley. *The Living Temple: George Herbert and Catechizing.* Berkeley: U of California P, 1978.

Fitzherbert, John. *Here Begynneth a Ryght Frutefull Mater: And Hath to Name the Boke of Surveyeng and Improvementes.* London, 1523.

———. *Surveyenge.* London, 1533.

Flachmann, Michael. "Ben Jonson and the Alchemy of Satire." *SEL* 17 (1977): 259–280.

Fletcher, Isaac. "Brigham Church." *Transactions of the Cumberland and Westmorland Antiquarian and Archaeological Society* 4 (1880): 149–177.

Fowler, Alastair. *The Country House Poem: A Cabinet of Seventeenth-Century Estate Poems and Related Items.* Edinburgh: Edinburgh UP, 1994.

Fréart, Roland. *A Parallel of the Antient Architecture with the Modern.* Tr. John Evelyn. London, 1664.

———. *A Parallel of the Antient Architecture with the Modern.* Tr. John Evelyn. London, 1707.

Friar, Stephen. *The Sutton Companion to the English Parish Church.* London: Chancellor Press, 2000.

Friedman, Alice T. "Constructing an Identity in Prose, Plaster, and Paint: Lady Anne Clifford as Writer and Patron of the Arts." In *Albion's Classicism: The Visual Arts in Britain 1550–1660.* Ed. Lucy Gent. New Haven: Yale UP, 1995, 359–376.

———. "Inside/Out: Women, Domesticity, and the Pleasures of the City." In *Material London, ca. 1600.* Ed. Lena Cowen Orlin. Philadelphia: U of Pennsylvania P, 2000, 229–250.

———. "John Evelyn and English Architecture." In *John Evelyn's "Elysium Britannicum" and European Gardening.* Ed. Therese O'Malley and Joachim Wolscke-Bulmahn. Washington, D.C.: Dumbarton Oaks Research Library and Collection, 1998, 153–170.

Fuller, Thomas. *The Church-History of Britain from the Birth of Jesus Christ, Untill the Year M.DC.XLVIII.* London, 1656.

Fumerton, Patricia. "Introduction." In *Renaissance Culture and the Everyday.* Ed. Patricia Fumerton and Simon Hunt. Philadelphia: U of Pennsylvania P, 1999.

Gapper, Claire, John Newman, and Annabel Ricketts. "Hatfield: A House for a Lord Treasurer." In *Patronage, Culture, and Power: The Early Cecils, 1553–1612.* Ed. Pauline Croft. New Haven: Yale UP, 2002, 67–98.

Gent, Lucy. *Picture and Poetry, 1560–1620.* Leamington Spa: James Hall, 1981.

———. "'The Rash Gazer': Economies of Vision in Britain, 1550–1660." In *Albion's Classicism: The Visual Arts in Britain, 1550–1660.* Ed. Lucy Gent. New Haven: Yale UP, 1995, 377–394.

Gibbons, Brian. *Jacobean City Comedy.* Cambridge, Massachusetts: Harvard UP, 1968.

———. "The Question of Place." *Cahiers Elisabéthains* 50 (1996): 33–43.

Girouard, Mark. *Life in the English Country House.* New Haven: Yale UP, 1978.

———. *Robert Smythson and the Elizabethan Country House.* New Haven: Yale UP, 1983.

Godfrey, Richard T. *Wenceslaus Hollar: A Bohemian Artist in England.* New Haven: Yale UP, 1994.

Gordon, D. J. "Poet and Architect: The Intellectual Setting of the Quarrel between Ben Jonson and Inigo Jones." In *The Renaissance Imagination.* Ed. Stephen Orgel. Berkeley: U of California P, 1975, 77–101.

Great Britain. "An Act for a Perpetuall Anniversary Thanksgiveing on the nine and twentieth day of May." In *The Statutes of the Realm*, 11 vols. London, 1819, 5.237.

Great Britain. "An Act of Free and Generall Pardon Indempnity and Oblivion." In *The Statutes of the Realm*, 11 vols. London, 5.226.

Griffin, Andrew. "Preserving and Reserving the Past in Stow's *Survey of London.*" In *The Idea of the City: Early-Modern, Modern and Post-Modern Locations and Communities.* Ed. Joan Fitzpatrick. Cambridge: Cambridge Scholars Press, 2009, 53–64.

Griffiths, Paul. "Politics Made Visible: Order, Residence and Uniformity in Cheapside 1600–45." In *Londinopolis.* Ed. Paul Griffiths and Mark S. R. Jenner. Manchester: Manchester UP, 2000, 176–196.

Griffiths, P., J. Landers, M. Pelling, and R. Tyson. "Population and Disease, Estrangement and Belonging, 1540–1700." In *The Cambridge Urban History of Britain.* 3 vols. Ed. Peter Clark. Cambridge: Cambridge UP, 2000, 2.195–233.

Guibbory, Achsah. *Ceremony and Community from Herbert to Milton.* Cambridge: Cambridge UP, 1998.

Güven, Suna. "Frontiers of Fear: Architectural History, the Anchor and the Sail." In *Rethinking Architectural Historiography.* Ed. Dana Arnold, Elvan Altan Ergut, and Belgin Turan Özkaya. New York: Routledge, 2006, 74–82.

Hailey, George. *Notes and Queries* 177 (1939): 284.

Hall, Edward. *The Union of the Two Noble and Illustre Famelies of Lancastre and Yorke.* London, 1548.

Harding, Vanessa. "City, Capitol, and Metropolis: The Changing Shape of Seventeenth-Century London." In *Imagining Early Modern London: Perceptions and Portrayals of the City from Stow to Strype.* Ed. J. F. Merritt. Cambridge: Cambridge UP, 2001, 117–143.

Harris, Eileen, with Nicholas Savage. *British Architectural Books and Writers, 1556–1785.* Cambridge: Cambridge UP, 1990.

Harris, Jonathan Gil. "Shakespeare's Hair: Staging the Object of Material Culture." *Shakespeare Quarterly* 52 (2001): 479–491.

———. *Untimely Matter in the Time of Shakespeare.* Philadelphia: U of Pennsylvania P, 2009.

Harris, Jonathan Gil, and Natasha Korda. "Introduction." In *Staged Properties in Early Modern English Drama.* Ed. Jonathan Gil Harris and Natasha Korda. Cambridge: Cambridge UP, 2002, 1–34.

Harrison, William. *The Description of England.* Ed. Georges Edelen. Ithaca: Cornell UP, 1968.

Hart, Vaughan. "'A peece rather of good *Heraldry,* than of *Architecture*': Heraldry and the Orders of Architecture as Joint Emblems of Chivalry." *RES* (1993): 53–66.

———. "From Virgin to Courtesan in Early English Vitruvian Books." In *Paper Palaces: The Rise of the Renaissance Architectural Treatise.* Ed. Vaughan Hart and Peter Hicks. New Haven: Yale UP, 1998, 312–318.

Heal, Felicity. *Hospitality in Early Modern England.* Oxford: Clarendon, 1990.

Helgerson, Richard. *Forms of Nationhood: The Elizabethan Writing of England*. Chicago: U of Chicago P, 1992.

Herbert, George. *The English Poems of George Herbert*. Ed. Helen Wilcox. Cambridge: Cambridge UP, 2007.

———. *Outlandish Proverbs Selected by Mr. G.H.* London, 1640.

Herendeen, Wyman H. *From Landscape to Literature: The River and the Myth of Geography*. Pittsburgh: Duquesne UP, 1986.

———. "Wanton Discourse and the Engines of Time: William Camden—Historian among Poets-Historical." In *Renaissance Rereadings: Intertext and Context*. Ed. Maryanne Cline Horowitz, Anne J. Cruz, and Wendy A. Furman. Urbana: U of Illinois P, 1988.

———. *William Camden: A Life in Context*. Woodbridge: Boydell Press, 2007.

Herrick, Robert. "The Entertainment; or, *Porch Verse* at the Marriage of Mr. *Hen. Northly* and the Most Witty Mrs. *Lettice Yard*." In *Herrick's Poems*. Ed. F. W. Moorman. Oxford: Clarendon, 1915, 124.

Hibbard, G. R. "The Country House Poem of the Seventeenth Century." *Journal of the Warburg and Courtauld Institutes* 19 (1956): 159–174.

Hind, Arthur M. *Engraving in England in the Sixteenth and Seventeenth Centuries*. 3 vols. Cambridge: Cambridge UP, 1952.

Hinman, Robert B. "The 'Verser' at *The Temple* Door: Herbert's 'The Church-porch.'" In *"Too Riche to Clothe the Sunne": Essays on George Herbert*. Ed. Claude J. Summers and Ted-Larry Pebworth. Pittsburgh: U of Pittsburgh P, 1980, 55–75.

Hobhouse, Hermione. Letter to Gordon Watkins, January 21, 1993. London Metropolitan Archives. LMA MS DL/A/C/MS30779/37.

Hodgkins, Christopher. *Authority, Church, and Society in George Herbert: Return to the Middle Way*. Columbia: U of Missouri P, 1993.

Hosley, Richard. "The Second Blackfriars Playhouse." In *The Revels History of Drama in English*. Ed. J. Leeds Barroll, Alexander Leggat, Richard Hosley, and Alvin Kernan. 8 vols. London: Methuen, 1975, 3.197–205.

Howard, Jean E. *Theater of a City*. Philadelphia: U of Pennsylvania P, 2007.

Howard, Maurice. *The Building of Elizabethan and Jacobean England*. New Haven: Yale UP, 2007.

———. *The Early Tudor Country House*. London: George Philip, 1987.

———. "The Treatise and Its Alternatives: Theory and Practice in Sixteenth-Century England." In *Théorie des arts et création artistique dans l'Europe du Nord du XVIe au début du XVIIIe siècle*. Ed. Michèle-Caroline Heck, Frédérique Lemerle, and Yves Pauwels. Lille: U Charles-de-Gualle, 2002, 141–153.

Hughes, Paul L., and James F. Larkin, eds. *Stuart Royal Proclamations*. 2 vols. Oxford: Clarendon, 1973, 1.111–112.

Hunneyball, Paul. *Architecture and Image Building in Seventeenth-Century Hertfordshire*. Oxford: Clarendon, 2004.

Hunter, Joseph. "A Catalogue of the Manuscripts Written or Collected by that Eminent Antiquary Roger Dodsworth and Now Deposited in the Bodleian Library." In *Three Catalogues; Describing the Contents of the Red Book of the Exchequer, of the Dodsworth Manu-*

scripts in the Bodleian Library and of the Manuscripts in the Library of the Honourable Society of Lincoln's Inn. London, 1838, 69–72.

Hunter, Michael. "John Evelyn in the 1650s: A Virtuoso in Quest of a Role." In *John Evelyn's "Elysium Britannicum" and European Gardening*. Ed. Therese O'Malley and Joachim Wolscke-Bulmahn. Washington, D.C.: Dumbarton Oaks Research Library and Collection, 1998, 79–106.

Jenkins, Hugh. *Feigned Commonwealths: The Country House Poem and the Fashioning of the Ideal Community*. Pittsburgh: Duquesne UP, 1998.

Johnson, A. W. *Ben Jonson: Poetry and Architecture*. Oxford: Clarendon, 1994.

Johnson, Jeffrey. "Recreating the Word: Typology in Herbert's 'The Altar'." *Christianity and Literature* 37 (1987): 55–65.

Jonson, Ben. *The Alchemist*. Ed. F. H. Mares. Manchester: Manchester UP, 1997.

———. *Ben Jonson: Works*. Ed. C. H. Herford and Percy Simpson. 10 vols. Oxford: Clarendon, 1937.

———. *Conversations with Drummond*. In *The Oxford Authors: Ben Jonson*. Ed. Ian Donaldson. Oxford: Oxford UP, 1985, 595–611.

———. *Discoveries*. In *The Oxford Authors: Ben Jonson*. Ed. Ian Donaldson. Oxford: Oxford UP, 1985, 521–594.

———. "Epigram 14." In *The Oxford Authors: Ben Jonson*. Ed. Ian Donaldson. Oxford: Oxford UP, 1985, 226.

———. "To Penshurst." In *The Oxford Authors: Ben Jonson*. Ed. Ian Donaldson. Oxford: Oxford UP, 1985, 282–285.

Keeble, N. H. *The Restoration: England in the 1660s*. Oxford: Blackwell, 2002.

Kendrick, T. D. *British Antiquity*. London: Methuen, 1950.

Kessner, Carole. "Entering 'The Church-porch': Herbert and Wisdom Poetry." *George Herbert Journal* 1 (1977): 10–25.

Klein, Bernhard. "Imaginary Journeys: Spenser, Drayton, and the Poetics of National Space." In *Literature, Mapping, and the Politics of Space*. Ed. Andrew Gordon and Bernhard Klein. Cambridge: Cambridge UP, 2001, 204–223.

———. *Maps and the Writing of Space in Early Modern England and Ireland*. Basingstoke: Palgrave, 2001.

Klein, Lisa M. "Lady Anne Clifford as Mother and Matriarch: Domestic and Dynastic Issues in Her Life and Writings." *Journal of Family History* 26 (2001): 18–38.

Knapp, Peggy A. "The Work of Alchemy." *Journal of Medieval and Early Modern Studies* 30 (2000): 575–599.

Knights, L. C. *Drama and Society in the Age of Jonson*. New York: George Stewart, 1936.

Kruft, Hanno-Walter. *A History of Architectural Theory from Vitruvius to the Present*. Tr. Ronald Taylor, Elsie Callander, and Anthony Wood. New York: Princeton Architectural Press, 1994.

Kunin, Aaron. "From the Desk of Anne Clifford." *ELH* 71 (2004): 587–608.

Lamb, Mary Ellen. "The Agency of the Split Subject: Lady Anne Clifford and the Uses of Reading." *ELR* 22 (1992): 347–368.

Leach, Elsie. "More Seventeenth-Century Admirers of Herbert." *Notes and Queries* 7 (1960): 62–63.

Leland, John. *The Itinerary of John Leland the Antiquary*. Ed. Thomas Hearne. 9 vols. Oxford, 1769.

———. *Leland's Journey through Wiltshire, A.D. 1540–42*. Ed. J. E. Jackson. Devizes: Henry Bull, [1875?].

Leland, John, and John Bale, *The Laboryouse Journey and Serche of Johan Leylande, for Englandes Antiquitees Geven of Hym as a New Yeares Gyfte to King Henry the VIII*. London, 1549.

Lemerle-Pauwels, Frédérique, and Milovan Stanic. "Introduction générale." In Roland Fréart, *Parallèle de l'architecture antique avec la modern; suivi de Idée de la perfection de la peinture*. Paris: Ecole nationale supérieur des beaux-arts, 2005.

Levin, Harry. "Jonson, Stow, and Drummond." *Modern Language Notes* 53:3 (1938): 167–169.

Levy, F. J. *Tudor Historical Thought*. San Marino, California: Huntington Library, 1967.

Lewalski, Barbara Kiefer. *Protestant Poetics and the Seventeenth-Century Religious Lyric*. Princeton: Princeton UP, 1971.

———. *Writing Women in Jacobean England*. Cambridge, Massachusetts: Harvard UP, 1993.

Lewis, Harold. "St. Mary Redcliffe: A Life's Failure." In *Cathedrals, Abbeys and Churches of England and Wales*. 6 vols. Ed. T. G. Bonney. London: Cassel, 1888, 3.398–404.

Linden, Stanton J. *Darke Hierogliphicks: Alchemy in English Literature from Chaucer to the Reformation*. Lexington: UP of Kentucky, 1996.

Lindley, Phillip. *Tomb Destruction and Scholarship*. Donnington: Shaun Tyas, 2007.

Llewellyn, Nigel. *Funeral Monuments in Post-Reformation England*. Cambridge: Cambridge UP, 2000.

Lockyer, Roger. *Buckingham: The Life and Political Career of George Villiers, First Duke of Buckingham, 1592–1628*. New York: Longman, 1981.

Lucar, Cyprian. *Treatise Named Lucarsolace*. London, 1590.

Lucas, Richard. "Testimony of the Revd Lucas." June 1993. London Metropolitan Archives. LMA MS DL/A/C/MS30779/37.

Maguire, Alison. "A Collection of Seventeenth-Century Architectural Plans." *Architectural History* 35 (1992): 140–182.

Malcolmson, Cristina. *George Herbert: A Literary Life*. Basingstoke: Palgrave, 2004.

———. *Heart-work: George Herbert and the Protestant Ethic*. Stanford, California: Stanford UP, 1999.

Marchitello, Howard. *Narrative and Meaning in Early Modern England*. Cambridge: Cambridge UP, 1997.

Mardock, James D. *Our Scene Is London: Ben Jonson's City and the Space of the Author*. New York: Routledge, 2008.

Mares, F. H. "Introduction" to *The Alchemist*. Ed. F. H. Mares. Manchester: Manchester UP, 1967, xvii–lxxix.

Martin, Ian. "News Week." *Building Design* 1110 (1993), 24.

Martz, Louis. *The Poetry of Meditation*. New Haven: Yale UP, 1954.

Marvell, Andrew. "Upon Appleton House." In *The Oxford Authors: Andrew Marvell*. Ed. Keith Walker. Oxford: Oxford UP, 1990, 53–77.

McBride, Kari Boyd. *Country House Discourse in Early Modern England*. Aldershot: Ashgate, 2001.

McClung, William A. *The Country House in English Renaissance Poetry*. Berkeley: U of California P, 1977.

McEvoy, Sean. *Ben Jonson: Renaissance Dramatist*. Edinburgh: Edinburgh UP, 2008.

McIntosh, Shona. "Space, Place and Transformation in *Eastward Ho!* and *The Alchemist*." In *The Idea of the City: Early-Modern, Modern, and Post-Modern Locations and Communities*. Ed. Joan Fitzpatrick. Cambridge: Cambridge Scholars Press, 2009, 65–78.

McRae, Andrew. *God Speed the Plough: The Representation of Agrarian England, 1500–1660*. Cambridge: Cambridge UP, 1996.

Melhuish, Claire. "St Helen's Bishopsgate." *Church Building* 39 (1996): 56–57.

Meyerstein, E. H. W. *A Life of Thomas Chatterton*. London: Ingpen and Grant, 1930.

Miller, John. *The Restoration and the England of Charles II*. London: Longman, 1997.

Mowl, Timothy. *Elizabethan and Jacobean Style*. London: Phaidon, 1993.

Mowl, Timothy, and Brian Earnshaw. *Architecture without Kings: The Rise of Puritan Classicism under Cromwell*. Manchester: Manchester UP, 1995.

Norden, John. *Speculi Britanniae Pars: The Description of Hartfordshire*. London, 1598.

———. *Speculum Britanniae: The First Parte: An Historicall, and Chorographicall Discription of Middlesex*. London, 1593.

———. *The Surveyors Dialogue*. London, 1607.

Norman, John. Letter to Gordon Watkins, January 18, 1993. London Metropolitan Archives. LMA MS DL/A/C/MS30779/37.

O'Connor, Mary. "Representations of Intimacy in the Life-Writing of Anne Clifford and Anne Dormer." In *Representations of the Self from the Renaissance to Romanticism*. Ed. Patrick Coleman, Jayne Lewis, and Jill Kowalik. Cambridge: Cambridge UP, 2000, 79–96.

Orgel, Stephen. "Marginal Maternity: Reading Lady Anne Clifford's *A Mirror for Magistrates*." In *Printing and Parenting in Early Modern England*. Ed. Douglas A. Brooks. Aldershot: Ashgate, 2005, 267–290.

Orgel, Stephen, and Roy Strong. *Inigo Jones: The Theatre of the Stuart Court*. 2 vols. Berkeley: U of California P, 1973.

Orlin, Lena Cowen. "Boundary Disputes in Early Modern London." In *Material London, ca. 1600*. Ed. Lena Cowen Orlin. Philadelphia: U of Pennsylvania P, 2000, 345–376.

———. *Locating Privacy in Tudor London*. Oxford: Oxford UP, 2007.

———. "Temporary Lives in London Lodgings." *Huntington Library Quarterly* 71 (2008): 219–242.

———. "The Tudor Long Gallery in the History of Privacy." *InForm: The Journal of Architecture, Design, and Material Culture* (2001): 284–298.

———. "Women on the Threshold," *Shakespeare Studies* 25 (1997): 50–58.

Page, John T. "Pattens in the Church Porch." *Notes and Queries* 117 (1908): 268.

Palladio, Andrea. *The Four Books of Architecture*. Tr. Robert Tavernor and Richard Schofield. Cambridge, Massachusetts: MIT Press, 1997.

———. *I quattro libri de achitettura*. Venice, 1570.

Palmer, G. H. "E.C. Lowe's Edition of George Herbert's 'Church Porch'." *Notes and Queries* 162 (1932): 442.

Parry, Graham. *The Trophies of Time: English Antiquarians of the Seventeenth Century*. Oxford: Oxford UP, 1995.

Paster, Gail Kern. "Ben Jonson and the Uses of Architecture." *Renaissance Quarterly* 27 (1974): 306–320.

Paterson, E. Verdon. "The Church Porch." *Notes and Queries* 177 (1939): 303.

Peacock, John. *The Stage Designs of Inigo Jones: The European Context.* Cambridge: Cambridge UP, 1995.

Pearce, Susan M. "Objects as Meaning; or, Narrating the Past." In *Interpreting Objects and Collections.* Ed. Susan M. Pearce. London: Routledge, 1994, 19–29. Essay reprinted from *New Research in Museum Studies: Objects of Knowledge.* London: Athlone Press, 1990, 125–140.

Peck, Linda Levy. "Building, Buying, and Collecting in London, 1600–1625." In *Material London, ca. 1600.* Ed. Lena Cowen Orlin. Philadelphia: U of Pennsylvania P, 2000, 268–290.

Penshurst Place and Gardens. Hadlow: Hephaistos Media, 1999.

Perks, Sydney. *Essays on Old London.* Cambridge: Cambridge UP, 1927.

Pevsner, Nikolaus. *The Buildings of England: Cumberland and Westmorland.* Harmondsworth: Penguin, 1967.

Piggott, Stuart. "William Camden and the *Britannia.*" In *The Changing Face of English Local History.* Ed. R. C. Richardson. Aldershot: Ashgate, 2000, 12–29.

Piloti, "The Great Architect of the Universe Arrives." Unidentified newspaper clipping. London Metropolitan Archives. LMA MS DL/A/C/MS30779/37.

Poole, Geoffrey Ayliffe. *A History of Ecclesiastical Architecture in England.* London: Joseph Masters, 1848.

Pounds, N. J. G. *A History of the English Parish: The Culture of Religion from Augustine to Victoria.* Cambridge: Cambridge UP, 2000.

Powers-Beck, Jeffrey. *Writing the Flesh: The Herbert Family Dialogue.* Pittsburgh: Duquesne UP, 1998.

Powys, A. R. *The English Parish Church.* London: Longman's and Green, 1930.

Price, John Edward. "St. Sepulchre's, London: The Church Porch." *Notes and Queries* 40 (1879): 366–367.

Pyrah, Roger and Enid. *The Parish Church of the Holy Trinity Skipton: A History and Guide.* N.p. 1994, revised 2000.

Rainbow, Edward. *A Sermon Preached at the Funeral of the Right Honorable Anne, Countess of Pembroke, Dorset, and Montgomery.* London, 1677.

Richards, Raymond. *Old Cheshire Churches.* London: B. T. Batsford, 1947.

Richardson, R. C., ed. *The Changing Face of English Local History.* Aldershot: Ashgate, 2000.

Rickey, Mary Ellen. *Utmost Art.* Lexington: U of Kentucky P, 1966.

Riggs, David. *Ben Jonson: A Life.* Cambridge, Massachusetts: Harvard UP, 1989.

Ripley, George. *Compound of Alchymy.* London, 1591.

Rockett, William. "*Britannia*, Ralph Brooke, and the Representation of Privilege in Elizabethan England." *Renaissance Quarterly* 53 (2000): 474–499.

Rodwell, Warwick, and E. Clive Rouse. "The Anglo-Saxon Rood and Other Features in the South Porch of St. Mary's Church, Breamore, Hampshire." *Antiquaries Journal* 64 (1984): 298–325.

Rogers, W. H. H., "Keeping School in the Parvise over the Church Porch." *Notes and Queries* 40 (1879): 394.

Roston, Murray. *Renaissance Perspectives in Literature and the Visual Arts*. Princeton: Princeton UP, 1987.

Rykwert, Joseph. "Introduction." In Leon Battista Alberti, *On the Art of Building in Ten Books*. Tr. Joseph Rykwert, Neil Leach, and Robert Tavernor. Cambridge: MIT Press, 1988, ix–xxi.

S., A. *Notes and Queries* 9 (1854): 597.

Salzman, Paul. *Reading Early Modern Women's Writing*. Oxford: Oxford UP, 2006.

Scamozzi, Vincenzo. *L'idea dell'architettura universale*. Venice, 1615.

Scattergood, John. "John Leland's *Itinerary* and the Identity of England." In *Sixteenth-Century Identities*. Ed. A. J. Piesse. Manchester: Manchester UP, 2000, 58–74.

Schoenfeldt, Michael C. *Prayer and Power: George Herbert and Renaissance Courtship*. Chicago: U of Chicago P, 1991.

Schofield, John. *The Building of London from the Conquest to the Great Fire*. London: British Museum Publications, 1984.

———. "The Topography and Buildings of London, ca. 1600." In *Material London, ca. 1600*. Ed. Lena Cowen Orlin. Philadelphia: U of Pennsylvania P, 2000, 296–321.

Schwyzer, Philip. *Archaeologies of English Renaissance Literature*. Oxford: Oxford UP, 2007.

———. *Literature, Nationalism and Memory in Early Modern England and Wales*. Cambridge: Cambridge UP, 2004.

Scott, Jonathan. *England's Troubles: Seventeenth-Century English Political Instability in European Context*. Cambridge: Cambridge UP, 2000.

Seelig, Sharon Cadman. *Autobiography and Gender in Early Modern Literature: Reading Women's Lives, 1660–1680*. Cambridge: Cambridge UP, 2006.

Sell, John Russell. "Proof of Evidence by John Russell Sell, RIBA, SPAB." June 1993. London Metropolitan Archives. LMA MS DL/A/C/MS30779/37.

Serlio, Sebastiano. *The Five Books of Architecture*. London, 1611.

———. *Tutte l'opere d'architettura*. Venice, 1584.

Sherlock, Peter. *Monuments and Memory in Early Modern England*. Aldershot: Ashgate, 2008.

Shiqiao, Li. *Power and Virtue: Architecture and Intellectual Change in England, 1660–1730*. Abingdon: Routledge, 2007.

Shuger, Debora. *Habits of Thought in the English Renaissance*. Berkeley: U of California P, 1990.

Shute, John. *The First and Chief Groundes of Architecture*. London, 1563.

Simpson, James. "Diachronic History and the Shortcomings of Medieval Studies." In *Reading the Medieval in Early Modern England*. Ed. David Matthews and Gordon McMullan. Cambridge: Cambridge UP, 2007, 17–30.

Sinfield, Alan. "*Poetaster*, the Author, and the Perils of Cultural Production." In *Material London, ca. 1600*. Ed. Lena Cowen Orlin. Philadelphia: U of Pennsylvania P, 2000, 75–90.

Singleton, Marion White. *God's Courtier: Configuring a Different Grace in George Herbert's Temple*. Cambridge: Cambridge UP, 1987.

Smallwood, R. L. "'Here, in the Friars'": Immediacy and Theatricality in *The Alchemist*." *RES* 32 (1981): 142–160.

Smith, Logan Pearsall. *The Life and Letters of Sir Henry Wotton*. 2 vols. Oxford: Clarendon, 1907.

Smithe, Frederick. "Notes on the Church of St. Bartholomew, Churchdown." *Transactions of the Bristol and Gloucester Archaeological Society* 13 (1888–89): 271–287.
Smyth, Adam. *Autobiography in Early Modern England*. Cambridge: Cambridge UP, 2010.
Solomon, Julie Robin. *Objectivity in the Making: Francis Bacon and the Politics of Inquiry*. Baltimore: Johns Hopkins UP, 1998.
Southcombe, George, and Grant Tapsell. *Restoration, Politics, Religion, and Culture*. Basingstoke: Palgrave, 2010.
Spence, Richard T. *Lady Anne Clifford*. Stroud: Sutton Publishing, 1997.
———. *The Privateering Earl*. Stroud: Sutton Publishing, 1995.
Stein, Arnold. *George Herbert's Lyrics*. Baltimore: Johns Hopkins Press, 1968.
Sterling, Eric. "Jonson and His Era: Overviews of Modern Research: Alchemist, The" *Ben Jonson Journal* 15 (2008): 112–122.
Stewart, Susan. *On Longing*. Durham, North Carolina: Duke UP, 1993, 2007.
St Helen's Church. Norfolk: Jarold Publishing, 2009.
Stow, John. *A Survey of London*. 2 vols. Ed. C. L. Kingsford. 1598; repr. Oxford: Clarendon, 1908. Elbiron Classics.
Strier, Richard. "George Herbert and the World." *Journal of Medieval and Renaissance Studies* 11 (1981): 225–232.
———. *Love Known: Theology and Experience in George Herbert's Poetry*. Chicago: U of Chicago P, 1983.
———. "Sanctifying the Aristocracy: 'Devout Humanism' in François de Sales, John Donne, and George Herbert." *Journal of Religion* 69 (1989): 36–58.
Summers, Joseph. "Introduction." In *The Selected Poetry of George Herbert*. New York: Signet, 1967, ix–xxvii.
Summerson, Henry. "The History of the Castle." In Henry Summerson, Michael Trueman, and Stuart Harrison, *Brougham Castle, Cumbria*. Kendal: Cumberland and Westmorland Antiquarian and Archaeological Society, 1998, 7–78.
Summerson, John. *Architecture in Britain, 1530–1830*. London: Penguin, 1953.
———. *Georgian London*. London: Pleiades Books, 1945.
———. *Inigo Jones*. Harmondsworth: Penguin, 1966. Repr., New Haven: Yale UP, 2000.
Summit, Jennifer. "Leland's *Itinerary* and the Remains of the Medieval Past." In *Reading the Medieval in Early Modern England*. Ed. David Matthews and Gordon McMullan. Cambridge: Cambridge UP, 2007, 159–178.
———. *Memory's Library: Medieval Books in Early Modern England*. Chicago: U of Chicago P, 2008.
Sutton, James M. *Materializing Space at an Early Modern Prodigy House: The Cecils at Theobalds, 1564–1607*. Aldershot: Ashgate, 2004.
Suzuki, Mihoko. "Anne Clifford and the Gendering of History." *Clio* 30 (2001): 195–229.
Swann, Marjorie. *Curiosities and Texts*. Philadelphia: U of Pennsylvania P, 2001.
Tanner, Thomas. *Notitia Monastica, or a Short History of the Religious Houses in England and Wales*. Oxford, 1695.
Targoff, Ramie. *Common Prayer: The Language of Public Devotion in Early Modern England*. Chicago: U of Chicago P, 2001.

Tavernor, Robert. "Introduction." In Andrea Palladio. *The Four Books of Architecture.* Tr. Robert Tavernor and Richard Schofield. Cambridge, Massachusetts: MIT Press, vii–xix.
Terry, Quinlan. "Architecture and Theology." In *Quinlan Terry: Selected Works.* Ed. Ken Powell. London: Academy Editions, 1993, 137.
———. "The Authority for Architecture." In *New Classicism.* Ed. Andreas Papadakis and Harriet Watson. New York: Rizzoli, 1990, 77–80.
———. "Origins of the Orders." *Architectural Review* 172 (1983): 29–32.
———. "Proof of Evidence of Quinlan Terry." June 15, 1993. London Metropolitan Archives. LMA MS DL/A/C/MS30779/37.
Thomas, Keith. "English Protestantism and Classical Art." In *Albion's Classicism: The Visual Arts in Britain, 1550–1660.* Ed. Lucy Gent. New Haven: Yale UP, 1995, 221–238.
Thompson, F. M. L. *Chartered Surveyors: The Growth of a Profession.* London: Routledge, 1968.
Thorpe, John. "The Book of Architecture of John Thorpe." Ed. John Summerson. *Walpole Society* 40 (1966).
Treswell, Ralph. *The London Surveys of Ralph Treswell.* Ed. John Schofield. London: London Topographical Society, 1987.
Turner, Henry S. *The English Renaissance Stage: Geometry, Poetics, and the Practical Spatial Arts, 1580–1630.* Oxford: Oxford UP, 2006.
Vendler, Helen. *The Poetry of George Herbert.* Cambridge, Massachusetts: Harvard UP, 1975.
Vignola, Giacomo Barozzi da. *La regola dell cinque ordini d'architettura.* Rome, 1652.
Vine, Angus. *In Defiance of Time: Antiquarian Writing in Early Modern England.* Oxford: Oxford UP, 2010.
Vitruvius Pollio, M. *De architectura libri decem.* Ed. Guillaume Philander. Lyon, 1552.
———. *I dieci libri dell'architettura de M. Vitruvio.* Ed. and tr. Daniele Barbaro. Venice, 1556.
———. *On Architecture.* 2 vols. Ed. and tr. Frank Granger. Cambridge, Massachusetts: Harvard UP, 1934, 2004.
———. *Ten Books on Architecture.* Tr. Ingrid D. Rowland. Cambridge: Cambridge UP, 1999.
———. *Zehen Bücher von der Architectur und künstlichem Bawen.* Ed. and tr. Gualtherus Rivius. Nuremburg, 1548.
Walker, John David. "The Architectonics of George Herbert's *The Temple.*" *ELH* 29 (1962): 289–305.
Wall, Cynthia. *The Literary and Cultural Spaces of Restoration London.* Cambridge: Cambridge UP, 1998.
Wall, J. Charles. *Porches and Fonts.* London: Wells, Gardner, Darton and Co., 1912. Repr., Honolulu: UP of the Pacific, 2003.
Ware, Rev., "Notes upon the Parish Church of Kirkby Lonsdale." *Transactions of the Cumberland and Westmorland Antiquarian and Archaeological Society* 1 (1874): 189–203.
Waters, T. "Thornbury Church." *Transactions of the Bristol and Gloucestershire Archaeological Society* 8 (1883–84): 79–90.
Watkin, David. *Radical Classicism: The Architecture of Quinlan Terry.* New York: Rizzoli, 2006.
Watts, Victor. "English Place-Names in the Sixteenth Century: The Search for Identity." In *Sixteenth-Century Identities.* Ed. A. J. Piesse. Manchester: Manchester UP, 2000.

Wayne, Don. *Penshurst: The Semiotics of Place and the Poetics of History*. Madison: U of Wisconsin P, 1984.
Weever, John. *Ancient Funerall Monuments*. London, 1631.
Wells-Cole, Anthony. *Art and Decoration in Elizabethan and Jacobean England: The Influence of Continental Prints, 1558–1625*. New Haven: Yale UP, 1997.
Whalen, Robert. "George Herbert's Sacramental Puritanism." *Renaissance Quarterly* 54 (2001): 1273–1307.
Whinney, Margaret. *Sculpture in Britain, 1530–1830*. Harmondsworth: Penguin, 1964.
White, James Boyd. *"This Book of Starres": Learning to Read George Herbert*. Ann Arbor: U of Michigan P, 1994.
Wilkinson, Catherine. "The New Professionalism in the Renaissance." In *The Architect: Chapters in the History of the Profession*. Ed. Spiro Kostof. Oxford: Oxford UP, 1999. Repr., Berkeley: U of California P, 2000, 124–160.
Williamson, George C. *Lady Anne Clifford, Countess of Dorset, Pembroke and Montgomery, 1590–1676*. Wakefield, Yorkshire: S. R. Publishers, 1967.
Wilson, A. N. "Vandals in Dog Collars." *Evening Standard*, February 2, 1993. Newspaper clipping. London Metropolitan Archives. LMA MS DL/A/C/MS30779/37.
Wilton-Ely, John. "The Rise of the Professional Architect in England." In *The Architect: Chapters in the History of the Profession*. Ed. Spiro Kostof. Oxford: Oxford UP, 1977. Repr., Berkeley: U of California P, 2000, 180–208.
Wiseman, Susan. "Knowing Her Place: Anne Clifford and the Politics of Retreat." In *Textures of Renaissance Knowledge*. Manchester: Manchester UP, 2003, 199–213.
Woolf, Daniel. *The Social Circulation of the Past: English Historical Culture, 1500–1730*. Oxford: Oxford UP, 2003.
Woolf, Virginia. "Donne After Three Centuries." In *The Second Common Reader*. New York: Harcourt Brace, 1932, 20–37.
Wordsworth, William. "Essay upon Epitaphs I." In *The Prose Works of William Wordsworth*. Ed. W. J. B. Owen and Jane Worthington Smyser. 3 vols. Oxford: Clarendon, 1974, 2.49–62.
Wotton, Henry. *The Elements of Architecture*. London, 1624.
Yates, Frances. *The Art of Memory*. Chicago: U of Chicago P, 1966.
Yegül, Fikret. "Hercules at the Roundabout: Multidisciplinary Choice in the History of Architecture." In *Rethinking Architectural Historiography*. Ed. Dana Arnold, Elvan Altan Ergut, and Belgin Turan Özkaya. New York: Routledge, 2006, 60–73.
Zanini, Giuseppi Viola. *Della architettura di Gioseffe Viola padovano pittore ed architetto*. Padua, 1629.
Zevi, Bruno. *Architecture as Space: How to Look at Architecture*. New York: Horizon, 1957.
Ziegler, Georgianna. "Lady Anne Clifford Reads John Selden." Unpublished conference paper delivered at the annual meeting of the Renaissance Society of America, Montreal, March 24, 2011.
Zwicker, Steven N. "Irony, Modernity, and Miscellany: Politics and Aesthetics in the Stuart Restoration." In *Politics and the Political Imagination in Later Stuart Britain*. Ed. Howard Nenner. New York: U of Rochester P, 1997, 181–195.

Index

Page numbers in *italics* indicate photographs.

Adrian, John M., 64, 112
Aelfrith, 37, 49
aesthetics: art history and, 13; Evelyn and, 173–75, 179; Fréart and, 165–66, 180–83, *181, 182, 184, 184, 185*; Marvell and, 72, 74; in modern London, 195–204; Wotton on, 72. *See also* architectural style
Alberti, Leon Battista: on architects, 56; *De re aedificatoria*, 54; education of, 57; Fréart on, 168; on judgments of beauty, 72; in *Parallèle*, 225n13; on sense of sight, 68; Wotton and, 59, 61
The Alchemist (Jonson): analogies in, 92–94; architectural setting of, 78, 79, 87–88, 103–4; as city house play, 78; country house narrative in, 88, 91, 94–95, 97; disintegration of association of person and place in, 78–79; final scene of, 94; first scene of, 88–94; genteel inheritance in, 100–101; household disorder in, 88–90, 91–92; Mammon character in, 95–100; mistress of household in, 88, 90–91; overview of, 77–78; return of householder in, 101–3; ruins of architectural narrative and, 88; "venture tripartite" in, 90, 91, 92, 102
All Saints, Harthill, Cheshire, 128
alms. *See* charity and church porches
ancestral narratives: in *Britannia*, 93–94; of Clifford, 147–48, 153–54
The Ancient Funerall Monuments (Weever), 144, 146, 154
Anderson, Christy, 69, 110–11
Andreae, Sophie, 198–99, 200
Anselment, Raymond, 111
antiquarian chorography: architects and, 50–51; estate surveyors and, 52–54. *See also* country house poems

antiquarianism: in *The Alchemist*, 98–99; architectural history and, 6; funeral monuments and, 10; in modern London, 195–204; texts of, 24, 63–64, 149–52. *See also* antiquarian chorography
antiquarians: architects and, 50–51; country house stories of, 37–44; Dodsworth and Dugdale as, 25; Evelyn as, 165; Herbert as, 131. *See also* Bale, John; Camden, William; Clifford, Anne; Herbert, George; Leland, John; Stow, John
Appleby Castle, 151, 153–54
Appleton House, 71–74
Archer, Ian, 80, 104
architects: agency and obtrusion of, 197–99; antiquarians and, 50–51; Carew and, 69; emphasis on career of, 13; estate surveyors compared to, 51, 52–54; Evelyn and, 175–78; Fréart and, 176; Jonson and, 68; marginalization of, 199–200; Marvell on, 71–73; models of profession of, 51–52; names mentioned in texts, 14; patrons and, 58–60, 177–78; professional, development of, 50; role of, 58–60; shortage of, 60; Vitruvius on, 55–56, 177; Wotton and, 55, 72, 175, 177. *See also* patron-builder relationship; *specific architects*
architectural history: antiquarian brand of, 6; in art history departments, 2; in *Britannia*, 83, 195; of Continent, 12–13; early modern texts and, 14; Fréart and, 166–68, 180; individual identity and, 11–12; of Leland, 8; literary studies and, 2–3; organizing principles of, 13–14, 22; patronage and, 172–73; political history and, 161–62, 164–65, 169, 170, 173; as process of decline, 168–69; spatial practice and experience concept in, 10–12; written forms of history, as

architectural history (*continued*)
  intertwined with, 1–2. *See also* country house stories
architectural literacy, modes of, 50–51, 195–99
architectural style: Camden and, 44–45; in country house poems, 64; Evelyn on, 179. *See also* aesthetics
architecture: antiquarian production and, 24; in *Britannia*, 24, 27; as collectible, 186–87; as compression of multiple time frames, 150; as dated in human terms, 14; disintegration of, 32–35, 186, 187; early modern descriptions of, 11; as form of storytelling, 2; historical dimension of, 11–12; literature and, 5, 7, 17; local and historical perspectives on, 105; as metaphor in Renaissance thought, 7; reappropriation of, 35–36; Reformation and English perceptions of, 44–49; sixteenth- and seventeenth-century writing about, 3–5; visual approach to, 4–5, 195, 196–99. *See also* architects; architectural history; architectural style; built environment; London architecture; setting, architectural
aristocracy: in *The Alchemist*, 92–95, 97–98, 99–100; in *Britannia*, 83; churches and, 46–47; country house stories of, 37–44; *Elements of Architecture* and, 57–58; estate surveyors and, 53, 54, 55; land ownership after Restoration, 178–79; monasteries and, 47–48; in *Survey of London*, 83; in "To Penshurst," 65–66. *See also* landlord-tenant relationships; patron-builder relationship
Arnold, Dana, 2, 12, 13
art historical aesthetic periods, 13
Arundel House, 162
Audley, Thomas, 79
Augustine, Saint, 31

Bacon, Francis, 28, 29, 33
Baldi, Barnardino, 54, 59
Baldwin, William, 149
Bale, John: on goals of, 8; on Leland, 53; Leland project and, 1; on monastery documents and records, 1; on preservation of architecture, 33–34
baptisms and church porches, 108–9, 110, 114
Barbaro, Daniele, 57, 59, 225n13
Barden Tower, 136, 137–38
Barker, Ashley, 193, 194, 200–201, 203
Barton, Anne, 94
Baths of Diocletian at Rome, 180, *181*, 183

Bede, the Venerable, 31, 33
Belsey, Catherine, 12, 13
Benedictines at Glastonbury, 36
Billingsley, Henry, 58
Biographical Dictionary of English Architects (Colvin), 13, 160, 162, 175–76
Blackfriars area of London, 78, 87
Bloch, Chana, 115, 116
Blum, Hans, *Booke of Five Collumnes*, 4, 23
A Boke Named Tectonicon (Digges), 4
Bolton Abbey, Staffordshire, 48
Bond, Francis, 108–9, 110, 115
Booke of Five Collumnes (Blum), 4, 23
Bowle, John, 161
Brigham Church, Cumberland, 109
Britannia (Camden): address to reader, 29–30; *The Alchemist* compared to, 101, 104; ancestral narratives of, 93–94; architectural descriptions in, 152–53; buildings in, as surviving only in text, 24, 32–35; castle stories in, 39; chorographic organization of, 30–31; churches and monasteries in, 45–49, 105; Clifford and, 149; collectors and collections in, 35–36; country house poems in, 63–64; country house stories in, 37–44; county maps in, 53; English perceptions of architecture and, 25; features of, 24, 49; as historical approach to architecture, 83, 195; influence on Stow, 81–82, 83; on inscriptions, 154; interdisciplinary approach in, 27–37; interests of, 26–27; overview of, 23–24; passage of time in, 36–37; philology in, 28–29, 30; preface to, 53; publication history of, 25–26; stories in, 24–25, 31–32; successive editions of, 28; translations of, 25, 26, 34; Vitruvius references in, 44–45; Wickham story in, 148–49
Brooke, Ralph, 27
Brougham Castle, 136, 138, 140–41, 146, 148, *148*
Brown, R. J., 111
Bryson, Norman, 9
Bucke, John, 60
Buckett, Richard, 60
Buckingham, Duke of (George Villiers), 60
built environment: biographies attached to, 5–6; influence on texts, 5; narrative dimensions of, 3. *See also* architecture
Bullant, Jean, 165, 168, 225n13
Burbage, James, 87
burials and church porches, 109–10

INDEX

Camden, William: documents and, 43–44; empirical observations of, 27–29, 30; Evelyn compared to, 172; on religious houses, 1; on William of Malmesbury, 9. *See also Britannia*
Cameron, Sheila, 194, 200
Canterbury Cathedral, 150
Carew, Thomas: *Coelum Britannicum*, 70–71; "To My Friend G.N., from Wrest," 68–70, 71
The Carpenters Rule (More), 4
Carruthers, Mary, 7
cartographic development, 8
castle stories, 39
Catholicism, classicism and, 44–45. *See also* monasteries
Cawarden, Thomas, 87
Cecil, Robert, 14, 60
Cecil, William, 14, 42
Chaney, Edward, 160
charity and church porches, 110, 115, 119–20
Charles, Amy, 108
Charles II, 162, 163, 164, 173, 174–75, 177
Charlton, John, 153
Chatterton, Thomas, 111
Chew, Elizabeth, 143
chimneypieces, 69
chorographic texts, 8. *See also Britannia*
chorography, defined, 26. *See also* antiquarian chorography
churches: of Bertha (wife of Ethelbert), 31; in *Britannia*, 45–47, 105; porches of, in community life, 107–11; post-Reformation, 106. *See also* "The Church-porch"; *specific churches*
"The Church-porch" (Herbert): architectural setting of, 105, 108, 115–16, 117, 128; criticism of, 106–7, 112, 115–16; daily affairs and, 116–18; events taking place in, 114–15; final stanzas of, 126–27, 128; financial transactions and, 118–21; as historical approach to architecture, 195; historical environment for, 107–11; interior of church in, 124–26; as looking outward, 113; overview of, 105–6, 130–31; pedagogic goals of, 123–24; as proverbial poem, 115–17; structural integrity of, 111–13; value, as reassessed and recreated in, 121–24
church porches: in community life, 107–11; financial transactions and, 110, 118–24, 126, 128, 129, 130; inscriptions in, 127–28, 129, 130; location of, 113; photographs of, *112, 113, 114*

classicism: Catholicism and, 44–45; development of, in England, 12–13; Evelyn on, 179; in St. Helen's Bishopsgate, 203–4. *See also* columns, classical
Cleland, James, 58
Clifford, Anne: ancestry of, 147–48, 153–54; as antiquarian writer, 134–35; architectural description of, 143; architectural works of, 133–34; *Britannia* and, 26; country house stories of, 38; diaries and projects of, 132, 133, 158–59; directions for inscription on body of, 156–57; distribution of objects by, 153–54; family motto of, 139–40, *140*; funeral sermon preached for, 155–56; inscriptions of, 137–40, *139, 140,* 141–46, *145,* 154–55, 158; Isaiah's prophecy and, 139–42, 144, 154; occupation, documentation of, 135–37; practices of building and inscribing of, 146–49; repetitions in diary of, 135–37, 142–43; "This made Roger" inscription and, 15. *See also* Great Books of Record
Clifford, George, 132, 140, 142, 143, 145–46, 158
Clifford, John de, 147, 151, 153
Clifford, Margaret, 136, 144, 145–46, 151–52
Clifford, Robert Lord, 147
Clifford, Roger Lord, 147–48
Clifford, Rosamund, 32
Clifford, Thomas Lord, 153–54
Clifton-Taylor, Alec, 111
Coelum Britannicum (Carew), 70–71
coins, 34, 35
collections: in *Britannia*, 35–36; Evelyn and, 162–63; as forms of history, 187; Fréart and, 163; history and novelty in, 164; in St. Helen's Bishopsgate, 202–4
Collinson, Patrick, 80–81
Colt, Maxmilian, 60
columns, classical: Doric, 165, *166, 167,* 167–69, 183; Fréart and, 163, 180; Ionic, 180, *181,* 182–83, *184*
Colvin, Howard, *Biographical Dictionary of English Architects*, 13, 160, 162, 175–76
Compound of Alchymy (Ripley), 91–92
Condy, Agnes de, 152
Continent: architectural history of, 12–13; Evelyn's travels to, 162; mode of architectural literacy of, 50–51. *See also* Renaissance
Cooley, Ronald W., 116
Corf Castle, Dorsetshire, 37

Cotton, Robert, 35
country house estates, seventeenth-century conceptions of, 60–62. *See also* estate surveyors
country house poems: *The Alchemist* compared to, 101; ancestral narratives of, 94; in *Britannia*, 63–64; Isaiah's prophecy and, 139; overview of, 51–52, 62–63, 75, 76; "To My Friend G.N., from Wrest," 68–70, 71; "Upon Appleton House," 71–74. *See also* "To Penshurst"
country house stories: in *The Alchemist*, 88, 91, 94–95, 97; in *Britannia*, 37–44; features of, 43–44; in *Survey of London*, 84–85, 86–87
court masques, 70–71
Cratillus (Plato), 29
Creed, Henry, 110
Cromwell, Thomas, 84–87

Daniel, Samuel, 143, 145, 157–58
de Certeau, Michel, 10–11
Dee, John, 58
de Grazia, Margreta, 14
de Krey, Gary S., 179
de l'Orme, Philibert, 54, 56, 59, 165, 168, 225n13
Denham, John, 163, 171, 173, 175–76
de Noyers, Sublet, 163, 169–70, 187
Deorhurst, Gloucestershire, 33
De re aedificatoria (Alberti), 54
Description of England (Harrison), 80
diaries: of Clifford, 132, 133, 135–37, 142–43, 158–59; of Evelyn, 162–63, 176
Digges, Leonard, *A Boke Named Tectonicon*, 4
disintegration/dematerialization/decline of buildings, 32–35, 168–69, 186, 187
documents: buildings as, 199; Camden and, 43–44; church porches as repositories for, 111; Clifford and, 151–52; Cromwell and, 86; in monastery libraries, 46, 151; physical property and, 133
Dodsworth, Roger: as antiquarian, 25; Clifford and, 149–50, 151; inscriptions and, 154; *Monasticon Anglicanum*, 47, 149–50, 151, 205n3
dole tables, 110, 128, 129, 130
Donaldson, Ian, 78
Donne, John, 7
Dorchester, 35
Doric order, 165, *166*, *167*, 167–69, 183
Dorset, Earl of, 136, 151
Dover, Kent, 32
Downes, Kerry, 161

Dugdale, William: as antiquarian, 25; Clifford and, 150; *History of St. Paul's Church*, 154; *Monasticon Anglicanum*, 47, 149–50, 151, 205n3
Dyer, F. Thistleton, 110

Edward VI, 1
Edward VI Prayer Book, 109
Einsham Abbey, Oxfordshire, 43
Elements of Architecture (Wotton): advice on materials and construction in, 56–57; on architect-patron role combination, 58–60, 175; architects mentioned in, 14; aristocracy and, 57–58; buildings mentioned in, 23; characteristics of, 4; on chimneys, 69; features and purpose of, 54–55, 63; overview of, 75–76; republication of, 26; on site selection, 61–62; as Vitruvian-style treatise, 51
epitaphs: of Clifford, 143–46; St. Augustine, 33
Eriksen, Roy, 7
estate surveyors: historiography and, 66; history and profession of, 52–54; relationship to architects, 51; in "To Penshurst," 65; Wotton and, 55. *See also* Norden, John
Ethelbert, 31
Evelyn, John: architectural knowledge of, 160–61; *Britannia* and, 26; on church porches, 111; contribution of, 160; country house stories of, 38; *Numismata*, 186; plans for rebuilding London, 188; Terry compared to, 202, 203. *See also A Parallel of the Antient Architecture with the Modern*
Evett, David, 3

Fairfax, William, 74
Ficino, Marsilio, 59
financial transactions and church porches: dole tables, 110, 128, *129*, 130; Herbert on, 114–15, 126; transfers and exchanges of wealth, 118–21; value and, 121–24
First and Chief Groundes of Architecture (Shute), 4, 23, 26
Fitzherbert, John, 52–53, 86
Five Books of Architecture (Serlio), 4, 23
Fletcher, Isaac, 109
Fowler, Alastair, 69, 73
fragmentation: in Fréart's illustrations, 180–83, *181*, *182*, *184*, *185*; Palladio and, 165–66; in St. Helen's Bishopsgate, 198, 202–4
Fréart, Roland. *See Parallèle de l'architecture antique avec la moderne*

INDEX

Friar, Stephen, 107, 108
Friedman, Alice T., 161, 164
Fuller, Thomas, 151
funeral monuments: Camden's transcriptions of, 46, 146; Clifford and, 143–46, *145*; sale of, 82, 83, 86, 95; St. Helen's Bishopsgate, 194; studies of, 10; Weever and, 144, 146

gambling in "The Church-porch," 119
Gent, Lucy, 3, 4, 12, 15
Geoffrey of Monmouth, 28
Georgian London (Summerson), 13
Gibbons, Brian, 102
Gibson, Edmund, 26, 34
Godwin, Frances, 35
Great Books of Record (Clifford): architectural descriptions in, 152–53; contents and copies of, 132–33, 134; family motto and, 140; and similarities to antiquarian texts, 149–52
Great Fire of 1666, 160
Greenwich Palace, 63, 176
Grey, Elizabeth, 149
Grey, Henry, 68, 71
Griffin, Andrew, 77
Güven, Suna, 2

Hall, Edward, 86
Harding, Vanessa, 79–80
Hardwick Hall, Derbyshire, 14, 40–41
Harris, Eileen, 4, 59
Harris, Jonathan Gil, 15, 16–17, 34, 36–37, 82
Harrison, William, *Description of England*, 80
Hatfield House, 14, 60
Helgerson, Richard, 41
Herbert, George: as antiquarian, 131; *Outlandish Proverbs*, 115, 116, 122; religious architecture and, 210n45; *The Temple*, 105, 131. *See also* "The Church-porch"
Herendeen, Wyman, 29
Herrick, Robert, *Hesperides*, 109
Hertland monastery, Devonshire, 47–48
Hesperides (Herrick), 109
Hexham, Northumberland, 81, 82, 83
historical approach to architecture, 11–12, 105, 195–99. *See also* architectural history
history: of images, 9–10; of St. Helen's Bishopsgate, 191. *See also* political history and architecture

History of St. Paul's Church (Dugdale), 154
Hobhouse, Hermione, 199
Holland, Philemon, 25, 26, 63
Hollar, Wenceslaus, 11, 150
Holly, Michael Ann, 9
Holy Trinity Church, Skipton, 154
Howard, Henry, 162
Howard, Jean E., 77–78
Howard, Maurice, 5
Howard, Thomas, 79
Hunneyball, Paul, 10, 45

idleness in "The Church-porch," 117–18
inscriptions: on Barden Tower, 137–38; on Brougham Castle, 138, 141–42; of Clifford, 137–40, *139*, 141–46, *145*, 154–55, 156–57, *158*; collection of, 35; Dodsworth and, 154; in church porches, 127–28, *129*, *130*; Parry on, 150; on Skipton Castle, 139–40, *140*
interdisciplinary approach: of book, 17; of Camden, 27–37; of country house stories, 43–44
Ionic order, 180, *181*, 182–83, *184*
I quattro libri dell'architecttura (Palladio), 54
Itinerary (Leland): Camden and, 27; differences between English and Continental architecture, 12, 13; on Malmesbury, 5–6, 9, 11; methodology of, 7–8; publication date, 205n3; as sustained study of objects, 14–15

Johnson, A. W., 7
Jones, Inigo: attention to works of, 12; career of, 50; classicism and, 13; Clifford and, 134; commissions of, 60; Evelyn on, 176; Jonson and, 64; Palladio and, 160; Webb and, 176; Wotton and, 14
Jonson, Ben, 7, 26, 38. *See also The Alchemist*; "To Penshurst"

Keeble, N. H., 162, 174
Kendrick, T. D., 27
Kilman Lhyd, Caermardenshire, 35
King, Daniel, 150
Klein, Bernhard, 27, 38
Korda, Natasha, 16

landlord-tenant relationships: in *The Alchemist*, 89; Jonson and, 66–67; in *Survey of London*, 85–86

land ownership after Restoration, 178–79
Leland, John: *Britannia* and, 23; contents of itineraries of, 2; country house poem by, 63; Evelyn compared to, 172; *"in memoria hominum,"* 14; journeys, goal of, 1; on Malmesbury, 5–6, 9, 11; methodological question and, 5; methodology of, 7–8; on monastic libraries, 46; purpose of, 53; setting and, 8; storytelling and, 204. *See also Itinerary*
Levy, F. J., 28
Lewalski, Barbara, 106
Lhanheron, Cornwall, 41
Libri decem de architectura (Vitruvius), 54
Ligorio, Pirro, 169
literature and architecture, 5, 7, 17, 32–35. *See also* documents; texts; *specific works*
Llewellyn, Nigel, 10, 45
London: Great Fire of 1666, 160; population growth and changes in, 79–80
London architecture: Blackfriars area, 78, 87; individual identity and, 80–81; narratives of, 77–78. *See also The Alchemist*; St. Helen's Bishopsgate; *Survey of London*
Lowe, E. C., 111
Lucar, Cyprian, 53
Lucas, Richard, 198, 199, 200, 202
Lyming, Robert, 60

Malcolmson, Cristina, 126
Mallerstang Chapel, Cumbria, 138, 139
Malmesbury Abbey, 5–6, 9, 11
maps: cartographic development, 8; county, in *Britannia*, 53; of England, early modern, 41
Marchitello, Howard, 8
Mares, F. H., 78, 100
Marlborough, Wiltshire, 39
marriage ceremonies and church porches, 108–9, 110
Martin, Ian, 192
Martz, Louis, 106, 112
Marvell, Andrew, "Upon Appleton House," 71–74
material culture, 14–17
May, Hugh, 160
McRae, Andrew, 52, 53, 61
Melhuish, Claire, 192
memory houses, 7
Michelangelo, 10, 170
Miller, John, 162

The Minories, 83–84
monasteries: Appleton House as, 73–74; associations for, 105; Augustinian, in Broadstreet Ward, 82–83, 104; in *Britannia*, 45–46, 47–49; dissolution of, 1, 81; Hertland, Devonshire, 47–48; Hexham, Northumberland, 81, 82; libraries of, 46, 151; Malmesbury, 5–6; Peterborough, 49; Whorwell, Hampshire, 48–49
Monasticon Anglicanum (Dodsworth and Dugdale), 47, 149–50, 151, 205n3
More, Richard, *The Carpenters Rule*, 4
Mowl, Timothy, 60
Moxley, Keith, 9

narratives: ancestral, 93–94; architecture and, as related forms of storytelling, 2, 3–4, 17; of London architecture, 77–78. *See also* country house stories
natural history in country house stories, 41–43
New Classicism, 192
Nonesuch (country house), 43
Norden, John, *The Surveyors Dialogue*, 52, 53–54, 62, 66, 74–75
Norman, John, 198
North, Roger, 160
Numismata (Evelyn), 186

objects: in "The Church-porch," 117; Fréart and, 183–87; in *Itinerary*, 14–15; literary texts and, 209n28; of ordinary lives, 130. *See also* collections
observation method of Camden, 27–29, 30
old Winchester, ramparts of, 34, 35
Orgel, Stephen, 149
Orlin, Lena Cowen, 11, 43
Outlandish Proverbs (Herbert), 115, 116, 122
ownership and occupation of buildings, 135–37
Oxfordshire, tomb of Rosamund in, 32

palimpsest and material culture, 16–17
Palladio, Andrea: on artifacts and fragments of buildings, 165–66; Evelyn and, 160; Fréart on, 168; on Ionic order, 182–83, 184; *I quattro libri dell'architecttura*, 54; in *Parallèle*, 225n13; Wotton and, 57
Palmer, G. H., 111
Parallèle de l'architecture antique avec la moderne (Fréart): aesthetic progression in, 165–66;

on aesthetics, 180–83, *181*, *182*, 184, *184*, *185*; architects and, 176; collections in, 183–87; content of, 163; dedicatory epistle of, 169–70, 179; Evelyn's selection and reframing of, 161–62; Evelyn translation of, 160, 163–65, 172–73, 188; on excuses for change, 172; history of architecture of, 166–68, 180; patronage and, 170–71, 176–78; process of decline and, 168–69; St. Helen's project and, 197, 203–4; on treatise as artifact, 187–88

A Parallel of the Antient Architecture with the Modern (Evelyn): "Account of Architects and Architecture," 163, 171–72, 176, 177–78, 179; aesthetic styles in, 173–75; architects mentioned in, 14; architectural progress in, 171–72, 175; architectural styles and, 14; dedication to Charles II, 160, 164, 177, 178, 203; dedication to Denham, 163, 171, 173, 176, 179; dedication to Wren, 188–89; English traditions and, 164; goals of, 175; names in, 176; perceptions of politics, aesthetics, and, 161–62; publication of, 160; reframing in, 188; as self-representation, 187; structure of, 162–63

Parry, Graham, 15, 26–27, 28, 29, 33, 150
patronage, 170–71, 172–73, 176–78
patron-builder relationship: Evelyn and, 178; Fréart and, 169–71; Hardwick Hall, 14; site selection, optics, and, 62; Wotton and, 57–60, 175
Peacock, John, 12–13
Pearce, Susan, 185
Pearson, J. L., 198
penance, public, and church porches, 110–11
Penshurst, Kent, 42, 64–68, 85
Perks, Sydney, 188
Peterborough monastery, 49
Philander, Guillaume, 54, 59
Piggott, Stuart, 26
Plato, *Cratillus*, 29
political history and architecture, 161–62, 164–65, 169, 170, 173
politics of the Restoration, 187
polychronic view, 36–37
Pounds, N. J. G., 107, 108
Powers-Beck, Jeffrey, 116
Powlet, William, 82–83
Powys, A. R., 130–31
Pratt, Roger, 160
predisciplinary approach of book, 13

preservation: of architecture, 24, 33–34, 150, 188; of documents, 46, 151, 152; of objects, 186
Priory of Christ Church, Aldgate, 79
proverbial poems, 115–16

Quilligan, Maureen, 14

Rainbow, Edward, 155–56
Reading Architectural History (Arnold), 13
Redcastle, 32
Reformation, the: architecture as metaphor for, 7; dissolution of monasteries in, 1, 81; effects of, on architecture, 13; effects of, on texts, 8–9; English perceptions of architecture and, 44–49; transformative effect of, 79
Renaissance: Evelyn and, 162, 179; Italian, influence of, 10, 23
Restoration, the, 173, 174–75, 178–79, 187
Richborough, Kent, 30–31
Richelieu, Cardinal de, 170, 178
Richmond, Countess of, 42
Ripley, George, *Compound of Alchymy*, 91–92
Rivius, Gualterus, 54
Roston, Murray, 3
Rowley, Thomas, 111

Salvage, Elizabeth, 83, 84
Scamozzi, Vincenzo, 168, 182–83, *184*, 225n13
Schofield, John, 11, 79
schools in church porch chambers, 111, 114
Schwyzer, Philip, 9
Scott, Jonathan, 187
Selden, John, 25, 149
Sell, John Russell, 198
Selsey, Sussex, 34–35
sepulcher near Terracina, Doric order on, 165, 167–69, *167*
Serlio, Sebastiano: *Five Books of Architecture*, 4, 23; Fréart on, 165, 168; Ionic order, 183, *185*; in *Parallèle*, 225n13
sermons: for Clifford, 155–56; Herbert on listening to, 124–26
setting, architectural: of *The Alchemist*, 78, 79, 87–88, 103–4; of "The Church-porch," 105, 108, 115–16, 117, 128; as dynamic category, 17; Leland and, 8
Sherborne Cathedral, 150
Sherlock, Peter, 10

Shiqiao, Li, 160–61
Shute, John, *First and Chief Groundes of Architecture*, 4, 23, 26
Sidney, Robert, 42, 65, 66, 67
Simpson, James, 9
Sinfeld, Alan, 15
site selection, 61–62
Skipton Castle, 139–40, *140*, 152, 154, 158
Smallwood, R. L., 78
Smithe, Frederick, 128
Smyth, Adam, 130
Smythson, Robert, 14
social space, concept of, 10–12
Solomon, Julie Robin, 28
Southcombe, George, 174
Spence, Richard: on Barden Tower, 136; on Clifford and father, 142, 158; on Clifford and Selden, 149; on Clifford family motto, 140; on Dodsworth, 150; on monastic records, 151
Spot, Thomas, 33
St. Augustine's, Canterbury, 33
St. Augustine's Cross, story of, 31, 32
St. Bartholomew, Churchdown, Gloucester, 128
Stein, Arnold, 117
Stewart, Susan, 186–87, 188, 203
St. Helen's Bishopsgate, London: chancel screen, 196; design of interior, 192–94; as fragmented, 198, 202–4; history of, 191; northeast corner, 195; north wall, *193*; renovation of, 202–3; style of worship in, 198, 202; west gallery, *194*. *See also* Terry, Quinlan
St. John the Baptist, Cirencester, Gloucestershire, *113*
St. Lawrence Church, Appleby, Cumbria, *145*, 154
St. Mary Redcliffe, Bristol, Gloucestershire, *114*
St. Nicholas, Addlethorpe, 127–28
St. Nicholas, King's Lynn, Norfolk, *112*
storytelling: architecture and narrative as related forms of, 2, 3–4, 17; in *Britannia*, 24–25, 31–32; broad range of, 8; Leland and, 5–6, 7–8; local and idiosyncratic, 48–49; polychronic view and, 36–37. *See also* country house stories
Stow, John: as antiquarian, 25; Camden and, 26; *Chronicles*, 149; country house stories of, 38; Cromwell and, 85; experience and personality of, 80–81; manuscript library of, 35. *See also Survey of London*
St. Paul's Cathedral, London, 188–89

St. Peter and St. Paul, Eye, Suffolk, 110, 128, *129*
Strier, Richard, 106, 119, 120
Summers, Joseph, 106, 115, 116, 119, 127
Summerson, Henry, 153
Summerson, John, *Georgian London*, 13
Summit, Jennifer, 9, 29
Survey of London (Stow): *The Alchemist* and, 79, 101; Archer on, 80; architectural setting and, 103–4; Augustinian monastery in, 82–83, 104; Blackfriars monastery in, 87; buildings as sources of wealth in, 83–84; country house narrative in, 84–85, 86–87; Cromwell in, 85–86; Harris on, 34; as historical approach to architecture, 195; overview of, 77–78; ruins of architectural narrative and, 88; Throgmorton Street house in, 84–86
surveyors. *See* estate surveyors
The Surveyors Dialogue (Norden), 52, 53–54, 62, 66, 74–75
Swann, Marjorie, 28, 178

Tanner, Thomas, 47, 151
Tapsell, Grant, 174
Taylor, William, 202
The Temple (Herbert), 105, 131
Terry, Quinlan: as collector of fragments, 202–3; New Classicism and, 192; opponents of plan of, 197–99, 200; renovation plans of, 191, 193–95, 204; supporters of plan of, 199–202; testimony of, 194, 201
texts: about architecture, 3–5, 8–9, 14, 32–35; anthologies of incongruous, 82; antiquarian, 63–64, 149–52; Camden access to, 43–44; correspondence between buildings and, 133, 157–58; objects and, 209n28. *See also* documents; *specific texts*
Theobalds, 14
Thornbury Church, Bristol, 128
Thorpe, John, 11
Throgmorton Street house (in Stow's *Survey*), 84–86
Thwaites, Isabella, 74
"To My Friend G.N., from Wrest" (Carew), 68–70, 71
"To Penshurst" (Jonson): *The Alchemist* compared to, 79, 85, 95, 98, 100, 103; as country house poem, 64–68, 78, 104
Trajan's Column, 169, 180, *182*

Treswell, Ralph, 11
Turner, Henry S., 80

"Upon Appleton House" (Marvell), 71–74
upper chambers of church porches, 111
users, viewing architecture from perspective of, 11
Ussher, James, 25

Vignola, Giacomo Barozzi da, 165, 168, 183, 185, 225n13
Vine, Angus, 16, 24, 30
The Vine, Hampshire, 40
Viola Zanini, Giuseppi, 165, 168, 225n13
"visual," reconsideration of, 10
visual approach to architecture, 4–5, 195, 196–99
visual culture, 9–10
Vitruvius: on architects, 55–56, 58–59, 177; Camden's references to, 44–45; influence of, 4, 51; *Libri decem de architectura*, 54; on site selection, 62; on success of designs, 72; on union of theoretical and practical, 50; on wealthy amateurs, 60

Wall, Cynthia, 188
Wall, J. Charles, 109, 127
Watkins, Gordon, 198
Wayne, Don, 67
Webb, John, 160, 176
Webster, William, 109
Weever, John, *The Ancient Funerall Monuments*, 144, 146, 154
Welland, Northamptonshire, 42

Wells-Cole, Anthony, 4, 69
Westminster Abbey, 46, 150
Whinney, Margaret, 10
White, James Boyd, 115
Whitefriars priory, 84
Whorwell monastery, Hampshire, 48–49
Wickham, William, 148–49
William of Malmesbury, 5, 9, 33, 46
Williamson, George, 158
Wilson, A. N., 199
Wilton-Ely, John, 12, 208n68
Winchester, 34, 35
wit in "The Church-porch," 122–23
Wollaton Hall, 14
Woodford Castle, Dorsetshire, 152
Woolf, Virginia, 156
Wotton, Henry: on aesthetics, 72; architects and, 55, 72, 175, 177; on country estates, 62; country house stories of, 38; education and credentials of, 56–57; as provost of Eton, 57; quoted by Terry, 201; Vitruvius and, 4. *See also Elements of Architecture*
Wren, Christopher, 160, 163, 176, 188, 208n68
Wrest Park, Bedfordshire, 68–70, 71

Yates, Frances, 7
Yegül, Fikret, 15–16
York Cathedral, 47

Zevi, Bruno, 10
Ziegler, Georgianna, 149
Zwicker, Steven, 187